timing is everything

timing is everything

THE COMPLETE TIMING GUIDE TO COOKING

jack piccolo

Three Rivers Press
New York

Published by Three Rivers Press, a division of Crown Publishers,
201 East 50th Street, New York, New York 10022.
Member of the Crown Publishing Group.

Random House, Inc. New York, Toronto, London, Sydney, Auckland

www.randomhouse.com

Printed in the United States of America

Design by Jan Derevjanik
Illustrations by Jack Piccolo

Library of Congress Cataloging-in-Publication Data
Piccolo, Jack.
Timing is everything : the complete timing guide to cooking / by
Jack Piccolo.
1. Cookery. I. Title.
TX652.P49 2000
641.5—dc21 99-36295
CIP

ISBN 0-609-80207-0
10 9 8 7 6 5 4 3 2 1

First Edition

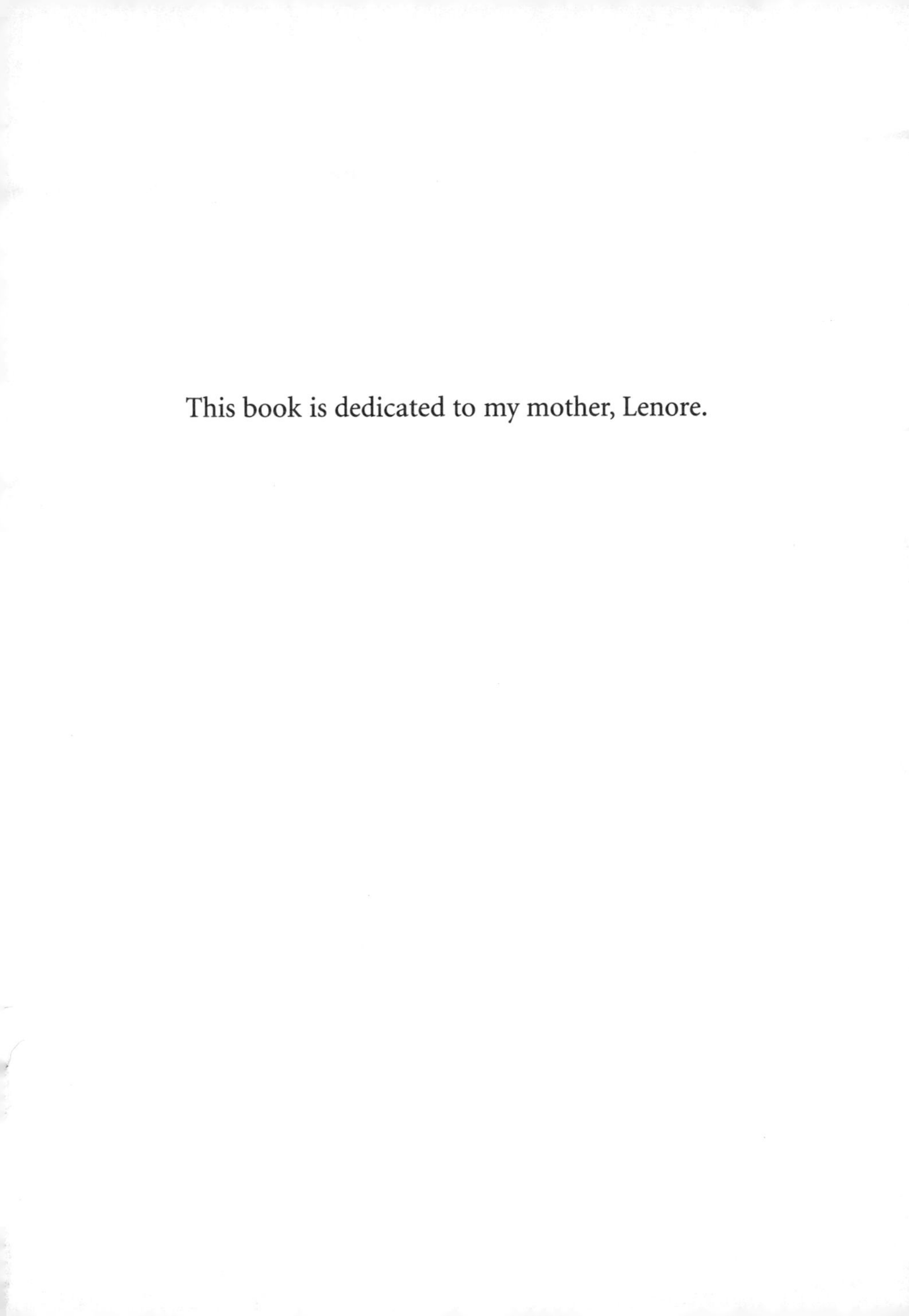

This book is dedicated to my mother, Lenore.

ACKNOWLEDGMENTS

I would especially like to thank Barbara Brock for her dedication, perseverance, and the long hours spent working with me on this book. Without her help I would still be working to complete it. I also would like to thank Justin Crasto for being there when I needed his help and Julian Bach, my agent, who had faith in me from the beginning. I also must thank friends and family, Eileen and Paul Guliner, Cece and Peter Frame, Stefania and Jamie McClennen, Tom Mooney, Ted Bell, Nancy Kahan, Rick, Karen, John, and Gisela for their willingness to taste not only my perfectly timed meals, but the undercooked and overcooked ones as well.

CONTENTS

Introduction

Many people have come up to me and said, "It's about time a book has been written about timing food. Finally, no more wading through recipe book after recipe book just to find out how long it takes to grill a lamb chop perfectly."

Timing Is Everything: The Complete Timing Guide to Cooking is for people who want to know how long it takes to cook a particular food perfectly. For example, if you want the answer to the question, "How long does it take to broil a 1½-inch-thick lamb chop to a perfect medium-rare?" just flip to the page about lamb, find lamb chop, find the entry to match the thickness of your chops, and voilà! Not only does this book give you correct cooking times for specific foods, but it also gives simple instructions for cooking the food in a variety of different ways.

Timing Is Everything tells you the time required to cook food perfectly—depending on size, weight, and thickness, whether you're looking to bake, barbecue, blanch, boil, braise, broil, deep-fry, grill, microwave, pan-broil, pan-fry, poach, pressure-cook, roast, sauté, simmer, steam, steep, stew, stir-fry. Everything from artichokes to zucchini, clams to venison, and apples to walnuts is included.

Over the years, I have acquired an appreciation for food that is cooked simply. This concept is basic to the Italian way of cooking, as well as other cuisines. Very fresh food cooked in a simple way brings out the true taste of the food. I have also discovered that the simpler the cooking, the more important the timing of the food. This discovery put me on the road to writing this book. It became clear to me that there are millions of cooks who prefer a wonderfully cooked simple meal to a complicated

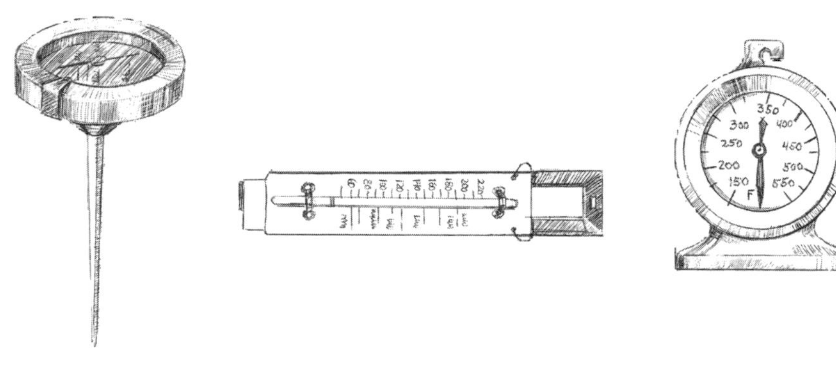

meat thermometer *deep-fat thermometer* *oven thermometer*

recipe that forces them to spend many hours in front of the stove. Granted, it's fun to prepare a dinner for friends from complicated recipes out of a French cookbook. However, how often does the average cook do this? I know that I certainly don't want to cook from a difficult recipe every time I make a meal. Many people want simple answers to simple cooking questions: How long should a 2-pound lobster stay in boiling water? How long should kidney beans simmer? How long should a 7-pound leg of lamb roast in the oven? And at what temperature? This book will also tell you the ways to broil a piece of salmon so that it's moist, pink, and flaky, not tough and overcooked.

Timing Is Everything is a guide to timing food, but cooking is not an exact science. Timing food depends on many factors: the quality of the food, the temperature of the food before you cook it, the weight and thickness of the food, whether you are cooking on a gas or electric stove, the exact temperature coming from the coals below your outdoor grill and many more factors too numerous to mention.

It helps to start with good equipment. Buy a reliable kitchen timer, an oven thermometer, an instant read-thermometer, and, if you fry foods, a deep-fat frying thermometer. Also start with the freshest food possible. Pay attention to the timings, but don't be afraid to experiment a little to get things cooked just right for you. Most of all, have fun. I hope this book helps you on your quest to becoming an excellent cook.

Part I

COOKING

1 Methods of Cooking Food

This book is filled with charts of cooking times based on following standard cooking methods.

Baking

Baking is a dry-heat cooking method used primarily for fish, vegetables, casseroles, breads, cakes, desserts, and other baked goods. The food is covered or left uncovered and cooked in an oven where the dry heated air surrounds the food to be cooked. Usually the oven is preheated before the food is added. An oven thermometer is essential for determining the accuracy of the baking temperature. *See also* Roasting.

Barbecuing

Some people confuse barbecuing with grilling, but they are two separate methods. Grilling is a fast method of cooking over flame, and barbecuing is a slow method. They both may be done on the same outdoor grill over charcoal or hardwood, but that's where the similarity ends. Barbecuing is done with a low heat (less than 225° F) and the grill is usually covered. With large cuts of meat, the coals are set to one side of the grill. A drip pan, half filled with water, is set in the middle of the coals or on the other side, and the meat is set over the drip pan and cooked very slowly. *See also* Grilling.

Blanching

This method partially cooks food by boiling or steaming to maintain the original color of vegetables before freezing and to loosen the skins of tomatoes, nuts, and fruits. It is also used to remove strong flavors or excess saltiness. To blanch, briefly immerse small quantities of food in boiling water for 30 seconds to 3 minutes. Drain and immerse in very cold water to stop the cooking. A few vegetables, such as soybeans and corn, require a longer blanching time, especially before freezing.

Boiling

This is a method of cooking food that is submerged in boiling water or another liquid in a pot on top of the stove. When the water or liquid reaches 212° F, it begins to boil.

When adding food to boiling water or liquid, the temperature of the liquid is immediately reduced. Therefore, time must be allowed for the water to return to a boil. Start counting your times when the water returns to a boil. Unless otherwise specified, add the food to already boiling water.

Braising or Pot-Roasting

Braising is a cooking method most often used with meat, fish, or vegetables, and it can be done on top of the stove or in a slow oven. Less tender cuts of meat, such as neck and shoulder, are most often used. Usually, the food is first browned in oil or butter on

all sides over moderate heat in a large kettle or heavy pot. Wine, broth, water, and/or vegetable juice is added, along with herbs, spices, and aromatic vegetables. The liquid is brought to a simmer. After the liquid starts to simmer, the heat should be reduced and the pot covered. You can simmer on top of the stove or in a 325° F oven. The liquid should always be at least 1 inch deep in the pot; additional liquid may be necessary as the cooking progresses. Braising takes 10 minutes to 4 hours depending on the food.

Deep-Frying

In this method, food is submerged in heated vegetable oil or fat (known as shortening). Deep-frying requires a heavy flat-bottomed iron kettle, deep saucepan, or electric fryer. A wire basket makes it easy to retrieve foods cut in small pieces. The pot or deep-fryer should never be filled more than half full with fat. Heat the fat gradually to 365° F to 375° F (use a frying thermometer).

The pieces to be cooked should be uniform in size and preferably not thicker than 1½ inches. They should also be patted dry before being added directly to hot fat or to batter. When coating with batter or crumbs, be sure the coating is even.

Fry several small batches rather than one larger one. Always reheat the fat to the correct temperature between batches. It may be necessary to adjust the heat, since the temperature of the oil will be reduced when food is added.

When food is deep-fried, it is cooked until it is an even golden-brown. Timing will vary depending on the temperature of the food going into the oil, the amount of food being cooked at a time, and the temperature of the oil. Therefore, I have not given specific times for all deep-fried foods; allow the foods to "cook until golden."

Grilling

To cook food over a grill with the fire below, charcoal or gas is usually used. The food may be placed directly over the coals (the direct method) or over a drip pan that is surrounded by coals (the indirect method). The indirect method eliminates the flare-ups that can occur when fat drips from the meat into the fire. Food cooks more slowly by the indirect grilling method. By either method, an instant-read thermometer is recommended for judging when the meat is done.

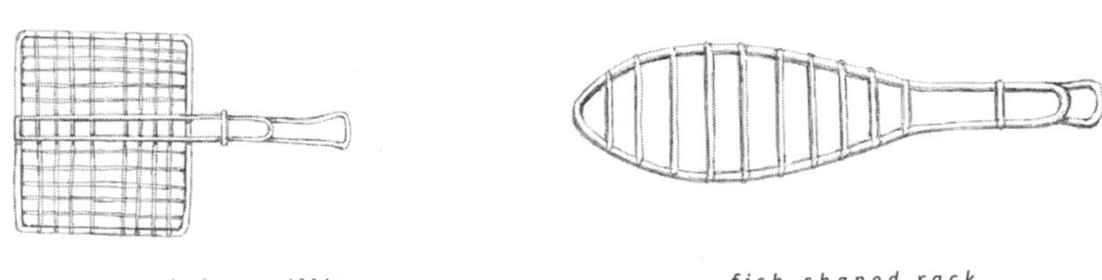

square rack for grilling

fish-shaped rack

Before lighting a fire in a grill, arrange the coals close together in pyramid fashion or use a chimney starter. Start the fire and allow the coals to burn until they are light gray in color (at night they will have a red glow). Spread the coals evenly on the rack, using long-handled tongs. To test the temperature of the coals, put a hand over the coals at close to the same height as the food will be placed. If you can hold your hand over the coals for 5 seconds, the fire is low; for 4 seconds, the fire is medium; for 3 seconds, the fire is medium-hot; and for 2 seconds, the fire is very hot.

When grilling foods that require slow cooking, arrange the grill rack at its highest position and lower it during cooking as the coals cool. When grilling a variety of foods that require slightly different timings, leave a space on the grill away from the fire to place faster-cooking items to the side where they will keep warm but not overcook.

To keep food from sticking, coat the grill rack lightly with cooking oil before using. A vegetable grilling rack or hinged basket makes it easy to grill small pieces of vegetable and delicate fish and shellfish.

Flare-ups are sudden bursts of flame caused by juices dripping onto hot coals. To control them, raise the grill rack with the meat and space the hot coals farther apart. If this doesn't work, remove the food from the grill and spray the coals with water; when the flame subsides, return the food to the grill and continue cooking. A clean grill helps prevent flare-ups; therefore, the grill should be cleaned after each use. Grilling by the indirect method also prevents flare-ups.

Indirect Method. Also called grill-roasting, indirect grilling usually involves large cuts of meat, poultry, or fish cooked in a covered grill. Place the coals around a drip pan large enough to catch the drippings. Place the food to be cooked over the drip pan. Use an instant-read thermometer to determine when the food is done.

Pan-Broiling

Pan-broiling is done in an already hot skillet on top of the stove. No fat or oil is used. The hot cooking surface sears the food, which prevents the loss of juices. The heat is kept on high throughout the cooking process. Ridged skillets that let the fat drip down below the cooking surface are perfect for this method of healthy, low-fat cooking.

Poaching

Poaching is a form of moist-heat cooking. Sometimes the food and liquid are combined and heated together; sometimes the food is added to the already simmering liquid. It may be done in a skillet or pan. The food should be completely covered by the liquid and the liquid should never reach a boil, but quiver at 195° F to 205° F.

Depending on the food being cooked, the cover is left on or off. The lid is not recommended when poaching meat or fish because too much steam will be entrapped in the cooking process. Delicate foods such as eggs, fruit, fish fillets, and chicken breasts are excellent candidates for poaching.

Pressure Cooking

This method of cooking is done in a pressure cooker at specific levels of pressure. The higher the pressure, the higher the temperature at which water boils, and therefore the higher the temperature at which the food in the pressure cooker cooks. The added heat in the pressure-cooking method allows food to cook faster (about one-third the time) and it retains the nutrients, color, and flavor in vegetables. The pressure cooker is a heavy pot with a locking lid, pressure gauge, and steam-release valve. The pressure cooker allows the temperature to rise as high as 250° F.

Roasting

Roasting is a type of baking, a dry-heat method used primarily for fish, poultry, meat, and vegetables. It is usually done in a shallow, uncovered pan at a temperature of 400° F or higher. Roasted food usually has a crusty brown exterior and a juicy interior.

Sautéing or Pan-Frying

This type of cooking is done in an open pan with a small amount of oil or butter. The pan is kept in frequent motion and the cooking process is quick, resulting in crisp but moist food. The heat must be high and the pan hot enough to sear the food. Select firm, tender cuts of meat or fish. Other suitable foods are tender chunks of chicken, chicken cutlets, veal cutlets and center cuts, lamb chops, pork chops, and certain vegetables. When sautéing, add foods that are perfectly dry or they will not brown. The pan must be large enough to allow air circulation between the pieces you are sautéing to prevent steaming. To keep the food from overbrowning, agitate the pan frequently.

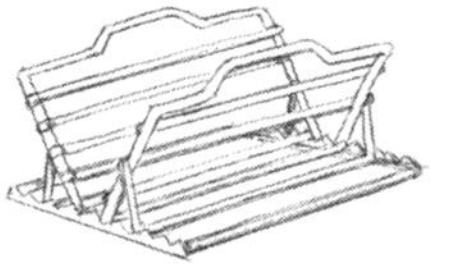

roasting rack

fish poacher

Simmering

Simmering involves cooking food in liquid that is just below the boiling point. Often the liquid is brought to a boil and then the heat is reduced to allow simmering to take place. At a simmering temperature (185° F to 205° F), bubbles will rise gently in simmering liquid and barely break the surface.

Steaming

Steaming is a moist-heat process where the cooking liquid never touches the food being cooked; instead, it produces a steam or vapor that cooks the food. Cookware for steaming is available—an all-purpose steamer, vegetable steamer, or a pressure cooker can be used. Steaming helps retain the natural vitamins in food. Fill the pot with water or other liquid to just below the bottom of the steamer basket, bring to a boil, add the food to be steamed, and cover. This cooking method is well suited to fish and vegetables.

Steeping

Steeping is done to allow a food or seasoning to stand in hot water (just below the boiling point) to extract flavor or color or to soften texture. Tea is made by steeping, as are several grains.

Stewing

Stewing is similar to braising, but more liquid is used. A heavy pot or pan with a tight lid is needed. The cuts of meats used are usually the less tender cuts, such as bottom round, chuck shoulder, and brisket. Appropriate cuts of poultry are mature turkey, chicken, duck, and pheasant. The meat should be cut into bite-size pieces. Brown the meat and aromatic vegetables and herbs in a small amount of fat. Then barely cover the meat with liquid. As soon as the liquid reaches a boil, reduce the heat, cover the pot, and simmer, turning the meat occasionally. You can simmer the stew meat slowly on top of the stove or in an oven preheated to 325° F. Additional vegetables can be added before the stew is finished. This process can also be done in a Crock-Pot.

Stir-Frying

Stir-frying involves brief cooking over high heat, resulting in crunchy but tender vegetables and moist, tender meat and fish. The food should be uniformly cut into small pieces so everything cooks in about the same amount of time. If the different ingredients require different cooking times, stir-fry them separately and toss them together at the end. When stir-frying, use a wok or a large, deep skillet and keep tossing and stirring the food as it cooks.

2 Timing Is Everything

Timing is everything—as long as you rely on your own good judgment to tell you when to remove the food from the heat. Timing ultimately depends on your stove or oven; the quality, size, and material of your cookware; and the freshness, temperature, weight, and thickness of your ingredients. So use the timings offered in the charts as guidelines, and let your own experience also be your guide.

DRIED BEANS AND LEGUMES

Dried beans will keep in an airtight container on a pantry shelf for up to a year. But the older the beans, the longer the cooking time. So buy beans from a store that has a rapid turnover of shelf items. The beans should be plump, not shriveled or moldy.

Bean Cooking Methods

Generally, 1 pound of beans (about 2½ cups) should be cooked in 8 cups of water and will yield 6 to 7 cups of cooked, drained beans. Before you begin cooking, pick through the beans and discard any stones or debris. Then presoak in water if needed (see box below). After soaking, drain off the soaking liquid, rinse the beans in tepid water, and proceed with your recipe.

To cook, place the beans in a large pot and add cold water to cover the beans by 2 inches. Bring to a boil over high heat. Skim off any foam that appears. Cover, reduce the heat, and simmer until the beans are completely tender. Taste one to test. **Timing will vary depending on the freshness of the beans.** Beans that have been stored for a long time will take longer to cook.

Two Ways to Presoak Beans

Conventional Soak. Soak dried beans in water that equals 4 times the volume of the beans (for example, 1 cup beans to 4 cups water). Let stand for at least 6 hours or overnight. Drain and cook.

Quick Soak. Place the beans in a heavy pan. Add enough water to cover the beans by 1 inch. Bring to a boil, then reduce the heat and let the beans simmer for 2 minutes. Remove the pan from the heat and let it sit, covered, for 1 hour.

Flavor Tips

Beans are usually cooked in water. It is a good idea to add aromatic vegetables, such as onions, garlic, carrots, and celery, to the water. Add them in big pieces and remove them before draining for the best appearance. You can also add herbs and spices to the cooking water. Do not add acid ingredients, such as vinegar or tomatoes, until the very end of the cooking times; they will toughen the skins of the beans. Salt can be added at any point; it will not toughen the skins.

Once the beans are cooked, be generous with seasoning. Add lots of salt, pepper, herbs, or spices. A little vinegar often brings out the subtly sweet flavors of beans.

A Description of Common Beans

Adzuki (Azuki)
Small red bean often used in Asian sweets.

Black (Turtle)
Small black beans often used in Central and South American cooking. Excellent for soups. Combines well with cumin for flavoring.

Black-Eyed Peas
Small beige beans with a black oval and beige dot in the center. Thin-skinned. Full-flavored. Used in dishes from India, Africa, the Caribbean, and the southern United States.

Broad (fava)
Large flat beans, ranging in color from white to brown; may be split or whole. Available fresh as well as dried. Used in the cooking of the Mediterranean and Middle East.

Cannellini
White kidney-shaped bean used in Italian cooking.

Cranberry (Borlotti)
Small tan-colored beans with maroon dots. In Italy they are used in pasta dishes, as a side dish, and in soups.

Garbanzo (Chickpeas)
Round, golden-colored beans, used in Mediterranean, Middle Eastern, and Indian cooking.

Great Northern
Medium-size round white bean used for baked beans and in soups. Can be used interchangeably with navy beans.

adzuki

white kidney

Kidney
Kidney-shaped red bean, with slightly sweet flavor. Used for chili.

Lentils (legume)
Small, flat, green, brown, red, and yellow legumes. Used in soups, Indian dahl, and French dishes.

Lima
Large, flat pale-green or white bean. Used in Central America and the southern United States.

Navy
Small white bean. Used for Boston baked beans and navy bean soup.

Pinto
Pink beans with red dots. Used to make refried beans. Similar in taste to kidney beans.

Red (chili or small red)
Small red beans with a robust flavor. Used in many Mexican dishes.

Soybean
Light-beige bean. Can be processed into soy milk, soy flour, tofu, and textured vegetable protein.

Split peas
Green or yellow. Used to make soup flavored with ham bone.

black-eyed peas

pinto

red kidney

TIMINGS: Beans and Legumes

All times are based on using presoaked beans unless otherwise specified. For information on pressure cooking dried beans and legumes, see page 295.

BEAN	*METHOD*	*INSTRUCTIONS*	*TIMING*
ADZUKI (azuki)	SIMMER	Place presoaked beans in large pot and add cold water to cover by 2 inches. Bring to boil over high heat, then reduce heat and simmer, partially covered, until beans are tender.	½–¾ hour
BLACK (turtle)	SIMMER	Place presoaked beans in large pot and add cold water to cover by 2 inches. Bring to boil over high heat, then reduce heat and simmer, partially covered, until beans are tender.	1–1½ hours
BLACK-EYED PEAS	SIMMER	Place beans in large pot and add cold water to cover by 2 inches. Bring to boil over high heat, then reduce heat and simmer, partially covered, until beans are tender. Presoaking not necessary, but will reduce cooking time.	½–1 hour
BROAD (fava)	SIMMER	Place presoaked beans in large pot and add cold water to cover by 2 inches. Bring to boil over high heat, then reduce heat and simmer, partially covered, until beans are tender.	½–1 hour
CANNELLINI	SIMMER	Place presoaked beans in large pot and add cold water to cover by 2 inches. Bring to boil over high heat, then reduce heat and simmer, partially covered, until beans are tender.	1–1½ hours

BEAN	*METHOD*	*INSTRUCTIONS*	*TIMING*
CRANBERRY (borlotti)	SIMMER	Place presoaked beans in large pot and add cold water to cover by 2 inches. Bring to boil over high heat, then reduce heat and simmer, partially covered, until beans are tender.	¾–1½ hours
GARBANZO (chickpeas)	SIMMER	Place presoaked beans in large pot and add cold water to cover by 2 inches. Bring to boil over high heat, then reduce heat and simmer, partially covered, until beans are tender.	1½–2½ hours
GREAT NORTHERN	SIMMER	Place presoaked beans in large pot and add cold water to cover by 2 inches. Bring to boil over high heat, then reduce heat and simmer, partially covered, until beans are tender.	1–1½ hours
KIDNEY	SIMMER	Place presoaked beans in large pot and add cold water to cover by 2 inches. Bring to boil over high heat, then reduce heat and simmer, partially covered, until beans are tender.	1–1½ hours
LENTILS (legume)	SIMMER	Do not presoak. Place lentils in large pot and add cold water to cover by 2 inches. Bring to boil over high heat, then reduce heat and simmer, partially covered, until tender. Reduce cooking time for salads, increase for soups and pureés.	Green or brown: 20–60 minutes Red: 10–20 minutes
LIMA	SIMMER	Place presoaked beans in large pot and add cold water to cover by 2 inches. Bring to boil over high heat, then reduce heat and simmer, partially covered, until beans are tender.	1–1¼ hours

BEAN	*METHOD*	*INSTRUCTIONS*	*TIMING*
NAVY	SIMMER	Place presoaked beans in large pot and add cold water to cover by 2 inches. Bring to boil over high heat, then reduce heat and simmer, partially covered, until beans are tender.	1–1½ hours
PINTO	SIMMER	Place presoaked beans in large pot and add cold water to cover by 2 inches. Bring to boil over high heat, then reduce heat and simmer, partially covered, until beans are tender.	1–1½ hours
RED (chili or small red)	SIMMER	Place presoaked beans in large pot and add cold water to cover by 2 inches. Bring to boil over high heat, then reduce heat and simmer, partially covered, until beans are tender.	1–1½ hours
SOYBEAN	SIMMER	Place presoaked beans in large pot and add cold water to cover by 2 inches. Bring to boil over high heat, then reduce heat and simmer, partially covered, until beans are tender.	3 or more hours
SPLIT PEAS	SIMMER	Do not presoak. Place beans in large pot and add cold water to cover by 2 inches. Bring to boil over high heat, then reduce heat and simmer, partially covered, until tender.	½–1 hour

GRAINS

Grains are the dried seeds of grass plants. They provide low-fat, high-fiber nutrition and are served in their various forms as both breakfast and dinner fare. Common grains include barley, buckwheat, corn (hominy, polenta), millet, oats, quinoa, and wheat (bulgur, couscous). Grains may be bought whole, milled, rolled, or ground.

Whole grains are best fresh. If they develop an unpleasant odor, they have become rancid and should be discarded. Rancid grains will taste bitter when cooked. Store whole grains in tightly sealed containers at room temperature for up to 1 month or in the refrigerator for up to 5 months. Cooked grains can be stored in the refrigerator for 2 to 3 days in an airtight container. They do not freeze well.

Rinse grains just prior to cooking to remove surface starch and debris.

Toasting will bring out the flavor of grains. To toast, place the grains in a nonstick pan over medium heat. Shake or stir until toasted and fragrant, about 4 minutes.

Cooking Grains

Most grains are simmered in a liquid until the liquid is absorbed and the grain is tender. To cook, measure the proper amount of water or broth into a saucepan. Add ¾ teaspoon salt for each cup of grain. Bring to a boil and slowly add the grain. (Note: in a few instances, the grain is added to the cold liquid; see the chart on the facing page). Return to a boil. Cover, reduce the heat, and simmer for the time specified, or until all of the liquid is absorbed and the grain is tender. Do not stir while cooking, unless otherwise instructed.

Flavor Tips

You can boost the flavor of any grain by cooking it in broth instead of water. Another way to flavor grains is to make a pilaf. Sauté the grains in a little oil with finely chopped onion, garlic, or other vegetables. Then add the cooking liquid, preferably broth. You can also add flavor to grains by combining them with sautéed vegetables or cooked fish, shellfish, poultry, or meat.

TIMINGS: Grains

NOTE: *For information on pressure cooking grains, see page* 299.

GRAIN	METHOD	INSTRUCTIONS	TIMING
BARLEY Quick-cooking pearl 1¼ cups	SIMMER	Bring **2 cups salted water** to a boil. Slowly add grain, cover, return to a boil. Then reduce heat and simmer.	10–12 minutes

GRAIN	METHOD	INSTRUCTIONS	TIMING
BARLEY Pearl ¾ cup	SIMMER	Bring **3 cups salted water** to a boil. Slowly add grain, cover, return to a boil. Then reduce heat and simmer. Fluff with a fork and let stand after cooking.	45 minutes, plus 10 minutes standing time
BARLEY Whole hulled 1 cup	SIMMER	Rinse grain thoroughly in several changes of water. Bring **3½ cups salted water** to a boil. Add grain and return to a boil. Cover, reduce heat, and simmer. Fluff with a fork and let stand after cooking.	30–35 minutes, plus 10 minutes standing time
BUCKWHEAT GROATS ⅔ cup	SIMMER	Add to **1½ cups cold water.** Bring to boil, cover, and then simmer.	12–15 minutes
BULGUR Fine and medium grain 1 cup	STEEP	Add to **2½ cups boiling water.** Cover and let stand. Do not cook.	15–30 minutes
CORNMEAL 1 cup	SIMMER	Combine with **1 cup salted cold water.** Stir until smooth. Add **2¾ cups salted boiling water.** Cover and simmer, stirring occasionally.	10 minutes
COUSCOUS, INSTANT 1 cup	STEEP	Bring **1¼ cups salted water** to a boil. Stir in couscous. Cover. Remove from heat. Let stand 5 minutes. Fluff with a fork.	5–7 minutes
CRACKED WHEAT 1 cup	SIMMER	Combine with **2 cups cold water.** Cover and bring to a boil. Reduce heat and simmer. Fluff with a fork.	15 minutes
GRITS Quick cooking ¾ cup	SIMMER	Bring **3 cups salted water** to a boil. Slowly add grits. Simmer, stirring occasionally.	5 minutes

GRAIN	*METHOD*	*INSTRUCTIONS*	*TIMING*
GRITS Regular 1 cup	SIMMER	Bring **3 cups salted water** to a boil. Stir in grits, reduce the heat, and simmer, stirring constantly.	10–15 minutes
JOB'S TEARS 1 cup	SIMMER	Rinse and soak grain overnight. Then drain. Bring **3 cups salted water** to a boil. Add grain and return to a boil. Then cover, reduce heat, and simmer. After cooking, fluff with a fork and let stand 10 minutes.	40 minutes, plus 10 minutes standing time
KAMUT ¾ cup	SIMMER	Soak overnight in water to cover. Drain. Add to **4 cups boiling salted water.** Simmer, uncovered. Drain.	45–60 minutes
MILLET ¾ cup	SIMMER	Bring **2 cups salted water** to a boil. Add millet and simmer in covered pan. After cooking, let stand covered 5 minutes.	15–20 minutes plus 5 minutes standing time
OATS Rolled 1⅔ cups	SIMMER	Combine with **3 cups cold water** and bring to a boil. Cover, reduce heat, and simmer for 5–7 minutes. Remove from heat and let stand covered 3 minutes.	5–7 minutes, plus 3 minutes standing time
OATS Steel-cut 1 cup	SIMMER	Combine with **4 cups cold water** and let soak overnight. Bring to a boil, cover, reduce heat, and simmer until tender.	60 minutes
POLENTA 1 cup	SIMMER	Bring **4 cups salted water** to a boil over medium heat. Slowly stir in polenta. Simmer, uncovered, stirring almost constantly.	20–25 minutes
QUINOA ¾ cup	SIMMER	Rinse well. Bring **1½ cups salted water** to a boil. Stir in quinoa. Cover and simmer. Fluff with a fork.	12–15 minutes

GRAIN	*METHOD*	*INSTRUCTIONS*	*TIMING*
RYE BERRIES 1 cup	SIMMER	Rinse well. Bring **3¼ cups water** to a boil. Add rye, return to a boil. Cover, reduce heat, and simmer. Let stand 10 minutes after cooking.	60 minutes, plus 10 minutes standing time
SPELT BERRIES ¾ cup	SIMMER	Soak overnight in water to cover. Drain. Add to **4 cups boiling salted water.** Simmer, uncovered. Drain.	45–60 minutes
WHEAT BERRIES ¾ cup	SIMMER	Combine with **2½ cups salted water** and bring to a boil. Cover, reduce heat, and simmer. Note: To reduce cooking time to 50–60 minutes, soak berries overnight in water to cover prior to cooking.	1¼–1½ hours

RICE

There are many thousands of types of rice, and more are becoming available to American shoppers all the time. In recent years, familiar long-grain white and brown rice have been joined by medium-grain Italian rices perfect for risotto, Japanese sticky rice for sushi, and Thai black rice. If rice is not white (it may be brown, red, or black), it means the rice has not been polished and the bran and germ are still attached. This means a shorter storage life (store "brown" rices in the refrigerator for 1 month) and a slightly longer cooking time. White rice stored in an airtight container will keep indefinitely.

Cooking Rice

There are as many ways to cook rice as there are varieties of rice. Sometimes the type of rice dictates the cooking method, but not always. Rinsing rice before cooking is optional. Rinsing removes the surface starch (as well as some vitamins), resulting in drier, fluffier rice.

Flavor Tips

Many people prefer salted rice, especially for non-Asian dishes. For salted rice, use ¼ to ½ teaspoon salt per cup of uncooked rice. If desired, you can also add 1 tablespoon butter per cup of uncooked rice. Substituting broth for some or all of the water will also boost flavor.

Another way to flavor rice is to make a pilaf. Sauté the rice in a little oil with finely chopped onion, garlic, or other vegetables. Then add the cooking liquid, preferably broth. You can also add flavor to cooked rice by adding sautéed vegetables or cooked fish, shellfish, poultry, or meat.

Cooking Methods for Rice

METHOD	INSTRUCTIONS
BAKE	Preheat oven to 350°F. Combine rice and water in ovenproof pot on top of stove. Bring to a boil, cover, and place in oven. Bake until liquid is absorbed and rice is tender. White rice takes about 20–30 minutes; brown rice takes about 55 minutes.
BOIL	Cook like pasta. Add rice to large pot of boiling water. Return water to a boil and cook until rice is tender. White rice will be fully cooked in 15–20 minutes; brown rice takes about 40 minutes. Drain well.
RICE COOKER	Combine the rice and cold water in machine. The rice cooks for about 20 minutes and comes out perfect. Fluff rice with a fork.
RISOTTO	Toast medium-grain rice in large skillet in small amount of butter or oil over medium-high heat. Add 1 cup simmering cooking liquid (water, broth, wine) and cook, stirring constantly, until all liquid is absorbed. Add another cup of simmering liquid and continue stirring until liquid is absorbed. Continue adding liquid, 1 cup at a time, until all the liquid is added and the rice is tender. Stir in additional cooked meat, poultry, shellfish, or vegetables if desired. Stir in butter and grated Parmesan cheese and serve at once.
SKILLET (pilaf)	Cook rice in a small amount of oil or butter along with aromatic vegetables and herbs or spices for 5 minutes, stirring constantly, until rice appears toasted. Add hot water or broth and bring to a boil. Cover, reduce heat, and simmer until liquid is absorbed and rice is tender, 15–20 minutes for white rice, 40–45 minutes for brown rice. Fluff rice with a fork.
STEAM (absorption method)	Steamed rice is actually boiled rice. Bring water to a boil in saucepan. Add rice, stir once. Cover and boil gently, until liquid is absorbed and rice is tender, about 12–18 minutes for white rice; 40 minutes for brown rice. Fluff rice with a fork.
STEAM	Steam in a colander or steamer over a pot of boiling water until rice is completely tender.

TIMINGS: Rice

***NOTE:** 1 cup uncooked rice yields about 3 cups cooked rice, or 4 servings.*

RICE	***METHOD***	***INSTRUCTIONS***	***TIMING***
WHITE RICE			
Long-grain 1 cup	BAKE	Bring **2 cups water** to a boil in an ovenproof saucepan. Add rice slowly. Return to a boil, then cover pan and place in 350°F oven.	20–25 minutes
	BOIL	Bring a large pot of water to a boil. Add the rice slowly so water continues to boil. Boil until rice is tender. Drain well.	12–18 minutes
	STEAM (Absorption method)	Bring **2 cups water** to a boil. Add rice slowly to boiling water. Cover and boil gently until liquid is absorbed and rice is tender. Do not stir.	12–18 minutes
Basmati 2 cups	STEAM (Absorption Method)	Bring **2 cups water** to a boil in a pot. Cover and boil gently until water is absorbed and rice is tender. Let stand uncovered.	15 minutes cooking time, plus 5 minutes standing time
Arborio or other medium-grain Italian rice (such as Carnaroli, Vialone Nano, Roma, or Balso) 1½ cups	RISOTTO	Heat **6 cups water or broth and ¼ cup white wine** in saucepan. Heat butter or olive oil in large heavy saucepan over medium heat. Stir in rice and cook until each grain has a white dot in middle. Stirring constantly, add 1 cup heated water or broth and wine. Stir until absorbed. Repeat until all broth and wine is added and rice is creamy and tender. Add cooked meat, shellfish, or vegetables. To finish, stir in a little butter and grated Parmesan cheese.	18–25 minutes

RICE	*METHOD*	*INSTRUCTIONS*	*TIMING*
Japanese (sticky rice, glutinous rice, sweet rice) 2 cups	STEAM (Absorption method)	Combine rice with **2½ cups water** in pan and leave to soak for 30 minutes. Bring water to a boil, cover, and simmer over medium-low heat until rice is tender and liquid is absorbed. Let stand, covered.	30 minutes soaking time, 10–15 minutes cooking time, plus 15 minutes standing time
Japanese (sticky rice, glutinous rice, sweet rice) 2 cups	STEAM	Soak rice in water to cover overnight. Drain. Place in steamer over boiling water and steam until rice is tender. Sprinkle water on top of rice from time to time.	20 minutes
BROWN RICE, RED RICE			
Long-grain 1 cup	BAKE	Bring **2¼ cups water** to a boil in an ovenproof saucepan. Add rice slowly and return to a boil. Cover pan and place in 350°F oven.	50–55 minutes
	BOIL	Soak in **2 cups water** for 8 hours or overnight. Drain rice. Combine **2½ cups water** and drained rice and bring to a boil. Cover, boil gently until water is absorbed and rice is fluffy.	25 minutes
	STEAM (Absorption method)	Bring **2¼ cups water** to a boil. Add rice slowly. Return to a boil, cover, and boil gently until rice is tender and water is absorbed.	40–45 minutes
Basmati 1 cup	STEAM (Absorption method)	Bring **2¼ cups water** to a boil. Slowly add rice, return to a boil, cover. Cook until rice is tender and all water is absorbed.	40–45 minutes

RICE	*METHOD*	*INSTRUCTIONS*	*TIMING*
THAI BLACK RICE 1 cup	STEAM (Absorption method)	Bring **2½ cups water** to a boil. Slowly add rice, return to a boil, cover. Boil gently until rice is tender and water is absorbed. Fluff with a fork, cover with dry pot lid, and let stand.	25–30 minutes
WILD RICE 1 cup	STEAM (Absorption method)	Combine rice with **3 cups water.** Bring to a boil. Cover and boil gently until water is absorbed and grains have burst open. Let stand uncovered until served.	35–60 minutes

PASTA AND NOODLES

Pasta is generally divided into two categories: fresh and dried. Dried pasta is found in at least 50 shapes, many of which are listed in the following chart. Dried pasta can be stored in a cool, dry, dark place for up to 18 months. Fresh pasta is usually egg pasta and comes in many forms. The dough is sometimes mixed with herbs or various vegetable juices. It should be stored in the refrigerator and used within 1 to 2 days or stored in the freezer for up to 2 months.

To cook pasta, all you need is a large uncovered pot and a couple tablespoons of salt. Fill the pot with 4 to 6 quarts of water for 1 pound of pasta. Do not cook more than 1 pound at a time. This prevents the pasta from becoming gluey and sticking together. When the water comes to a boil, add the salt and a drop of oil, then add the pasta and stir immediately. Bring the water back to a boil. Time it according to the type of pasta you are using. **Every brand and style of pasta cooks differently. Therefore the timings given are just a guide.**

Begin to test for doneness a minute or two before the suggested cooking time. Take a piece out of the pot before the time given and bite into it. The pasta should be slightly firm, tender, and chewy (al dente). When the pasta is cooked (fresh pasta may take as little as 2 minutes to cook; dried pasta can take from 3 to 15 minutes to cook), drain at once into a large colander. Do not rinse unless the pasta is to be baked or served in a pasta salad. Serve hot. Asian noodles are extremely variable in cooking times. **Use these times as guidelines only. Test for doneness frequently.**

TIMINGS: Pasta and Noodles

TYPE	*INSTRUCTIONS*	*TIMING*
ITALIAN PASTA, DRIED		
Bow Ties (Farfalle)	Boil	12–15 minutes
Capellini	Boil	3 minutes
Cavatelli	Boil	13 minutes
Conchiglie	Boil	13 minutes
Ditalini (thimbles)	Boil	9 minutes
Egg noodles, fine	Boil	3–4 minutes

PASTA	**INSTRUCTIONS**	**TIMING**
Egg noodles, medium	Boil	4–7 minutes
Fettuccine	Boil	11–12 minutes
Fusilli	Boil	11–13 minutes
Gemelli	Boil	10 minutes
Gnocchi	Boil	6 minutes
Lasagna	Boil	12 minutes
Linguine	Boil	Regular: 9–12 minutes Whole wheat: 12 minutes
Macaroni, elbow	Boil	8–10 minutes
Manicotti	Boil	18 minutes
Mostaccioli	Boil	12 minutes
Orecchiette	Boil	12–15 minutes
Orzo	Boil	8 minutes
Pappardelle	Boil	12 minutes
Penne	Boil	12–13 minutes
Rigatoni	Boil	12–14 minutes
Rotini	Boil	11 minutes
Shells (large)	Boil	18 minutes
Shells (medium)	Boil	10–13 minutes

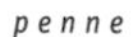

penne

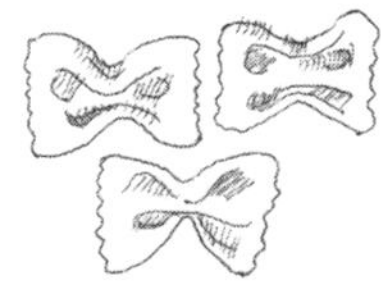

farfalle (butterfly or bowtie)

rigatoni

PASTA	INSTRUCTIONS	TIMING
Spaghetti	Boil	Regular: 11–12 minutes Whole wheat: 15 minutes
Spaghettini	Boil	9 minutes
Stellini	Boil	4–7 minutes
Tortellini	Boil	15 minutes
Vermicelli	Boil	4–7 minutes
Wagon wheels	Boil	13 minutes
Ziti	Boil	13–14 minutes
ITALIAN PASTA, FRESH		
Bow Ties	Boil	2 minutes
Fettuccine	Boil	1½ minutes
Lasagna	Boil	2 minutes
Linguine	Boil	2 minutes
Manicotti	Boil	2 minutes
Noodles	Boil	1½ minutes
Ravioli	Boil	8 minutes
Spaghetti	Boil	1½ minutes
Tagliatelle	Boil	1½ minutes
Tortellini	Boil	7 minutes

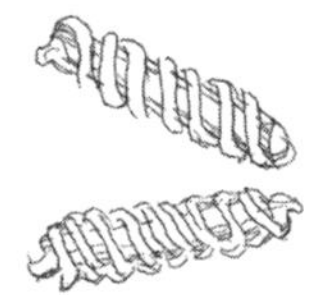

fusilli (corkscrews)

conchiglie (shells)

ravioli

pappardelle

PASTA	INSTRUCTIONS	TIMING
ASIAN NOODLES		
Cellophane noodles	Soak in hot tap water to cover until softened. Drain well.	About 15 minutes
Chinese thin egg noodles	Bring large pot of salted water to a boil. Add noodles and boil until tender. Drain well.	Dried: 4–5 minutes Fresh: 3–4 minutes
Chinese wheat flour noodles	Bring large pot of salted water to a boil. Add noodles and cook until tender. Drain well.	5–7 minutes
Ramen noodles	Bring water to a boil. Add noodles and boil, separating strands, until tender. Drain.	2–3 minutes
Rice noodles, thin (rice vermicelli)	*For Stir-Fries:* Soak in boiling water until softened, then drain. *For Salads, Spring Rolls:* Boil in large pot of boiling water until softened. Drain.	Stir-fries: 15 minutes to partially cook Salads, spring rolls: 3–5 minutes to fully cook
Soba	Bring large pot of salted water to a boil. Add noodles and cook until tender. Drain well. Rinse under running water and drain again.	5–7 minutes

routi (wagon wheel)

ziti

ditali

cavatappi

PASTA	***INSTRUCTIONS***	***TIMING***
Somen	Bring large pot of salted water to a boil. Add noodles and cook until tender. Drain well. Rinse under running water and drain again.	About 5 minutes
Udon	Bring large pot of water to a boil. Add noodles and cook until tender. Drain well.	Dried: 10–12 minutes Fresh: 2–2½ minutes

VEGETABLES

Vegetables, like most foods, are best when fresh. Try to cook them shortly after purchasing. The taste and tenderness of cooked vegetables depend on the age, thickness, and freshness of the vegetable you begin with.

Cooking Vegetables and Flavor Tips

Cooking vegetables is not an exact science. When vegetables are crowded in a pan, they will take longer to cook than those packed loosely or fit in a single layer. If you prefer your vegetables crisp but fully cooked, follow the charts in this book. If you like them slightly crunchy or fairly soft, adjust your time accordingly. You can slightly undercook or overcook vegetables without major impact in taste.

Blanching and Boiling. Add the vegetables to a large pot of salted boiling water, do not cover the pan, and begin timing when the water returns to a boil.

Braising. Braised vegetables are usually sautéed, then simmered in a small amount of liquid. There are many ways to make braised vegetables flavorful. Start with a high-quality oil, such as extra-virgin olive oil, or a flavored oil, such as lemon oil or garlic oil. Or replace some of the oil with butter. You can add herbs, spices, or other aromatic vegetables, such as finely chopped onions or garlic to the sauté. The braising liquid can be water, broth, or even a vegetable juice, such as tomato juice. Add seasoning, such as salt and pepper and fresh herbs and spices at any point in the cooking process.

Braising times listed in the charts are total cooking times, including an initial searing or sautéing step.

Grilling. Vegetables are usually grilled in whole or cut into big slices. If you have a vegetable grilling rack or hinged grill basket, however, you can grill small slices and dices and they won't fall into the fire.

Vegetables need a protective brushing with oil or melted butter to help them brown on the grill. Enhance their taste by using a flavored oil and adding finely chopped herbs or spices to the oil. Or brush with a marinade.

Roasting. Vegetables that are roasted are also tossed with a little oil to aid in browning. Using a flavored oil and adding finely chopped herbs or spices to the oil will add a lot of flavor. And don't forget the salt and pepper.

TIMINGS: Vegetables

This chart is based on preparing and cooking enough vegetables to serve four as part of a meal of several different dishes. See page 323 for microwave cooking of vegetables; see page 302 for pressure cooking of vegetables.

VEGETABLE	METHOD	INSTRUCTIONS	TIMING
ARTICHOKES 4 (10-ounce) globes		*Preparation:* Wash and trim bottom, cut off top 1 inch and snip off tips of leaves. Brush with lemon juice.	
	BAKE	Preheat oven to 375°F. Slice off tops, pull out sharp inner leaves, and scrape out chokes. Stuff and place top up in pan. Add ½ inch water to pan. Cover pan.	45–50 minutes
	BLANCH	Cut artichoke into uniform-size globes. Plunge into boiling water. Remove when blanching time is up and plunge immediately into ice water.	8–10 minutes
	BOIL	Add to a large pot of boiling salted water. Begin counting the time when the water returns to a boil. Drain immediately when boiling time is up.	30–40 minutes
	DEEP-FRY	Preheat oil to 365°F. Use trimmed stems or hearts. Dip in batter. Fry until golden. Drain well.	Until golden

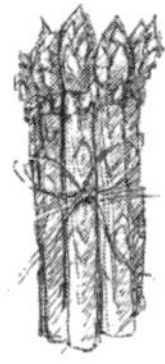

asparagus

artichoke

beet

VEGETABLE	METHOD	INSTRUCTIONS	TIMING
ARTICHOKES 4 (10-ounce) globes (*cont'd.*)	GRILL	Prepare a medium-hot fire in grill. Slice off tops of boiled or steamed artichokes. Cut into quarters, and remove choke. Brush with oil. Grill 4 inches from coals, turning to grill all sides.	10 minutes
	PAN-FRY	Add blanched artichoke hearts to heated oil, stem side up. Fry over medium-high heat, turning once.	8–12 minutes
	PAN-FRY	*To Pan-Fry Batter-Dipped:* Cut trimmed globes into quarters and remove choke. Dip into batter. Fry in hot oil without crowding pan. Turn frequently. Drain briefly on paper towels.	5–8 minutes
	STEAM	Place globes top down in basket over a pan of boiling water and cover pan.	25–40 minutes
ARTICHOKES, JERUSALEM 1 pound		*Preparation:* Scrub, but do not peel. Slice ½ inch thick into acidulated water (1 tablespoon vinegar or lemon juice to 4 cups water). Or leave whole for roasting.	
	ROAST	Preheat oven to 425°F. Toss with oil. Stir occasionally.	20–30 minutes
	SAUTÉ	Add to hot oil or butter in skillet and cook, stirring occasionally.	5–10 minutes
ASPARAGUS 1 pound medium-thick spears; 1½ cups in pieces		*Preparation:* Wash; snap off woody ends. Leave spears whole or chop into 1½-inch pieces.	
	BLANCH	Cut into uniform-size pieces. Plunge into boiling water. When blanching time is up, remove and plunge immediately into ice water.	1–3 minutes
	BOIL	Add to a large pot of boiling salted water. Begin counting the time when the water returns to a boil. Drain immediately when boiling time is up.	4–5 minutes

VEGETABLE	METHOD	INSTRUCTIONS	TIMING
	DEEP-FRY	Preheat oil to 365°F. Cut tips uniformly. Coat in batter. Fry until golden. Drain well.	Until golden
	GRILL	Prepare a medium-hot fire in grill. Brush with oil. Grill whole spears 4 inches from coals, turning occasionally.	7–10 minutes
	ROAST	Preheat oven to 500°F. Brush whole spears with olive oil. Stir occasionally.	8–10 minutes
	STEAM	Place in basket over a pan of boiling water and cover pan.	4–5 minutes
	STIR-FRY	Add to hot oil in wok or skillet. Cook, stirring constantly.	6 minutes
BEANS, FRESH GREEN AND YELLOW ¾ pound; 2¼ cups in pieces		*Preparation:* Wash; snap off the ends. Leave whole or cut into 1-inch lengths.	
	BLANCH	Cut beans into uniform-size pieces. Plunge into boiling water. When blanching time is up, remove and plunge immediately into ice water.	2–3 minutes
	BOIL	Cut beans into uniform-size pieces. Add to a large pot of boiling salted water. Begin counting the time when the water returns to a boil. Drain immediately when boiling time is up.	4–8 minutes
	GRILL	Prepare a medium-hot fire in grill. Brush whole beans with oil. Grill 4 inches from coals, turning occasionally.	8–10 minutes
	SAUTÉ	Start with steamed beans. Add to hot oil or butter and cook, stirring occasionally.	2–3 minutes

VEGETABLE	*METHOD*	*INSTRUCTIONS*	*TIMING*
BEANS, FRESH GREEN AND YELLOW ¾ pound; 2¼ cups in pieces (*cont'd.*)	STEAM	Place in basket over a pan of boiling water and cover pan.	5–12 minutes
	STIR-FRY	Add to hot oil in wok or skillet. Cook, stirring, until softened. Add broth or other liquid, cover wok, then steam until tender.	5–6 minutes uncovered, then 5–10 minutes covered
BEANS, FRESH SHELL 2 pounds in pod		*Preparation:* Shell the beans.	
	BLANCH	Plunge into boiling water. When blanching time is up, remove and plunge immediately into ice water.	1–2 minutes
	BOIL	Add to a large pot of boiling salted water. Begin counting the time when the water returns to a boil. Drain immediately when boiling time is up.	10–40 minutes, depending on variety
	STEAM	Place in basket over pan of boiling water and cover pan.	10–40 minutes, depending on variety
BEET GREENS 2 pounds		*Preparation:* Wash. Separate stems from leaves. Slice into ¼- to ½-inch strips.	

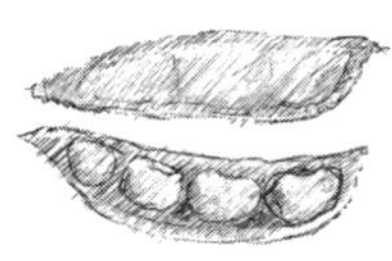

lima beans

American green bean

VEGETABLE	METHOD	INSTRUCTIONS	TIMING
	BLANCH	Plunge into a large pot of boiling salted water. When blanching time is up, remove and plunge immediately into ice water.	2–3 minutes
	BOIL	Add to a large pot of boiling salted water. Begin counting the time when the water returns to a boil. Drain immediately when boiling time is up.	3–7 minutes
	SAUTÉ	Add to heated oil or butter in skillet and cook, stirring occasionally.	5–7 minutes
	STEAM	Place in a basket over a pan of boiling water and cover pan.	8–10 minutes
BEETS 1 pound		*Preparation:* Wash; do not peel. Cut off stems, leaving about 1½ inches.	
	BAKE	Preheat oven to 325°F and wrap unpeeled beets individually in aluminum foil.	Small beets: 20–30 minutes Large beets: 40–60 minutes
	BOIL	Add to large pot of boiling water. Begin counting the time when the water returns to a boil. When boiling time is up, plunge into cold water until cool enough to handle. Slip off skins.	Small beets: 20–30 minutes Large beets: 40–60 minutes
	ROAST	Preheat oven to 400°F. Do not peel. Toss with oil. Stir occasionally.	Small beets: 25–45 minutes Large beets: 35–60 minutes
	STEAM	Place in basket over a pan of boiling water and cover pan.	Small beets: 20–30 minutes Large beets: 40–60 minutes
BROCCOLI 1 pound		*Preparation:* Wash; trim leaves and tough end of stalk. Use paring knife to remove outer tough skin of stalk. Cut lengthwise into spears.	

VEGETABLE	METHOD	INSTRUCTIONS	TIMING
BROCCOLI 1 pound (*cont'd.*)	BLANCH	Cut into uniform-size pieces. Plunge into boiling water. When blanching time is up, plunge immediately into ice water.	2–4 minutes
	BOIL	Cut into uniform-size pieces. Add to a large pot of boiling salted water. Begin counting the time when the water returns to a boil. Drain immediately when boiling time is up.	5–7 minutes
	DEEP-FRY	Preheat oil to 350°F. Chop florets into 1½-inch pieces or quarters. Dip into batter, then deep-fry in hot oil until golden. Drain briefly on paper towels.	Until golden
	SAUTÉ	Start with blanched broccoli. Add to hot butter or oil and cook until heated through, stirring occasionally.	2–4 minutes
	STEAM	Place in basket over a pan of boiling water and cover pan.	5–7 minutes
	STIR-FRY	Chop florets and stems into 1½-inch pieces. Add to heated oil in wok or skillet. Stir while cooking.	4–6 minutes
BROCCOLI RABE 1 pound		*Preparation:* Wash and cut off tough part of stalks. Remove wilted outer leaves. Chop into 1½- to 3-inch pieces.	
	BLANCH	Cut into uniform-size pieces. Plunge into boiling water. When blanching time is up, remove and plunge immediately into ice water.	2–4 minutes

broccoli

Savoy cabbage

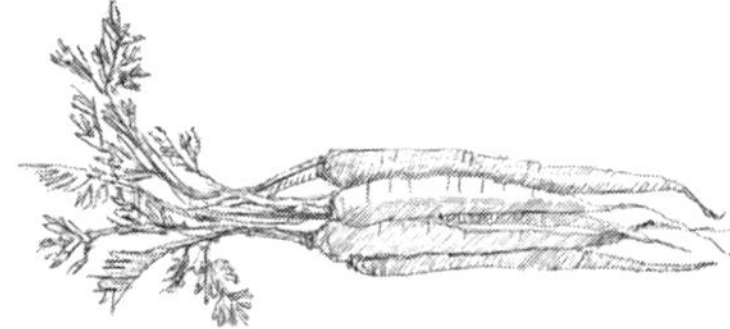

carrots

VEGETABLE	METHOD	INSTRUCTIONS	TIMING
	BOIL	Cut into uniform-size pieces. Add to a large pot of boiling salted water. Begin counting the time when the water returns to a boil. Drain immediately when boiling time is up.	6–9 minutes
	SAUTÉ	Start with blanched broccoli rabe. Add to hot butter or oil.	2–4 minutes
	STEAM	Cut into uniform-size pieces. Place in a basket over a pan of boiling water and cover the pan.	6–9 minutes
	STIR-FRY	Chop into 1½-inch pieces. Add to hot oil in wok or skillet. Cook, stirring constantly.	4–6 minutes
BRUSSELS SPROUTS 1 pound		*Preparation:* Wash and remove wilted leaves. Cut an *X* in the bottom of each sprout for even cooking.	
	BLANCH	Plunge into a large pot of boiling salted water. When blanching time is up, remove and plunge immediately into ice water.	3–4 minutes
	BOIL	Add to a large pot of boiling salted water. Begin counting the time when the water returns to a boil. Drain immediately when boiling time is up.	6–12 minutes
	BRAISE	Sauté in heated butter or oil. Then add 1 inch broth and seasonings, cover, and cook until sprouts are tender.	15–20 minutes
	STEAM	Place in a basket over a pan of boiling water and cover pan.	9–14 minutes
	STIR-FRY	Cut into halves or quarters. Add to heated oil in wok or skillet. Cook, stirring constantly.	2–4 minutes

VEGETABLE	METHOD	INSTRUCTIONS	TIMING
CABBAGE 1 pound or 4–8 wedges (1½ inch thick) or 1½ cups shredded		*Preparation:* Wash and remove tough outer leaves, remove white core. Cut into 1½-inch wedges or shred.	
	BLANCH	Plunge into a large pot of boiling salted water. When blanching time is up, remove and plunge immediately into ice water.	3–5 minutes
	BOIL	Add to a large pot of boiling salted water. Begin counting the time when the water returns to a boil. Drain immediately when boiling time is up.	SHREDDED: Green: 9–11 minutes Red: 12–15 minutes WEDGES: Green: 12–15 minutes Red: 15–17 minutes WHOLE LEAVES: Green: 5–7 minutes Red: 15 minutes
	STIR-FRY	Shred cabbage or very thinly slice. Add to heated oil in wok or skillet and cook, stirring constantly.	7–10 minutes
CARROTS 1 pound		*Preparation:* Wash; scrub or peel. Slice or dice. For baby whole carrots, wash and scrub. Use same timings.	
	BLANCH	Plunge into a large pot of boiling salted water. When blanching time is up, remove and plunge immediately into ice water.	1–3 minutes

VEGETABLE	METHOD	INSTRUCTIONS	TIMING
	BOIL	Add to a large pot of boiling salted water. Begin counting the time when the water returns to a boil. Drain immediately when boiling time is up.	4–6 minutes
	GRILL	Prepare a medium-hot fire in grill. Leave carrots whole. Brush with oil. Grill 4 inches from coals, turning frequently.	About 10 minutes
	ROAST	Preheat oven to 400°F. Leave carrots whole or cut into even-size chunks. Brush with oil. Stir occasionally.	About 1 hour
	SAUTÉ	Start with blanched carrots. Add to hot butter or oil and cook until heated through.	2–4 minutes
	STEAM	Place in a basket over a pan of boiling water and cover pan.	7–10 minutes
	STIR-FRY	Slice thinly or grate. Add to hot oil in wok or skillet and cook, stirring constantly.	6–7 minutes
CAULIFLOWER 1 pound		*Preparation:* Wash. Trim off leaves, cut florets from tough stem.	
	BLANCH	Plunge into a large pot of boiling salted water. When blanching time is up, remove and plunge immediately into ice water.	Florets: 1–3 minutes Whole head: 15–20 minutes

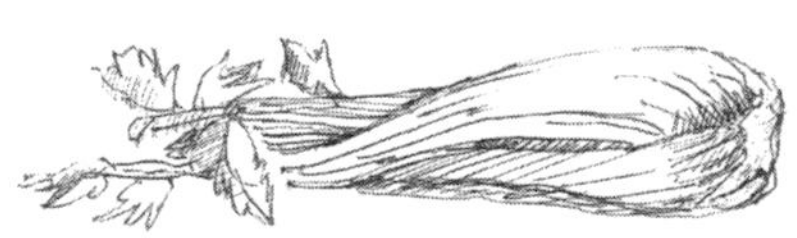

celery

cauliflower

VEGETABLE	***METHOD***	***INSTRUCTIONS***	***TIMING***
CAULIFLOWER 1 pound (*cont'd.*)	BOIL	Add to a large pot of boiling salted water. Begin counting the time when the water returns to a boil. Drain immediately when boiling time is up.	Florets: 3–5 minutes Whole head: 10–15 minutes
	DEEP-FRY	Preheat oil to 365°F. Dip each floret in batter and deep-fry until golden. Drain well after frying.	Until golden
	SAUTÉ	Start with blanched florets. Add to hot butter or oil in pan.	6 minutes
	STEAM	Place in a basket over a pan of boiling water and cover pan.	Florets: 7–9 minutes Whole head: 15–20 minutes
CELERY 1 pound		*Preparation:* Wash each stalk and remove leaves. Cut away white stalk at end if tough. Remove strings on outside if tough. Slice, chop, or dice.	
	BLANCH	Plunge into a large pot of boiling salted water. When blanching time is up, remove and plunge immediately into ice water.	1–3 minutes
	BOIL	Add to a large pot of boiling salted water. Begin counting the time when the water returns to a boil. Drain immediately when boiling time is up.	6–8 minutes
	SAUTÉ	Chop into 1½-inch pieces. Add to hot butter or oil in pan.	2–3 minutes
	STEAM	Place in a basket over a pan of boiling water and cover pan.	7–9 minutes
	STIR-FRY	Chop into 1–1½-inch pieces. Add to hot oil in wok or skillet. Cook, stirring constantly.	5–6 minutes

VEGETABLE	METHOD	INSTRUCTIONS	TIMING
CELERY ROOT (Celeriac) 1 pound		*Preparation:* Wash. Peel, cut into slices or strips, and place pieces in acidulated water (1 tablespoon vinegar or lemon juice to 4 cups cold water).	
	BOIL	Add to a large pot of boiling salted water. Begin counting the time when the water returns to a boil. Drain immediately when boiling time is up.	6–10 minutes
	ROAST	Preheat oven to 350°F. Use whole trimmed, unpeeled roots. Brush with olive oil. Turn once after 30 minutes.	About 1 hour
	STEAM	Place in a basket over a pan of boiling water and cover pan.	8–12 minutes
CHAYOTE (Mirliton, Christophene) 2 whole		*Preparation:* Peel unless chayote is young. Cut in half and remove seed. Cut into cubes.	
	BLANCH	Plunge into a large pot of boiling salted water. When blanching time is up, remove and plunge immediately into ice water.	4–5 minutes
	BOIL	Add to a large pot of boiling salted water. Begin counting the time when the water returns to a boil. Drain immediately when boiling time is up.	6–10 minutes
	STEAM	Place in a basket over a pan of boiling water and cover pan.	8–10 minutes
COLLARD GREENS 2 pounds		*Preparation:* Wash. Strip leaves from stems and chop each. Reduce cooking times for baby greens.	

VEGETABLE	METHOD	INSTRUCTIONS	TIMING
COLLARD GREENS 2 pounds (*cont'd.*)	BOIL	Add to a large pot of boiling salted water. Begin counting the time when the water returns to a boil. Drain immediately when boiling time is up.	10–15 minutes
	BRAISE	Briefly sauté greens in hot butter or oil in skillet. Add 1 inch broth or other cooking liquid and seasonings. Cover pan and simmer. Add more liquid as needed.	20–30 minutes
CORN 6 large ears or 2½ cups kernels		*Preparation:* Remove husks and silks from ears. Scrape kernels from cob.	
	BLANCH	Plunge into a large pot of boiling salted water. When blanching time is up, remove and plunge immediately into ice water.	1–2 minutes
	BOIL	Add to a large pot of boiling salted water. Begin counting the time when the water returns to a boil. Drain immediately when boiling time is up.	3–4 minutes
	SAUTÉ	Add to hot butter or oil in skillet and cook, stirring occasionally.	3–5 minutes
	STEAM	Place in a basket over a pan of boiling water and cover pan.	3–4 minutes

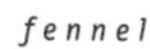

fennel

eggplant

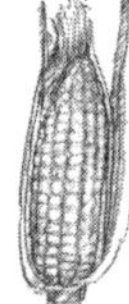

corn on the cob

VEGETABLE	*METHOD*	*INSTRUCTIONS*	*TIMING*
CORN ON THE COB 4–8 ears		*Preparation:* Remove husks and silks from ears and wash, if desired. Cooking in husks intensifies flavor, but silks should be removed.	
	BLANCH	Plunge into a large pot of boiling salted water. When blanching time is up, remove and plunge immediately into ice water.	1–2 minutes
	BOIL	Add to a large pot of boiling salted water. Begin counting the time when the water returns to a boil. Drain immediately when boiling time is up.	1–3 minutes
	GRILL	Soak corn in husk for 1 hour (optional). Prepare a medium-hot fire in grill. Pull down husk to remove silks, replace husk, tying off or twisting ends. Or wrap each ear in foil. Grill 4 inches from coals, turning frequently.	15–25 minutes
	ROAST	Soak corn in husk for 1 hour (optional). Pull down husk to remove silks, replace husk, tying off or twisting ends. Or wrap each ear in foil. Preheat oven to 450°F.	15–25 minutes
	STEAM	Place in a basket over a pan of boiling water and cover pan.	3–5 minutes
EGGPLANT 2 pounds		*Preparation:* Trim stems; peel if desired. Leave whole for grilling and roasting, or slice or cube. Salting will draw off bitter flavors if eggplant is old (drain for 30–60 minutes).	
	BAKE	Preheat oven to 375°F. Coat eggplant slices with crumbs. Place on well-oiled baking sheets. Turn once during baking.	30–45 minutes

VEGETABLE	METHOD	INSTRUCTIONS	TIMING
EGGPLANT 2 pounds (*cont'd.*)	BLANCH	Cut eggplant into uniform-size pieces. Plunge into a large pot of boiling salted water. When blanching time is up, remove and plunge immediately into ice water.	3–4 minutes
	BROIL	Leave whole, pricking with a fork in several places, or cut in ½-inch slices and brush generously with oil. Broil 4 inches from heat, turning several times.	Slices: 10–15 minutes Whole: 30–45 minutes
	DEEP-FRY	Preheat oil to 365°F. Batter-dip or crumb-coat slices or cubes. Drain on paper towels after frying.	Until golden
	GRILL	Prepare a medium-hot fire in grill. Leave whole, pricking with a fork in several places, or cut in ½-inch slices and brush generously with oil. Grill 4 inches from coals, turning once.	Slices: 10–15 minutes Whole: 30–45 minutes
	ROAST	Preheat oven to 400°F. Place whole eggplant in roasting pan. Prick in several places with a fork. Roast until soft and collapsed.	20–40 minutes
	SAUTÉ OR PAN-FRY	Add cubed eggplant to hot oil in skillet. Cook, stirring constantly, until eggplant is completely tender.	About 15 minutes
	STEAM	Cut eggplant into uniform-size pieces. Place in a basket over a pan of boiling water and cover pan.	4–5 minutes
ENDIVE, ESCAROLE, RADICCHIO 1 pound		*Preparation:* Rinse, trim away wilted or bruised leaves. Cut in half or wedges.	
	BRAISE	Sauté briefly in hot oil or butter. Add 1 inch broth or other liquid and seasonings to pan. Cover and simmer. Add more liquid as needed.	6–10 minutes

VEGETABLE	METHOD	INSTRUCTIONS	TIMING
	GRILL	Prepare a medium-hot fire in grill. Brush with oil. Grill 4 inches from the coals, turning occasionally.	5–10 minutes
	ROAST	Preheat oven to 425°F. Brush with oil. Turn once.	10–15 minutes
FENNEL 2 medium bulbs		*Preparation:* Wash. Remove upper and wilted stalks. May be cut into thin slices or quarters or left whole.	
	BLANCH	Plunge into a large pot of boiling salted water. When blanching time is up, remove and plunge immediately into ice water.	Slices: 2–3 minutes Whole bulbs: 9–10 minutes
	BOIL	Add to a large pot of boiling salted water. Begin counting the time when the water returns to a boil. Drain immediately when boiling time is up.	Slices: 4–6 minutes Quarters: 6–8 minutes Whole bulbs: 5–20 minutes
	BRAISE	Sauté briefly in hot oil or butter. Add 1 inch broth or other cooking liquid and seasonings to pan, cover, and simmer. Add more cooking liquid as needed.	Quarters: 15–20 minutes
	GRILL	Prepare a medium-hot fire in grill. Slice ¼-inch thick. Toss with oil. Grill 4 inches from coals on vegetable grilling rack or grill basket, turning occasionally.	10–12 minutes
	ROAST	Preheat oven to 375°F. Use blanched bulbs and cut into slices. Brush with oil. Turn once.	30–40 minutes
	STEAM	Place in a basket over a pan of boiling water and cover pan.	Quarters: 15–20 minutes

VEGETABLE	METHOD	INSTRUCTIONS	TIMING
GARLIC 4 bulbs	BLANCH	Plunge unpeeled cloves into a large pot of boiling salted water. When blanching time is up, remove and plunge immediately into ice water. Drain and peel.	2 minutes
	GRILL	Prepare a medium-hot fire in grill. Rub off papery skin after cutting off ¼ inch from head. Brush with olive oil; wrap tightly in foil. Or skewer individual peeled cloves and brush with oil. Grill 4 inches from coals, turning occasionally.	Whole bulbs: 10–15 minutes Cloves: 5–10 minutes
	ROAST	Preheat oven to 325°F, rub off papery skin after cutting off ¼ inch from head. Place the heads in baking dish. Pour a little olive oil or chicken stock over each head. Cover and bake.	1 hour
	SAUTÉ	Peel cloves. Slice or chop. Add to hot oil or butter in pan. Stir and cook over medium heat so as not to burn.	3–4 minutes
KALE 2 pounds		*Preparation:* Remove wilted or yellow leaves. Wash thoroughly in several changes of water. Strip leaves from stems and discard stems. Slice leaves into ribbons. Timing depends on age of kale.	

garlic

leek

VEGETABLE	*METHOD*	*INSTRUCTIONS*	*TIMING*
	BLANCH	Plunge into a large pot of boiling salted water. When blanching time is up, remove and plunge immediately into ice water.	2–3 minutes
	BOIL	Add to a large pot of boiling salted water. Begin counting the time when the water returns to a boil. Drain immediately when boiling time is up.	10–25 minutes
	BRAISE	Sauté briefly in hot butter or oil. Add 1 inch broth or other cooking liquid and seasonings to pan. Cover pan and simmer. Add more liquid as needed.	10–25 minutes
KOHLRABI 1 pound		*Preparation:* Wash; remove leaves and stems. Peel older kohlrabi with tough skins. Then chop or slice. (For cooking leaves, see Mustard Greens.)	
	BLANCH	Plunge into a large pot of boiling salted water. When blanching time is up, remove and plunge immediately into ice water.	1–2 minutes
	BOIL	Add to a large pot of boiling salted water. Begin counting the time when the water returns to a boil. Drain immediately when boiling time is up.	7–10 minutes
	STEAM	Place in a basket over a pan of boiling water and cover pan.	9–14 minutes
LEEKS 1 pound	*Preparation:* Wash well. Remove tough outer leaves and roots. Leave whole, slice into quarters, or thinly slice crosswise.		
	BOIL	Add to a large pot of boiling salted water. Begin counting the time when the water returns to a boil. Drain immediately when boiling time is up.	Slices: 3–5 minutes Halves: 6–8 minutes Whole: 10–25 minutes

VEGETABLE	METHOD	INSTRUCTIONS	TIMING
LEEKS 1 pound (*cont'd.*)	BRAISE	Sauté briefly in hot oil or butter. Add 1 inch broth or other cooking liquid and seasonings to pan. Cover and simmer. Add more liquid as needed.	15–20 minutes
	GRILL	Prepare a medium-hot fire in grill. Halve lengthwise and brush with oil. Grill 4 inches from coals, turning occasionally.	5–10 minutes
	ROAST	Preheat oven to 300°F. Brush with oil. Baste occasionally.	40–60 minutes
	STEAM	Place in a basket over a pan of boiling water and cover pan.	Slices: 3–5 minutes Halves: 6–8 minutes Whole: 10–25 minutes
MUSHROOMS (Button, Chanterelles, Enoki, Morels, Oyster, Porcini, Portobello, Shiitake) 1–1½ pounds		*Preparation:* Wipe clean with damp paper towel, trim bottom stem. Discard stem of shiitakes. Leave whole, slice, chop, or mince.	
	BAKE	Preheat oven to 350°F. Coat caps with butter and place in baking dish. May be stuffed and returned to oven to heat stuffing through.	15–20 minutes

chanterelle

porcini

morel

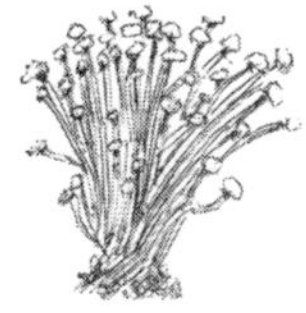
enoki

VEGETABLE	METHOD	INSTRUCTIONS	TIMING
	BLANCH	Plunge into a large pot of boiling salted water. When blanching time is up, remove and plunge immediately into ice water.	4 minutes
	BROIL	Remove stems. Brush caps with butter or oil. Broil 4 inches from flame, turning once.	4–5 minutes
	DEEP-FRY	Preheat oil to 365°F. Dip in batter. Drain well after frying.	Until golden
	GRILL	Prepare a medium-hot fire in grill. Toss or brush with oil. Grill 4 inches from coals on vegetable grilling rack or hinged basket or arranged on skewers. Turn once while grilling.	5–8 minutes
	ROAST	Preheat oven to 500°F. Brush mushrooms with oil. Turn once during roasting.	10–15 minutes
	SAUTÉ	Add to hot butter or oil in skillet over medium-high heat. Shake pan or stir continuously.	3–4 minutes
MUSTARD OR TURNIP GREENS 2 pounds		*Preparation:* Wash. Strip leaves from stems and chop both. Reduce cooking times for baby greens.	
	BLANCH	Plunge into a large pot of boiling salted water. When blanching time is up, remove and plunge immediately into ice water.	2–3 minutes
	BOIL	Add to a large pot of boiling salted water. Begin counting the time when the water returns to a boil. Drain immediately when boiling time is up.	5–10 minutes

VEGETABLE	METHOD	INSTRUCTIONS	TIMING
MUSTARD OR TURNIP GREENS 2 pounds (*cont'd.*)	BRAISE	Sauté briefly in hot oil or butter. Add 1 inch broth or other liquid and seasonings to the pan. Cover and simmer. Add more liquid as needed.	15–25 minutes
OKRA 1 pound		*Preparation:* Wash, cut off stem. Leave whole for blanching, steaming, boiling, deep-frying, or grilling. May be sliced into ½-inch rounds for sautéing or stewing.	
	BLANCH	Plunge into a large pot of boiling salted water. When blanching time is up, remove and plunge immediately into ice water.	2–3 minutes
	BOIL	Add to a large pot of boiling salted water. Begin counting the time when the water returns to a boil. Drain immediately when boiling time is up.	4–8 minutes
	BRAISE	Sauté briefly in hot butter or oil. Add broth, sauce, or other ingredients and bring to a boil. Cover, reduce heat, and simmer.	30 minutes
	DEEP-FRY	Preheat oil to 365°F. Dip in batter or coat with crumbs. Drain well after frying.	Until golden
	GRILL	Prepare a medium-hot fire in grill. Toss with oil. Grill 4 inches from coals on vegetable grilling rack, in hinged basket, or arranged on skewers. Turn occasionally.	7–10 minutes
	SAUTÉ	Add to hot butter or oil in skillet and cook, stirring occasionally.	4–5 minutes
	STEAM	Place in a basket over a pan of boiling water and cover pan.	4–8 minutes

VEGETABLE	*METHOD*	*INSTRUCTIONS*	*TIMING*
ONIONS (Yellow onions, White onions, Red onions, Boiling onions, Cipollini, Pearl onions) 1 pound			
	BAKE	Preheat oven to 375°F. Place whole unpeeled onions on rack above a pan with ¼ inch water. Cover. Uncover for last 15–30 minutes.	1¼–1½ hours
	BLANCH	Add unpeeled onions to a large pot of boiling salted water. Boil, then drain and peel.	3 minutes
	BOIL	Add peeled whole onions to a large pot of boiling salted water. Begin counting the time when the water returns to a boil. Drain immediately when boiling time is up.	Pearl, boiling, cipollini: 2–5 minutes Large whole: 30 minutes
	BRAISE	Begin with blanched and peeled onions. Melt butter in skillet, add onions, Cook and cover. over low heat, shaking skillet often; uncover for last 5 minutes and cook until tender.	25–30 minutes
	DEEP-FRY	Preheat oil to 365°F. Cut peeled onions into rings and dip in batter. Drain on paper towels after frying and sprinkle with salt.	Until golden

Vidalia onion

parsnip

garden pea

VEGETABLE	METHOD	INSTRUCTIONS	TIMING
ONIONS (Yellow onions, White onions, Red onions, Boiling onions, Cipollini, Pearl onions) 1 pound (*cont'd.*)	GRILL	Prepare a medium-hot fire in grill. Peel and cut into ½-inch-thick slices or leave whole. Brush with oil. Grill 4 inches from coals; slices are best on vegetable grilling rack or hinged grill basket. Turn occasionally.	Slices: 10 minutes Whole onions: 20 minutes
	ROAST	Preheat oven to 400°F. Place peeled or unpeeled onions on baking sheet.	1 hour
	SAUTÉ	Peel onions. Chop, slice, or mince. Add to hot butter or oil in skillet and cook, stirring occasionally	4–5 minutes
	STIR-FRY	Peel onions. Chop, slice, or mince. Add to hot oil in wok or skillet and cook, stirring constantly.	4–5 minutes
PARSNIPS 1 pound		*Preparation:* Wash and trim off tops and roots; peel or scrub. Cut into ¼-inch slices or cubes.	
	BLANCH	Plunge into a large pot of boiling salted water. When blanching time is up, remove and plunge immediately into ice water.	2–3 minutes
	BOIL	Add to a large pot of boiling salted water. Begin counting the time when the water returns to a boil. Drain immediately when boiling time is up.	4–6 minutes
	BRAISE	Briefly sauté blanched parsnips in hot oil or butter. Add 1 inch broth or other cooking liquid and seasonings to pan. Bring to a boil, cover, reduce heat, and simmer.	10–15 minutes
	ROAST	Preheat oven to 375°F. Toss with oil. Stir occasionally while roasting.	30–45 minutes
	STEAM	Place in a basket over a pan of boiling water and cover pan.	6–8 minutes

VEGETABLE	METHOD	INSTRUCTIONS	TIMING
PEAS, GREEN 2 pounds (3 cups shelled)		*Preparation:* Wash and shell.	
	BLANCH	Plunge into a large pot of boiling salted water. When blanching time is up, remove and plunge immediately into ice water.	1–2 minutes
	BOIL	Add to a large pot of boiling salted water. Begin counting the time when the water returns to a boil. Drain immediately when boiling time is up.	4–10 minutes
	BRAISE	Sauté briefly in hot oil or butter. Add 1 inch broth or other cooking liquid and seasonings to pan. Bring to a boil, cover, reduce heat, and simmer.	15–25 minutes
	STEAM	Place in a basket over a pan of boiling water and cover pan.	5–10 minutes
PEAS, EDIBLE POD (Sugar snap, Snow) 1 pound		*Preparation:* Wash; remove strings from one or both seams as needed.	
	BLANCH	Plunge into a large pot of boiling salted water. When blanching time is up, remove and plunge immediately into ice water.	½–1 minute
	BOIL	Add to a large pot of boiling salted water. Begin counting the time when the water returns to a boil. Drain immediately when boiling time is up.	1–2 minutes
	STEAM	Place in a basket over a pan of boiling water and cover pan.	2–5 minutes
	STIR-FRY	Add to hot oil in wok or skillet. Cook over high heat, stirring constantly.	2–5 minutes

VEGETABLE	METHOD	INSTRUCTIONS	TIMING
PEPPERS, HOT AND SWEET 2–4 peppers		*Preparation:* Wash; remove stems, cut and remove seeds and white membrane. Slice into rings or strips.	
	BAKE	*To Bake Stuffed:* Preheat oven to 375°F. Stuff steamed peppers and place in baking dish. Tops may be browned under broiler after baking.	20–30 minutes
	BLANCH	Plunge into a large pot of boiling salted water. When blanching time is up, remove and plunge immediately into ice water.	2 minutes
	BOIL	Add to a large pot of boiling salted water. Begin counting the time when the water returns to a boil. Drain immediately when boiling time is up.	6–7 minutes
	GRILL	Prepare a medium-hot fire in grill. Toss slices or halves with oil. Place halves directly on grill 4 inches from coals or place slices on vegetable grilling rack 4 inches from coals. Turn frequently.	8–10 minutes
	ROAST	Place whole peppers directly over stovetop gas flame, under broiler flame, on barbecue grill, or in dry skillet over high heat. Turn frequently to char skin all over. Remove and place in paper or plastic bag to allow steam to loosen skin. Remove from bag, peel off skin, and remove seeds and membranes.	10–12 minutes, plus 10 minutes standing time
	SAUTÉ	Add to hot butter or oil in skillet and cook, stirring occasionally.	7–10 minutes
	STEAM	Place in a basket over a pan of boiling water and cover pan.	6–7 minutes
	STIR-FRY	Add to hot oil in wok or skillet. Cook over high heat, stirring constantly.	7–10 minutes

VEGETABLE	METHOD	INSTRUCTIONS	TIMING
PLANTAINS 4 small		*Preparation:* To peel green and yellow plantains, cut into pieces, slit skin along ridgeline, and peel. To peel ripe plantains, cut off ends, cut slit the length of skin, and peel.	
	BAKE	Preheat oven to 400°F. Choose green or yellow plantains and do not peel. Serve in skin after baking, as you would a baked potato.	40 minutes
	DEEP-FRY	Preheat oil to 365°F. Slice peeled ripe plantains into $\frac{1}{4}$-inch rounds. After frying, drain well on paper towels.	Until golden
	SAUTÉ	Slice peeled ripe plantains into $\frac{1}{4}$-inch rounds. Add to hot butter or oil in skillet. Cook over medium-low heat, turning once.	6–8 minutes
POTATOES $1\frac{1}{2}$ pounds		*Preparation:* Wash; peel if desired. Chop, slice, cube, or leave whole.	
	BAKE	Preheat oven to 400°F. For best results, use russet potatoes, such as Idaho. Prick with fork to let steam escape.	45–60 minutes
	BAKE	*To Bake Oven Fries:* Cut baking potato into $\frac{3}{4}$-inch strips. Preheat oven to 450°F. Toss potatoes with oil. Arrange on baking sheet in single layer. Turn several times during baking. Sprinkle with salt.	30–35 minutes

bell pepper

baking potato, red potato, new potato

sweet potato

VEGETABLE	METHOD	INSTRUCTIONS	TIMING
POTATOES 1½ pounds (*cont'd.*)	BOIL	Cook new potatoes, unpeeled, in a small amount of salted water and cover pan. Peeling is optional for mature potatoes; remove sprouts and blemishes. Leave whole, cut in chunks, or slice. Cook in salted water to cover and cover pan.	Whole new potatoes: 10–15 minutes Whole mature potatoes: 20–45 minutes Slices: 5–7 minutes
	DEEP-FRY	*To Make French Fries:* Cut baking potato into ⅜-inch strips. Preheat oil to 365°F. After frying, drain on paper towels and sprinkle with salt.	Until golden
	GRILL	Prepare a medium-hot fire in grill. Wrap whole baking potatoes in foil. Grill 4 inches from coals, turning occasionally.	1–1½ hours
	GRILL	Prepare a medium-hot fire in grill. Slice boiled or steamed potatoes or cut in wedges. Toss with oil. Grill 4 inches from coals, turning occasionally.	10–12 minutes
	PAN-FRY	Slice cooled preboiled potatoes. Add to hot butter or oil in skillet and turn frequently.	5–6 minutes
	PAN-FRY	Thinly slice potatoes or grate on large holes of grater. Heat butter or oil in large, heavy skillet. Add potatoes in thin layer, and cook over medium heat, turning once.	15 minutes
	ROAST	Preheat oven to 425°F. Peel and cut potatoes into uniform chunks. Toss potatoes with oil and season with salt and pepper. Turn a few times during roasting.	25–45 minutes

VEGETABLE	METHOD	INSTRUCTIONS	TIMING
	STEAM	Place in basket over pot of boiling water and cover pan.	Whole mature potatoes: 30–45 minutes Slices: 10–15 minutes Whole new potatoes: 15–20 minutes
POTATOES, SWEET AND YAMS 4 large		*Preparation:* Wash. Select whole unpeeled potatoes. Peel after cooking.	
	BAKE	Preheat oven to 400°F. Prick with fork before cooking.	35–50 minutes
	BOIL	Add to a large pot of salted water. Bring to a boil, then cover.	15–35 minutes
	DEEP-FRY	Preheat oil to 365°F. Boil potatoes in water to cover for 10 minutes. Then peel and cut into strips. After frying, drain on paper towels and sprinkle with salt.	Until golden
	GRILL	Prepare a medium-hot fire in grill. Wrap whole potatoes in foil. Grill 4 inches from coals, turning occasionally.	45–60 minutes
	GRILL	Prepare a medium-hot fire in grill. Slice or cut in wedges. Toss with oil. Grill 4 inches from the coals, turning occasionally.	15–20 minutes
	STEAM	Leave whole or cut in halves or 1- to 2-inch cubes. Place in basket over pot of boiling water and cover pan.	Whole potatoes 30–35 minutes Halves: 15–20 minutes Cubes: 13–18 minutes

VEGETABLE	METHOD	INSTRUCTIONS	TIMING
RUTABAGAS 1 pound	*Preparation:* Peel. Cut into slices or cubes.		
	BLANCH	Plunge into a large pot of boiling salted water. When blanching time is up, remove and plunge immediately into ice water.	3–5 minutes
	BOIL	Add to a large pot of boiling salted water. Begin counting the time when the water returns to a boil. Drain immediately when boiling time is up.	12–18 minutes
	DEEP-FRY	Preheat oil to 365°F. Cut into ⅜-inch strips. Drain on paper towels after frying. Sprinkle with salt.	Until golden
	ROAST	Preheat oven to 375°F. Toss blanched rutabagas with oil. Turn occasionally.	30–45 minutes
	STEAM	Place in a basket over a pan of boiling water and cover pan.	12–16 minutes
SCALLIONS 16 scallions		*Preparation:* Wash and remove tough outer parts. Trim roots. Slice crosswise or leave whole.	
	BRAISE	Sauté in butter or oil. Add 1 inch broth or other cooking liquid and seasonings to the pan. Cover and simmer.	7–10 minutes
	GRILL	Prepare a medium-hot fire in grill. Brush with oil. Grill 4 inches from coals, turning occasionally.	5–8 minutes
	SAUTÉ	Add to hot oil or butter in skillet and cook over medium-high heat, stirring occasionally.	5 minutes
	STIR-FRY	Add to hot oil in wok or skillet and cook over high heat, stirring constantly.	5 minutes

VEGETABLE	METHOD	INSTRUCTIONS	TIMING
SHALLOTS 1 pound		*Preparation:* Trim off top and base. Peel. Slice, chop, or mince, or leave whole.	
	BLANCH	Plunge whole shallots into a large pot of boiling salted water. When blanching time is up, remove and plunge immediately into ice water.	2 minutes
	BRAISE	Sauté briefly in butter or oil. Add 1 inch broth or other cooking liquid and seasonings to pan. Cover and simmer. Add more liquid as needed.	20–30 minutes
	ROAST	Preheat oven to 450°F. Toss peeled shallots with oil. Stir occasionally.	15–20 minutes
	SAUTÉ	Add sliced, chopped, or minced shallots to hot oil or butter in skillet and cook over medium-high heat, stirring occasionally.	3–5 minutes
	STIR-FRY	Add sliced, chopped, or minced shallots to hot oil in wok or skillet and cook over high heat, stirring constantly.	3–5 minutes
SPINACH 1½–2 pounds		*Preparation:* Wash thoroughly. Remove tough stems. Leave whole or chop.	
	BLANCH	Plunge into a large pot of boiling salted water. When blanching time is up, remove and plunge immediately into ice water.	1–2 minutes
	BOIL	Add to a large pot of boiling salted water. Begin counting the time when the water returns to a boil. Drain immediately when boiling time is up.	1–2 minutes
	SAUTÉ	Add to hot butter or oil in large pot and cook, stirring occasionally, until wilted and heated through.	3–4 minutes

VEGETABLE	METHOD	INSTRUCTIONS	TIMING
SPINACH 1½–2 pounds (*cont'd.*)	STEAM	Place in a basket over a pan of boiling water and cover pan.	3–4 minutes
	STIR-FRY	Add to hot oil in wok or skillet. Cook over high heat, stirring constantly.	3–4 minutes
SUMMER SQUASH (Yellow, Crookneck, Pattypan, Zucchini) 1–1½ pounds		*Preparation:* Wash. Cut off stem and blossom end. Leave baby squash whole. Slice, dice, or grate mature squash.	
	BAKE	Preheat oven to 375°F. Stuff halves or brush with seasoned oil.	30 minutes
	BLANCH	Plunge into a large pot of boiling salted water. When blanching time is up, remove and plunge immediately into ice water.	1–2 minutes
	BOIL	Add to a large pot of boiling salted water. Begin counting the time when the water returns to a boil. Drain immediately when boiling time is up.	2–4 minutes
	BRAISE	Sauté briefly in hot butter or oil. Add 1 inch broth or other cooking liquid and seasonings to pan. Cover and simmer. Add more cooking liquid as needed.	15 minutes

pumpkin

butternut squash

acorn squash

VEGETABLE	METHOD	INSTRUCTIONS	TIMING
	DEEP-FRY	Preheat oil to 365°F. Cut squash into ¼-inch slices or ⅜-inch strips. Coat in crumbs or batter-dip. Drain on paper towels after frying and sprinkle with salt.	Until golden
	GRILL	Prepare a medium-hot fire in grill. Slice into rounds or slabs ¾ inch thick. Leave baby squash whole. Brush with oil. Grill 4 inches from the coals, turning once.	8–10 minutes
	SAUTÉ	Add to hot butter or oil in skillet and cook, stirring occasionally.	4–7 minutes
	STEAM	Place in a basket over a pan of boiling water and cover pan.	4–6 minutes
	STIR-FRY	Add to hot oil in wok or skillet. Cook over high heat, stirring constantly.	4–7 minutes
SWISS CHARD		*Preparation:* Wash. Separate stems from leaves. Slice into ¼- to ½-inch strips.	
	BLANCH	Plunge into a large pot of boiling salted water. When blanching time is up, remove and plunge immediately into ice water.	2–3 minutes
	BOIL	Add to a large pot of boiling salted water. Begin counting the time when the water returns to a boil. Drain immediately when boiling time is up.	3–7 minutes
	SAUTÉ	Add to heated oil or butter in skillet and cook, stirring occasionally.	5–7 minutes
	STEAM	Place in a basket over a pan of boiling water and cover pan.	8–10 minutes
TOMATOES 1 pound		*Preparation:* Wash.	
	BLANCH	Blanch to loosen skin if desired. Cut an X in bottom of tomatoes. Blanch, then slip off skin.	15–30 seconds

VEGETABLE	*METHOD*	*INSTRUCTIONS*	*TIMING*
TOMATOES 1 pound *(cont'd.)*	BAKE	*To Bake Stuffed:* Preheat oven to 375°F. Scoop out pulp. Fill cavity with filling of choice. Place in baking dish.	25 minutes
	GRILL	Prepare a medium-hot fire in grill. Arrange cherry tomatoes on skewers. Or slice tomatoes thickly, brush with oil, and place on vegetable grilling rack or in hinged grill basket. Grill 4 inches from coals, turning once.	5–10 minutes
	PAN-FRY	*To Pan-Fry Green Tomatoes:* Slice ½ inch thick. Coat with crumbs. Fry in hot oil over medium heat, turning once.	5–8 minutes
	ROAST	Preheat oven to 250°F. Slice tomatoes ¾ inch thick and arrange on baking sheets lined with parchment paper. Drizzle with oil.	2 hours
	SAUTÉ	*To Sauté Cherry Tomatoes:* Cut in halves or quarters if large. Add to hot oil or butter in skillet and cook, stirring occasionally.	2–3 minutes
	STEW	Place peeled and chopped tomatoes in heavy pan and cook over very low heat, stirring occasionally.	20 minutes
TURNIPS 1–1½ pounds		Peel older turnips. Cut into slices or cubes.	
	BLANCH	Plunge into a large pot of boiling salted water. When blanching time is up, remove and plunge immediately into ice water.	3–5 minutes
	BOIL	Add to a large pot of boiling salted water. Begin counting the time when the water returns to a boil. Drain immediately when boiling time is up.	12–18 minutes

VEGETABLE	***METHOD***	***INSTRUCTIONS***	***TIMING***
	BRAISE	Combine blanched turnips with 1 inch broth or other cooking liquid and seasonings to pan. Simmer. Add additional liquid as needed.	20–30 minutes
	DEEP-FRY	Preheat oil to 365°F. Cut into ⅜-inch strips. Drain on paper towels after frying. Sprinkle with salt.	Until golden
	ROAST	Preheat oven to 375°F. Toss blanched turnips with oil. Turn occasionally.	30–45 minutes
	STEAM	Place in a basket over a pan of boiling water and cover pan.	12–16 minutes
WINTER SQUASH (Acorn, Buttercup, Butternut, Delicata, Hubbard, Pumpkin, etc.) 3–4 pounds		*Preparation:* Wash; slice in half. Remove seeds and fiber.	
	BAKE	Preheat oven to 400°F. Place halves, slabs, or quarters cut side down in roasting pan. Add ¼ inch water and cover with foil. Bake until tender when pierced with a fork.	½–1½ hours, depending on size
	STEAM	Place in a basket over a pan of boiling water and cover pan.	1-inch cubes: 12–15 minutes Small halves: 15–20 minutes Large pieces: 25–30 minutes

FRUIT

Most fruit can be eaten raw or cooked, but however you enjoy it, look for brightly colored, plump, healthy-looking fruit. There should be no mold or bruising; avoid fruit that smells musty. When preparing fruit for cooking or eating, wash it thoroughly.

Cooking Fruit

The fruit you choose to cook should be just ripe and not overripe. Cooking fruit briefly with very little liquid can maximize much of the vitamin content. Any liquid left after cooking can be saved and turned into syrup that can be used later in other recipes.

When cooking fruit, make sure you use nonreactive stainless steel, enameled cast-iron, or nonstick pots and pans and stainless steel utensils.

Deep-Frying. Deep-fried fruit fritters are a favorite. Make a lightly sweetened batter of eggs, flour, and water. Cut the fruit into slices or cubes. Dredge the fruit in flour, then dip in the batter and fry in preheated oil. Fry in small batches to avoid lowering the temperature of the fat. Drain well on paper towels. A sprinkling of confectioners' sugar just before serving is a lovely final touch.

Poaching. Fruit that is poached should hold its shape. So start with fruit that is ripe but firm. If you want to core the fruit to remove the seeds and allow the poaching liquid to penetrate the fruit, use a vegetable peeler with a sharp point, a melon baller, or a corer (made especially for coring). Most fruits are peeled before poaching. **To avoid browning, toss the peeled fruit with the juice of a lemon or lime or hold in acidulated water (1 part lemon juice to 10 parts water).**

The fruit is poached in a flavorful liquid, which may be a simple sugar syrup or spiced wine mixture (see box). In any poaching liquid you use, you can replace some of the water with liqueur or wine. Adding sweet spices, such as cinnamon, or vanilla extract is also a good idea. The sugar is necessary for maintaining the texture of the fruit.

Bring the poaching liquid to a boil. Reduce the heat to medium-low. Carefully add the fruit. Cover and simmer. If the fruit is tender when pierced with the tip of a sharp knife, it is done. Remove it from the cooking syrup. Boil the cooking liquid until it has a syrupy consistency. Strain over the fruit. Serve at once, or chill before serving.

Sautéing. Butter is the sautéing medium of choice with fruit. Melt butter in a large nonreactive skillet. Add sliced fruit, sprinkle with granulated white or brown sugar, and sauté, stirring and shaking continuously, until the fruit is just tender and the juices have caramelized. You may also want to add a dusting of cinnamon, nutmeg, or ginger.

Stewing. Stewed fruit is mushy compared to poached fruit. It no longer holds its shape. To stew fruit, place washed, peeled, and pitted fruit in a nonreactive saucepan. Sprinkle with sugar or sweetener. Add a sweet spice, such as cinnamon, if you like. If you let the fruit sit, the sugar will draw out juices from the fruit and provide a cooking liquid. If you are impatient, add water or fruit juice to keep the fruit from scorching. Simmer until the fruit is thoroughly cooked.

Poaching Liquids for Fruits

To make a poaching liquid, combine the ingredients in a nonreactive saucepan and heat until the sugar is dissolved. Bring to a boil, then reduce the heat to medium-low, add the fruit, and simmer until tender.

Light Poaching Syrup

1¼ cups sugar
Water, wine, or a combination to make 1 quart
Zest of lemon or orange, or cinnamon stick, or ½ vanilla bean, or 1 tablespoon grated fresh ginger

Heavy Poaching Syrup

2 cups water
2 cups sugar
Zest of lemon or orange, or cinnamon stick, or ½ vanilla bean, or 1 tablespoon grated fresh ginger

Wine Poaching Liquid

1½ cups red wine
1½ cups water
¾ cup sugar
1 lemon, thinly sliced
1 cinnamon stick

TIMINGS: Fruit

FRUIT	METHOD	INSTRUCTIONS	TIMING
APPLES		*Preparation:* Wash, dry, and core apples. Peel as desired. Apples may be left whole, sliced, cut in wedges, or chopped. To prevent browning, toss with lemon juice or hold in acidulated water.	
	BAKE	Preheat oven to 350°F. Place stuffed apples in baking dish. Baste occasionally, if desired, with water, cider, or other liquid. Or slice apples, sprinkle with sugar, and dot with butter.	40–60 minutes
	DEEP-FRY	Preheat oil to 375°F. Core, peel, and slice apples ¼ inch thick. Dip into batter. After frying, drain on paper towels.	Until golden
	GRILL	Prepare a low fire in the grill. Skewer wedges and brush with butter. Grill 4 inches from coals, turning occasionally.	5–6 minutes
	POACH	Core and peel apples and cut into quarters. Add to simmering poaching liquid and simmer until tender.	20 minutes
	SAUTÉ	Core and peel apples. Slice into thin wedges. Add to hot butter in skillet. Sprinkle with white or brown sugar, if desired. Cook over medium heat, stirring frequently. If sugar is added, take care to avoid scorching.	10–15 minutes
	STEW	Core and peel apples and cut into quarters. Add 1 inch water or cider to the apples in a pan, cover and simmer until tender. May be puréed and served as sauce.	20 minutes

FRUIT	METHOD	INSTRUCTIONS	TIMING
APPLES, DRIED		*Preparation:* To plump, soak in hot water, juice, or spirits for 10 minutes.	
	STEW	Combine apples with water to cover. Cover pan and simmer. Add sugar to taste in last 15 minutes of cooking.	25–30 minutes
APRICOTS		*Preparation:* To peel, dip in boiling water for 30 seconds. Then plunge into ice water. Skins should slip off. Use the tip of a sharp paring knife to begin peeling.	
	BAKE	Preheat oven to 350°F. Place peeled and pitted halves in baking dish and sprinkle with lemon juice and brown sugar. Pour ½ inch water or other fruit juice in the dish.	25–30 minutes
	GRILL	Prepare a low fire in grill. Poach halved and pitted fruit in hot syrup for 2 minutes to make moist. Place on hinged grilling basket or vegetable grilling rack and grill 4 inches from coals, turning once.	2–4 minutes
	POACH	Place peeled and pitted halves in simmering poaching liquid and simmer.	3–5 minutes
	STEW	Place in pan of water that just covers fruit, cover, and cook gently until soft.	15 minutes
APRICOTS, DRIED		*Preparation:* To plump, soak in hot water, juice, or spirits for 10 minutes.	
	POACH	Place in simmering poaching syrup to cover and simmer.	2–3 minutes
	STEW	Combine in a saucepan with water to cover. Cover pot and simmer. If desired, add liqueur and or sweetener. May be puréed and served as sauce.	12–15 minutes

FRUIT	METHOD	INSTRUCTIONS	TIMING
BANANAS		*Preparation:* Peel.	
	BAKE	Preheat oven to 350°F. Place unpeeled bananas on baking sheet. Eat with spoon out of skins.	20 minutes
	BAKE	Preheat oven to 350°F. Cut bananas in half lengthwise and crosswise. Arrange in single layer in baking dish. Dot with butter and sugar, drizzle with lemon juice.	15–20 minutes
	BROIL	Cut bananas in half lengthwise and arrange on baking sheet in single layer. Dot with butter and sprinkle with sugar. Broil 6 inches from the flame.	5–10 minutes
	DEEP-FRY	Preheat oil to 375°F. Cut bananas in half lengthwise. Dip into batter. After frying, drain on paper towels. Sprinkle with sugar.	Until golden
	GRILL	*To Grill Slices:* Prepare a low fire in grill. Cut bananas in half lengthwise and crosswise. Brush with melted butter and sprinkle with brown sugar. Place on vegetable grilling rack or hinged grill basket 4 inches from coals and grill, turning once.	8–10 minutes

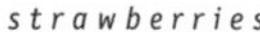

strawberries

black cherries

raspberries

FRUIT	METHOD	INSTRUCTIONS	TIMING
	GRILL	*To Grill Whole:* Prepare a low fire in grill. Place unpeeled bananas on grill 4 inches from coals. Turn to cook evenly. Eat with spoon out of skins.	15–30 minutes
	SAUTÉ	Cut bananas in half lengthwise and crosswise. Add to melted butter in skillet. Cook, stirring frequently, until lightly browned. Sprinkle with sugar, if desired.	10–15 minutes
BERRIES (Blackberries, Blueberries, Boysenberries, Huckleberries, Raspberries, Strawberries)		*Preparation:* Clean and wash all berries. Remove hulls.	
	POACH	Combine 1 pound berries with 1 cup sugar in a nonreactive saucepan and let stand 30 minutes. Add a little water if berries have not released any juice. Turn heat to low and simmer until berries are heated through. Serve as sauce. May be puréed.	10 minutes
CHERRIES		*Preparation:* Pit cherries.	
	STEW	Combine 1 pound cherries with ½ cup water or juice and ½–¾ cup sugar. Simmer covered. May be puréed and served as sauce.	10–20 minutes
CRANBERRIES, ELDERBERRIES		*Preparation:* Wash and pick over before cooking. Remove elderberries from stems by shaking or raking with a fork.	
	BOIL	*To Make a Sauce or Conserve:* Place 1 pound berries in saucepan, cover with 2 cups boiling water. Cover and boil until the skins burst. Strain. Add 2 cups sugar, return pan to boil, then remove from heat.	5–6 minutes

FRUIT	*METHOD*	*INSTRUCTIONS*	*TIMING*
CURRANTS, GOOSEBERRIES		*Preparation:* Currants can be teased off the stem with a fork. Their hard seeds are not edible. Seed, or plan to strain fruit. Gooseberries can be strained after cooked, or topped and tailed before, to remove inedible parts.	
	POACH	Add berries to simmering poaching syrup, simmer until soft. Strain and serve as sauce.	10–15 minutes
FIGS	BAKE	Preheat oven to 350°F. Quarter the figs (but not all the way through). Spread the figs open, place in a shallow baking pan, and pour a sugar syrup over figs.	20 minutes
	BROIL	Cut in half lengthwise, arrange on baking sheets, and sprinkle with sugar. Broil 6 inches from heat.	5–10 minutes
	DEEP-FRY	Preheat oil to 370°F. Slice from root to stem in ¼-inch slices without cutting all the way through. Dip in batter. After frying, drain on paper towels.	Until golden
	GRILL	Prepare a low fire in grill. Skewer figs. Grill 4 inches from the coals, turning occasionally.	10 minutes
FIGS, DRIED	STEW	Place in pan of cold water, cover, and simmer until tender.	15–30 minutes

currants

kiwi

FRUIT	*METHOD*	*INSTRUCTIONS*	*TIMING*
GRAPEFRUIT, POMELOS		*Preparation:* Slice fruit in half, remove seeds, and cut along the outer and inner membranes so that the fruit can easily be removed with a spoon after cooking.	
	BAKE	Preheat oven to 450°F. Sprinkle the top of the fruit with sugar.	15–20 minutes
	BROIL	Sprinkle with sugar. Broil 6 inches from heat.	3–5 minutes
GUAVAS (Slightly underripe)		*Preparation:* Peel the skin with a vegetable peeler and cut into chunks or cubes.	
	BAKE	Preheat oven to 350°F. Place peeled cubes or unpeeled halves in baking dish.	30 minutes
	POACH	Add to simmering poaching syrup and simmer until tender.	5–7 minutes
KUMQUATS		*Preparation:* Wash well. Leave whole.	
	STEW	Combine 1 quart kumquats with 1 cup water and 2 cups sugar. Bring to a boil, reduce heat, cover, and simmer until tender.	45 minutes
NECTARINES		*Preparation:* Slice in half and remove stone.	
	BAKE	Preheat oven to 350°F. Fill the pit cavity with sugar or other mixtures of spirits or nuts and place in oven.	15–20 minutes
	BROIL	Fill the pit cavity with sugar or other mixtures of spirits or nuts and place 6 inches from heat.	2–4 minutes
	GRILL	Prepare a low fire in grill. Brush halves with butter. Grill 4 inches from coals on vegetable grilling rack or hinged grill basket, turning once.	8–10 minutes
	POACH	Slice pitted halves. Toss slices with lemon juice. Add to simmering poaching liquid and simmer.	3–5 minutes

FRUIT	METHOD	INSTRUCTIONS	TIMING
NECTARINES *(cont'd.)*	SAUTÉ	Heat sugar syrup (3 parts water to 1 part sugar) in skillet over low heat. Add 1 tablespoon butter and heat. Add fruit and shake pan until fruit is evenly coated. Do not overcrowd pan. Increase heat and simmer until syrup bubbles.	3–5 minutes
ORANGES (Mandarins, Tangerines, and related varieties)		*Preparation:* Peel.	
	POACH	Combine 1¼ cups water with 1 cup sugar. Bring to a simmer. Add peeled fruit sections. Simmer and stir until fruit is completely coated with the glaze.	1–2 minutes
PAPAYAS		*Preparation:* Peel and remove the seeds.	
	BAKE	Preheat oven to 375°F. Brush slices with melted butter. Turn occasionally during baking.	20–30 minutes
	GRILL	Prepare a low fire in grill. Cut fruit into quarters or cubes. Arrange on skewers and brush with melted butter. Grill 4 inches from coals, turning occasionally.	4–5 minutes
	SAUTÉ	Cut into 1-inch slices. Add to melted butter in skillet. Sprinkle with sugar. Cook, over low heat, stirring to avoid scorching.	4–5 minutes
PEACHES		*Preparation:* To peel peaches, dip in boiling water for 30 seconds. Plunge into cold water. Skins should peel off easily.	
	BAKE	Preheat oven to 350°F. Slice peeled peaches in half and remove stone. Fill the pit cavity with sugar or preferred mixture and place in oven.	15–20 minutes

FRUIT	METHOD	INSTRUCTIONS	TIMING
	BROIL	Slice peeled peaches in half and remove stone. Fill the pit cavity with sugar or preferred mixture. Broil 6 inches from heat.	2–4 minutes
	GRILL	Brush peeled halves with butter and grill 4 inches from the coals on vegetable grilling rack or hinged grill basket. Turn once.	8–10 minutes
	POACH	Leave peeled fruit whole, or pit and halve or slice. Brush with lemon juice. Place in pan of simmering syrup and simmer.	3–5 minutes
	SAUTÉ	Heat syrup to cover in skillet over low heat. Add 1 tablespoon butter, heat, and add sliced, peeled fruit. Shake pan to coat fruit. Do not overcrowd the pan. Increase heat and simmer until syrup bubbles.	3–5 minutes
PEARS		*Preparation:* Wash, dry, and core. Peel as desired. Pears may be left whole or sliced, cut in wedges, or chopped. To prevent browning, toss with lemon juice or hold in acidulated water.	
	BAKE	Preheat the oven to 325°F. Peel and core pear halves and brush with lemon juice. Add a little water and honey to baking dish. Baste occasionally during baking.	30–45 minutes
	DEEP-FRY	Preheat oil to 375°F. Core, peel, and slice ¼ inch thick. Dip into batter. After frying, drain on paper towels.	Until golden
	GRILL	Prepare a low fire in grill. Skewer wedges and brush with butter. Grill 4 inches from coals, turning occasionally.	5–6 minutes

FRUIT	METHOD	INSTRUCTIONS	TIMING
PEARS *(cont'd.)*	POACH	Core and peel. Leave whole or slice in wedges. Add to simmering poaching liquid and simmer.	8–10 minutes
	SAUTÉ	Add peeled, sliced pears to melted butter in skillet. Sprinkle with sugar. Flip and stir constantly as you sauté over medium-high heat.	10–15 minutes
PINEAPPLES		*Preparation:* Cut off leaves at base. Slice off bottom rind. Stand pineapple on its base and cut off rind from all sides, removing as much of the eyes as possible. Slice into rings and remove cores from each. Or slice the entire pineapple in quarters lengthwise, remove the cores, then slice into wedges.	
	BAKE	Preheat oven to 350°F. Place in baking dish. Baste occasionally, if desired, with water, pineapple juice, or other liquid.	40–60 minutes
	BROIL	Arrange rings or wedges on baking sheet and drizzle with butter. Sprinkle with sugar. Broil 6 inches from heat.	5–8 minutes
	GRILL	Prepare low fire in grill. Skewer wedges and brush with butter. Grill 4 inches from coals, turning once.	5–6 minutes

Bartlett pear

plum

pineapple

FRUIT	METHOD	INSTRUCTIONS	TIMING
	SAUTÉ	Combine in large skillet with butter and brown sugar. Add rum if desired. Cook over low heat, stirring, until pieces are well coated with glaze and heated through.	4–5 minutes
PLUMS	BAKE	Preheat the oven to 325°F. Make a cross at the top of each plum and extract the pit. Place the plums in a buttered baking dish. Sprinkle with sugar.	1–1¼ hours
	POACH	Add plums to simmering poaching liquid or fruit juice. Cover and simmer until plums are soft.	5–10 minutes
	STEW	Place plums in saucepan and barely cover them with water or fruit juice. Add sweetener to taste. Cover and simmer until plums are soft.	10–15 minutes
PRUNES	STEEP	*To Plump:* Cover with boiling water and let sit.	10 minutes
	STEW	Place prunes in saucepan and add water to cover. Cover the pan and simmer until tender.	12–20 minutes
QUINCES		*Preparation:* Rub off any fuzz. Peel with vegetable peeler. Cut into quarters and trim out core.	
	BAKE	Preheat oven to 300°F. Place in baking dish and sprinkle with sugar. Cover with water.	1½–2 hours
RAISINS	STEEP	Cover with boiling water and let sit.	10 minutes
RHUBARB		*Preparation:* Remove leaves if still attached. Rinse stalks, and trim tops and bottoms. If stalks are stringy, peel as with celery. Slice crosswise into ½-inch pieces.	

FRUIT	METHOD	INSTRUCTIONS	TIMING
RHUBARB *(cont'd.)*	BAKE	Preheat oven to 350°F. Place rhubarb in shallow baking dish. Sprinkle generously with sugar. Cover and bake.	20–30 minutes
	STEW	Combine 4 cups rhubarb with ½ cup sugar and ½ cup water. Bring to a boil, then reduce heat and simmer covered until rhubarb is tender and sauce is thick.	12–15 minutes

NUTS

Nuts are the hard seeds of fruits with hard husks. Almonds, pecans, peanuts, walnuts, hazelnuts, pistachios, and pine nuts (pignoli) are the nuts most used in cooking. They all add a crunchy texture and flavor to food, and they are a good source of fiber. Nuts are high in oil and fat, however, so they become rancid easily. Keep them away from heat, light, and moisture. Shelled nuts deteriorate faster then unshelled and are best kept in the refrigerator (for 3 to 12 months, depending on the variety) or in the freezer (for up to 12 months). Discard any nuts that are moldy, shriveled, dry, or bitter.

A few types of nuts require blanching before cooking, so that the skin can be removed. Almonds and pistachio nuts have a bitter skin and must be blanched to remove the skin or they will leave a bitter taste. With other nuts, such as hazelnuts (filberts) and Brazil nuts, toasting and then rubbing them with a dishtowel is the method for removing skins.

Make sure you let nuts cool before processing them in a blender or they will turn into a paste. The two most popular ways of cooking nuts are roasting or toasting. Both methods bring out the nuts' flavor and leave them crisp for eating, cooking, or baking.

TIMINGS: Nuts

NUT	*METHOD*	*INSTRUCTIONS*	*TIMING*
ALMONDS	BLANCH	Remove the shells. To remove the inner skins, put almonds in a bowl and cover with boiling water. Let them stand 10 minutes. Drain and let cool. Pinch the skin between your thumb and index finger and slip it off, or simply rub it off.	10 minutes
	ROAST	Preheat the oven to 325°F. Spread peeled nuts on a cookie sheet in a single layer, and place in oven. Check often to prevent burning and shake the pan 2–3 times.	5–10 minutes
	TOAST	Place peeled nuts in dry skillet and cook over medium heat. Stir and shake until fragrant and lightly colored.	4–5 minutes

NUT	METHOD	INSTRUCTIONS	TIMING
BRAZIL NUTS	BAKE	*To Shell:* Preheat oven to 400°F. Place on a single layer on baking sheet. After baking, remove from oven and use a nutcracker to shell them.	15 minutes
	BLANCH	*To Remove Skins:* Remove the shells (above). To remove the inner skins, drop the nuts in boiling water and boil for 1–2 minutes. Drain. While nuts are still warm, rub them in a clean kitchen towel to remove the skins. If some don't skin, repeat the process.	1–2 minutes
	ROAST	Preheat oven to 325°F. Spread skinned nuts on a cookie sheet in a single layer and place in oven. Check nuts often, shaking the pan 2–3 times.	5–10 minutes
	TOAST	*To Remove Skins:* Place shelled nuts in a nonstick skillet and stir over low heat until all sides are slightly toasted. Then wrap nuts in a clean kitchen towel. Let steam for a few minutes. Then rub nuts to remove the skins.	4–5 minutes
	TOAST	Place skinned nuts in dry skillet and cook over medium heat. Stir and shake until fragrant and lightly colored.	4–5 minutes

almonds

brazil nuts

hazelnuts

NUT	METHOD	INSTRUCTIONS	TIMING
CASHEWS	ROAST	Preheat oven to 325°F. Spread skinned nuts on a cookie sheet in a single layer and place in oven. Check often to prevent burning and shake the pan 2–3 times.	5–10 minutes
	TOAST	Place skinned nuts in dry skillet and cook over medium heat. Stir and shake until fragrant and lightly colored.	4–5 minutes
CHESTNUTS		*Preparation:* Cut an X on the flat side of each nut to allow for easier peeling.	
	BOIL	Place in saucepan with water to cover. Bring to a boil. Simmer.	To peel: 4–5 minutes To fully cook: 20–30 minutes
	ROAST	Preheat the oven to 425°F. Place in a single layer on a baking sheet. Shake pan to stir nuts occasionally during roasting.	To peel: 10–15 minutes To fully cook: 15–25 minutes
COCONUT	TOAST	Grate coconut with grater or food processor. Place shreds in a heavy skillet. Mix in 2 tablesoons sugar. Stir to avoid burning and cook over low heat until golden.	2–3 minutes
HAZELNUTS (Filberts)	BLANCH	*To Remove Skins:* Drop nuts in boiling water for 1–2 minutes. Drain. While nuts are still warm, rub in clean kitchen towel to remove skins. If some don't skin, repeat the process.	1–2 minutes
	ROAST	Preheat oven to 325°F. Spread skinned nuts on a cookie sheet in a single layer, place in oven. Check often to prevent burning and shake the pan 2–3 times.	5–10 minutes

NUT	METHOD	INSTRUCTIONS	TIMING
HAZELNUTS (Filberts) (*cont'd.*)	TOAST	*To Remove Skins:* Place nuts in a dry skillet and stir over low heat until all sides are lightly toasted. Wrap nuts in a clean kitchen towel. Let steam for a few minutes. Then rub nuts to remove the skins.	4–5 minutes
	TOAST	Place in dry skillet and cook over medium heat until lightly colored. Stir and shake until done.	4–5 minutes
MACADAMIA NUTS	TOAST	Place nuts in dry skillet and stir or shake over low heat.	4–5 minutes
	ROAST	Preheat oven to 325°F. Spread nuts on a cookie sheet in a single layer. Check often to prevent burning and shake or stir 2–3 times.	5–7 minutes
PECANS	ROAST	Preheat oven to 325°F. Spread nuts on cookie sheet in single layer. Place in oven. Check often to prevent burning and shake or stir 2–3 times.	5 minutes
	TOAST	Place shelled nuts in a skillet and shake over low heat until lightly toasted.	3–4 minutes
PINE NUTS (Pignoli)	TOAST	Place nuts in dry skillet and stir or shake over low heat until all sides are lightly toasted.	2–3 minutes

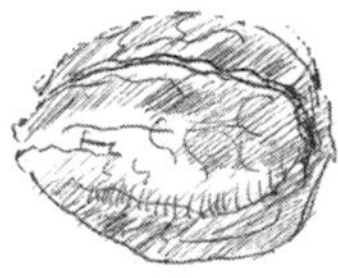

walnut

pine nuts (pignoli)

pecans

pistachio

NUT	METHOD	INSTRUCTIONS	TIMING
	ROAST	Preheat oven to 375°F. Spread nuts on cookie sheet in single layer and place in oven. Check often to prevent burning and shake or stir 2–3 times.	5 minutes
PISTACHIOS	BLANCH	*To Remove Skins:* Put the shelled nuts in a bowl and cover with boiling water. Let stand for 10 minutes. Drain and let cool. Pinch the skin between your thumb and index finger and slip it off, or simply rub off.	10 minutes
	ROAST	Preheat the oven to 325°F. Spread nuts on a cookie sheet in a single layer, place in oven. Check often to prevent burning and shake the pan 2–3 times.	5–10 minutes
	TOAST	Place in skillet and cook over medium heat. Stir and shake until done.	4–5 minutes
WALNUTS	ROAST	Spread shelled nuts on cookie sheet in single layer. Place in oven. Check often to prevent burning and shake or stir 2–3 times.	5 minutes
	TOAST	Place shelled nuts in dry skillet and shake over low heat until both sides are lightly toasted.	3–4 minutes

EGGS

When cooking eggs, remember that very fresh eggs take slightly longer to cook than eggs that are a week or more old. However, unless you buy directly from the farmer, it is unlikely that you are getting absolutely fresh eggs. Another point to remember is that overcooking results in tough, rubbery eggs.

Freshness can be tested by dropping an egg into a bowl of water. If the egg floats on its side, it is fresh. If it floats vertically with the rounded end up, it is 2–3 weeks old. An egg that floats to the surface of the water is not fresh and should be discarded. When an egg that is cracked onto a plate is fresh, the yolk sits high and is rounded and plump and the white is thick and clings to the yolk.

Tips and Instructions for Cooking Eggs

Baked Eggs (Shirred Eggs)

- Bake the eggs until the whites are firm but the yolks are still runny.
- Use individual buttered custard cups or small ramekins.
- Method #1: Preheat the oven to 350°F. Put 1 egg in each ramekin. Add 2 teaspoons cream to each egg. Place the ramekins into a larger baking dish, cover, and bake.
- Method #2: Preheat the oven to 375°F. Put 1 egg in each ramekin. Place the ramekins in a heavy skillet filled with 1 inch water. Bring the water to a boil on top of the stove. Then place the skillet in the oven and bake.
- Method #3: Preheat the oven to 300°F. Place 1 egg in each ramekin. Set the ramekins in a large baking pan. Pour hot water in the baking pan around the ramekins to a depth of 1 inch. Bake.

Boiled Eggs

- Eggs should never be boiled. Add them to gently simmering water instead. The difference between soft-cooked (coddled) eggs and hard-cooked eggs is simply a matter of timing.
- Start the timer when the water returns to a simmer, not when you add the eggs to the water.

- Make sure water in pan covers eggs by at least 1 inch, and don't crowd the pan.
- Poking a pinhole in the broad end of the egg will reduce the chance of the egg cracking.
- Gently lower the eggs into the simmering water with a slotted spoon.
- When it is time to remove the egg, do so immediately with a slotted spoon and run the egg briefly under cold water to stop the cooking.

Fried Eggs

- Cook in a small amount of butter or fat on medium to low heat.
- Use a nonstick skillet to allow easy removal of the eggs.
- To cook the edges around the yolk of sunny-side-up eggs, use a spoon to baste the eggs with the fat in the pan until the yolk loses its shine.
- For over-easy eggs, after turning the eggs, cook them only 30 seconds more.

Omelets

- Have all the ingredients ready before you start cooking.
- Make one omelet at a time.
- Crack the eggs into a bowl containing a little water and beat with a fork until well blended.
- For a 2-egg omelet, use a 6- to 8-inch-diameter nonstick pan. For a 3- to 5-egg omelet, use an 8- to 9-inch-diameter nonstick pan. Heat the omelet pan over medium-high heat and have the butter foaming before you add the eggs.
- If you are adding a filling, spread it across the center of the omelet about 15 seconds after the eggs have entered the pan.
- Keep shaking the pan with a short forward and backward motion as you cook. Tip the pan while shaking, letting the liquid egg in the center run to the edge of the omelet. Pull the edge of the omelet away from the edge of the pan with a spatula or fork as you cook.
- With a spatula or fork, start to roll the omelet when the center is still a little runny.

Poached Eggs

- Add vinegar to the poaching water (2 tablespoons per quart of water) to help coagulate the egg whites and keep poached eggs from spreading.
- Crack the eggs carefully onto a plate and slide gently into the simmering water. Do not crowd the pan.
- Maintain the water at a simmer or just below.
- Method #1: Fill a 12-inch nonstick skillet two-thirds full of water. Add 1 tablespoon vinegar and bring to a simmer. Add the eggs. Spoon the simmering water over each egg for about 3 minutes or until they set. When the whites become opaque and feel firm to the touch (remove an egg with a slotted spoon to test), the eggs are done.
- Method #2: Bring the water to a boil in a 12-inch nonstick skillet two-thirds full of water. Add 1 tablespoon vinegar to the boiling water. Turn off the heat. Add the eggs, cover, and let stand until the whites are opaque and feel firm to the touch. (Remove an egg with a slotted spoon to test.)

Scrambled Eggs

- The lower the heat, the creamier the eggs.
- If you like your eggs moist, cook them for less time. If you like them on the dry side, cook them longer.
- Scrambled eggs always continue to cook after they leave the pan.
- Crack the eggs into a bowl containing a little water, cream, or milk and sprinkle on salt and pepper. Then whisk them until completely blended.
- Cook the eggs in melted butter over low heat, stirring them until they just begin to reach the desired consistency; remove them from pan.
- Flavor add-ins include chopped fresh herbs; sautéed onions, mushrooms, or peppers; chopped smoked meat or fish; cooked meat, poultry, or fish.

TIMINGS: Eggs

NOTE: Timings are for large eggs.

TYPE	***INSTRUCTIONS***	***TIMING***
BAKED (shirred)	Preheat oven to 350°F. Place eggs in buttered ramekins. Add 2 teaspoons cream to each egg. Place ramekins in baking dish, cover, and bake.	15 minutes
	Preheat oven to 375°F. Place eggs in buttered ramekins. Set ramekins in heavy skillet. Add 1 inch of water. Bring to boil on top of stove, then bake in oven.	8–12 minutes
	Preheat oven to 300°F. Place eggs in buttered ramekins. Set ramekins in baking dish and fill dish with 1 inch of water. Bake.	23 minutes
BOILED	Add eggs in shell to simmering water. Run soft-cooked eggs briefly under cold water to stop the cooking. Run hard-cooked eggs under water until thoroughly cooled.	Soft: 3½–4 minutes Medium-soft: 4–5 minutes Medium: 5–6 minutes Hard: 8–10 minutes
FRIED	Heat butter in skillet over medium-low heat. Cook until whites are completely firm. For over-easy eggs, turn eggs and cook for 30 seconds on second side.	Sunny-side up: 3–4 minutes Over easy: 3½–5½ minutes
OMELET	Add beaten eggs to heated butter over medium-high heat in a nonstick pan. Let cook undisturbed for 30 seconds, then use a fork to draw in edges of omelet, tilt and shake pan. Then fold.	3–4 minutes
POACHED	Add 1 tablespoon vinegar to simmering water. Carefully add eggs. Maintain water at a simmer and spoon simmering water over eggs until eggs are set.	Soft: 3–3½ minutes Medium: 4–5 minutes

TYPE	*INSTRUCTIONS*	*TIMING*
POACHED (*cont'd.*)	Add 1 tablespoon vinegar to simmering water in a wide shallow pan. Turn off heat. Carefully add eggs. Cover pan and let stand off the heat until eggs are cooked.	Soft: 3–3½ minutes Medium: 4–5 minutes
SCRAMBLED	Whisk eggs with a little cream or milk. Add to heated butter in skillet over medium heat. Reduce heat to low and cook, stirring gently.	2–5 minutes

FISH

No other food overcooks as easily as fish, so it must be timed carefully and tested while cooking. White fish, especially, is sensitive to heat. With a fillet, less than 1 minute can make the difference between being cooked perfectly or being overdone.

Buying Fish

When buying fish, look for bright color, firm flesh, and skin without slime or odor. The eyes should be bright and bulging, and the gills should be clean and bright red.

Cooking Fish with Flavor

Fish must be scaled, trimmed, and gutted before cooking. Before marinating or cooking, rinse the fish under cold running water and pat dry. Remove any bones left in fillets.

The flavor of fish is quite delicate and is often enhanced with the addition of fresh herbs and a squeeze of lemon or lime juice. Fish that is to be steamed, broiled, baked, or grilled can be marinated first. Marinades add both flavor and moisture to fish. They can be used as a basting sauce for broiled and grilled fish, and can even double as a steaming liquid. Spice and herb rubs, made with a blend of spices and fresh herbs in an oil base, can also be used to flavor fish.

The classic Latin American dish ceviche is made by marinating fresh seafood in a high-acid citrus marinade. The acid literally "cooks" the seafood, turning the flesh firm and white. No further cooking is needed. Unless you are making ceviche or want to forgo further cooking, choose a marinade that is low in acid. An olive oil base, with citrus juice or white wine for acid balance and fresh herbs for flavor, makes a good marinade for fish. In general, you can leave fish in such a marinade from 30 minutes to 4 hours. The fish should be refrigerated if you are marinating it longer than 30 minutes. If you see any signs of the flesh turning white, remove the fish from the marinade immediately; it is "cooking." Although there is no acid in a rub, it should not be applied more than 4 hours before cooking; otherwise its flavor will overwhelm the delicate flavor of the fish.

Before using a marinade as a basting sauce, bring it to a boil on top of the stove and boil for at least 3 minutes.

Baking. Always preheat the oven and grease the baking dish to prevent sticking. Generally, it is a good idea to coat the fish with oil, butter, or sauce. To prevent the fish from drying out, either cover the baking dish or add liquid, such as white wine (to provide steam), or encase the fish in foil or parchment paper. A squeeze of lemon or lime juice, some chopped fresh herbs, or a sauté of mixed vegetables make a fine topping for the baking fish.

Braising. Braising fish is similar to baking, with the addition of ½ to 1 inch cooking liquid to provide moisture. The braising liquid is often half wine and half fish stock or water. To prepare a fish for braising, place it in a greased baking dish. Sprinkle with salt and pepper and cover with chopped aromatic vegetables (onions, celery, carrots, parsley, garlic) and herbs. Add the braising liquid and place the fish in a preheated oven. Baste 2 or 3 times during braising.

Broiling. Preheat the broiler and use a heavy-duty broiler pan or heavy ovenproof skillet. The pan should be oiled and very hot before the fish is added—otherwise the fish may stick or break in the pan. Leave the skin on to help the fish hold its shape. The skin may be removed after cooking.

Fillets should be about 1 inch thick, brushed with butter or oil, cooked skin-side down and not turned. Very lean fillets or steaks may be dusted with flour. Whole fish or steaks should also be brushed with oil and/or melted butter before broiling and basted with oil, melted butter, or a marinade 2 or 3 times during cooking. For additional moisture, you can add about ¼ to ½ inch liquid (water, wine, marinade, etc.) to the bottom of the broiler pan. If desired, spinkle with fresh herbs during the last minute or so of broiling.

Deep-Frying. Lean fish, such as flatfish, bass, snapper, grouper, cod, hake, whiting, and skinned catfish, are excellent for deep-frying.

Fish that are to be fried can be dipped in batter (see page 90) or coated in crumbs. To coat with crumbs, mix fresh or dried breadcrumbs, cracker crumbs, or cornflake crumbs with salt and pepper and finely chopped fresh herbs. Season the fish with salt and pepper and dust with flour. Dip in an egg wash, then roll in the crumbs.

Use an electric deep-fryer; a deep, heavy pan; or a wok for frying. You will need 1 or more quarts of oil, depending on the amount of fish to be fried. Preheat the oil to 375°F, using a deep-fat thermometer to determine the exact temperature of the oil (or drop a cube of stale bread in the oil—if it browns within 20 seconds, the oil is ready). Lower a small batch of fish into the hot oil at a time. A wire basket makes the retrieval of the fish easier.

Grilling. Always coat the grill with a little oil to prevent sticking. Even better, lightly coat a grilling rack or hinged basket with oil and place it on the grill. Fish is less likely to stick to these specially coated nonstick surfaces. Place the fish skin side down on the greased grill. Baste several times with oil or marinade. Try adding soaked wood chips to coals to give the fish a smoked flavor.

Pan-Broiling. Preheat the skillet or grilling pan. Pat the fish dry, then brush with oil and/or butter before adding it to the hot pan.

Pan-Frying and Sautéing. For best results, use a nonstick skillet. A light coating of seasoned flour (1 cup flour, 1 teaspoon salt, ¼ teaspoon pepper) helps fillets brown. For breaded fillets, dust the fillets with flour, then dip in beaten eggs, then in the breading. Breading can be made with rice flour, breadcrumbs, oats, ground nuts, or cornmeal, and can be seasoned with salt, pepper, and herbs or spices. Heat ⅛ to ¼ inch oil or a combination of butter and oil in the skillet over medium heat. Add the fish and fry, cooking, turning once.

Poaching. For most poaching jobs, 4 cups liquid will be enough. You can poach in water or fish stock, or a combination, or with the addition of wine. Court bouillon (see page 90) is a classic poaching liquid. Sea water or salted water also makes an excellent poaching liquid. I like to use a combination of 3 cups water and 1 cup white wine. You can flavor the liquid with fresh herbs or aromatic vegetables (onions, celery, carrots, parsley, garlic), if desired. Add a little vinegar, white wine, or lemon juice to the poaching liquid to whiten the fish and firm up its texture.

The temperature of the poaching liquid is critical. Maintain the liquid at 170°F to 180°F. The liquid will appear to shiver at the correct simmering temperature, but use a thermometer to be sure.

When poaching fish, large pieces are often started in cool liquid, small pieces in hot liquid. Begin timing when fish is added to liquid.

If you are poaching fish to serve cold, let it cool in the poaching liquid.

If you do a lot of poaching, a large oval fish poacher will enable you to poach whole fish with ease.

Roasting. Always coat the fish with oil and/or butter or some fat and always preheat the oven.

Steaming. Lean fish, such as flatfish, bass, snapper, grouper, cod, hake, and whiting, are perfect for steaming. Even oily freshwater fish, such as salmon, pike, perch, and trout, are excellent cooked by this method.

Most steamed fish will have better flavor if marinated for up to 4 hours before cooking. A soy-based marinade, made with rice wine and seasoned with ginger and garlic or other spices, is wonderful and can double as a steaming liquid.

It is important to keep the fish from coming in direct contact with the steaming liquid. Place the fish on a poaching rack or tray so that the rack is just above the waterline. When steaming a large whole fish, wrap it in a double layer of cheesecloth.

Stir-Frying. Cut the fish into uniform-size pieces and cook in small batches to cook more evenly. Make sure the oil in the wok is hot before the fish is added. Consult an Asian cookbook for finishing sauces.

Timing Fish

How long to cook fish depends on the texture and thickness of the fish. The general rule that some chefs follow, but with caution, is to **cook fish for 8 to 9 minutes per inch of thickness.** This rule follows no matter what size or type of fish is to be cooked, but it's only a guide. In order to cook fish the way you like it, check it frequently. If fish must be turned, cook for 4 to 4½ minutes per inch per side. If the fish comes from the freezer, the timing should be 16 to 18 minutes per inch of thickness.

Testing for doneness. To test whether or not a fish is done, cut the thickest section of the fish with a very thin-bladed knife and, with a fork, see if the meat flakes. If it does, the fish is cooked. Or use appearance as a gauge: If the center of the fish is still transparent, it is not ready.

You can also test for doneness with an instant-read thermometer. Insert the thermometer into the thickest part of the fish. When the thermometer reads 135°F, the fish is cooked and still moist. Some people prefer fish cooked to 120°F. Remember to remove the fish from heat just before it's at the desired temperature, because it will continue to cook a bit after being removed from the heat.

Beer Batter

For deep-fried fish: Mix together 1 cup flour, 3 tablespoons cornstarch, 1 teaspoon salt, ½ teaspoon pepper, 1 cup beer, 1 tablespoon vegetable oil.

Court-Bouillon

For poaching fish: In a large pan, combine 8 cups water, 3 cups white wine, 2 peeled and chopped carrots, 2 chopped onions, 6 sprigs parsley, 4 bay leaves, 1 pinch thyme, 10 black peppercorns, 1 tablespoon salt. Bring to a boil, then reduce heat and simmer uncovered for 15 to 20 minutes. Cool before using. Store in the refrigerator for up to 5 days.

A Guide to Choosing Fish

In order to decide on a specific way to cook fish, it is a good idea to know whether the flavor is mild or strong, and whether the texture is soft or firm.

TEXTURE/TYPE	FLAVOR
Soft-Textured Fish	
American sole	Delicate
Bluefish	Full
Flounder	Delicate
Freshwater bass	Delicate
Herring	Moderate
Kingfish	Full
Plaice	Delicate
Mackerel	Full
Sardine	Full
Shad	Moderate
Whiting	Delicate
Moderately Firm	
Atlantic croaker	Delicate
Black sea bass	Delicate
Brill	Moderate
Carp	Delicate
Catfish	Delicate
Cod/scrod	Delicate
Dover sole	Delicate
Drum	Moderate
Grouper	Delicate
Haddock	Delicate
Hake	Delicate
Halibut	Delicate
John Dory	Delicate
Lake trout	Delicate
Mahimahi	Delicate
Monkfish	Delicate
Mullet	Moderate
Ocean perch	Delicate

TEXTURE/TYPE	FLAVOR
Yellow perch	Delicate
Pike	Delicate
Pollock	Delicate
Rockfish	Delicate
Roughy	Delicate
Salmon	Delicate
Skate	Moderate
Snapper	Moderate
Striped bass	Delicate
Tilefish	Delicate
Trout	Delicate
Turbot	Moderate
Walleye	Delicate
Whitefish	Delicate
Wolffish	Delicate
Firm	
Amberjack (jack family)	Full
Eel	Delicate
Garfish	Delicate
Jack	Moderate
Lamprey	Delicate
Marlin	Moderate
Pomfret	Delicate
Pompano	Delicate
Sea bream	Delicate
Shark	Moderate
Skate	Moderate
Sturgeon	Delicate
Swordfish	Moderate
Tuna	Moderate
Yellowtail (jack family)	Moderate

Categories of Fish

Timing fish is done according to the texture of the fish. The following timing charts organize the fish into categories according to type and texture. The categories are as follows:

The Cod Family
Cod, haddock, hake, pollock, scrod, whiting

Flatfish, Large
Brill, halibut, John Dory, turbot

Flatfish, Small
Flounder, plaice, sole

Freshwater Fish
Carp (smallmouth buffalo), catfish, pike (Northern, walleye), suckers, sunfish, whitefish (chub, lake herring), yellow perch

Meaty Fish
Marlin, tuna, shark, swordfish, sturgeon

Oily Fish and Small Fry
Bluefish, herring, kingfish, mackerel, sardine, shad, smelt

Salmon and Trout
Atlantic salmon, Pacific salmon (silver, pink, sockeye), salmon, trout (brook, cutthroat, lake, rainbow)

Thin-Boned Fish
Pompano, pomfret, sea bream, other jacks

White Fish, Flaky
Croaker, drum, mullet, rockfish, sea bass, tilefish, weakfish

White Fish, Firm
Grouper, mahimahi, ocean perch, orange roughy, snapper, wolffish

Assorted Fish
Eel, garfish, lamprey, monkfish, skate

TIMINGS: Fish

All timings are approximate, depending on the thickness of the fish. *When in doubt, use 8–9 minutes per inch of thickness for total cooking. If fish must be turned, use 4–4½ minutes per inch per side. If fish comes directly from the freezer, the timing should be 16–18 minutes per inch of thickness. All of the timings in the chart are for fish cooked at room temperature. NOTE: Types of fish are listed by category (see the facing page), not in alphabetical order.*

FISH	*METHOD*	*INSTRUCTIONS*	*TIMING*
THE COD FAMILY			
COD, HADDOCK, HAKE, POLLOCK, SCROD, WHITING Fillets and steaks; 6–8 ounces	BAKE	Preheat oven to 350°F. Place fish in a greased baking dish. Brush fish with butter or oil and drizzle with fresh herbs, seasoning paste, or sauce. Cover the bottom of pan with white wine or other liquid. Bake uncovered.	8–12 minutes
	BROIL	Preheat broiler. Brush the fish with melted butter or oil. Pour ¼–½ inch water or wine into the pan. Broil 4 inches from heat. Turn steaks halfway through broiling; do not turn fillets. Season the fish just before the end of the cooking time, if desired.	Fillets: 4–6 minutes Steaks: 3–4 minutes per side
	DEEP-FRY	Heat oil to 375°F. Wash and pat fish dry. Dip in batter or seasoned flour. Deep-fry until golden. Drain on paper towels before serving.	2–3 minutes
	OVEN-FRY	*To Oven-Fry Fillets:* Preheat oven to 500°F. Soak fillets in milk or buttermilk, then coat in crumbs. Place in well-greased baking pan and bake on top rack, uncovered.	8 minutes

FISH	*METHOD*	*INSTRUCTIONS*	*TIMING*
COD, HADDOCK, HAKE, POLLOCK, SCROD, WHITING Fillets and steaks; 6–8 ounces (*cont'd.*)	PAN-FRY	Heat oil in heavy skillet, add fish, and sear over high heat for 2 minutes on each side. For thick steaks, add 1–2 minutes per side.	2–4 minutes per side
	POACH	Bring 4 cups poaching liquid to a boil. Add fish and simmer gently.	Fillets: 4–6 minutes Steaks: 5–10 minutes
	ROAST	Preheat oven to 450°F. Place fish in well-greased pan. Brush fish with butter or oil. Baste during roasting. Do not cover.	7–10 minutes
	SAUTÉ	*To Sauté Fillets:* Rub fillets with lemon juice and dust with seasoned flour. Heat oil and/or butter in a nonstick skillet over medium-high heat. Add fish and brown on both sides, turning once.	2–3 minutes per side
	STEAM	Sprinkle fish with salt and pepper. Place fish on steamer rack or basket over simmering water. Cover and steam.	3–5 minutes
COD, HADDOCK, HAKE, POLLOCK, SCROD, WHITING Whole fish; 1 pound	BAKE	Preheat oven to 350°F. Place fish in a greased baking dish. Brush fish with butter or oil and drizzle with fresh herbs, seasoning paste, or sauce. Cover the bottom of pan with white wine or other liquid. Bake uncovered.	15–20 minutes
	BAKE	*To Bake Stuffed:* Preheat oven to 350°F. Spoon stuffing into the stomach cavity. Secure with 2–3 toothpicks. Brush fish with oil and/or butter. Wrap tightly in foil. Bake. Unwrap foil when ready to serve.	15–25 minutes

FISH	METHOD	INSTRUCTIONS	TIMING
	BROIL	Preheat broiler. Brush fish with butter or oil. Pour ¼–½ inch water or wine into the pan. Broil 4 inches from the heat, basting occasionally. Do not turn. Season fish just before the end of the cooking time, if desired.	10–12 minutes
	DEEP-FRY	Heat oil to 375°F. Wash and pat fish dry. Dip in batter or coat with seasoned flour. Fry until golden. Drain on paper towels before serving.	5–7 minutes
	POACH	Place fish in poacher or similar pan. Pour in enough water to cover fish by 1 inch. Add 2 tablespoons salt and 1 teaspoon white vinegar. Bring water rapidly to a simmer. Reduce heat and simmer uncovered. The liquid must not get hotter than 170°–180°F. If fish is to be served cold, turn off heat and let fish cool in liquid, covered.	12–15 minutes
	ROAST	Preheat oven to 450°F. Brush both sides of fish with oil and season with salt and pepper. Place fish in greased roasting pan. Roast uncovered.	12–15 minutes

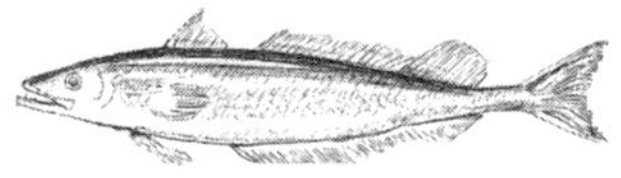

hake (whiting)

cod

FISH	METHOD	INSTRUCTIONS	TIMING
COD, HADDOCK, HAKE, POLLOCK, SCROD, WHITING Whole fish; 1 pound (*cont'd.*)	SAUTÉ	Dust fish with seasoned flour or leave plain. Heat oil and/or butter in a large nonstick skillet over medium-high heat. Add fish and brown on both sides, turning once.	2½–3½ minutes per side
	STEAM	Place fish on steamer rack or basket over boiling water. Cover and steam.	10–13 minutes
COD, HADDOCK, HAKE, POLLOCK, SCROD, WHITING Over 1 pound	ALL METHODS	Whole fish or large pieces; Follow instructions for 1-pound fish.	8–9 minutes per inch of thickness
LARGE FLATFISH			
BRILL, HALIBUT, JOHN DORY, TURBOT Fillet and steaks; 8 ounces	BAKE	Preheat oven to 350°F. Place fish in greased baking pan. Brush with butter or oil. Drizzle with fresh herbs, seasoning paste, or sauce. Cover the bottom with white wine or other liquid. Bake uncovered.	15–25 minutes
	BROIL	Preheat broiler. Brush fish with oil or butter. Place in hot pan skin side down. Broil 3 inches from heat, basting 2–3 times. Turn steaks halfway through cooking; do not turn fillets. Season just before the end of cooking, if desired.	Fillets: 4–5 minutes total Steaks: 3–5 minutes per side
	GRILL	*To Grill Steaks:* Prepare hot fire in the grill. Brush fish with oil or marinade. Lay fish on greased grill or fish grilling rack, skin side down, and grill 4 inches from coals, turning once.	3–5 minutes per side
	OVEN-FRY	*To Oven-Fry Fillets:* Preheat oven to 500°F. Soak fillets in milk or buttermilk, then coat in crumbs. Place in well-greased baking pan and bake on top rack, uncovered.	8 minutes

FISH	METHOD	INSTRUCTIONS	TIMING
	PAN-FRY	*To Pan-Fry Steaks:* Heat oil in heavy skillet, add fish, and sear over high heat for 2 minutes on each side. For thicker steaks, add 1–2 minutes per side.	2–4 minutes per side
	POACH	Bring 4 cups poaching liquid to a boil Add fish and simmer gently.	Fillets: 6–8 minutes Steaks: 8–10 minutes
	SAUTÉ	*To Sauté Fillets:* Rub fillets with lemon juice and dust with seasoned flour. Add fish to hot oil and/or butter in nonstick skillet and cook over medium-high heat until brown, turning once.	2–4 minutes per side
	STEAM	Sprinkle fish with salt and pepper. Place fish on steamer rack or basket over simmering water. Cover and steam.	5–7 minutes
BRILL, HALIBUT, JOHN DORY, TURBOT Whole fish; 1 pound	BAKE	Preheat oven to 350°F. Place fish in a greased baking dish. Brush with butter or oil. Drizzle with fresh herbs, seasoning paste, or sauce. Cover the bottom of pan with white wine or other liquid and bake uncovered.	15–20 minutes

halibut

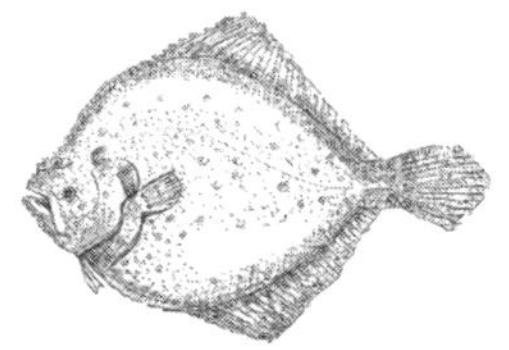

turbot

FISH	*METHOD*	*INSTRUCTIONS*	*TIMING*
BRILL, HALIBUT, JOHN DORY, TURBOT Whole fish; 1 pound (*cont'd.*)	BAKE	*To Bake Stuffed:* Preheat oven to 350°F. Spoon stuffing into the stomach cavity. Secure with 2–3 toothpicks. Brush fish with oil and/or butter. Wrap tightly in foil. Bake. Unwrap foil when ready to serve.	15–25 minutes
	BROIL	Preheat broiler. Brush fish with melted butter or oil. Add ¼–½ inch water or wine to pan. Broil 4 inches from heat, basting occasionally. Do not turn. Season fish just before end of cooking time, if desired.	10–12 minutes
	GRILL	Prepare hot fire in the grill. Brush fish with oil or marinade. Lay fish on greased grill or fish grilling rack, skin side down, and grill 4 inches from coals, turning once.	4–5 minutes per side
	POACH	Bring 4 cups poaching liquid to a boil. Add fish and simmer gently.	12–15 minutes
	ROAST	Preheat oven to 425°F. Place fish in large shallow greased pan. Rub olive oil all over the fish. Wrap the head and tail loosely with aluminum foil allowing a 2-inch space for circulation. Sprinkle the fish with white wine and roast.	15–20 minutes
	STEAM	Score each side of fish 2–3 times from top to bottom. Place fish in steaming rack or basket over boiling liquid and steam covered.	10–13 minutes
BRILL, HALIBUT, JOHN DORY, TURBOT Over 1 pound	ALL METHODS	Larger turbot, halibut, John Dory, and brill are usually cut into steaks that can be steamed, poached, or sautéed. Halibut can also be cut into fillets.	8–9 minutes per inch of thickness

FISH	*METHOD*	*INSTRUCTIONS*	*TIMING*
SMALL FLATFISH *NOTE: These fish overcook easily, so check frequently.*			
SOLE, FLOUNDER, PLAICE Strips or small fillets; 3–4 ounces	DEEP-FRY	Heat oil to 375°F. Wash and pat fish dry. Dip in batter or seasoned flour. Deep-fry until golden. Drain on paper towels before serving.	2–3 minutes
	POACH	Bring 4 cups poaching liquid to a boil. Add fish and simmer gently.	3–5 minutes
	SAUTÉ	Dust strips with seasoned flour. Heat butter and/or oil in a nonstick skillet over medium-high heat. Add fish and brown on both sides.	1–2 minutes
	STEAM	Sprinkle fish with salt and pepper. Place fish on steamer rack or basket over simmering water. Steam covered.	3–5 minutes
	STIR-FRY	Add to hot oil in wok. Cook, stirring gently, until done.	1–2 minutes
SOLE, FLOUNDER, PLAICE Fillets; 6–8 ounces	BAKE	Preheat oven to 350°F. Place fish skin side down in greased roasting pan. Brush with butter or oil. Drizzle over fresh herbs, seasoning paste, or sauce. Cover the bottom of pan with white wine or other liquid. Bake uncovered.	8–10 minutes
	BRAISE	Preheat oven to 350°F. Score skin side of fish. Place in buttered baking pan, skin side down. Dust with salt and pepper. Spread cooked vegetables and herbs over fish, if desired. Pour ½ inch liquid around fish. Bake, basting 2–3 times. Remove fish from liquid when done.	4–6 minutes

FISH	*METHOD*	*INSTRUCTIONS*	*TIMING*
SOLE, FLOUNDER, PLAICE Fillets; 6–8 ounces (*cont'd.*)	BROIL	Preheat broiler. Brush fish with melted butter or oil. Place skin side down on pan and broil 4 inches from heat. Do not turn. Season fish just before end of cooking, if desired.	4–5 minutes
	DEEP-FRY	Heat oil to 375°F. Wash and pat fish dry. Dip in batter or seasoned flour. Deep-fry until golden. Drain on paper towels before serving.	3–4 minutes or until golden
	OVEN-FRY	*To Oven-Fry Fillets:* Preheat oven to 500°F. Soak fillets in milk or buttermilk, then coat in crumbs. Place in well-greased baking pan and bake on top rack, uncovered.	8 minutes
	POACH	Bring 4 cups poaching liquid to a boil. Add fish and simmer gently.	4–6 minutes
	SAUTÉ	Rub fillets with lemon juice and dust with seasoned flour. Heat butter and/ or oil in skillet over medium-high heat and add fish, skin side down. Brown on each side.	2–3 minutes per side
	STEAM	Sprinkle fish with salt and pepper. Place fish on steamer rack or basket above simmering water. Cover and steam.	5–7 minutes

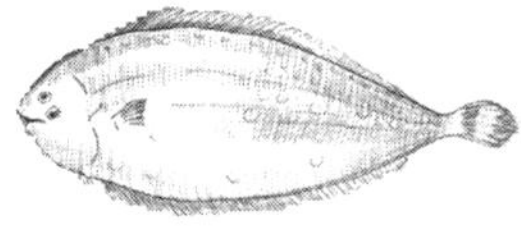

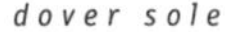

dover sole

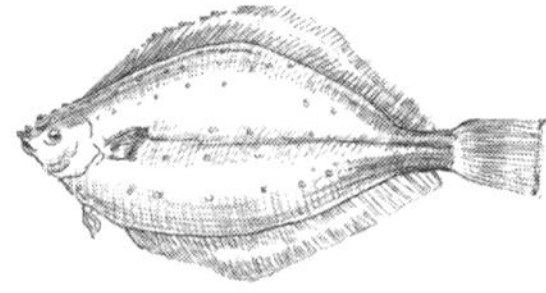

flounder

FISH	METHOD	INSTRUCTIONS	TIMING
SOLE, FLOUNDER, PLAICE Whole; ¾–1 pound	BAKE	Preheat oven to 350°F. Place fish in greased roasting pan. Brush with butter or oil and drizzle over fresh herbs, seasoning paste, or sauce. Cover the bottom of pan with white wine or other liquid. Bake uncovered.	10–15 minutes
	BAKE	*To Bake Stuffed:* Preheat oven to 350°F. Spoon stuffing into cavity of fish. Secure with 2–3 toothpicks. Brush fish with oil or butter. Wrap tightly in foil. Bake. Unwrap foil when ready to serve.	15–20 minutes
	BROIL	Preheat broiler. Brush fish with melted butter or oil. Add ¼–½ inch water or wine to pan. Broil 4 inches from heat, basting occasionally. Do not turn. Season fish just before end of cooking, if desired.	6–10 minutes
	POACH	Bring 4 cups poaching liquid to a boil. Add fish and simmer gently.	10–15 minutes
	SAUTÉ	Dust fish with seasoned flour, if desired. Heat butter and/or oil in large skillet over medium-high heat and add fish. Brown on one side. Turn and cook.	3–5 minutes per side
	STEAM	Score each side of the fish 3 times from top to bottom. Place on a steaming rack or basket over boiling water. Cover and steam.	10–12 minutes

FISH	*METHOD*	*INSTRUCTIONS*	*TIMING*
FRESHWATER FISH			
CARP, CATFISH, PERCH, PIKE, SUCKER, SUNFISH, WHITEFISH Fillets; 6–8 ounces	BROIL	Preheat broiler. Season both sides of fish with salt and pepper and rub with butter or oil. Broil 2 inches from heat for 1 minute, then spread butter or oil over top of fish. Do not turn.	4–6 minutes
	DEEP-FRY	Heat oil to 375°F. Wash and pat fish dry. Dip in batter or seasoned flour. Deep-fry until golden. Drain on paper towels before serving.	2–3 minutes
	OVEN-FRY	Preheat oven to 500°F. Soak fillets in milk or buttermilk, then coat in crumbs. Place in well-greased baking pan and bake on top rack, uncovered.	8 minutes
	PAN-FRY	Dust fish with seasoned flour. Heat oil in large skillet over medium-high heat. Add fish and fry. Drain on paper towels before serving.	2–3 minutes per side
	POACH	Bring 4 cups poaching liquid to a boil. Add fish and simmer gently.	Fillets: 4–6 minutes Steaks: 5–10 minutes
	SAUTÉ	Dust fillets with seasoned flour. Heat oil and/or butter in large nonstick skillet over medium-high heat. Add fish skin side down and sauté until golden, turning once.	2–3 minutes per side
	STEAM	Sprinkle fish with salt and pepper. Place fish on steamer rack or basket above simmering water. Cover and steam.	3–5 minutes
	STIR-FRY	Cut fish into 1-inch chunks and add to hot oil in wok over high heat. Cook, stirring gently, until done.	2–3 minutes

FISH	METHOD	INSTRUCTIONS	TIMING
CARP, CATFISH, PERCH, PIKE, WHITEFISH Whole fish; 1 pound	BAKE	Preheat oven to 350°F. Place fish in a greased baking dish. Brush the fish with butter or oil and drizzle with fresh herbs, seasoning paste, or sauce. Cover the bottom of pan with white wine or other liquid. Bake uncovered.	15–20 minutes
	BAKE	*To Bake Stuffed:* Preheat the oven to 350°F. Spoon stuffing into the stomach cavity. Secure with 2–3 toothpicks. Brush fish with oil and/or butter. Wrap tightly in foil. Bake. Unwrap foil when ready to serve.	15–25 minutes
	BROIL	Preheat broiler. Brush fish with butter or oil. Pour ¼–½ inch water or wine into pan. Broil 4 inches from the heat, basting occasionally. Do not turn. Season fish just before the end of the cooking, if desired.	10–12 minutes
	DEEP-FRY	Heat oil to 375°F. Wash and pat fish dry. Dip in batter or seasoned flour and deep-fry until golden. Drain on paper towels before serving.	5–7 minutes
	POACH	Bring 4 cups poaching liquid to a boil Add fish and simmer gently.	12–15 minutes

catfish

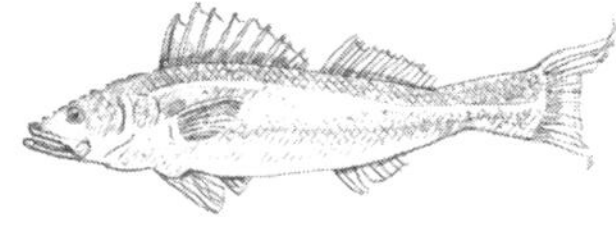

walleye (perch)

FISH	*METHOD*	*INSTRUCTIONS*	*TIMING*
CARP, CATFISH, PERCH, PIKE, WHITEFISH Whole fish; 1 pound (*cont'd.*)	ROAST	Preheat oven to 425°F. Place fish in a large shallow greased pan. Brush fish with oil and/or butter. Wrap the head and tail loosely with aluminum foil, allowing for a 2-inch space for circulation. Sprinkle the fish with white wine and roast uncovered.	12–18 minutes
	SAUTÉ	Dust fish with seasoned flour or leave plain. Heat butter and/or oil in large nonstick skillet over medium-high heat. Add fish and brown on both sides, turning once.	8–10 minutes per side
	STEAM	Score each side of the fish 3 times from top to bottom. Place the fish on a steamer rack or basket over boiling water. Cover and steam.	10–13 minutes
CARP, CATFISH, PERCH, PIKE, WHITEFISH Whole fish and large pieces; over 1 pound	ALL METHODS	Follow instructions for 1-pound fish.	8–9 minutes per inch of thickness
MEATY FISH			
MARLIN, TUNA, SWORDFISH Fillets and steaks; 6–8 ounces	BRAISE	Preheat oven to 350°F (if oven-braising). In a large Dutch oven, sear fish in hot oil. Add precooked vegetables, if desired, seasonings, and ½–1 inch braising liquid. Cover. Let simmer in oven or on top of stove, basting several times.	10–12 minutes

FISH	METHOD	INSTRUCTIONS	TIMING
	BROIL	Preheat broiler. Brush fish with butter or oil. Broil 4 inches from heat, basting with additional butter or oil. Turn steaks halfway through cooking; do not turn fillets. Season fish just before the end of cooking time, if desired.	Fillets: 3–5 minutes total Steaks: 4–5 minutes per side
	GRILL	*To Grill Steaks:* Prepare hot fire in grill. Brush steaks with oil and/or butter. Place on oiled grill or fish grilling rack 2–3 inches from coals. Turn once, basting frequently.	3–5 minutes per side
	PAN-FRY	*To Pan-Fry Steaks:* Heat oil in a heavy skillet over high heat, add steaks, and sear for 2 minutes on each side. If more than 1 inch thick, add 1–2 minutes per side.	2–4 minutes per side
	POACH	Bring 4 cups poaching liquid to a boil. Add fish and simmer gently.	8–12 minutes
	SAUTÉ	*To Sauté Fillets:* Dust fish with seasoned flour. Add to heated oil and/or butter in large skillet and cook over medium-high heat until lightly browned, turning once.	2–5 minutes per side
	STEAM	Sprinkle fish with salt and pepper. Place fish on steamer rack or basket over simmering water. Cover and steam.	7–10 minutes

blue fin tuna

swordfish

FISH	METHOD	INSTRUCTIONS	TIMING
MARLIN, TUNA, SWORDFISH Fillets and steaks; 6–8 ounces *(cont'd.)*	STIR-FRY	Cut fish into 1-inch cubes. Divide into 2 or more small batches. Add to hot oil in wok and cook, stirring constantly.	2–3 minutes
SHARK, STURGEON Fillets and steaks; 6–8 ounces	BRAISE	Preheat oven to 350°F (if oven-braising). In a large Dutch oven, sear fish in hot oil. Add ½–1 inch braising liquid, seasonings, and precooked vegetables, if desired. Cover. Let simmer in oven or on top of stove, basting several times.	8–10 minutes
	BROIL	Preheat broiler. Brush fish with butter or oil. Pour ¼–½ inch water or wine into the pan. Broil 4 inches from heat, basting with butter or oil. Turn steaks halfway through cooking; do not turn fillets.	Fillets: 3–5 minutes total Steak: 4–5 minutes per side
	DEEP-FRY	*To Deep-Fry Fillets:* Heat oil to 375°F. Wash and pat fish dry. Dip in batter or seasoned flour. Deep-fry until golden. Drain on paper towels before serving.	3–5 minutes
	POACH	Bring 4 cups poaching liquid to a boil. Add fish and simmer gently.	Fillets: 4–6 minutes total Steaks: 5–10 minutes
	SAUTÉ	Rub fillets with lemon juice and dust with seasoned flour. Heat oil and/or butter in nonstick skillet over medium-high heat. Add fish and brown on each side, turning once.	3–4 minutes per side
	STIR-FRY	Cut fish into 1-inch cubes. Divide into 2 or more small batches. Add to hot oil in wok and cook, stirring constantly.	1–3 minutes

FISH	*METHOD*	*INSTRUCTIONS*	*TIMING*
MARLIN, TUNA, SHARK, STURGEON, SWORDFISH Whole fish or large pieces; over 1 pound	BRAISE	Preheat oven to 350°F. Coat fish with seasoned flour. Heat oil in large Dutch oven, add fish, and brown on both sides for about 5 minutes per side. Add precooked vegetables, if desired, seasonings, and 1 inch braising liquid. Bring to a boil. Reduce heat, cover, and simmer in oven.	3-pound fish: 15–20 minutes 5-pound fish: 25–30 minutes
	BROIL	Preheat broiler. Brush fish with butter or oil. Add ¼–½ inch water or wine to pan. Broil 4 inches from heat, basting occasionally. Season fish just before end of cooking time, if desired.	8–9 minutes per inch of thickness
	GRILL	Prepare a hot fire in grill. Brush fish with oil or marinade. Lay the fish on an oiled grill or fish grilling rack 4 inches from the coals and grill, turning once and basting occasionally.	8–9 minutes per inch of thickness

OILY FISH AND SMALL FRY

FISH	*METHOD*	*INSTRUCTIONS*	*TIMING*
BLUEFISH, HERRING, KINGFISH MACKEREL, SARDINE, SHAD Fillets and steaks; 6–8 ounces	BROIL	Preheat broiler. Season both sides of fish with salt and pepper and rub with oil. Place fillets skin side down. Broil 2 inches from heat for 1 minute and spread butter over top of fish. Continue broiling, turning steaks halfway through broiling time. Do not turn fillets.	Fillets: 4–6 minutes total Steaks: 3–4 minutes per side
	BRAISE	Cut fish into 2–4 pieces. Heat oil in a large nonstick skillet over high heat. Add the fish and sear for 1 minute on each side. Add precooked vegetables, if desired, seasonings, and ½–1 inch braising liquid. Reduce the heat, cover, and simmer.	8–12 minutes

FISH	*METHOD*	*INSTRUCTIONS*	*TIMING*
BLUEFISH, HERRING, KINGFISH, MACKEREL, SARDINE, SHAD Fillets and steaks; 6–8 ounces (*cont'd.*)	GRILL	Prepare a hot fire in the grill. Brush steaks with oil and/or butter. Place on oiled grill or fish grill rack 2–3 inches from coals. Place fillets skin side down. Grill, turning once.	3–5 minutes per side
	POACH	Bring 4 cups poaching liquid to a boil. Add fish and simmer gently. When poaching herring, add vinegar to the poaching liquid.	Fillets: 4–6 minutes Steaks: 5–10 minutes
	SAUTÉ	Coat the fish with seasoned flour or herbs. Heat butter and/or oil in a nonstick skillet over medium-high heat. Add the fish (skin side down with fillets). Fry, turning once.	3–5 minutes per side
BLUEFISH, HERRING, KINGFISH, MACKEREL, SARDINE, SHAD Whole fish; 1 pound	BAKE	Preheat oven to 350°F. Place fish in a greased baking dish. Brush fish with butter or oil and drizzle with fresh herbs, seasoning paste, or sauce. Cover the bottom of pan with white wine or other liquid. Bake uncovered.	15–20 minutes

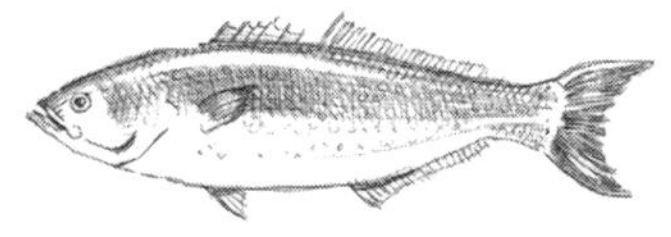

bluefish

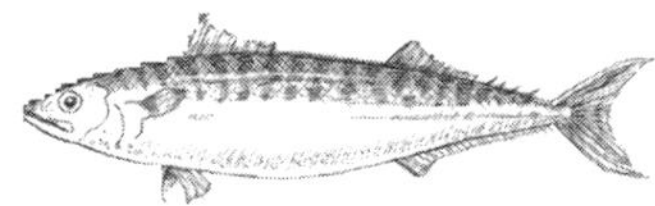

mackerel

FISH	METHOD	INSTRUCTIONS	TIMING
	BAKE	*To Bake Stuffed:* Preheat oven to 350°F. Spoon stuffing into the stomach cavity. Secure with 2–3 toothpicks. Brush fish with oil and/or butter. Wrap tightly in foil. Bake. Unwrap foil when ready to serve.	15–25 minutes
	BROIL	Preheat broiler. Brush fish with butter or oil. Pour ¼–½ inch water or wine into broiler pan. Broil 4 inches from heat, basting occasionally. Do not turn. Season just before the end of the cooking, if desired.	10–12 minutes
	ROAST	Preheat oven to 425°F. Place fish skin side down in greased pan. Brush fish with olive oil and lemon juice and roast uncovered.	10–15 minutes
	SAUTÉ	Dust the fish with seasoned flour or herbs. Heat butter and/or oil in large skillet over medium-high heat. Add fish skin side down and fry, turning once.	2–3 minutes per side
BLUEFISH, HERRING, KINGFISH, MACKEREL, SARDINE, SHAD Whole fish or large pieces; over 1 pound	ALL METHODS	Follow instructions for 1-pound fish.	8–9 minutes per inch of thickness
	BAKE	Preheat oven to 350°F. Place fish in a greased baking dish. Brush fish with oil and/or butter and drizzle with fresh herbs, seasoning paste, or sauce. Cover the bottom of pan with white wine or other liquid. Bake uncovered.	18–28 minutes, depending on size
	GRILL	Prepare a medium fire in the grill. Brush both sides of fish with oil. Place fish in a greased grill basket or grill rack 6 inches from coals. Grill, turning once.	9–10 minutes per side

FISH	*METHOD*	*INSTRUCTIONS*	*TIMING*
SALMON AND TROUT			
ATLANTIC SALMON, PACIFIC SALMON, SALMON, SALMON, TROUT (Brook, Cutthroat, Lake, Rainbow) Fillets and steaks; 6–8 ounces	BAKE	Preheat oven to 350°F. Place fish in a greased baking dish. Brush fish with butter or oil and drizzle with fresh herbs, seasoning paste, or sauce. Cover the bottom of pan with white wine or other liquid. Bake uncovered.	8–10 minutes
	BROIL	Preheat broiler. Brush fish with oil or butter. Place skin side down in broiler 4 inches from heat, basting occasionally. Turn steaks halfway through cooking; do not turn fillets. Season fish just before end of cooking, if desired.	Fillets: 4–5 minutes total Steaks: 3–4 minutes per side
	POACH	Bring 4 cups poaching liquid to a boil. Add fish and simmer gently.	3–5 minutes
	ROAST	Preheat oven to 450°F. Brush both sides of fish with oil. Season with salt and pepper. Place in a greased roasting pan and roast uncovered.	4–6 minutes
	SAUTÉ	*To Sauté Fillets:* Dust fillets with seasoned flour. Add skin side down to hot butter and/or oil in skillet and sauté over medium-high heat until fish is golden, turning once.	2–3 minutes per side
	STEAM	Sprinkle fish with salt and pepper. Place fish on steamer rack or basket over simmering water. Cover and steam.	3–5 minutes

FISH	*METHOD*	*INSTRUCTIONS*	*TIMING*
ATLANTIC SALMON, PACIFIC SALMON, SALMON, TROUT (Brook, Cutthroat, Lake, Rainbow) Whole fish; 1 pound	BAKE	Preheat oven to 350°F. Place fish in a greased baking dish. Brush the fish with butter or oil and drizzle with fresh herbs, seasoning paste, or sauce. Cover the bottom of pan with white wine or other liquid. Bake uncovered.	12–18 minutes
	BAKE	*To Bake Stuffed:* Spoon stuffing into the stomach cavity. Secure with 2–3 toothpicks. Brush with oil and/or butter. Wrap tightly in foil. Bake. Unwrap foil when ready to serve.	12–20 minutes
	BRAISE	Preheat oven to 350°F. Place fish in a greased baking dish. Cover with sauce. Cover dish with lid or foil. Simmer in oven or on top of the stove.	10–15 minutes
	BROIL	Preheat broiler. Brush fish with melted butter or oil. Pour $\frac{1}{4}$–$\frac{1}{2}$ inch water or wine into pan. Broil 4 inches from heat, basting occasionally. Do not turn. Season fish just before the end of the cooking time, if desired.	10–12 minutes
	PAN-FRY	Heat oil and/or butter in a large heavy skillet. Season the fish and add to pan. Fry, turning once. Drain when done.	4–5 minutes per side

rainbow trout

salmon

FISH	METHOD	INSTRUCTIONS	TIMING
ATLANTIC SALMON, PACIFIC SALMON, SALMON, TROUT (Brook, Cutthroat, Lake, Rainbow) Whole fish; 1 pound (*cont'd.*)	POACH	Bring 4 cups poaching liquid to a boil. Add fish and simmer gently.	12–15 minutes
	ROAST	Preheat oven to 450°F. Place fish in a greased baking dish. Brush fish with butter or oil and season with salt and pepper. Roast uncovered.	12–18 minutes
	STEAM	Place fish on steamer rack or basket over boiling water. Cover and steam.	10–13 minutes
ATLANTIC SALMON, PACIFIC SALMON, SALMON, TROUT (Brook, Cutthroat, Lake, Rainbow) Whole fish or large pieces; over 1 pound	ALL METHODS	Follow instructions for 1-pound fish.	8–9 minutes per inch of thickness
	BRAISE	Brush both sides of fish with oil. Sprinkle cavity with salt and pepper. Place fish on rack at bottom of large pot. Wrap cheesecloth around both rack and fish. Pour 1 inch cooking liquid into pot. Cover and simmer over medium heat.	5–6 pound fish: 30–45 minutes
	POACH	Bring 4 cups poaching liquid to a boil. Add fish and simmer gently, with pot partially covered.	4–5 pound fish: 30–40 minutes
	POACH	*To Poach in Court-Bouillon:* Place fish on a lightly oiled rack. Then place in a pot and cover with cold court-bouillon. Bring to simmer over medium heat. Reduce heat and poach.	4–5 pound fish: 30–40 minutes

FISH	METHOD	INSTRUCTIONS	TIMING
	ROAST	Preheat oven to 450°F. Roll fish in flour or cover with an herb paste. Place in greased roasting pan and drizzle with oil or melted butter. Roast uncovered.	2–4-pound fish: 20–25 minutes 4–6-pound fish: 25–30 minutes 6–8-pound fish: 35–45 minutes 8–10-pound fish: 45–60 minutes
THIN-BONED FISH			
POMPANO, POMFRET, SEA BREAM, OTHER JACKS Fillets and steaks; 6 ounces	BAKE	Preheat oven to 350°F. Place fish in a greased baking dish. Brush fish with butter or oil and drizzle with fresh herbs, seasoning paste, or sauce. Cover the bottom of pan with white wine or other liquid. Bake uncovered.	8–12 minutes
	BROIL	Preheat broiler. Brush fish with melted butter or oil. Pour ¼–½ inch water or wine into pan. Broil 4 inches from heat, basting occasionally. Turn steaks halfway through broiling time; do not turn fillets. Season fish just before the end of cooking, if desired.	Fillets: 4–6 minutes total Steaks: 3–4 minutes per side

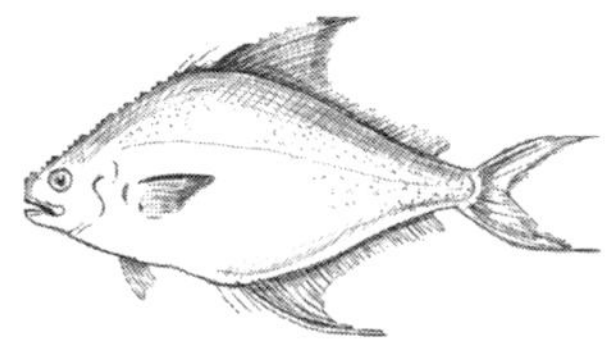

pompano (jack)

FISH	METHOD	INSTRUCTIONS	TIMING
POMPANO, POMFRET, SEA BREAM, OTHER JACKS Fillets and steaks; 6 ounces (*cont'd.*)	PAN-FRY	*To Pan-Fry Steaks:* Heat oil in heavy skillet, add fish, and sear over high heat for 2 minutes on each side. For thick steaks, add 1–2 minutes per side.	2–4 minutes per side
	POACH	Bring 4 cups poaching liquid to a boil. Add fish and simmer gently.	Fillets: 4–6 minutes Steaks: 5–10 minutes
	SAUTÉ	Dust fillets with seasoned flour. Heat oil and/or butter in a nonstick skillet over medium-high heat. Add fillets skin side down to pan. Sauté until fish is golden on both sides, turning once.	2–3 minutes per side
POMPANO, POMFRET, SEA BREAM, OTHER JACKS Whole fish; 1 pound	BAKE	Preheat oven to 350°F. Place fish in a greased baking dish. Brush fish with butter or oil and drizzle with fresh herbs, seasoning paste, or sauce. Cover the bottom of pan with white wine or other liquid. Bake uncovered.	15–20 minutes
	BAKE	*To Bake Stuffed:* Preheat oven to 350°F. Spoon stuffing into the stomach cavity. Secure with 2–3 toothpicks. Brush fish with oil and/or butter. Wrap tightly in foil. Bake. Unwrap foil when ready to serve.	15–25 minutes
	BROIL	Preheat broiler. Brush fish with melted butter or oil. Pour ¼–½ inch water or wine into pan. Broil 4 inches from heat, basting occasionally. Do not turn. Season fish just before the end of cooking, if desired.	10–12 minutes

FISH	*METHOD*	*INSTRUCTIONS*	*TIMING*
	ROAST	Preheat oven to 450°F. Brush both sides of fish with oil and season with salt and pepper. Place fish in greased roasting pan. Roast uncovered.	12–18 minutes
	STEAM	Place fish on steamer rack or basket over boiling water. Cover and steam.	10–13 minutes
POMPANO, POMFRET, SEA BREAM, OTHER JACKS Whole fish or large pieces; over 1 pound	ALL METHODS	Follow instructions for 1-pound fish.	8–9 minutes per inch of thickness
	GRILL	Prepare a medium fire in the grill. Brush both sides of fish with oil. Place fish in a greased grill basket or grill rack 6 inches from coals. Grill, turning once.	4–5 pound fish: 9–10 minutes per side

FIRM WHITE FISH

FISH	*METHOD*	*INSTRUCTIONS*	*TIMING*
GROUPER, MAHIMAHI, OCEAN PERCH, ORANGE ROUGHY, SNAPPER, WOLFFISH Fillets and steaks; 6–8 ounces	BAKE	Preheat oven to 350°F. Place fish in greased baking dish. Brush with butter or oil and drizzle with fresh herbs, seasoning paste, or sauce. Cover bottom with white wine or other liquid. Bake uncovered.	12–18 minutes
	BROIL	Preheat broiler. Brush fish with oil and/or butter and place in hot broiling pan (fillets skin side down). Grill 3 inches from heat, basting. Turn steaks halfway through broiling; do not turn fillets. Season fish just before end of cooking time, if desired.	Fillets: 3–5 minutes total Steaks: 4–5 minutes per side

FISH	*METHOD*	*INSTRUCTIONS*	*TIMING*
GROUPER, MAHIMAHI, OCEAN PERCH, ORANGE ROUGHY, SNAPPER, WOLFFISH Fillets and steaks; 6–8 ounces (*cont'd.*)	DEEP-FRY	*To Deep-Fry Fillets:* Heat oil to 375°F. Wash and pat fish dry. Dip in batter or seasoned flour. Deep-fry until golden. Drain on paper towels before serving.	3–5 minutes
	GRILL	Prepare a hot fire in the grill. Brush fish with oil or marinade and place on greased grill or fish grilling rack 4 inches from coals. Cover grill. Cook until the side facing heat is blistered. Turn and grill other side.	3–5 minutes per side
	OVEN-FRY	*To Oven-Fry Fillets:* Preheat oven to 500°F. Soak fillets in milk or buttermilk, then coat in crumbs. Place in well-greased baking pan and bake on top rack, uncovered.	8 minutes
	PAN-BROIL	Brush fish with oil and/or butter. Place fish in preheated skillet and cook one side until golden. Then turn and brown second side.	3–5 minutes per side
	POACH	Bring 4 cups poaching liquid to a boil. Add fish and simmer gently.	Fillets: 4–6 minutes Steaks: 5–10 minutes

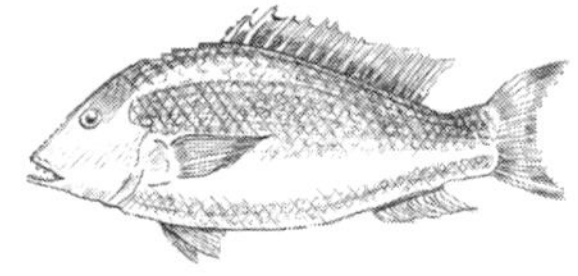

red snapper

mahimahi

FISH	*METHOD*	*INSTRUCTIONS*	*TIMING*
	SAUTÉ	Rub fish with lemon juice and dust with seasoned flour. Heat butter and/or oil in a large nonstick skillet over medium-high heat. Add fish and sauté until brown on each side, turning once.	2–3 minutes per side
	STEAM	Sprinkle fish with salt and pepper. Place fish on steamer rack or basket above simmering water. Cover and steam.	4–5 minutes
	STIR-FRY	Cut fish into 1-inch chunks. Add the fish to hot oil in wok and stir gently until done.	2–3 minutes
GROUPER, MAHIMAHI, OCEAN PERCH, ORANGE ROUGHY, SNAPPER, WOLFFISH Whole fish; 1 pound	BAKE	Preheat oven to 350°F. Place fish in a greased baking dish. Brush with butter or oil. Drizzle with fresh herbs, seasoning paste, or sauce. Cover the bottom of the pan with white wine or other liquid. Bake uncovered.	15–25 minutes
	BAKE	*To Bake Stuffed:* Preheat oven to 350°F. Spoon stuffing into the stomach cavity. Secure with 2–3 toothpicks. Brush fish with oil and/or butter. Wrap tightly in foil. Bake. Unwrap foil when ready to serve.	20–25 minutes
	BROIL	Preheat broiler. Brush fish with melted butter or oil. Pour $\frac{1}{4}$–$\frac{1}{2}$ inch water or wine into pan. Broil 4 inches from the heat, basting occasionally. Do not turn. Season fish just before end of cooking time, if desired.	10–12 minutes

FISH	*METHOD*	*INSTRUCTIONS*	*TIMING*
GROUPER, MAHIMAHI, OCEAN PERCH, ORANGE ROUGHY, SNAPPER, WOLFFISH Whole fish; 1 pound (*cont'd.*)	DEEP-FRY	Heat oil to 375°F. Wash and pat fish dry. Dip in batter or seasoned flour. Deep-fry until golden. Drain on paper towels before serving.	7–10 minutes
	GRILL	Prepare a hot fire in the grill. Brush fish with oil and place on oiled grill or fish grilling rack 4 inches from coals. Cover grill. Grill until the side facing heat is blistered. Turn and grill other side.	4–6 minutes per side
	POACH	Bring 4 cups poaching liquid to a boil. Add fish and simmer gently.	12–15 minutes
	ROAST	Preheat oven to 450°F. Score fish on both sides with 2-inch slashes. Rub lemon juice and oil over fish. Coat skin with coarse salt or pepper. Place in well-oiled pan and roast uncovered.	15–20 minutes
	SAUTÉ	Rub fish with lemon juice. Dust with seasoned flour or leave plain. Heat oil and/or butter in large nonstick skillet over medium-high heat. Add fish and sauté until brown on both sides, turning once.	5–6 minutes per side
	STEAM	Place fish on steaming rack or basket over boiling water. Steam covered.	10–13 minutes

FISH	*METHOD*	*INSTRUCTIONS*	*TIMING*
GROUPER, MAHIMAHI, OCEAN PERCH, ORANGE ROUGHY, SNAPPER, WOLF-FISH Whole fish or large pieces; over 1 pound	ALL METHODS	Follow instructions for 1-pound fish.	8–9 minutes per inch of thickness
	BAKE	*To Bake in Foil:* Preheat oven to 425°F. Place fish on a sheet of greased aluminum foil. Pour melted butter and lemon juice over fish and season with salt and pepper. Bring the two sides of the foil over the fish and make a double fold in the middle and at both ends of the fish. Pour ¼ inch water in a baking pan and place aluminum foil package in the water. Bake. Let stand 15 minutes before serving.	35–40 minutes
	BRAISE	Heat oil in a large heavy skillet over high heat. Add fish and brown on each side, 5 minutes a side. Add cooked vegetables, if desired, 1 inch cooking liquid, and seasonings. Bring to a boil. Reduce heat, cover, and simmer until done.	3-pound fish: 15–20 minutes 5-pound fish: 25–30 minutes
	ROAST	Preheat oven to 475°F. Cut 3–4 slashes on each side of fish. Rub fish inside and out with oil and season with salt and pepper. Line a roasting pan with aluminum foil and place the fish on a rack in the pan. Roast undisturbed until done.	3–4-pound fish: 25–30 minutes

FISH	*METHOD*	*INSTRUCTIONS*	*TIMING*
FLAKY WHITE FISH			
BASS, CROAKER, DRUM, MULLET, ROCKFISH, SEA BASS, TILEFISH, WEAKFISH Fillets and steaks; 6 ounces	BAKE	Preheat oven to 350°F. Place fish in a greased baking dish. Brush fish with butter or oil and drizzle with fresh herbs, seasoning paste, or sauce. Cover the bottom of pan with white wine or other liquid. Bake uncovered.	8–12 minutes
	BROIL	Preheat broiler. Pour $\frac{1}{4}$–$\frac{1}{2}$ inch water or wine into a broiler pan. Brush fish with butter or oil. Broil 4 inches from the heat. Turn steaks halfway through broiling time; do not turn fillets. Season fish just before end of cooking, if desired.	Fillets: 4–6 minutes total Steaks: 3–4 minutes per side
	DEEP-FRY	*To Deep-Fry Fillets:* Heat oil to 375°F. Wash and pat fish dry. Dip fillets in batter or seasoned flour. Deep-fry until golden. Drain on paper towels before serving.	3–5 minutes
	OVEN-FRY	*To Oven-Fry Fillets:* Preheat oven to 500°F. Soak fillets in milk or buttermilk, then coat in crumbs. Place in well-greased baking pan and bake on top rack, uncovered.	8 minutes
	PAN-FRY	*To Pan-Fry Steaks:* Heat oil in heavy skillet, add fish, and sear over high heat 2 minutes on each side. For thick steaks, add 1–2 minutes per side.	2–4 minutes per side
	POACH	Bring 4 cups poaching liquid to a boil. Add fish and simmer gently.	Fillets: 4–6 minutes Steaks: 5–10 minutes

FISH	METHOD	INSTRUCTIONS	TIMING
	ROAST	*To Roast Fillets:* Preheat oven to 450°F. Sprinkle fillets with salt and pepper and brush with oil. Place skin side down in a greased baking dish in a single layer. Sprinkle with lemon juice and herbs. Roast uncovered.	6–9 minutes
	SAUTÉ	*To Sauté Fillets:* Rub fish with lemon juice and dust with seasoned flour. Heat butter and/or oil in a nonstick skillet over medium-high heat. Add the fish and brown on both sides, turning once.	2–3 minutes per side
	STEAM	Sprinkle fish with salt and pepper. Place fish on steamer rack or basket over simmering water. Cover and steam.	5–7 minutes
BASS, CROAKER, DRUM, MULLET, ROCKFISH, SEA BASS, TILEFISH, WEAKFISH Whole fish; 1 pound	BAKE	Preheat oven to 350°F. Place fish in a greased baking dish. Brush fish with butter or oil and drizzle with fresh herbs, seasoning paste, or sauce. Cover the bottom of pan with white wine or other liquid. Bake uncovered.	15–20 minutes

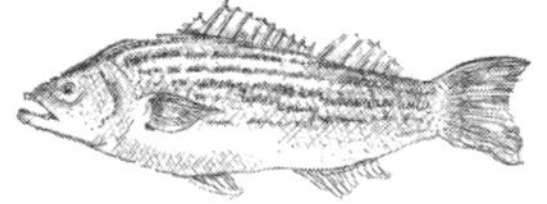

striped bass

tilefish

FISH	*METHOD*	*INSTRUCTIONS*	*TIMING*
BASS, CROAKER, DRUM, MULLET, ROCKFISH, SEA BASS, TILEFISH, WEAKFISH Whole fish; 1 pound (*cont'd.*)	BAKE	*To Bake Stuffed:* Preheat oven to 350°F. Spoon stuffing into the stomach cavity. Secure with 2–3 toothpicks. Brush fish with oil and/or butter. Wrap tightly in foil. Bake. Unwrap foil when ready to serve.	15–25 minutes
	BROIL	Preheat broiler. Brush fish with butter or oil. Pour ¼–½ inch water or wine into pan. Broil 4 inches from the heat, basting occasionally. Do not turn. Season fish just before the end of cooking, if desired.	10–12 minutes
	GRILL	Prepare a hot fire in the grill. Brush the fish with oil or marinade and place on greased grill or fish grilling rack and grill 4 inches from coals. Cover and grill until the side facing heat is blistered. Turn and grill other side.	4–6 minutes per side
	PAN-FRY	Dust fish with seasoned flour. Add to hot oil in large heavy skillet over medium-high heat. Brown on both sides, turning once.	4–6 minutes per side
	POACH	Place fish in poacher or similar pan. Pour in enough water to cover fish by 1 inch. Add 2 tablespoons salt and 1 teaspoon white vinegar. Bring water rapidly to a simmer. Reduce heat and simmer uncovered. The liquid must not get hotter than 170°–180°F. To serve cold, let fish cool in poaching liquid, covered.	12–15 minutes

FISH	METHOD	INSTRUCTIONS	TIMING
	ROAST	Preheat oven to 425°F. Place the fish in a large greased pan. Rub olive oil all over the fish. Wrap the head and tail loosely with aluminum foil, allowing a 2-inch space for air circulation. Sprinkle the fish with white wine and roast uncovered.	15–20 minutes
	SAUTÉ	Dust the fish in seasoned flour or leave plain. Heat butter and/or oil in large nonstick skillet over medium-high heat. Add fish and brown on both sides, turning once.	5–7 minutes
	STEAM	Score each side of fish 2–3 times from top to bottom. Place fish on steaming rack or basket over boiling liquid and steam covered.	10–13 minutes
BASS, CROAKER, DRUM, MULLET, ROCKFISH, SEA BASS, TILEFISH, WEAKFISH Over 1 pound	ALL METHODS	Follow instructions for 1-pound fish.	8–9 minutes per inch of thickness
	BRAISE	Heat oil in a large heavy skillet over medium-high heat. Add fish and brown on both sides, turning once, about 5 minutes a side. Add cooked vegetables, if desired, seasonings, and 1 inch cooking liquid. Bring to a boil, reduce heat, cover, and simmer until done.	3-pound fish: 15–20 minutes 5-pound fish: 25–30 minutes
	ROAST	Cut 3–4 slashes on each side of fish. Rub fish inside and out with oil and season with salt and pepper. Line a roasting pan with aluminum foil and place the fish on a rack in the pan. Roast undisturbed until done.	3–4-pound fish: 25–30 minutes 7-pound fish: 40–45 minutes

FISH	METHOD	INSTRUCTIONS	TIMING
MISCELLANEOUS FISH			
EEL, GARFISH, LAMPREY Fillets; 4–6 ounces	BAKE	Preheat oven to 350°F. Place fish in a greased baking dish. Cover the bottom of the dish with white wine or other liquid. Bake uncovered.	15–20 minutes
	BROIL	Preheat broiler. Rub fish with oil and sprinkle with salt and pepper. Broil 2 inches from heat. Do not turn.	2–3 minutes per side
	POACH	Bring 4 cups poaching liquid to a boil. Add fish and simmer gently.	5–7 minutes
	SAUTÉ	*To Sauté:* Cut into 2-inch pieces and coat with seasoned flour. Heat oil in a nonstick skillet over medium-high heat. Add the fish; brown and turn.	2–3 minutes per side
EEL, GARFISH, LAMPREY Steaks; 4–6 ounces	BAKE	Preheat oven to 350°F. Place fish in a greased baking dish. Cover the bottom of the dish with white wine or other liquid. Bake uncovered.	15–20 minutes
	BROIL	*To Broil:* Preheat broiler. Cut fish into 2-inch pieces. Rub with oil and sprinkle with salt and pepper. Broil 4–6 inches from heat, turning once.	2–4 minutes per side
	GRILL	Prepare a hot fire in the grill. Cut fish into 2-inch pieces. Rub with oil and sprinkle with salt and pepper. Place on oiled grill or fish grilling rack 4–6 inches from coals. Grill, turning once.	2–4 minutes per side
	POACH	Cut steaks into 2-inch pieces. Bring 4 cups poaching liquid to a boil. Add fish and simmer gently.	8–12 minutes

FISH	*METHOD*	*INSTRUCTIONS*	*TIMING*
	SAUTÉ	Cut into 2-inch pieces and coat with seasoned flour. Heat oil in a nonstick skillet over medium-high heat. Add the fish; brown and turn. When meat starts to come away from bone, it's done.	3–5 minutes per side
MONKFISH 8-ounce tail piece, fillets, steaks, or cut into 2-inch cubes or medallions	BRAISE	Heat oil in large skillet or heavy saucepan over medium-high heat. Add fish and brown. Add precooked vegetables, if desired, seasonings, and 1 inch braising liquid. Reduce heat, cover, and simmer until done.	10–15 minutes
	BROIL	*To Broil Fillets:* Preheat broiler. Season both sides of fish with salt and pepper and rub with oil. Broil 2 inches from heat.	2–3 minutes per side
	GRILL	Prepare a hot fire in the grill. Brush fish with oil and/or butter. Place on oiled grill or fish grill rack, 2–3 inches from coals. Grill, turning once.	5–7 minutes per side
	POACH	Bring 4 cups poaching liquid to a boil. Add fish and simmer gently.	5–10 minutes
	ROAST	Preheat oven to 450°F. Brush sides of fish with oil. Season with salt and pepper. Place in a greased roasting pan. Shake pan occasionally.	8–10 minutes
	SAUTÉ	Rub fish with lemon juice and dust with seasoned flour. Heat oil and/or butter a nonstick skillet over medium-high heat. Add fish and sauté until golden brown on both sides, turning once.	4–6 minutes
MONKFISH 2-pound fillet	ROAST	Preheat oven to 450°F. Place fish in greased roasting pan and brush with oil. Season with lemon juice and herbs. Roast uncovered.	15–20 minutes

FISH	*METHOD*	*INSTRUCTIONS*	*TIMING*
SKATE (RAY) Wings; 8–12 ounces	BROIL	Preheat broiler. Brush fish with oil and/or butter. Pour ¼–½ inch water or wine into the pan. Broil 4 inches from the heat, turning once.	4–6 minutes per side
	GRILL	Prepare a hot fire in the grill. Brush the fish with oil and/or butter. Place on an oiled grill or fish grilling rack 2–3 inches from coals. Grill, turning once.	4–6 minutes per side
	POACH	Bring 4 cups poaching liquid or court-bouillon to a boil. Add fish and simmer gently until fish turns white along edges.	10–15 minutes
	SAUTÉ	Rub with lemon juice and dust with seasoned flour. Heat oil and/or butter in a nonstick skillet over medium-high heat. Add fish and brown on both sides, turning once.	4–6 minutes per side
	STEAM	Place poached skate on a steaming rack or basket over boiling water. Cover and steam.	8–10 minutes

SHELLFISH AND OTHER SEAFOOD

Seafood is delicate: mild in flavor, quick to overcook, and quick to spoil if not stored properly. When you bring shellfish home from the market, wash it thoroughly and rinse under cold running water, then pat dry with a paper towel. Store on a bed of ice in the refrigerator. Seafood must be eaten as soon as possible; it can go bad within a few days. When cooking, watch your timing carefully. Overcooked seafood becomes tough.

Types of Shellfish and Seafood

Shellfish come in two major varieties: **mollusks** and **crustaceans.** Mollusks, like clams, oysters, and scallops, don't have legs. Crustaceans move about by means of claws or a tail, such as lobsters, crabs, and shrimp. Other edible aquatic creatures include the cephalopods, which include octopus, squid, and cuttlefish, and various snails and frogs.

Clams. There are many varieties of clams, from the hard-shell clams like littlenecks, cherrystones, and chowder clams, to the soft-shell clams such as the steamer clam or razor clam. Clams can be eaten raw or cooked in or out of their shells. They can be baked, deep-fried, steamed, and simmered in soups or stews.

Crab. There are many species of crab, but the most popular for eating in this country are the blue crab, Dungeness crab, king crab, snow crab, and stone crab. All species of crab must be sold live or already cooked. In most cases, the tender meat inside the crab, once it has been cooked, is just as good cold as it is hot. The stone crab is a recycled crab, meaning the claws are snapped off and the crab is returned to the water to grow new claws. Therefore, only the claws of stone crabs are eaten. The best methods for cooking stone crab are steaming and grilling.

Make sure soft-shell crabs have been cleaned and prepared for cooking. The best way to cook soft-shell crabs is by sautéing.

Crayfish (Crawfish). Crayfish are freshwater crustaceans. They look somewhat similar to lobsters, except they are much smaller. They are best bought fresh and boiled or steamed. They are also available frozen—cooked and uncooked.

spider crab

blue crab

crayfish

Frogs' Legs. It's true—frogs' legs really do taste like chicken wings. They even have a similar texture. You can buy them at a good fish market already skinned, cleaned, and ready to cook. The best way to cook frogs' legs is to sauté them.

Lobster. There are many types of lobsters in the world, but Maine or Canadian lobsters are considered superior to all others. The tender Maine lobster is often available in sizes ranging from 1¼ to 3 pounds or larger. Lobsters from Maine and the North Atlantic coast have large claws, which distinguish them from Florida or southern lobsters (rock lobsters), which are clawless. All the meat on the Maine lobster, including the claws, can be eaten, but only the tail is eaten on the Florida lobster. Lobsters should be bought alive and show a lot of life.

When you cook lobster, it should still be lively, unless you decide to kill it immediately before cooking, which is the most humane thing to do. (Immersing lobster in boiling water also kills instantaneously.) To kill a lobster, plunge a chef's knife straight down right behind the lobster's head on its spine (backside). The most common ways of cooking lobster are steaming, boiling, baking, broiling, or grilling.

Mussels. Mussels are plentiful and inexpensive, so don't hesitate to buy more than you need—you will have to discard any that don't close when lightly tapped. Mussels are usually steamed in a small amount of seasoned liquid.

Octopus. Octopus is a cephalopod, one that is often called an "ink fish"; it can be found fresh or frozen, usually cleaned, in your local fish market. Like squid, the meat is tender when cooked properly. Small octopuses are usually more tender than large, but whatever size you buy, you must precook it. That should be done by covering the octopus with water and letting it simmer for about 45 to 60 minutes. The best ways to cook octopus after precooking are grilling or stewing.

Oysters. Oysters come in many shapes and sizes throughout the world, but the most common species here are the Pacific (or Japanese), the Atlantic (or Eastern), and the Olympia (from Puget Sound). It is necessary to clean oysters thoroughly, and no matter how they are served, they must be shucked first. This is done with a shucking or

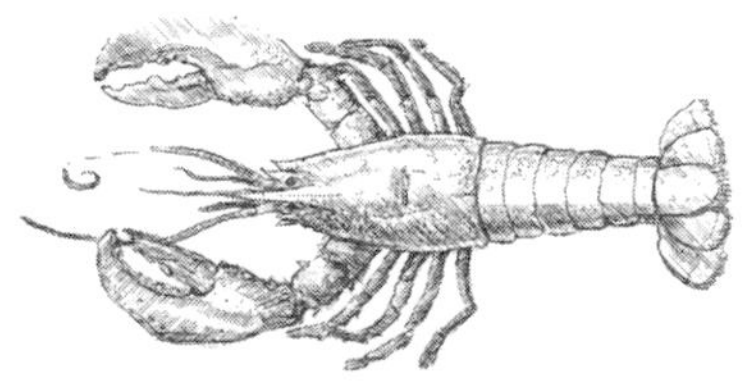

clawed lobster

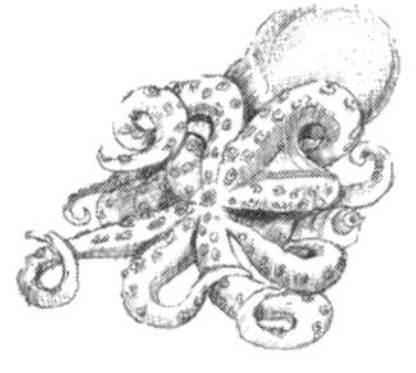

octopus

oyster (Eastern)

clam knife. To shuck, insert the shucking knife in at the hinge and twist open. If you don't have a shucking knife, use a stubby bladed screwdriver. For easier opening, chill before shucking.

Oysters are most often eaten raw, but there are many ways to cook them, both in and out of their shells. The best ways to cook oysters are broiling, grilling, deep-frying, and stewing in chowders.

Scallops. The most common types of scallops are calico, which are tiny; sea, which are large but tender; and bay, small and the most tender. Bay scallops come from the Cape Cod area and off Long Island and have a short season—November through February. Scallops are almost always sold shucked, but not cooked. They should be very fresh and have a sweet odor. They should be sitting in liquid, with no signs of dryness or browning. The best ways to cook scallops are broiling, grilling, deep-frying, and sautéing.

Shrimp and Prawns. There are more than 1,000 varieties of shrimp. Prawns are a closely related, longer-bodied crustacean. Jumbo shrimp are sometimes labeled as prawns. Shrimp and prawns may be peeled before or after cooking, depending on the way you want to eat them. Most are sold with their heads already cut off. To devein, make a slit along the back with a small sharp knife, then run cold water over the shrimp while picking out the thin black vein. Shrimp and prawns can be prepared by all methods of cooking.

Squid and Cuttlefish. Squid and cuttlefish, its European cousin, are cephalopods that are similar in look and taste. In restaurants, they are often served as *calamari.* They have a sweet flavor and must be cooked quickly with high heat, or braised or stewed slowly over low heat. Overcooked squid and cuttlefish will be tough.

Squid are sold fresh, precooked, or frozen. You may buy squid already cleaned, or clean it yourself at home. Squid loses about 25 percent of its weight in the cleaning process, so start with 2 pounds of squid to end up with 1½ pounds, or enough to serve four people.

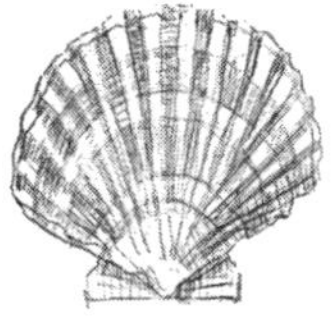

scallop

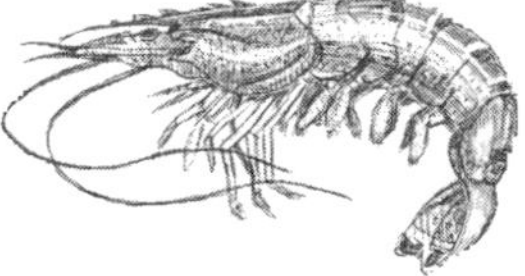

shrimp

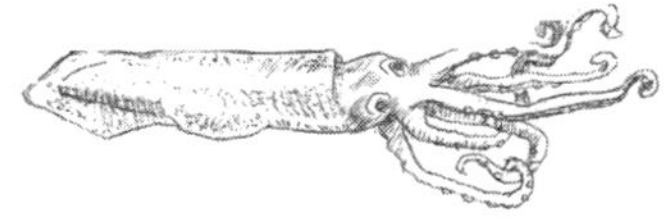

squid

Cooking Seafood

The same principles that apply to cooking fish apply to cooking these types of seafood. The flavor of seafood is quite delicate and often enhanced by the addition of fresh herbs and a squeeze of lemon or lime juice. Seafood that is to be steamed, broiled, baked, or grilled can be marinated first. Before marinating or cooking, rinse the seafood under running water and pat dry.

Marinades can add flavor and moisture to seafood. They can be used as basting sauces for broiled and grilled seafood or double as a steaming liquid. Unless you are making ceviche or want to forgo further cooking, choose a marinade that is low in acid. An olive-oil base, with citrus juice or white wine for acid balance and fresh herbs for flavor, makes a good marinade for all types of seafood. In general, you can leave seafood in a marinade for 30 minutes up to 4 hours. If you see any signs of the flesh turning white, remove the seafood from the marinade immediately; it is "cooking."

If you are marinating for more than 30 minutes, keep the seafood refrigerated. Before using a marinade as a basting sauce, bring it to a boil on top of the stove and boil for at least 3 minutes.

Seafood cooked in the shell will have more flavor than seafood that is first removed from the shell. Shells from shrimp and lobster can be used to make stock. Place the shells in a pot, cover with water, bring to a boil, then reduce the heat and simmer for 20 minutes. Strain before using.

When sautéing, dust the shellfish with seasoned flour (1 cup flour, 1 teaspoon salt, ¼ teaspoon black pepper) for a crispy outside. After sautéing, add a squeeze of lemon juice and a little butter to the pan juices to create a sauce to pour over the cooked seafood.

TIMINGS: Shellfish

All timings are for shellfish cooked at room temperature. All timings are approximate depending on the age of the shellfish and the thickness of the shell. Begin counting times for boiling after the water has returned to a boil. Note: When cooking clams, mussels, or oysters, discard any that do not open during cooking.

TYPE/SIZE	METHOD	INSTRUCTIONS	TIMING
CLAMS		*Preparation:* Before cooking, scrub clamshells. Discard any that are not closed. To purge clams of their sand, soak for a few hours in salted water to which a handful of cornmeal has been added. Then drain and rinse.	

TYPE/SIZE	*METHOD*	*INSTRUCTIONS*	*TIMING*
CLAMS In shell	BROIL	Preheat broiler. Place clams on broiler pan and broil 4 inches from heat until opened. Check frequently, and remove clams as they open.	3–10 minutes
	GRILL	Prepare a medium-hot fire in the grill. Place the clams on the grill 4 inches from coals and grill until open, removing the clams as soon as they open.	3–10 minutes
	ROAST	Preheat oven to 450°F. Place clams in a single layer in a roasting pan. Drizzle with oil and sprinkle with fresh herbs. Roast until opened.	8–10 minutes
	STEAM	Place in a large pot with 2 cups water. Bring to boil. Cook, covered, over high heat until shells open. Shake pot occasionally. Discard unopened clams.	Small: 5–7 minutes Large: 7–10 minutes
CLAMS On the half shell	BAKE	Preheat oven to 450°F. Place clams on half shell on a baking tray lined with coarse salt (for stability). Pour melted butter or sauce over each clam. Bake until topping is browned and clams are heated through.	4–6 minutes
	BAKE	*To Bake Stuffed:* Preheat oven to 450°F. Remove clams from shells, mince them, and mix with crumbs and seasonings. Return mixture to shells. Place shells on baking dish. Bake until topping is browned.	10–15 minutes
CLAMS Whole, shucked	DEEP-FRY	Heat oil to 365°F. Wash and dry clams completely. Dip in batter or coat with crumbs. Deep-fry until brown. Drain on paper towels before serving.	1–2 minutes

TYPE/SIZE	*METHOD*	*INSTRUCTIONS*	*TIMING*
CLAMS Whole, shucked *(cont'd.)*	SAUTÉ	Trim tough little necks from clams. Melt butter in a skillet over medium heat. Add drained whole clams. Cook, stirring, until they plump up.	2–3 minutes
CLAMS Chopped	SAUTÉ	Melt butter in a skillet over medium heat. Add chopped clams. Cook until tender.	1–2 minutes
	STEW	Add to simmering soup or sauce. Simmer until tender.	1–2 minutes
CRAB		*Preparation:* Grab live crabs from behind, firmly holding the back two legs on each side. Rinse under running water. For recipes requiring crab legs, times are based on using crab legs at room temperature. Frozen crab legs should be fully defrosted. For recipes requiring crabmeat, use store-bought or pick meat from boiled or steamed crab. Figure 7–10 Dungeness crabs will yield 1 pound crabmeat.	
CRAB Live, whole	BOIL	Plunge crabs into a large pot of boiling water. Begin counting time when water returns to a boil and boil until crabs turn red. Drain.	5–6 minutes
	STEAM	Place the crabs on a steaming rack or basket over boiling water. Cover and steam until crabs turn red.	8–10 minutes
LARGE CRAB LEGS	BAKE	Preheat oven to 350°F. Remove some of shell from legs and place on baking sheet. Brush with melted butter or olive oil before and during baking. Bake uncovered.	15–25 minutes
	BOIL	Plunge legs into boiling water. Cover and start counting the time when water returns to a boil. Boil until crabs turn red.	4–6 minutes

TYPE/SIZE	METHOD	INSTRUCTIONS	TIMING
	BROIL	*To Broil in Shell:* Preheat broiler. Remove just enough of the shell of each leg so that basting is possible. Place meat on broiling pan and brush the meat with butter. Broil 4 inches from heat, basting often with butter and lemon juice.	4–6 minutes
	GRILL	Prepare a hot fire in the grill. Place legs on grill 4 inches from coals. Grill, turning often.	5–8 minutes
	STEAM	Place in a steamer rack or basket above boiling water. Cover and steam until crabs turn red.	5–6 minutes
SOFT-SHELL CRAB (Blue crab)	BOIL	Place crabs in sea water or court-bouillon to cover. Bring to a boil and begin counting boiling time. Let cool in the water before removing the meat.	8 minutes per pound
	BROIL	Dust crabs lightly with seasoned flour. Place on flat broiling rack or pan. Dot crabs with butter and broil 3 inches from heat. Baste often and turn once.	3 minutes per side
	DEEP-FRY	Heat oil to 375°F. Coat crabs with crumbs. Deep-fry until golden. Drain on paper towels before serving.	2–4 minutes
	GRILL	Prepare a medium fire in the grill. Brush the crabs with butter or oil. Grill 4 inches from coals, turning frequently.	6–10 minutes
	SAUTÉ	Dust crabs with seasoned flour and coat with breadcrumbs. Heat butter and/or oil in large skillet over medium-high heat. Add crabs and cook on each side until golden.	2–4 minutes per side

TYPE/SIZE	METHOD	INSTRUCTIONS	TIMING
CRABMEAT	BROIL	Preheat broiler. Place crabmeat on a broiling pan. Brush with melted butter or lemon and oil mixture. Broil 4 inches from heat until golden brown.	5–6 minutes
	SAUTÉ	Heat butter and/or oil in skillet over medium heat. Add crabmeat and seasoning. Toss lightly. Add a little lemon or lime juice, hot pepper sauce, or vinegar to finish, if desired.	3–4 minutes
CRAYFISH		*Preparation:* Rinse live crayfish under running water before cooking. To clean, before or after cooking, twist the tail off the head and peel. Devein tail, if desired.	
CRAYFISH Whole	BOIL	Plunge headfirst into a large pot of boiling water. Begin counting time when water returns to a boil. Reduce heat to medium, cover, and simmer until shells turn red.	6–8 minutes
	BROIL	Preheat broiler. Split open lengthwise, leaving head and shells on. Place cut side up on broiler pan and brush with melted butter or oil. Broil 6 inches from heat, basting occasionally.	6–8 minutes
	STEAM	Place on a steaming rack or basket over boiling water. Cover and steam.	10–14 minutes
CRAYFISH Tails	BROIL	Preheat broiler. Split open boiled crayfish tails lengthwise. Place cut side up on broiler pan and brush with melted butter or oil. Broil 4 inches from heat until lightly browned.	3–5 minutes

TYPE/SIZE	METHOD	INSTRUCTIONS	TIMING
FROGS' LEGS		*Preparation:* Most frogs' legs are sold dressed. If not, skin the frog by slitting the skin at the neck and by pulling it back. Cut the backbone, making sure the 2 legs are still joined and they can be cooked in pairs. Cut off the feet and soak the legs in very cold water for 12 hours so the flesh whitens and swells. Dry legs before cooking.	
	BROIL	Brush with butter, oil, or marinade. Broil 4 inches from heat. Do not turn.	2–3 minutes
	DEEP-FRY	Heat oil to 375°F. Dust legs with seasoned flour. Deep-fry until golden. Drain on paper towels before serving.	2–3 minutes
	SAUTÉ	Dust legs with seasoned flour. Heat oil and/or butter in a skillet over medium-high heat. Add the legs and sauté until tender.	1–2 minutes
	STEW	Add frogs' legs to the sauce of your choice. Simmer until tender.	10–15 minutes
LOBSTER		*Preparation:* Grasp live lobster just behind the head. Rinse under cold running water.	
LOBSTER Whole; 1–5 pounds	BAKE	*To Bake Stuffed:* Split lobster in half lengthwise, leaving the back of the shell intact as a hinge. Remove head sac and intestines. Crack the center of each claw on one side only. Season with salt and pepper and place in a large roasting pan. Add stuffing. Dot with butter or drizzle with oil.	1½ pounds: 17 minutes 1¾ pounds: 20 minutes 2 pounds: 24 minutes 2½ pounds: 30 minutes

TYPE/SIZE	*METHOD*	*INSTRUCTIONS*	*TIMING*
LOBSTER Whole; 1–5 pounds (*cont'd.*)	BOIL	Plunge live lobster headfirst into a large pot of briskly boiling sea water or salted water (¼ cup kosher or sea salt per gallon water). Do not crowd pot. Begin counting time when water returns to a boil. Cover, reduce heat, and simmer.	1 pound: 7–8 minutes 1¼ pounds: 9–10 minutes 1½ pounds: 11–12 minutes 1¾ pounds: 12–13 minutes 2 pounds: 15–18 minutes 2½ pounds: 20 minutes 3 pounds: 22–25 minutes 5 pounds: 30–35 minutes
	BROIL	Preheat broiler. Split lengthwise and remove the head sac and intestines. Place lobster in a broiling pan shell side down. Brush cut side with melted butter or oil. Broil 4 inches from heat, brushing on more butter or oil occasionally.	1¼ pounds: 8–9 minutes 1½ pounds: 10 minutes 1¾ pounds: 11 minutes 2 pounds: 13 minutes 2¼ pounds: 15 minutes 2½ pounds: 17 minutes

TYPE/SIZE	METHOD	INSTRUCTIONS	TIMING
	GRILL	Prepare a medium-hot fire in the grill. Split the lobster in half lengthwise. Remove the head sac and intestines. Crack the claws on the side that will be away from the fire. Brush the shell and the exposed meat with oil or butter. Place lobster, shell side down, on grill 4 inches from coals. Cover lobster loosely with foil or a pie plate. Grill, basting with oil or butter frequently. Do not turn lobster over.	1¼ pounds: 7–9 minutes 1½ pounds: 8–10 minutes 1¾ pounds: 10–11 minutes 2 pounds: 12–13 minutes 2¼ pounds: 14–15 minutes 2½ pounds: 15–17 minutes
	PARBOIL	Plunge live lobster headfirst into a large pot of briskly boiling sea water or salted water (¼ cup kosher or sea salt per gallon water). Do not crowd pan. Count time as soon as water returns to a boil. When time is up, drain. Allow lobster to cool slightly before removing the meat; it will be easier to remove if the lobster is still slightly warm. Lobsters weighing more than 3 pounds are not suitable for parboiling because the meat does not cook properly a second time.	1 pound: 3½ minutes 1¼ pounds: 4 minutes 1½ pounds: 4½ minutes 1¾ pounds: 5 minutes 2 pounds: 5½ minutes 2½ pounds: 6½–7 minutes 3 pounds: 7½–8 minutes **Note:** If lobster shell is soft and not hard, reduce timings by 1 minute.

TYPE/SIZE	METHOD	INSTRUCTIONS	TIMING
LOBSTER Whole; 1–5 pounds *(cont'd.)*	STEAM	Add lobsters to a steaming rack or basket in a large pot above boiling water. Cover and steam. Rearrange lobsters halfway through steaming if cooking more than 1 lobster. Make sure lid is very tight. Test for doneness by pulling one of the small legs. If it comes off, the lobster is done.	1 pound: 10 minutes 1¼ pounds: 12 minutes 1½ pounds: 15 minutes 1¾ pounds: 16 minutes 2 pounds: 18 minutes 2½ pounds: 20 minutes 3–5 pounds: 21–25 minutes
LOBSTER Pieces in shell; 1½ pounds	ROAST	Preheat oven to 425°F. Split lengthwise and remove head sac and intestines. Snap the claws off. Place lobster halves and claws on baking sheet and brush with melted butter or olive oil. Brush again during roasting.	Claws: 18 minutes Body: 10 minutes
LOBSTER TAILS— ROCK LOBSTER TAILS 1½ pounds	BOIL	Add tails to a large pot of boiling salted water. Begin counting time when water returns to a boil. Reduce heat and simmer, uncovered.	3–4-ounce tails: 4–8 minutes 6-ounce tails: 6–10 minutes 8-ounce tails: 12 minutes
	BROIL	Split open hard outer shell lengthwise. Using fingers, press tails open to expose meat. Devein if necessary. Place tails, meat side up, in broiler pan. Brush with butter or oil. Broil 6 inches from heat, until meat is opaque.	8–12 minutes

TYPE/SIZE	METHOD	INSTRUCTIONS	TIMING
LOBSTER MEAT 2 cups	SAUTÉ	Heat butter and/or oil in a nonstick skillet over medium heat. Add parboiled lobster and sauté, adding seasoning and white wine, vermouth, cream, or all of the above to pan for flavor.	10–12 minutes
MUSSELS		*Preparation:* Before cooking, scrub mussels under cold running water, discarding any with broken shells and any that do not close when tapped lightly. Using your fingers, pull out beards. To purge mussels of their sand, soak for a few hours in salted water to which a handful of cornmeal has been added. Then drain and rinse.	
MUSSELS In shell	BOIL	Add mussels to a large pot of boiling water, making sure the water covers them. Begin counting time when water returns to a boil. Boil until shells open.	4–6 minutes
	GRILL	Prepare a hot fire in the grill. Place mussels on grill 4 inches from coals and grill until opened. Remove mussels as they open; those over the hottest part of the fire will open first.	2–10 minutes
	STEAM	In a large pot, combine water, wine, and seasonings to cover the bottom of the pot by several inches. Add the mussels. Bring to a boil. Cover and steam over high heat until shells open. Shake pot occasionally.	5–7 minutes
MUSSELS On the half shell	BAKE	Preheat oven to 350°F. Remove top shell of steamed mussel. Place mussels in bottom shell on baking dish. Sprinkle mussels with seasoning and bake just long enough to heat through.	3–5 minutes

TYPE/SIZE	*METHOD*	*INSTRUCTIONS*	*TIMING*
MUSSELS On the half shell (*cont'd.*)	BROIL	Preheat broiler. Place mussels in broiling pan and brush them with butter. Broil 4 inches from heat, just long enough to lightly brown.	2–3 minutes
	ROAST	Preheat oven to 450°F. Put a small amount of herb butter in each empty mussel shell. Lay cooked mussel on top. Cover mussels with more butter and place them in a single layer in shallow pan. Roast uncovered.	4–6 minutes
MUSSELS Without shell	BAKE	Preheat oven to 350°F. Place cooked mussels in a buttered baking dish with seasoning. Bake uncovered.	4–6 minutes
	DEEP-FRY	Heat oil to 375°F. Pat dry cooked mussels. Dip into batter or coat with crumbs. Deep-fry until golden. Drain well on paper towels before serving.	2–3 minutes
OCTOPUS		*Preparation:* Most octopus has been cleaned and frozen when sold. If not, turn the head and all its contents inside out. Then wash well. Octopus must be *precooked by simmering to tenderize it* before using it in a recipe. Always test octopus for tenderness. It becomes tough and chewy if overcooked.	
	GRILL	Prepare a hot fire in the grill. Cut precooked octopus into large or small pieces or leave whole. Brush the pieces with a marinade or oil and lemon juice mixture. Place on a greased grill 4 inches from very hot coals. Grill until crisp on all sides.	Whole: 5–8 minutes per side Large pieces: 8–15 minutes Medium pieces: 5–8 minutes Small pieces: 3–5 minutes

TYPE/SIZE	METHOD	INSTRUCTIONS	TIMING
	SIMMER	Cover the octopus with water in a large pot. Add 1 tablespoon salt, 2 crushed garlic cloves, 1 bay leaf, and some peppercorns. Simmer on low heat, covered. Test by piercing it with a thin-bladed knife. When the knife penetrates easily, it's done.	2–3 pounds: 45–50 minutes 3 pounds or larger: 60–70 minutes
	STEW	Simmer a sauce in a large pot. Make sure the sauce covers the bottom of the pot up to ½ inch. Cut octopus into bite-size pieces and stir into simmering sauce. Simmer until the octopus is heated through.	4–5 minutes
OYSTERS		*Preparation:* Scrub live oysters under cold running water.	
OYSTERS In shell	GRILL	Prepare a medium-hot fire in the grill. Place oysters, rounded side down, on grill 4 inches from coals. Grill until they begin to open, removing them as they open.	5 minutes
	ROAST	Preheat oven to 425°F. Place in a single layer in a shallow pan and roast uncovered until shells open.	4–5 minutes
	STEAM	In a large pot, add enough water or white wine to cover the bottom by several inches. Add the oysters. Cover and bring to a boil. Reduce heat to medium and cook until shells open. Discard unopened shells.	4–5 minutes
OYSTERS On the half shell	BROIL	Open the oysters and drain out juices. Loosen the meat from lower shell. Leave in shell. Dot with butter and cover with breadcrumbs. Broil 3 inches from heat until lightly browned.	4–5 minutes

TYPE/SIZE	*METHOD*	*INSTRUCTIONS*	*TIMING*
OYSTERS Shucked	DEEP-FRY	Heat oil in heavy skillet to 375°F. Dip each oyster in batter or coat with crumbs. Deep-fry until golden. Drain on paper towels before serving.	1–2 minutes
	GRILL	Prepare a medium-hot fire in grill. Sprinkle oysters with lemon juice. Arrange on skewers. Brush with butter or oil and grill 4 inches from coals, turning frequently.	4–5 minutes
	POACH	Bring poaching liquid to a boil. Reduce heat and add oysters. Simmer until oysters are plump and opaque.	1–2 minutes
	SAUTÉ	Dip oysters in seasoned flour, then in egg wash, then coat with crumbs. Add to hot butter and/or oil in heavy skillet and cook, turning once.	5–6 minutes
	STEW	Simmer in soup or sauce.	1–2 minutes
SCALLOPS		*Preparation:* Rinse scallops and pat dry with towels. Scallops should be completely dry before cooking. Cut large sea scallops into chunks or slices.	
SCALLOPS, BAY OR CALICO Tiny; without shell	BROIL	Dip scallops in melted butter or oil. Place in a shallow pan and broil 3 inches from heat until slightly brown, turning once.	30–60 seconds per side
	DEEP-FRY	Heat oil to 375°F. Dip scallops in batter or coat with crumbs. Deep-fry until golden. Drain on paper towels before serving.	30–60 seconds
	POACH	Bring poaching liquid to a boil. Reduce heat and add scallops. Simmer until scallops are opaque and firm.	30–60 seconds

TYPE/SIZE	METHOD	INSTRUCTIONS	TIMING
	ROAST	Preheat oven to 425°F. Arrange in roasting pan in single layer and place in oven uncovered; bake until scallops are slightly opaque in center. If overcooked, they become tough.	3–4 minutes
	SAUTÉ	Pat scallops dry. Dust with seasoned flour. Heat butter and/or oil in skillet over medium-high heat. Add the scallops and sauté until lightly browned, stirring constantly.	1 minute
SCALLOPS, SEA Medium or large; without shell	DEEP-FRY	Heat oil to 375°F. Dip scallops in batter or coat with crumbs. Deep-fry until golden. Drain on paper towels before serving.	1–2 minutes
	GRILL	Prepare a medium-hot fire in the grill. Skewer the scallops through their equators. Brush with lemon juice and melted butter. Grill 2–4 inches from the coals, turning often.	4–5 minutes
	GRILL	*To Grill (Indirect Method):* Prepare a hot fire in the grill. Place a drip pan in the center of the grill and arrange the coals around drip pan. Toss scallops in lemon juice, olive oil, and salt and pepper. Place scallops on a fish rack above the drip pan. Grill until scallops are opaque and firm, turning once.	5–7 minutes
	POACH	Bring poaching liquid to a boil. Reduce heat and add scallops. Simmer until scallops are opaque and firm.	1–2 minutes

TYPE/SIZE	*METHOD*	*INSTRUCTIONS*	*TIMING*
SCALLOPS, SEA Medium or large; without shell (*cont'd.*)	ROAST	Preheat oven to 425°F. Pour ¼ inch fish stock, water, or wine into a shallow baking pan. Add the scallops in a single layer. Sprinkle with salt and pepper. Roast uncovered.	6–8 minutes
	SAUTÉ	Dust scallops with seasoned flour. Heat butter and/or oil in large skillet on medium-high heat. Add the scallops and sauté until lightly browned.	3–5 minutes
	STEAM	Slice the scallops in half through their equators. Place the scallops on steaming rack or basket over boiling water. Cover and steam until opaque and firm.	3–5 minutes
	STIR-FRY	Heat oil in wok. Add the scallops and cook, stirring until opaque and firm.	2–3 minutes
SHRIMP AND PRAWNS		*Preparation:* Rinse shrimp under cold running water and drain. Peel, if desired. Most medium to large shrimp and prawns have a black intestinal vein running along their backs. Remove this before cooking, if desired.	
SHRIMP AND PRAWNS In shell	BOIL	Drop shrimp into a large pot of briskly boiling salted water. Begin counting Reduce heat, cover, and simmer. time when water returns to a boil.	Jumbo: 5–8 minutes Large: 4–6 minutes Medium: 3–5 minutes Tiny: 1–2 minutes

TYPE/SIZE	METHOD	INSTRUCTIONS	TIMING
	BROIL	Preheat broiler. Arrange shrimp in a single layer in a shallow pan and broil 4 inches from heat until browned, turning once.	Jumbo: 3–5 minutes per side Large: 2½–4 minutes per side Medium: 2–3 minutes per side
	GRILL	Prepare a medium fire in the grill. Place the shrimp directly on the grill or on a fish basket 4 inches from coals. Grill, turning once, until shrimp are opaque.	Jumbo: 3–5 minutes per side Large: 2½–4 minutes per side Medium: 2–3 minutes per side
	SAUTÉ	Heat butter and/or oil in large skillet over medium-high heat. Add shrimp and cook, stirring constantly, until shrimp are pink and opaque.	Jumbo: 4–6 minutes Large: 3–5 minutes Medium: 2–4 minutes
	STEAM	Place on a steaming rack or basket over boiling water. Cover and steam until the shrimp are pink and opaque.	Jumbo: 7–9 minutes Large 4–6 minutes Medium: 3–4 minutes Tiny: 2–3 minutes

TYPE/SIZE	*METHOD*	*INSTRUCTIONS*	*TIMING*
SHRIMP AND PRAWNS Peeled	BAKE	Preheat oven to 350°F. Sprinkle shrimp with salt and pepper. Arrange on skewers and brush with oil or melted butter and lemon juice. Place in shallow baking pan and bake, basting often.	Jumbo: 10–15 minutes Large: 8–12 minutes Medium: 7–10 minutes
	BROIL	Preheat broiler. Brush shrimp with melted butter, oil, or marinade. Place in shallow pan. Broil 4 inches from heat, basting and turning once.	Jumbo: 3–4 minutes per side Large: 2–3 minutes per side Medium: 1–2 minutes per side
	DEEP-FRY	Heat oil to 375°F. Dip shrimp in batter or coat with crumbs. Deep-fry until golden. Drain on paper towels before serving.	Jumbo: 2–3 minutes Large: 2–3 minutes Medium: 2–3 minutes
	GRILL	Prepare a medium-hot fire in the grill. Brush shrimp with oil, melted butter, or marinade. Arrange on skewers or on fish grill and grill 5 inches from coals, turning once.	Jumbo: 3–4 minutes per side Large: 2–3 minutes per side Medium: 1½–3 minutes per side

TYPE/SIZE	METHOD	INSTRUCTIONS	TIMING
	POACH	Bring poaching liquid to a boil. Add shrimp, reduce heat, and simmer until the shrimp are opaque and firm.	Jumbo: 4–5 minutes Large: 3–4 minutes Medium: 2–4 minutes
	ROAST	Preheat oven to 450°F. Place shrimp in roasting pan. Toss with oil or butter and seasonings. Roast uncovered.	Jumbo: 8–12 minutes Large: 7–10 minutes Medium: 6–9 minutes
	SAUTÉ	Heat butter and/or oil in large skillet over medium-high heat. Add shrimp and cook, stirring constantly.	Jumbo: 3–5 minutes Large: 3–4 minutes Medium: 2–4 minutes
	STEAM	Place on a steaming rack or basket over boiling water. Cover and steam.	Jumbo: 6–8 minutes Large: 3–5 minutes Medium: 2–3 minutes
	STIR-FRY	Add to hot oil in wok and cook, stirring, until opaque and firm.	Jumbo: 3–4 minutes Large: 3–3½ minutes Medium: 2–3 minutes

TYPE/SIZE	*METHOD*	*INSTRUCTIONS*	*TIMING*
SQUID AND CUTTLEFISH		*Preparation:* To clean, grasp the squid's head and innards as far inside the body as you can and pull gently. It should all come out, along with the translucent "quill." Scrape away any remaining innards. Cut the tentacles off above the beak, and discard the beak, head, and innards. Peel off the mottled purple skin. Rinse the tentacles and body and pat dry. Slice into rings, cut into squares or diamonds, or leave whole. **Note:** Medium squid are 5–8 inches long, large are longer than 8 inches. Measure body only.	
SQUID AND CUTTLEFISH 1 pound; whole or cut up	DEEP-FRY	Heat oil to 365°F. Leave squid whole or cut into rings. Coat with flour, then dip in batter or coat with crumbs. Deep-fry until golden. Drain on paper towels before serving.	2–3 minutes
	GRILL	Prepare a hot fire in the grill. Cut squid body open and clean. Brush with marinade or oil and lemon juice mixture. Thread the skewer through the squid 2–3 times. Thread tentacles separately. Place on a greased grill as close to the fire as possible, over the hottest spot on the grill. Turn once.	1–2 minutes per side
	SAUTÉ	Cut cleaned squid into squares or diamonds. Heat oil and/or butter in a nonstick skillet over medium heat. Add ¼ cup fish stock. Sprinkle salt and pepper over squid and place in pan. Stir and cook until tender.	3–5 minutes
	STEW	Cut cleaned squid into squares or diamonds no longer than 1½ inches a side. Simmer in sauce over medium heat, stirring occasionally until opaque and tender.	4–5 minutes

TYPE/SIZE	METHOD	INSTRUCTIONS	TIMING
	STIR-FRY	Cut into diamonds, squares, or rings. Heat oil in a wok, add squid, and cook, stirring, until opaque and tender.	1–3 minutes
SQUID AND CUTTLEFISH Whole, tiny	DEEP-FRY	Heat oil to 365°F. Coat squid with flour. Dip in batter or coat with cornmeal. Deep-fry until golden. Drain on paper towels before serving.	3–4 minutes
	GRILL	Prepare a hot fire in the grill. Cut the skinned meat into strips. Score it in a diagonal pattern and thread onto skewer, making the strips lie flat. Brush with marinade or oil and lemon juice combination. Place on greased grill over hottest part of the fire, as close to the coals as possible. Grill, turning once.	1 minute per side
	STEW	Simmer in sauce over medium heat, stirring occasionally until opaque and tender.	5–7 minutes

POULTRY

Poultry is very perishable and should be treated with care. When buying poultry, check the "sell by" date and don't buy it if it's near the end of its time, unless you plan to cook immediately. The poultry should not be sticky or have an off-odor. Don't judge poultry by the color of its skin—this is related to the bird's type and the feed it was raised on, as well as consumer preferences.

Types of Poultry

Chicken, Capons, Cornish Hens, and Guinea Fowl. Chicken come in all sizes, from a little over a pound to slightly larger broilers and fryers; roasters may weigh more than 3½ pounds. Larger birds are usually cut into pieces. Thighs, legs, wings, breasts, halves, and quarters of chicken are readily available, as are boneless cutlets and ground meat. Capons, bred to yield large quantities of white meat, can weigh up to 10 pounds. Cornish hens are much smaller, weighing just over a pound and serving one or two people. Guinea fowl, a domesticated descendant of a game bird, has dark meat, very little fat, a tender texture, and strong flavor. You can substitute guinea fowl in any chicken recipe.

Duck. Wild ducks are generally lean and require moist methods of cooking, but domesticated ducks have rich meat and a lot of fat under the skin. Most ducks will run between 4½ and 5½ pounds, which will serve four. Buy the heaviest duck available, because a duck yields surprisingly little meat.

Although duck meat is all dark, the breast meat is tender and the leg meat is not. Many people prefer to cut the duck into serving pieces before cooking. Then they cook duck breast to rare (the juices will run pink when done) and the legs to medium or well done (the juices will run clear).

Game Birds. The most common birds that are commercially available are squab, quail, and pheasant. Squab generally weighs about 1 pound; its rich meat will serve 2. Quail are quite small; allow 2 per main course serving. Pheasants generally weigh 2 to 3 pounds. Their legs are tough and require longer cooking times than the breasts, so it is best to cook them separately.

Goose. A mature goose for roasting averages 8 pounds. Look for pale skin and plump breasts when buying one. Goose is generally roasted but can be braised or stewed.

A goose cooks well as a whole bird, but should be scalded in hot water and dried before roasting. This tightens the skin so that the goose will be less fatty and have a crisp skin. Cooking goose as individually cut pieces also works well, since all the meat is dark.

Turkey. Turkeys can weigh from 7 to 40 pounds, but most supermarkets stock birds that weigh up to 20 pounds—larger birds don't fit in average-size ovens. Male turkeys (toms) have larger breasts. Packaged turkey pieces are available and can be cooked much like chicken, but with longer cooking times.

Preparing Poultry for Cooking

Before cooking poultry, remove neck, liver, and giblets (if provided), then rinse inside and out. Pat dry all birds.

To Butterfly Poultry for Broiling and Grilling. A butterflied, or split, chicken will cook more evenly and quickly than a whole chicken. To split a chicken, place the bird breast side down. Use poultry shears or a heavy knife to cut on either side of the backbone, from front to rear. Remove the backbone and lay the chicken flat. Flatten the bird with your hand by pushing down on it; this will crack the breastbone. Push metal skewers through the bird to keep it flat: one through the thighs, the other through the wings.

To Marinate Poultry. Marinades and spice rubs can add flavor to poultry—especially white meat chicken, which tends to be rather dry. Choose a low-acid olive oil– or soy-based marinade for chicken and turkey. A high-acid marinade may "cook" the flesh, turning the surface of the meat white and causing it to cook unevenly. Farm-raised ducks and geese are enhanced by sweet, fruity marinades that cut through the rich flavor of the meat, while wild birds should be treated with low-acid, oil-based marinades.

To Truss Poultry for Poaching and Roasting. Trussing is usually not essential, but does add to the appearance of the final dish. To truss, take a 3-foot length of cotton string for chicken (longer for turkeys) and place the center point of the string under the rear end of the bird. Loop the string around the ends of the legs. Cross the string over the top of the breast and under and around the wings. Tie the two ends together over the breast.

In general, you can marinate poultry in the refrigerator for up to 4 hours. If you want to use a marinade as a basting sauce, be sure to bring it to a boil on top of the stove and boil for 3 minutes.

Cooking Poultry

The main problem when cooking poultry is to know when to remove the bird from the heat so that the dark meat is cooked enough but the white meat is still juicy, tender, and moist, not dry and overcooked. Since the white meat cooks in a much shorter time than the dark meat, this presents a challenge. The white meat on poultry can become dry and tough at a temperature only 5 degrees higher (165°F) than its proper cooked degree of 160°F.

One solution is to take the birds out of the oven or pan when the white meat is cooked perfectly. At that point separate the legs and thighs from the bird. Continue cooking only the dark sections. Another solution, when you are cooking pieces separately, is to cook the dark meat until it is almost done. At that point, add the white meat to the pot or pan. Some cooks use separate pots and pans; the dark meat cooks in one pan and the white meat in another. That way both sections are timed perfectly.

When poultry is cut into pieces before cooking, it is easier to time and cook. Smaller parts and pieces can be cooked in a variety of ways and timed with excellent results.

Both duck and goose are entirely dark meat birds. It would seem that cooking and timing them would be simple. Unfortunately, that's not true. Ducks have a very lean, delicate, tender breast. Their legs can be stringy and tough and should be cooked thoroughly. On the other hand, the breast is delicious when cooked rare, medium-rare, or medium. The obvious cooking solution is to cook them separately.

Ground turkey and chicken should always be cooked until well done.

The same standard cooking methods that are used for all meats—baking, braising, broiling, grilling, roasting, sautéing, stewing—are used with poultry. Here are some techniques to remember when cooking poultry.

Broiling and Grilling. When broiling or grilling, the timing can be difficult to gauge because home-cooking ranges and grills vary so much in terms of the intensity of the heat; and much depends on how close the bird is to the heat source. To make cooking easier and the timing more accurate, cook parts or a small bird. If you want to use a whole bird, split and butterfly the bird as on page 151. Marinating is not necessary but can enhance the flavor of the bird.

When broiling, start with a preheated broiler. Always broil on a two-piece broiling pan, which allows dripping fat to drain away where it isn't at risk of catching on fire from the broiler flame. For crisp skin, broil the bird on the bone side first. Then turn and broil skin side up.

Grilling times are provided for grilling directly over the flames, or indirectly, with the chicken placed over a drip pan on one side of the grill and the coals banked on the other side. Indirect grilling avoids the problem of flare-ups, and is particularly good for marinated chicken. When grilling directly, watch the birds carefully and be prepared to move pieces around.

How to Tell When Poultry Is Done

- When an instant-read thermometer registers 170°F in the dark meat area or the leg, the meat is cooked.
- When an instant-read thermometer registers 160°F in the white meat area or the breast, the meat is cooked.
- When the juices that are released by pricking the meat run clear and not pink, the bird is cooked.
- When the stuffing reaches 165°F.

Deep-Frying and Oven-Frying. Marinating the chicken in buttermilk for up to 2 hours in the refrigerator before coating in crumbs or flour will promote tenderness. If you are using a simple flour coating, season 1 cup flour with 1 teaspoon salt and ¼ teaspoon black pepper. Use a cast-iron skillet for even browning without charring the crust. Frying in vegetable shortening rather than oil results in a crisper chicken with less odor in the kitchen. After frying, drain the chicken on a rack rather than paper towels for a crisper crust.

Poaching. Poaching results in a moist bird, as long as it isn't overcooked. For extra flavor, poach in broth. If you don't have chicken broth on hand, use water and add salt and aromatic vegetables, such as onion, celery, and carrots. Bring the poaching liquid to a boil, add the poultry, reduce the heat, and cover. Maintain the poaching liquid at a gentle simmer.

Roasting. All poultry, with the exception of duck and geese, should be basted while roasting in order to retain the moisture in the bird. Baste every 15 to 20 minutes or so. Let the bird stand 10 to 15 minutes before carving.

According to the USDA, stuffings must reach an internal temperature of 165°F. If you have stuffed your bird, you must continue roasting the bird until the stuffing reaches the proper temperature, even if the rest of the meat is done. Roasting the bird unstuffed, with the dressing baked separately, obviously solves this problem.

Roasting turkey and capon can be done in a variety of ways. They can be fast-roasted at 400°F or fast-roasted at 400°F–425°F to brown the skin, then finished at lower temperatures (275°F–325°F). This second method allows the rest of the bird to cook slowly and evenly. You can also medium-roast at 350°F or slow-roast at 325°F. Experiment with the oven temperature to arrive at the exact texture and taste desirable.

The method of roasting chicken and Cornish hen is similar to that for turkey, but temperatures usually range from 350°F to 400°F.

Duck, goose, squab, and guinea fowl are best roasted at a high temperature (375°F–425°F) to render as much fat from the skin as possible. If you wish, prick the skin before roasting. This lets even more fat escape and creates a crispy skin.

Sautéing. Choose a heavy skillet that is large enough to hold the chicken in a single layer. How much oil to use depends on taste and whether you are using a nonstick skillet. Generally I like to sauté in a combination of 2 tablespoons oil and 1 tablespoon butter. When dusting with seasoned flour, use 1 cup flour, 1 teaspoon salt, and ¾ teaspoon black pepper. You can also add 1 teaspoon or more dried herbs or spices.

Judging When Poultry Is Done

The easiest way to tell when poultry is done is to use an instant-read thermometer. Stick the stem into the thickest part of the thigh just beneath the bone. This will check the leg, or dark meat, temperature. When checking the white meat temperature, insert the thermometer into the breast at its thickest point. In either case, do not let the stem touch bone. Let all birds rest for 10 to 20 minutes after they are removed from the oven, to reabsorb juices and finish the cooking.

TIMINGS: Quick Chart for Roasting Poultry

NOTE: The USDA recommends that all poultry be cooked to a minimum temperature of 160°F for safety. In order to guarantee that every part of the bird reaches that safe temperature, it recommends roasting all birds until they reach 180°F in the thigh. This chart recommends a slightly lower temperature, recognizing that the bird continues to cook once it is removed from the oven. However, if food safety is your first concern, and you don't mind overcooked white meat, by all means roast to an internal temperature of 180°F at the thigh.

TYPE	*OVEN TEMPERATURE*	*DONENESS TEMPERATURE*	*TIMING*
CAPON	375°F	Breast: 160°F–165°F Thigh: 170°F–175°F	18–20 minutes per pound
CHICKEN	400°F	Breast: 160°F–165°F Thigh: 170°F–175°F	15–18 minutes per pound, plus 18 minutes
CORNISH HEN	400°F	Thigh: 175°F	18–20 minutes per pound
DUCK	425°F	Breast: 160°F–165°F Thigh: 170°F–175°F	12–15 minutes per pound
GOOSE	425°F	Breast: 160°F–165°F Thigh: 170°F–175°F	12–15 minutes per pound
GUINEA FOWL	400°F	Breast: 160°F–165°F Thigh: 170°F–175°F	18–20 minutes per pound

TYPE	*OVEN TEMPERATURE*	*DONENESS TEMPERATURE*	*TIMING*
SQUAB	400°F	Breast: 160°F–170°F Thigh: 170°F–180°F	30–40 minutes
TURKEY	350°F	Breast: 165°F Thigh: 175°F–180°F	8–12 pounds: 2½–2¾ hours 12–14 pounds: 2¾–3½ hours 14–18 pounds: 3½–4 hours 18–20 pounds: 4–4½ hours 20–25 pounds: 4½–5 hours
TURKEY	325°F (Slow-Roast)	Breast: 165°F Thigh: 175°F–180°F	12–16 pounds: 4 hours 16–20 pounds: 5 hours 20–26 pounds: 6 hours

TIMINGS: Chicken, Cornish Hens, Guinea Fowl

NOTE: Test poultry for doneness. An instant-read thermometer inserted into the breast should read 160°F to 165°F; inserted into the thigh, it should read 170°F to 175°F.

TYPE	*METHOD*	*INSTRUCTIONS*	*TIMING*
CHICKEN Whole bird; 3–4 pounds	BRAISE	Heat butter and/or oil in a large Dutch oven over medium-high heat. Brown the chicken on all sides. Drain off excess fat. Return chicken to pot and add 2 inches braising liquid, seasonings, and vegetables, if desired. Cover and simmer.	15–20 minutes per pound
	BROIL	Preheat broiler. Place a butterflied bird (see page 151) in a broiler pan skin side down. Brush bone side with seasoned oil or melted butter. Broil 7 inches from heat for 15 minutes. Turn skin side up. Brush with seasoned oil or melted butter. Broil until golden.	Bone side: 15 minutes Skin side: 10–20 minutes
	GRILL	Prepare a hot fire in the grill. Brush butterflied bird (see page 151) with oil and seasoning or marinade. Place skin side down and grill over hot fire 4 inches from coals for 15 minutes. Turn skin side up. Baste occasionally and grill until done.	Skin side: 10–12 minutes Bone side: 12–15 minutes

TYPE	METHOD	INSTRUCTIONS	TIMING
	GRILL	*To Grill Indirectly:* Prepare a medium-hot fire in the grill. Push all the coals to one side of the grill and place a drip pan on the other side. Brush trussed chicken with seasoned oil or marinade. Place on greased grill 4 inches from hot coals and sear on all sides. Then move the bird over the drip pan, breast side up, and grill with lid down, basting occasionally, until the internal temperature reaches 165°F. Let stand 15 minutes before carving.	1–1½ hours, plus 15 minutes standing time
	POACH	Place trussed bird in a large saucepan. Add liquid to cover the chicken halfway. Cover and bring to a simmer. Turn once while cooking.	12–20 minutes per pound
	ROAST	Preheat oven to 400°F. Rub the bird with butter and seasonings. Place in an oiled roasting pan, breast side up, and roast uncovered. Let stand 15 minutes before carving.	15–18 minutes per pound, plus 15 minutes standing time
CHICKEN PARTS Breasts, legs, thighs, wings	BAKE	Preheat oven to 375°F. Rub skin with butter, oil, or spice mixture. Place pieces skin side up in a baking pan. Bake uncovered.	35–40 minutes
	BRAISE	Heat oil in a large skillet or Dutch oven over medium-high heat. Add chicken and brown on all sides. Drain fat. Return chicken to the pan along with vegetables, if desired, seasonings, and 1 inch braising liquid. Bring to a boil. Reduce heat, cover, and simmer.	White meat: 25–30 minutes Dark meat: 35–40 minutes

TYPE	*METHOD*	*INSTRUCTIONS*	*TIMING*
CHICKEN PARTS Breasts, legs, thighs, wings (*cont'd.*)	BROIL	Preheat broiler, brush chicken with oil and seasoning or marinade. Broil skin side down, 5 inches from heat. Brush often with oil or marinade. Turn pieces occasionally, finishing skin side up.	Dark meat: 25–30 minutes Light meat: 15–20 minutes
	DEEP-FRY	Heat 3 inches of oil or vegetable shortening in a deep heavy pan to 350°F. Dip chicken in batter, then immerse in the oil. Maintain a frying temperature between 320°F and 365°F and fry until golden brown. Drain on a rack before serving.	Dark meat: 15 minutes Light meat: 10 minutes
	GRILL	Prepare a hot fire in the grill. Rub pieces with oil and seasoning or marinade. Place skin side up on greased grill. Baste and turn every 10 minutes. Move pieces to prevent charring.	Dark meat: 30–40 minutes Light meat: 25–30 minutes
	GRILL	*To Grill Indirectly:* Build a medium-hot fire, with the coals banked on one side of the grill, a drip pan on the other. Place chicken on greased grill directly over drip pan. Cook until done, turning and basting several times.	45 minutes
	GRILL	*To Grill in Aluminum Foil:* Prepare a medium-hot fire in grill. Wrap pieces in individual foil packets, using double folds to secure packages. Place packets seam side down on grill 4 inches from coals. Turn occasionally. When done, open packet carefully to allow steam to escape.	40–50 minutes

TYPE	METHOD	INSTRUCTIONS	TIMING
	OVEN-FRY	Preheat oven to 350°F. Coat chicken with crumb coating and place on greased baking sheet, skin side up.	45–60 minutes
	PAN-FRY	Dip chicken pieces in buttermilk or milk, then coat with seasoned flour. Heat ½ inch oil in heavy skillet to 365°F. Or heat ½ inch vegetable shortening (3 cups) to 350°F. Place chicken skin side down in pan, cover, and cook for 10 minutes. Turn and cook until golden brown, leaving pan uncovered. Drain on a rack before serving.	20–25 minutes
	ROAST	Preheat oven to 450°F. Place parts skin side up in roasting pan and season well. Roast uncovered, turning and basting with pan juices every 15 minutes.	30–40 minutes
	SAUTÉ	Heat butter and/or oil in a heavy skillet. Add chicken pieces skin side down in single layer. Sauté over high heat until chicken is brown. Turn pieces and brown second side. Reduce heat to medium and continue cooking. Turn chicken often until done.	High heat: 10 minutes Medium heat: 20–25 minutes
	STEW	In a large Dutch oven, brown chicken pieces in hot oil. Remove from pan. Add vegetables and sauté until tender. Return chicken to pan, add seasonings and liquid to barely cover chicken. Cover and simmer until chicken is tender.	45–60 minutes
CHICKEN BREAST Boneless, skinless	BAKE	Preheat oven to 350°F. Toss with marinade or sauce. Bake uncovered, adding a little water if pan becomes dry.	25 minutes

TYPE	METHOD	INSTRUCTIONS	TIMING
CHICKEN BREAST Boneless, skinless (*cont'd.*)	BAKE	*To Bake Stuffed:* Preheat oven to 350°F. Pound breasts slightly to flatten. Place about ¼ cup stuffing in the center of each breast and fold the ends of the breast over the stuffing. Place folded side down in greased baking dish. Brush with oil. Bake uncovered.	20–30 minutes
	BRAISE	Heat oil in a large skillet or Dutch oven over medium-high heat. Add chicken and brown on both sides. Add vegetables, if desired, seasonings, and 1 inch braising liquid. Bring to a boil. Reduce heat, cover, and simmer.	20–25 minutes
	BROIL	Preheat broiler. Brush breasts with seasoned oil or marinade. Place 4 inches from heat and broil, turning once.	3–4 minutes per side
	GRILL	Prepare a hot fire in the grill. Rub chicken breasts with seasoned oil or marinade. Place on greased grill 4–6 inches from coals. Move breasts to prevent charring. Baste and turn once.	3–4 minutes per side
	GRILL	*To Grill Kabobs:* Prepare a hot fire in the grill. Cut the breasts into 1-inch chunks. Arrange on skewers. Brush kabobs with seasoned oil or marinade. Place on a greased grill about 4–6 inches from coals. Turn to grill all sides.	8–10 minutes
	POACH	Place in boiling liquid to cover. Reduce heat to simmer and cover pan.	15–20 minutes
	SAUTÉ	Dust chicken with seasoned flour. Heat butter and/or oil in a large heavy skillet over medium-high heat. Place underside of the breast down. Sauté, turning once.	2–4 minutes per side

TYPE	METHOD	INSTRUCTIONS	TIMING
	SAUTÉ	*To Sauté Breaded:* Coat chicken with seasoned breadcrumbs. Heat oil and/or butter in large heavy skillet over medium-high heat. Add chicken and sauté until lightly browned, turning once.	2–4 minutes per side
	STEAM	*To Steam Stuffed:* Pound breasts to flatten slightly. Place about ¼ cup stuffing in the center of each breast and fold the sides of the breast over the stuffing. Place folded side down in steamer basket. Place over boiling water. Cover and steam.	20–25 minutes
	STIR-FRY	Cut breasts into ⅛-inch-thick strips. Add to hot oil in wok. Stir pieces until cooked through.	4–5 minutes
CHICKEN LEGS, THIGHS Boneless	BAKE	*To Bake Stuffed:* Preheat oven to 375°F. Place a rounded tablespoon of stuffing in the center of each thigh and fold meat and skin over to enclose it. Place thigh seam side down in greased baking dish and bake uncovered. Let stand 15 minutes before serving.	35 minutes, plus 15 minutes standing time
	GRILL	Prepare a medium-hot fire in the grill. Pound chicken to ¼-inch thickness. Brush with marinade or seasoned oil. Place 4–6 inches from the coals. Grill, turning once.	4–5 minutes per side
	GRILL	*To Grill Kabobs:* Prepare a hot fire in the grill. Cut thighs into 1-inch chunks. Arrange on skewers. Brush kabobs with marinade or seasoned oil. Place on a greased grill 4–6 inches from coals. Turn to grill all sides.	10–15 minutes

TYPE	*METHOD*	*INSTRUCTIONS*	*TIMING*
CHICKEN LEGS, THIGHS Boneless (*cont'd.*)	SAUTÉ	Dust chicken with seasoned flour. Heat butter and/or oil in a large heavy skillet over medium-high heat. Sauté for 3–5 minutes. Turn chicken and sauté until cooked through.	3–5 minutes per side
	STIR-FRY	Cut into 1-inch chunks. Add to hot oil in wok. Stir pieces until cooked through.	8–10 minutes
CHICKEN WINGS		*Preparation:* Separate wings into wing, drummette, and tips. Discard tips or save for soup-making.	
	BAKE	Preheat oven to 400°F. Toss wings with marinade or glaze or leave plain. Place on rack on baking sheet and bake until tender, turning once. For a crisp finish, broil the wings 4 inches from the heat in a preheated broiler for 1–2 minutes per side.	20–30 minutes
	BROIL	Preheat broiler. Brush pieces with seasoned oil or marinade. Broil 6–8 inches from heat, turning once.	5–8 minutes
	DEEP-FRY	Heat oil to 375°F. Fry in batches without crowding until golden brown. Drain on paper towels before serving.	7–10 minutes
	GRILL	Prepare a medium-hot fire in the grill. Toss the wings with seasoned oil or marinade. Grill 4 inches from the coals, turning occasionally.	5 minutes
	PAN-FRY	Heat oil in a large heavy skillet over medium-high heat. Add the wings and cook until golden brown, turning frequently.	10 minutes

TYPE	METHOD	INSTRUCTIONS	TIMING
GROUND CHICKEN	BAKE	*To Bake as Meatloaf:* Preheat oven to 350°F. Make into meatloaf using favorite recipe (1 pound meat). Place in greased baking dish and bake uncovered. Let stand 10 minutes before serving.	35 minutes, plus 10 minutes standing time
	BROIL	*To Broil Patties:* Shape into patties ¾ inch thick. Preheat broiler. Broil 4 inches from heat until well done, turning once.	6–7 minutes per side
	GRILL	*To Grill Patties:* Prepare a hot fire in the grill. Shape into patties ¾ inch thick. Place on lightly oiled grill rack and grill 4 inches from coals until well done, turning once.	5 minutes per side
	PAN-FRY	*To Pan-Fry Patties:* Shape into patties ¾ inch thick. Add enough oil to film a heavy skillet and heat over medium-high heat. Add patties and fry until well done, turning once.	7 minutes per side
	PAN-FRY	*To Pan-Fry Meatballs:* Shape into meatballs using recipe for beef meatballs. Add to heated oil in large heavy skillet over medium-high heat. Brown on all sides, then add to sauce.	10–12 minutes
CAPON	ROAST	Preheat oven to 375°F. Rub bird with a coating of butter and salt. Place in a greased roasting pan breast side up. Roast until the internal temperature in the thigh reaches 170°F. Let stand 10–15 minutes before carving.	18–20 minutes per pound, plus 10–15 minutes standing time

TYPE	METHOD	INSTRUCTIONS	TIMING
CAPON *(cont'd.)*	ROAST	*To Roast Pieces:* Preheat oven to 325°F. Cut capon into serving-size pieces. Toss with marinade or seasoned oil in baking dish. Roast uncovered, turning and basting every 20 minutes.	1 hour
GUINEA FOWL Whole; 3–4 pounds	ROAST	Preheat oven to 400°F. Rub bird with a coating of butter and salt. Place in a greased roasting pan, breast side up. Roast until the internal temperature in the thigh reaches 175°F. Let stand 10–15 minutes before carving.	18–20 minutes per pound, plus 10–15 minutes standing time
GUINEA FOWL BREAST 7–9 ounces	ROAST	Preheat oven to 425°F. Place skin side up in greased roasting pan. Rub breast with salt, pepper, and butter. Place guinea fowl in oven and reduce heat to 350°F. Baste often and roast until tender. Let stand 10–15 minutes before slicing.	30–40 minutes, plus 10–15 minutes standing time
ROCK CORNISH HEN Whole; 2 pounds	BRAISE	Preheat oven to 375°F. Cut hen into 8 pieces and dust with seasoned flour. Brown in hot oil in heavy skillet. Place browned pieces in baking dish. Cover with precooked vegetables, if desired, seasonings, and 1 inch braising liquid. Bake uncovered until hen pieces are golden brown.	30 minutes
	ROAST	Preheat oven to 400°F. Rub the bird with a coating of butter and salt. Place in a greased roasting pan, breast side up. Roast until the internal temperature in the thigh reaches 175°F. Let stand 10–15 minutes before carving.	45–60 minutes, plus 10–15 minutes standing time

TIMINGS: Turkey

TYPE	METHOD	INSTRUCTIONS	TIMING
TURKEY, WHOLE Unstuffed	BRAISE	Preheat oven to 350°F. In a large Dutch oven, brown the turkey on all sides in hot oil. Add 2 inches chicken or turkey stock. Cover and simmer until bird is very tender.	12–15 minutes per pound
	GRILL	*To Grill on Rotisserie:* Prepare a medium-hot fire in the grill. Place trussed bird (see page 151) on spit and place spit 5 inches from medium-hot coals. Make sure drip pan is directly below bird. Grill, basting frequently until the internal temperature reaches 165°F for breast or 175°F–180°F for leg or thigh. Let stand 10–15 minutes before carving.	6–8 pounds: 3–4 hours 10–12 pounds: 4–5½ hours, plus 10–15 minutes standing time
	ROAST	Preheat oven to 350°F. Place turkey breast side up on a rack in a roasting pan. Brush bird with melted butter or oil. Roast, basting every 30 minutes, until the internal temperature reaches 165°F for breast or 175°F–180°F for leg or thigh. Let stand 10–15 minutes before carving.	8–12 pounds: 2½–2¾ hours 12–14 pounds: 2¾–3½ hours 14–18 pounds: 3½–4 hours 18–20 pounds: 4–4½ hours 20–25 pounds: 4½–5 hours, plus 10–15 minutes standing time

TYPE	*METHOD*	*INSTRUCTIONS*	*TIMING*
TURKEY, WHOLE Unstuffed (*cont'd.*)	ROAST	*To Slow-Roast:* Preheat oven to 325°F. Place turkey breast side up on a rack in a roasting pan. Brush bird with melted butter or oil. Roast, basting every 30 minutes, until the internal temperature reaches 165°F for breast or 175°F–180°F for leg or thigh. Let stand 10–15 minutes before carving.	12–16 pounds: 4 hours 16–20 pounds: 5 hours 20–26 pounds: 6 hours, plus 10–15 minutes standing time
TURKEY, WHOLE Stuffed	ROAST	*To Roast:* Preheat oven to 325°F. Stuff cavity of bird with hot stuffing and close vents. Place breast side up on rack in roasting pan. Brush bird with melted butter or oil. Roast, basting every 30 minutes until the internal temperature reaches 165°F for breast or 175°F–180°F for leg or thigh and 165°F for stuffing. Let stand 10–15 minutes before carving.	12–15 minutes per pound, plus 10–15 minutes standing time
TURKEY BREAST Bone in; 4–7 pounds	ROAST	Preheat oven to 350°F. Place breast skin side up in a shallow roasting pan. Brush with melted butter and seasonings. Roast until the internal temperature is 160°F. Let stand 10–15 minutes before carving.	15–20 minutes per pound, plus 10–15 minutes standing time
	GRILL	Prepare a medium-hot fire in grill. Brush breast generously with butter or oil and seasonings. Grill 6–8 inches from coals. Baste and turn often. Let stand 10–15 minutes before carving.	1¾–3 hours, plus 10–15 minutes standing time

TYPE	METHOD	INSTRUCTIONS	TIMING
TURKEY BREAST Boneless; 3–6 pounds	ROAST	Preheat oven to 450°F. Rub breast with butter and seasonings. Place skin side up in baking dish and add 1 inch broth or water. Roast, basting frequently, until the internal temperature of the breast reaches 160°F. Let stand 10–15 minutes before slicing.	30 minutes, plus 10–15 minutes standing time
	ROAST	*To Slow-Roast:* Preheat oven to 325°F. Place breast skin side up on rack in roasting pan. Brush with seasoned oil or butter. Loosely cover with foil, uncovering for the last 45 minutes. Roast until the internal temperature reaches 160°F. Let stand 10–15 minutes before carving.	2½–3½ pounds: 2–2½ hours 4–6 pounds: 2½–3½ hours, plus 10–15 minutes standing time
TURKEY BREAST CUTLETS	BRAISE	Dust cutlets with seasoned flour. Add to hot oil in heavy skillet over medium heat. Brown on both sides. Add precooked vegetables, if desired, seasonings, and 1 inch braising liquid. Bring to a boil, then reduce heat and simmer until turkey is tender.	10–15 minutes
	BROIL	Preheat broiler. Brush cutlets with seasoned oil or marinade. Grill 4 inches from heat, turning once.	6–8 minutes per side
	GRILL	Prepare a medium-hot fire in the grill. Brush the turkey with seasoned oil or marinade. Place on greased grill 4–6 inches from coals. Baste and turn once.	6–8 minutes per side
	POACH	Place cutlets in boiling liquid to cover. Reduce heat to simmer and cover pan.	15–20 minutes

TYPE	*METHOD*	*INSTRUCTIONS*	*TIMING*
TURKEY BREAST CUTLETS *(cont'd.)*	SAUTÉ	Dust with seasoned flour. Heat butter and/or oil in a large heavy skillet over medium-high heat. Add cutlets and sauté until tender, turning once.	4 minutes per side
	SAUTÉ	*To Sauté Breaded Cutlets:* Coat with breadcrumbs. Heat oil in heavy skillet over medium-high heat. Add cutlets and sauté until lightly browned. Turn and brown second side.	4 minutes per side
	STIR-FRY	Cut into ⅛-inch-thick strips. Add to hot oil in wok and stir strips until cooked through.	5 minutes
TURKEY DRUMSTICKS	BRAISE	Preheat oven to 350°F. Heat oil in Dutch oven over medium heat and brown drumsticks on all sides. Add 1 inch braising liquid, seasonings, and vegetables, if desired, and bring to a boil. Cover and place in oven.	40–45 minutes
	ROAST	*To Quick-Roast:* Preheat oven to 375°F. Brush with seasoning paste or marinade. Roast, uncovered, basting every 15 minutes. Let stand 10–15 minutes before serving.	40–45 minutes, plus 10–15 minutes standing time
	ROAST	*To Slow-Roast:* Preheat oven to 325°F. Place drumsticks on a rack in a roasting pan. Brush with seasoned oil or butter. Loosely cover with foil, uncovering during the last 45 minutes. Roast until the internal temperature reaches 180°F–185°F. Let stand 10–15 minutes before serving.	1¼–1¾ hours, plus 10–15 minutes standing time

TYPE	*METHOD*	*INSTRUCTIONS*	*TIMING*
TURKEY THIGHS Boneless	BRAISE	Heat oil in Dutch oven over medium heat and brown turkey on all sides. Add vegetables, if desired, seasonings, and 1 inch braising liquid. Cover and simmer gently over low heat.	1½–2 hours
	ROAST	Preheat oven to 325°F. Place thighs on a rack in a roasting pan. Brush with seasoned oil or butter. Loosely cover with foil, uncovering during the last 45 minutes. Roast until the internal temperature reaches 180°F–185°F. Let stand 10–15 minutes before serving.	1½–1¾ hours, plus 10–15 minutes standing time
GROUND TURKEY	BAKE	*To Bake as Meatloaf:* Preheat oven to 350°F. Make into meatloaf using favorite recipe (1 pound meat). Place in greased baking dish and bake uncovered. Let stand 10 minutes before serving.	35 minutes, plus 10 minutes standing time
	BROIL	Shape into patties ¾ inch thick. Preheat broiler. Broil until well done, 4 inches from the heat, turning once.	6–7 minutes per side
	GRILL	Prepare a hot fire in the grill. Shape into patties ¾ inch thick. Place on lightly oiled grill rack 4 inches from coals and grill until well done, turning once.	5 minutes per side
	PAN-FRY	*To Pan-Fry Patties:* Shape into patties ¾ inch thick. Add enough oil to film a heavy skillet and heat over medium-high heat. Add patties and cook until well done, turning once.	7 minutes per side

TYPE	METHOD	INSTRUCTIONS	TIMING
GROUND TURKEY *(cont'd.)*	PAN-FRY	*To Pan-Fry Meatballs:* Shape into meatballs using recipe for beef meatballs. Add to heated oil in large heavy skillet. Brown on all sides, then add to sauce.	10–12 minutes

TIMINGS: Duck and Goose

For duck cooked rare, cook until juice runs pink. For medium or well-done duck, cook until juices run clear.

TYPE	METHOD	INSTRUCTIONS	TIMING
DUCK Whole bird; 3–5 pounds	GRILL	*To Grill Indirectly:* Prepare a hot fire in the grill. Push the coals to one side of the grill and place a drip pan on the other side. Place the trussed duck over the drip pan, cover the grill, and grill, pricking skin occasionally, until the internal temperature of the thigh reaches 165°F–170°F. Let stand 10–15 minutes before carving.	1½ hours, plus 10–15 minutes standing time
	ROAST	*To Quick-Roast:* Place bird in large pot and cover with water. Bring to a boil, reduce heat, and simmer for 30 minutes. Drain and pat duck dry. Preheat oven to 400°F. Place duck on rack in roasting pan. Season well. Roast until the internal temperature of the thigh reaches 175°F. Let stand 20 minutes before carving.	40–45 minutes, plus 30 minutes simmering and 20 minutes standing time

TYPE	METHOD	INSTRUCTIONS	TIMING
	ROAST	*To Slow-Roast:* Rub duck with salt. Preheat oven to 250°F. Prick duck skin—not meat—with sharp fork or pointed knife all over body. Place the duck, breast down, on a rack in a roasting pan and roast for 3 hours, pricking the skin 3–4 times. Drain fat out of pan and turn duck breast side up. Roast for another 45 minutes, at 350°F, until the internal temperature in the thigh reaches 165°F–170°F. Baste duck often with ice water for crisp skin. Let stand 10–15 minutes before carving.	3 hours at 250°F, plus 45 minutes at 350°F and 10–15 minutes standing time
DUCK PIECES	BRAISE	Prick the skin of the duck all over. Heat a little butter or oil in a heavy pot over medium heat and brown the duck pieces on all sides. Drain off excess fat. Add 1 inch stock or braising liquid and seasonings. Cover, reduce heat, and simmer until meat falls easily from the bone.	1–1½ hours
DUCK BREAST Boneless, skinless	SAUTÉ	Heat oil in skillet over medium-high heat. Add duck breast and sear until it's brown on both sides.	4–6 minutes
	STIR-FRY	Cut into ¼-inch-thick strips. Add to hot oil in wok. Cook, stirring.	4–6 minutes
DUCK LEGS	BRAISE	Heat oil in Dutch oven over medium-high heat. Add legs and brown all over. Add vegetables, if desired, seasonings, and 1 inch braising liquid. Cover, reduce heat, and simmer until meat falls easily from the bone.	45–60 minutes

TYPE	*METHOD*	*INSTRUCTIONS*	*TIMING*
GOOSE Whole bird; 8–12 pounds	BRAISE	Prick the skin of the goose. Heat oil in a Dutch oven over medium heat and brown on all sides. Add vegetables, if desired, seasonings, and 2 inches braising liquid. Cover and simmer until juice runs clear when thigh is pricked and pieces fall easily from the bone.	1–2 hours
	ROAST	Preheat oven to 325°F. Prick goose skin—not meat—all over. Place on a rack in a shallow roasting pan. Roast until juices run clear when thigh is pricked and pieces fall easily from the bone. The internal temperature should be 170°F. Let stand 15 minutes before carving.	3–3½ hours, plus 15 minutes standing time

TIMINGS: Game Birds

NOTE: For tender texture, game birds are most often cooked until medium-rare, with the juices running rose-colored. The juices will be clear yellow in a well-done bird, if that is your preference.

TYPE	*METHOD*	*INSTRUCTIONS*	*TIMING*
SMALL GAME BIRDS Partridge, Pigeon, Dove, Quail, Squab; ¾–1 pound	BRAISE	In a casserole, brown the birds in hot oil or butter on both sides. Season well. Add mixture of chicken stock, wine, and herbs to cover the bottom of the pot by 1 inch. Cover and simmer.	15–20 minutes per pound
	BROIL	Preheat broiler. Brush butterflied bird (see page 151) well with butter. Broil 3 inches from heat, skin side up, turning once.	5–6 minutes per side

TYPE	METHOD	INSTRUCTIONS	TIMING
	GRILL	Prepare a medium-hot fire in the grill. Rub butterflied bird (see page 151) with seasoned oil. Place on greased rack about 4 inches from coals and grill, turning once.	7–8 minutes per side
	ROAST	*To Quick-Roast:* Preheat oven to 450°F. Brush bird with seasoned oil. Place on rack in roasting pan. Season well. Roast, basting often.	15–30 minutes
	ROAST	Preheat oven to 325°F. Brush bird with seasoned oil. Place on a rack in roasting pan. Cover loosely with foil. Roast, basting occasionally. Let stand 10 minutes before serving.	45–60 minutes, plus 10 minutes standing time
	SAUTÉ	Heat oil and/or butter in a heavy skillet over medium-high heat. Place butterflied bird (see page 151) skin side down and brown on both sides, turning once.	6–7 minutes per side
MEDIUM GAME BIRDS Grouse, Pheasant, Black Mallard; 1–3 pounds	BRAISE	Brown birds in hot oil in Dutch oven over medium heat. Add vegetables, if desired, seasoning, and 1 inch braising liquid. Bring to a boil, then reduce heat, cover, and simmer until tender.	35–40 minutes
	GRILL	Prepare medium-hot fire in the grill. Brush butterflied birds with seasoned oil. Place birds skin side down on greased grill 6–8 inches from coals. Grill, turning often.	16–20 minutes

TYPE	*METHOD*	*INSTRUCTIONS*	*TIMING*
MEDIUM GAME BIRDS Grouse, Pheasant, Black Mallard; 1–3 pounds (*cont'd.*)	ROAST	*To Quick-Roast:* Preheat oven to 400°F. Brush birds with seasoned oil. Place on rack in roasting pan. Season well. Roast, basting often, until juices run clear. Let stand 10 minutes before carving.	Rare: 15 minutes per pound Medium: 18 minutes per pound Well: 20 minutes per pound Stuffed: 25–30 minutes per pound, plus 10 minutes standing time
	ROAST	*To Slow-Roast:* Preheat oven to 325°F. Brush bird with seasoned oil. Place on rack in shallow roasting pan. Roast until juices run clear (when thigh is pricked and pieces fall easily from two-pronged fork). Internal temperature should be 170°F.	3–3½ hours
LARGE GAME BIRDS Wild Turkey, Sage Grouse	BRAISE	Cut birds into 6–8 pieces. Brown them in hot oil in Dutch oven over medium heat. Add vegetables, if desired, seasoning, and 1 inch braising liquid. Bring to a boil, then reduce heat, cover, and simmer until tender.	35–40 minutes

TYPE	METHOD	INSTRUCTIONS	TIMING
	ROAST	Preheat oven to 425°F. Place bird on rack in roasting pan. Brush with seasoned oil or butter. Season well. Roast, basting often. Let stand 10 minutes before carving.	Rare: 12 minutes per pound Medium: 13 minutes per pound Well: 15 minutes per pound Stuffed: 20–25 minutes per pound, plus 10 minutes standing time

MEAT

When buying meat, it helps to find a butcher you can trust. The meat he sells should have good color and be without odor. Let the butcher know what type of dish you want to prepare, and he will recommend the cut of meat and method of cooking you should use. The best and most expensive cuts of meat, if improperly cooked or timed, can turn out tough. It is also true that an inexpensive cut, properly timed and cooked, can be delicious.

Cuts of Meat

The most tender cuts of meat (veal, beef, pork, lamb) come usually from the loin, back, rump, and round end of the animal. These are the parts that are exercised the least. Some terminology pertaining to certain cuts of meat may be confusing. The following descriptions may help:

Chop. A tender cut of meat usually from the loin or rib area of lamb, pork, or veal. Usually it includes a bone but may be boneless.

Cutlet. A boneless piece of meat that is cut thin. It can refer to meat from the leg of a young calf (veal) a chicken breast, or a turkey breast.

Hock. The lower portion of an animal's leg, corresponding to the human ankle. Generally ham hocks from hogs are available.

Fillet. A boneless piece of fish or meat.

Kabobs. Cubes of meat, fish, poultry, and/or vegetables often threaded on a skewer, which are usually grilled or broiled.

Roast. A large piece of meat that is roasted, although some less tender cuts are braised.

Scallop. A very thin slice of meat or fish that is flattened or pounded so it cooks quickly in a skillet. It may also be called an escalope.

Shank. A cut from the front leg of an animal. The meat is tough but flavorful. It is most often cooked by braising.

Cooking Meat with Flavor

Try to bring all cuts of meat to room temperature before cooking. It will make the timing more accurate.

Marinades and spice rubs add flavor to meat. If the meat has been trimmed of fat, a marinade can replace lost moisture. Tender, well-marbled cuts should be marinated briefly—4 to 6 hours in the refrigerator. Tough cuts of meat can handle 1 or 2 days of marinating. If the meat starts to show signs of turning gray, it is beginning to "cook" from the acids in the marinade and should be removed and patted dry. If you want to reuse a marinade as a basting sauce, be sure to bring it to a boil for 3 minutes once the meat has been removed.

All meat, whether it has been marinated or not, should be patted dry before seasoning, breading, or batter is added. Generally, meat benefits from seasoning with salt and pepper before cooking. The USDA recommends that all meat be cooked to at least 160°F to kill any microorganisms that may exist.

Barbecuing. Long, slow cooking over coals can turn a tough cut into a flavorful feast. Begin with meat that has been marinated in a traditional marinade. If you have a smoker, follow the manufacturer's directions for setting up the smoker. To barbecue in a covered grill, prepare a fire in the grill and let the coals burn down to medium-low. Push all the coals to one side. Place a drip pan on the other side. Provide wood smoke by wrapping wood chunks or soaked wood chips in an aluminum foil packet that has been pierced in several places. Place the packet directly on the coals. Set the cooking grate in place and place the meat over the drip pan. Cover the grill and adjust vents or add coals as necessary to maintain an ambient cooking temperature of 220°F to 250°F. Turn the meat and baste occasionally with a marinade (boiled for 3 minutes) or a mopping sauce.

Braising. Beef is particularly suited to braising. Cuts of meat that have little fat and are considered tough, but have a lot of flavor, can be delicious when cooked with this method. Browning the meat first adds flavor, then the slow and gentle heat breaks down the tissue and makes the meat tender.

Traditional braising liquids include water, stock, wine, beef, and tomato or other juices. The less liquid you use, the more intensely flavored the sauce, so add just 1 to 2 inches of braising liquid. Make sure the cooking liquid does not boil but simmers instead.

If you want to add vegetables, add them during the last 45 minutes to a braise simmered on top of the stove. If you are simmering the meat in the oven, cook the vegetables on top of the stove and add them to the meat just before serving.

Broiling. Only the most tender cuts are suitable for broiling. For extra flavor, marinate for 4 to 6 hours before cooking. The best cuts of meat for broiling are beef steak and lamb chops and cutlets. Pork chops can be broiled but need regular basting. Veal chops also require continuous basting with oil or butter or they will dry out. Broiling must be done quickly—beef and lamb should be seared on both sides. Pork and veal should be cooked more slowly, but should brown well for optimal flavor. Often pork and veal are finished in the oven after browning under the broiler so they stay moist.

To broil, preheat the broiler for about 15 minutes with the broiling pan in place. Brush the meat with oil on both sides to promote browning and prevent sticking to the pan.

Deep-Frying. Meat should be at room temperature and patted dry before deep-frying. Only the most tender cuts should be used and they should be uniform in size.

Grilling. Tender cuts of meat are perfect for grilling over coals or wood that produce high heat. The high heat sears the meat on the outside, forming a delicious crust. If the meat has been marinated with a liquid marinade or dry spice rub, the crust will be even more delicious. Many cuts of meat are seared on the outside, then slowly grill-roasted with the grill covered for the remainder of the cooking. Take care when grilling not to burn the meat or allow it to dry out. Timing is crucial.

Pan-Broiling. Cooking without moisture will give the meat a tasty crust, but use tender cuts of meat for this method. Use a well-seasoned cast-iron skillet, a ridged skillet, or a grill designed for this purpose. Preheat the pan, using no oil or butter. To prevent the meat from sticking, you can lightly brush lean cuts with oil or make a bed of coarse salt (in a flat-bottomed skillet). Cook over high heat, and tip off any fat that accumulates if using a flat-bottomed skillet.

Pan-Frying and Sautéing. Sautéing is the perfect way to cook scallops of lamb or veal. It is simple and takes a short time. You can make a gravy by adding butter or wine to the pan juices.

Meat Grading

The USDA grading of meat falls into eight categories (pork being the exception). As consumers, we need only to be concerned with three.

Prime. The best grade available is usually reserved for expensive restaurants and hotels and is in short supply at neighborhood markets. It comes from young and specially fed animals. The meat is well marbled and the fat surrounding the meat is white. It is usually tender, well handled, and aged. Freezing it will affect its high quality, so it should be cooked soon after purchasing.

Choice. This grade of meat is high quality and can be found easily. It has less marbling than Prime and less flavor but is still tender and delicious.

Select. This grade is still a tender grade of meat but has thinner layers of fat than Prime or Choice. The meat, in general, is leaner, which means less juice, less tenderness, and less flavor.

Roasting. Meat for roasting should be the best, both in quality and cut. Small roasts should cook at a higher temperature than large ones, and red meats at a higher temperature than white meats. Frequent basting is necessary to keep the meat moist. If you start the meat roasting at a higher temperature (450°F for 10 minutes, then reducing to 350°F) you will help give the meat a crisp crust.

Stir-Frying. Stir-frying is perfect for thinly sliced or cubed pieces of meat. The number one rule for good stir-frying is: Keep the pan very hot. The oil should be heated until it shimmers; just before it smokes is perfect. The food must sizzle when cooking. This will sear the meat, imparting flavor and keeping the inside of the meat moist.

Timing Meat

There are many factors that make precision timing almost impossible. The quality, shape, age, thickness, bone content, and precooked temperature of the meat are all factors in exact timings. Therefore, the timings offered are only accurate to a point. You might have to adjust the timings according to the types of meat you are cooking.

Timing Tips

- Remove steaks and chops from refrigerator 1 hour before cooking.
- Remove roasts from refrigerator 2 hours before cooking.
- The oven must be preheated before roasting, usually to 450°F.
- Pork must be cooked thoroughly to ensure that the parasite that causes trichinosis is destroyed. The internal temperature of the meat must reach at least 137°F. The meat should not be pink, but can be slightly rosy, white, or grayish in color. To be safe to eat, the minimum internal temperature for pork is 150°F.
- Cooking with moist heat requires an ambient temperature of 180°F. Even at this low temperature, bacteria is killed because moist heat has a penetrating quality that other methods do not have.
- Use an instant-read thermometer whenever possible, especially when roasting.
- When broiling or grilling, choose the best quality and most tender cuts of meat.

Cooked Temperatures

The temperature of cooked meat will continue to rise after the meat has been removed from the heat. To achieve perfectly cooked meat, use the timing charts to estimate cooking times and an instant-read thermometer to determine exactly when the meat is done. Let the cooked meat rest under a loose tent of aluminum foil, and the temperature will continue to rise about 5 degrees.

The cooked temperatures for beef are:

DONENESS	TEMPERATURE	DESCRIPTION
Rare	120°F–130°F	Meat is soft and bright pink to red in center. Very juicy.
Medium-rare	130°F–135°F	Meat is pink in center and has begun to turn gray at edges. Firmer, but still juicy.
Medium	135°F–150°F	Meat is pink in center, gray at edges. Texture is firm.
Medium-well	150°F–165°F	Meat is uniformly gray, pinkish tint near bones.
Well-done	165°F	Meat is overcooked unless it is fatty and very juicy.

One of the most accurate ways to get perfectly cooked meat, every time, is to use an instant-read thermometer. To use it properly, insert the thermometer into the thickest part of the meat without touching bone or fat. After the meat is done to the proper temperature, push the thermometer deeper into the meat. If the temperature drops, continue cooking until the thermometer has the correct reading. Remove the meat. Cover it loosely with foil. Let it stand about 15 minutes before carving.

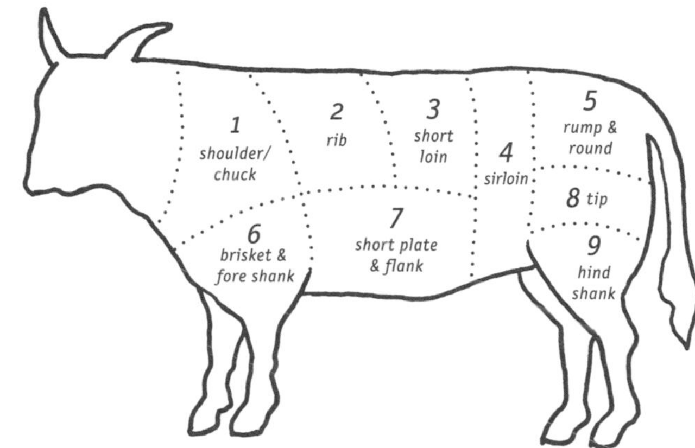

back ribs (2)

boneless arm pot roast (1)

boneless chuck pot roast (1)

boneless chuck roast (1)

boneless shoulder steak (1)

boneless top blade steak (1)

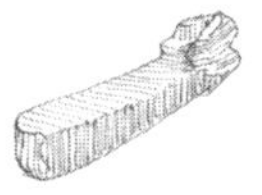
country-style ribs (1)

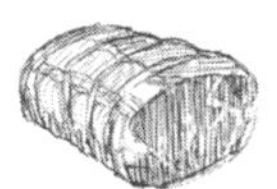
rib eye roast (2)

rib eye steak (2)

rib roast (2)

short ribs (1)

t-bone top roast (1)

BEEF

The most tender cuts of beef come from the loin, back, rump, and round end of the animal. The most flavorful, tender, juiciest beef is aged or Prime. When buying beef, look for bright red color and fine texture with a slightly moist look. The exterior fat should be white, not yellow, and the meat should have no odor.

TIMINGS: Roast Beef

The following cuts of meat are best for roasting. Let the roast sit for 1 to 2 hours outside the refrigerator just before cooking. Preheat the oven to 550° F. Put the meat into the hot oven, then reduce the temperature to the temperature specified on the chart. Remove the roast from the oven when an instant-read thermometer registers 5 degrees below the temperature of doneness. Let the meat stand for 15 minutes covered with foil. It will continue to cook to the correct temperature.

TYPE	***INSTRUCTIONS***	***INTERNAL TEMPERATURE***	***TIMING***
RIB EYE, EYE ROUND ROASTS 4–6 pounds	*To Roast:* Preheat oven to 550°F. Place meat fat side up on a rack in a shallow roasting pan. Place in oven and reduce oven temperature to **350°F.** Roast uncovered. Insert thermometer to test for doneness.	115°F–120°F	Rare: 18–20 minutes per pound
		125°F–130°F	Medium-rare: 20–22 minutes per pound
		135°F–140°F	Medium: 22–24 minutes per pound
		140°F–160°F	Well: 24–26 minutes per pound

TYPE	*INSTRUCTIONS*	*INTERNAL TEMPERATURE*	*TIMING*
RUMP ROAST Boneless, rolled; 4–6 pounds	*To Roast:* Preheat oven to 550°F. Place meat fat side up on a rack in a shallow roasting pan. Place in oven and reduce oven temperature to **325°F.** Roast uncovered. Insert thermometer to test for doneness. Best cooked medium.	115°F–120°F	Rare: 19–21 minutes per pound
		125°F–130°F	Medium rare: 21–23 minutes per pound
		135°F–140°F	Medium: 23–25 minutes per pound
		140°F–160°F	Well: 25–27 minutes per pound
SIRLOIN TIP ROAST Boneless; 3–5 pounds	*To Roast:* Preheat oven to 550°F. Place meat fat side up on a rack in a shallow roasting pan. Place in oven and reduce oven temperature to **325°F.** Roast uncovered. Insert thermometer to test for doneness.	115°F–120°F	Rare: 20–23 minutes per pound
		125°F–130°F	Medium-rare: 23–26 minutes per pound
		135°F–140°F	Medium: 26–31 minutes per pound
		140°F–160°F	Well: 33–38 minutes per pound
STANDING RIB ROAST, 2-RIB ROAST 4–5 pounds	*To Roast:* Preheat oven to 550°F. Place meat fat side up on a rack in a shallow roasting pan. Place in oven and reduce oven temperature to **325°F.** Roast uncovered, basting every 30 minutes. Insert thermometer to test for doneness.	115°F–120°F	Rare: 1–1¼ hours
		125°F–130°F	Medium-rare: 1–1¼ hours
		135°F–140°F	Medium: 1–1¼ hours
		140°F–160°F	Well: 1–1¼ hours

TYPE	INSTRUCTIONS	INTERNAL TEMPERATURE	TIMING
3-RIB ROAST 7–8½ pounds	*To Roast:* Preheat oven to 550°F. Place meat fat side up on a rack in a shallow roasting pan. Place in oven and reduce oven temperature to **325°F.** Roast uncovered, basting every 30 minutes. Insert thermometer to test for doneness.	115°F–120°F 125°F–130°F 135°F–140°F 140°F–160°F	Rare: 1½–1¾ hours Medium-rare: 1½–1¾ hours Medium: 1½–1¾ hours Well: 1½–1¾ hours
4-RIB ROAST 9–10 pounds	*To Roast:* Preheat oven to 550°F. Place meat fat side up on a rack in a shallow roasting pan. Place in oven and reduce oven temperature to **325°F.** Roast uncovered, basting every 30 minutes. Insert thermometer to test for doneness.	115°F–120°F 125°F–130°F 135°F–140°F 140°F–160°F	Rare: 1¾–2¼ hours Medium-rare: 1¾–2¼ hours Medium: 1¾–2¼ hours Well: 1¾–2¼ hours
5-RIB ROAST 11–13 pounds	*To Roast:* Preheat oven to 550°F. Place meat fat side up on a rack in a shallow roasting pan. Place in oven and reduce oven temperature to **325°F.** Roast uncovered, basting every 30 minutes. Insert thermometer to test for doneness.	115°F–120°F 125°F–130°F 135°F–140°F 140°F–160°F	Rare: 2¼–2¾ hours Medium-rare: 2¼–2¾ hours Medium: 2¼–2¾ hours Well: 2¼–2¾ hours

TYPE	INSTRUCTIONS	INTERNAL TEMPERATURE	TIMING
STANDING RIB ROAST Rolled; 4–6 pounds	*To Roast:* Preheat oven to 550°F. Place meat fat side up on a rack in a shallow roasting pan. Place in oven and reduce oven temperature to **325°F.** Roast uncovered, basting every 30 minutes. Insert thermometer to test for doneness.	115°F–120°F 125°F–130°F 135°F–140°F 140°F–160°F	Rare: 26–32 minutes per pound Medium-rare: 32–34 minutes per pound Medium: 34–38 minutes per pound Well: 40–42 minutes per pound
TOP SIRLOIN ROAST 4–6 pounds	*To Roast:* Preheat oven to 550°F. Place meat fat side up on a rack in a shallow roasting pan. Place in oven and reduce oven temperature to **325°F.** Roast uncovered, basting every 30 minutes. Insert thermometer to test for doneness.	115°F–120°F 125°F–130°F 135°F–140°F 140°F–160°F	Rare: 18–20 minutes per pound Medium-rare: 20–22 minutes per pound Medium: 22–24 minutes per pound Well: 24–26 minutes per pound
TENDERLOIN ROAST 4–6 pounds	*To Roast:* Preheat oven to 450°F. Rub exposed ends with butter and place on rack in a shallow roasting pan. Place in oven and reduce oven temperature to **350°F.** Roast uncovered. Insert thermometer to test for doneness. Cooking beyond medium-rare is not recommended.	120°F–125°F 130°F–140°F	Rare: 5–6 minutes per pound Medium-rare: 7–8 minutes per pound

TIMINGS: Beef—All Methods but Roasting

NOTE: For roasting times, see pages 182–85.

TYPE	*METHOD*	*INSTRUCTIONS*	*TIMING*
BACK RIBS 3–3½ pounds	BARBECUE	Prepare a medium-low fire in the grill. Push the coals to one side and place a drip pan on the other side. Place meat over drip pan and cover grill. Maintain a temperature inside the grill of 220°F–250°F, adding more coals and wood chips as needed. Baste and turn occasionally and barbecue until tender.	5½ hours
	BRAISE	Preheat oven to 325°F (optional). Cut meat into 2 × 2 × 4–inch pieces. Heat oil in Dutch oven on top of stove over medium-high heat. Add meat and brown on all sides. Add seasonings and 1 inch cooking liquid. Bring to a simmer. Cover and cook on low heat or in oven until tender.	1½–2½ hours
BRISKET Whole; 8–10 pounds	BARBECUE	Prepare a medium-low fire in the grill. Push the coals to one side and place a drip pan on the other side. Place meat over drip pan and cover grill. Maintain a temperature inside the grill of 220°F–250°F, adding more coals and wood chips as needed. Baste and turn occasionally and barbecue until tender, or to an internal temperature of 160°F–170°F.	5–8 hours

TYPE	METHOD	INSTRUCTIONS	TIMING
	BRAISE	Trim most of the visible fat from the meat. Preheat oven to 325°F (optional). Heat oil in Dutch oven on top of stove over medium-high heat. Add meat and brown on all sides. Add seasonings and 1 inch cooking liquid. Bring to a simmer. Cover and cook on low heat or in oven until tender. Add vegetables 45 minutes before end of cooking time, if desired.	3–4 hours
	SIMMER	*To Make Corned Beef:* Submerge meat in pickling brine for 8–12 days, turning beef occasionally. Remove from brine, cover with fresh water, add fresh spices, and simmer until tender.	2½–3 hours, plus 8–12 days in pickling brine
CUBE STEAK ½ inch	PAN-BROIL	Preheat a heavy iron skillet over high heat. Add cube steaks, reduce heat to medium, and cook, turning once.	Medium-rare: 1½ minutes per side Medium: 2½ minutes per side Well: 3½ minutes per side
	PAN-FRY	Brush a heavy skillet with oil and preheat over medium-high heat. Add cube steaks and cook, turning once.	Medium-rare: 2 minutes per side Medium: 3 minutes per side Well: 4 minutes per side

TYPE	*METHOD*	*INSTRUCTIONS*	*TIMING*
GROUND BEEF Hamburgers; ¾ inch	BROIL	Preheat broiler. Place patties on preheated broiler pan. Broil 3 inches from heat, turning once.	Rare: 3½ minutes per side Medium-rare: 4 minutes per side Medium: 5 minutes per side Well: 6 minutes per side
	GRILL	Prepare a medium-hot fire in the grill. Place patties on the grill 4 inches from the coals. Sear for 1 minute. Cover. Halfway through cooking, turn, sear for 1 minute, then cover grill and cook until desired doneness.	Rare: 3 minutes per side Medium-rare: 3½ minutes per side Medium: 4 minutes per side Well: 5 minutes per side
	PAN-BROIL	Preheat a heavy skillet over high heat. Add patties and cook, turning once.	Rare: 3 minutes per side Medium-rare: 4 minutes per side Medium: 5 minutes per side Well: 7 minutes per side

TYPE	METHOD	INSTRUCTIONS	TIMING
Hamburgers; 1 inch	BROIL	Preheat broiler. Place meat on preheated broiler pan. Broil 3 inches from heat, turning once.	Rare: 4 minutes per side Medium-rare: 4½ minutes per side Medium: 5½ minutes per side Well: 6½ minutes per side
	GRILL	Prepare a medium-hot fire in the grill. Place patties on grill 4 inches from the coals. Sear for 1 minute. Cover. Halfway through cooking, turn, sear for 1 minute, then cover grill and cook until desired doneness.	Rare: 3½ minutes per side Medium-rare: 4 minutes per side Medium: 4½ minutes per side Well: 5½ minutes per side
	PAN-BROIL	Preheat a heavy skillet over high heat. Add patties and cook, turning once.	Rare: 3½ minutes per side Medium-rare: 4½ minutes per side Medium: 5½ minutes per side Well: 7½ minutes per side

TYPE	*METHOD*	*INSTRUCTIONS*	*TIMING*
Meatballs	PAN-FRY	*To Pan-Fry Meatballs:* Combine meat with seasonings, using favorite recipe. Shape into meatballs. Add to heated oil in large heavy skillet over medium-high heat. Brown on all sides, then add to sauce.	10–12 minutes
Meatloaf	BAKE	*To Bake Meatloaf:* Preheat oven to 350°F. Make a meatloaf using favorite recipe (1 pound meat). Place in greased baking dish and bake uncovered. Let stand 10 minutes before serving.	35 minutes, plus 10 minutes standing time
POT ROASTS, FLAT Arm pot roast, Blade roast, Chuck-eye roast, Boneless chuck roast, Flatiron roast, 7-bone pot roast; 3–5 pounds	BRAISE	Preheat oven to 325°F (optional). Heat oil in a Dutch oven or roasting pan over medium-high heat. Add meat and brown on all sides. Add seasonings and 1 inch cooking liquid and bring to a simmer. Cover and cook on low heat or in oven until tender. If desired, add vegetables about 45 minutes before the end of the cooking time.	1½–2½ hours
POT ROASTS, ROUND Bottom round roast, Eye-of-round roast, Rump roast; 3–5 pounds	BRAISE	Preheat oven to 325°F (optional). Heat oil in a Dutch oven or roasting pan over medium-high heat. Add meat and brown on all sides. Add seasonings and 1 inch cooking liquid and bring to a simmer. Cover and cook on low heat or in oven. If desired, add vegetables about 45 minutes before the end of the cooking time.	3–3½ hours

TYPE	METHOD	INSTRUCTIONS	TIMING
ROUND STEAK 2½ pounds	BRAISE	Preheat oven to 325°F (optional). Heat oil in a Dutch oven or roasting pan over medium-high heat. Add meat and brown on all sides. Add seasonings and 1 inch cooking liquid and bring to a simmer. Cover and cook on low heat or in oven until tender. If desired, add vegetables about 45 minutes before the end of the cooking time.	1–1½ hours
SHANKS 3–5 pounds	BRAISE	Preheat oven to 325°F (optional). Heat oil in a Dutch oven or roasting pan over medium-high heat. Add meat and brown on all sides. Add seasonings and 1 inch cooking liquid and bring to a simmer. Cover and cook on low heat or in oven until tender. If desired, add vegetables about 45 minutes before the end of the cooking time.	2½–3½ hours
SHORT RIBS 3–3½ pounds	BARBECUE	Prepare a medium-low fire in the grill. Push the coals to one side and place a drip pan on the other side. Place meat over drip pan and cover grill. Maintain a temperature inside the grill of 220°F–250°F, adding more coals and wood chips as needed. Baste and turn occasionally.	5 hours
	BRAISE	Preheat oven to 325°F (optional). Heat oil in a Dutch oven or roasting pan over medium-high heat. Add meat and brown on all sides. Add seasonings and 1 inch cooking liquid and bring to a simmer. Cover and cook on low heat or in oven until tender. If desired, add vegetables about 45 minutes before the end of the cooking time.	2½–3½ hours

TYPE	*METHOD*	*INSTRUCTIONS*	*TIMING*
STEAK Châteaubriand, Filet, Filet mignon; 1 inch	BROIL	Preheat the broiler. Brush steak with a little oil or butter and place on preheated broiler pan. Broil 4 inches from the heat, turning once. Transfer steak to a cutting board when done. Serve rare to medium—filets should not be overcooked. Cover loosely with foil and let stand 5 minutes before slicing.	Rare: 3–4 minutes per side Medium-rare: 4–5 minutes per side Medium: 5–6 minutes per side Well: 6–7 minutes per side, plus 5 minutes standing time
	GRILL	Prepare a medium fire in the grill. Lightly oil steak and place on grill 4 inches from coals. Cover. Grill, turning once. Transfer steak to a cutting board when done. Cover loosely with foil and let stand 5 minutes before slicing.	Rare: 3–4 minutes per side Medium-rare: 4–5 minutes per side Medium: 5–6 minutes per side Well: 6–7 minutes per side, plus 5 minutes standing time

TYPE	METHOD	INSTRUCTIONS	TIMING
	PAN-BROIL	Preheat a heavy iron skillet over high heat with 2 tablespoons oil in the pan (optional). Add steak and brown on both sides. Then reduce the heat to medium and cook on both sides. Begin timing after browning both sides. Transfer steak to a cutting board when done. Cover loosely with foil and let stand 5 minutes before slicing.	Rare: 3½ minutes per side Medium-rare: 4 minutes per side Medium: 5 minutes per side Well: 6 minutes per side, plus 5 minutes standing time
STEAK Châteaubriand, Filet, Filet mignon; 2 inch	BROIL	Preheat the broiler. Brush steak with a little oil or butter and place on the preheated broiler pan. Broil 4 inches from the heat, turning once. Transfer steak to a cutting board when done. Serve rare to medium—filets should not be overcooked. Cover loosely with foil and let stand 5 minutes before slicing.	Rare: 6–7 minutes per side Medium-rare: 7–9 minutes per side Medium: 9–10 minutes per side Well: 10–13 minutes per side

TYPE	METHOD	INSTRUCTIONS	TIMING
STEAK Châteaubriand, Filet, Filet mignon; 2 inch *(cont'd.)*	GRILL	Prepare a medium fire in the grill. Lightly oil steak and place on grill 4 inches from coals. Cover. Grill, turning once. Transfer steak to a cutting board when done. Cover loosely with foil and let stand 5 minutes before slicing.	Rare: 6–7 minutes per side Medium-rare: 7–9 minutes per side Medium: 9–10 minutes per side Well: 10–11 minutes per side
	PAN-BROIL	Preheat a heavy iron skillet over high heat with 2 tablespoons oil in the pan (optional). Add steak and brown on both sides. Then reduce the heat to medium and cook on both sides. Begin timing after browning both sides. Transfer steak to a cutting board when done. Cover loosely with foil and let stand 5 minutes before slicing.	Rare: 4–6 minutes per side Medium-rare: 6–7 minutes per side Medium: 8–9 minutes per side Well: 9–11 minutes per side
STEAK Chuck, Eye round, Rump, Tip, Top round; Boneless, 1 inch	BRAISE	Preheat oven to 325°F (optional). Heat oil in a Dutch oven or roasting pan over medium-high heat. Add meat and brown on both sides. Add seasonings and 1 inch cooking liquid and bring to a simmer. Cover and cook on low heat or in a 325°F oven. If desired, add vegetables about 45 minutes before the end of the cooking time.	1–1½ hours

TYPE	METHOD	INSTRUCTIONS	TIMING
	BROIL	Preheat the broiler. Brush steak with a little oil or butter and place on the preheated broiler pan. Broil 2 inches from the heat, turning once. Transfer steak to a cutting board when done. Cover loosely with foil and let stand 5 minutes before slicing.	Rare: 3–4 minutes per side Medium-rare: 4–5 minutes per side Medium: 5–6 minutes per side Well: 6–8 minutes per side
	GRILL	Prepare a hot fire in the grill. Lightly oil steak and place on grill 4 inches from coals. Grill, turning once. Transfer steak to a cutting board when done. Cover loosely with foil and let stand 5 minutes before slicing.	Rare: 3–4 minutes per side Medium-rare: 4–5 minutes per side Medium: 5–6 minutes per side Well: 6–8 minutes per side
STEAK Chuck, Eye round, Rump, Tip, Top round; Boneless; 2 inch	BRAISE	Preheat oven to 325°F (optional). Heat oil in a Dutch oven or roasting pan over medium-high heat. Add meat and brown on all sides. Add seasonings and 1 inch cooking liquid and bring to a simmer. Cover and cook on low heat or in a 325°F oven. If desired, add vegetables about 1 hour before the end of the cooking time.	2–2½ hours

TYPE	METHOD	INSTRUCTIONS	TIMING
STEAK Chuck, Eye round, Rump, Tip, Top round; Boneless; 2 inch (*cont'd.*)	BROIL	Preheat the broiler. Brush steak with a little oil or butter and place on the preheated broiler pan. Broil 2 inches from the heat, turning once. Transfer steak to a cutting board when done. Cover loosely with foil and let stand 5 minutes before slicing.	Rare: 8–9 minutes per side Medium-rare: 9–10 minutes per side Medium: 10–11 minutes per side Well: 12–15 minutes per side
	GRILL	Prepare a hot fire in the grill. Lightly oil steak and place on grill 4 inches from coals. Grill, turning once. Transfer steak to a cutting board when done. Cover loosely with foil and let stand 5 minutes before slicing.	Rare: 8–9 minutes per side Medium-rare: 9–10 minutes per side Medium: 10–11 minutes per side Well: 12–15 minutes per side
STEAK Club, Porter-house, Sirloin, T-bone; 1 inch	BROIL	Preheat the broiler. Brush steak with a little oil or butter and place on the preheated broiler pan. Broil 3 inches from the heat, turning once. Transfer steak to a cutting board when done. Cover loosely with foil and let stand 5 minutes before slicing.	Rare: 4–5 minutes per side Medium-rare: 5–6 minutes per side Medium: 6–9 minutes per side Well: 9–11 minutes per side

TYPE	METHOD	INSTRUCTIONS	TIMING
	GRILL	Prepare a medium-hot fire in the grill. Cut the fat at 1½-inch intervals to prevent curling. Place steak on grill 3 inches from coals. Sear steak 1 minute, then cover grill. About halfway through cooking, turn steak over, sear for 1 minute, then cover grill again. Transfer steak to a cutting board when done. Cover loosely with foil and let stand 5 minutes before slicing.	Rare: 4–5 minutes per side Medium-rare: 5–6 minutes per side Medium: 6–9 minutes per side Well: 9–11 minutes per side
	PAN-BROIL	Preheat heavy skillet over high heat. Lightly oil steak. Add to skillet and brown on both sides, turning once. Transfer steak to a cutting board when done. Cover loosely with foil and let stand 5 minutes before slicing.	Rare: 3–4 minutes per side Medium-rare: 4–5 minutes per side Medium: 5–7 minutes per side Well: 7–9 minutes per side
STEAK Club, Porterhouse, Rib, Sirloin, T-bone; 1½ inch	BROIL	Preheat the broiler. Brush steak with a little oil or butter and place on the preheated broiler pan. Broil 3 inches from the heat, turning once. Transfer steak to a cutting board when done. Cover loosely with foil and let stand 5 minutes before slicing.	Rare: 5–6 minutes per side Medium-rare: 6–7 minutes per side Medium: 8–9 minutes per side Well: 10–12 minutes per side

TYPE	METHOD	INSTRUCTIONS	TIMING
STEAK Club, Porterhouse, Rib, Sirloin, T-bone; 1½ inch (*cont'd.*)	GRILL	Prepare a medium-hot fire in the grill. Cut the fat at 1½-inch intervals to prevent curling. Place steak on grill 4 inches from coals. Sear for 1 minute, then cover grill. Halfway through cooking, turn steak over, sear on the second side for 1 minute, then cover grill again. Transfer steak to a cutting board when done. Cover loosely with foil and let stand 5 minutes before slicing.	Rare: 5–6 minutes per side Medium-rare: 6–7 minutes per side Medium: 8–9 minutes per side Well: 10–12 minutes per side
STEAK Club, Porterhouse, Rib, Sirloin, T-bone; 2 inch	BROIL	Preheat the broiler. Brush steak with a little oil or butter and place on the preheated broiler pan. Broil 4 inches from the heat, turning once. Transfer steak to a cutting board when done. Cover loosely with foil and let stand 5 minutes before slicing.	Rare: 7 minutes per side Medium-rare: 8 minutes per side Medium: 9 minutes per side Well: 11 minutes per side
	GRILL	Prepare a medium-hot fire in the grill. Cut the fat at 2-inch intervals to prevent curling. Place steak on grill 4 inches from coals. Sear the steak for 1 minute. Then cover the grill. Turn, sear the steak on the second side for 1 minute, then cover the grill again. Transfer steak to a cutting board when done. Cover loosely with foil and let stand 5 minutes before slicing.	Rare: 7 minutes per side Medium-rare: 8 minutes per side Medium: 9 minutes per side Well: 11 minutes per side

TYPE	***METHOD***	***INSTRUCTIONS***	***TIMING***
STEAK Flank, London broil; ¾ inch	BROIL	Preheat the broiler. Brush steak with a little oil or butter and place on the preheated broiler pan. Broil 2–3 inches from the heat, turning once. Serve rare to medium. Transfer steak to a cutting board when done. Cover loosely with foil and let stand 5 minutes before slicing.	Rare: 4–5 minutes per side Medium-rare: 5–6 minutes per side Medium: 6–7 minutes per side
	GRILL	Prepare a medium fire in the grill. Lightly oil steak and place on grill 4 inches from coals. Cover. Grill, turning once. Serve rare to medium. Transfer steaks to a cutting board when done. Cover loosely with foil and let stand 5 minutes before slicing.	Rare: 4–5 minutes per side Medium-rare: 5–6 minutes per side Medium: 6–7 minutes per side
STEAK Rib eye; 1 inch	BROIL	Preheat the broiler. Brush steak with a little oil or butter and place on the preheated broiler pan. Broil 4 inches from the heat, turning once. Transfer steak to a cutting board when done. Cover loosely with foil and let stand 5 minutes before slicing.	Rare: 5–6 minutes per side Medium-rare: 6–7 minutes per side Medium: 7–9 minutes per side
	GRILL	Prepare a hot fire in the grill. Lightly oil steak and place on grill 4 inches from coals. Grill, turning once. Transfer steak to a cutting board when done. Cover loosely with foil and let stand 5 minutes before slicing.	Rare: 5–6 minutes per side Medium-rare: 6–7 minutes per side Medium: 7–9 minutes per side

TYPE	*METHOD*	*INSTRUCTIONS*	*TIMING*
STEAK Rib eye; 1 inch (*cont'd.*)	PAN-BROIL	Preheat a heavy skillet over high heat. Lightly oil the steak. Add to skillet and brown on both sides, turning once. Transfer steak to a cutting board when done. Cover loosely with foil and let stand 5 minutes before slicing.	Rare: 4 minutes per side Medium-rare: 4½–5 minutes per side Medium: 5–6 minutes per side
	STIR-FRY	Cut the meat in ¼-inch-thick strips. Add to oil in a hot wok and cook, stirring.	Medium-rare: 3 minutes Medium: 4 minutes Well: 5 minutes
STEWING BEEF Chuck, Bottom, Round, Short rib; 2 pounds	BRAISE	Preheat oven to 325°F (optional). Cut meat into cubes and dust with seasoned flour. Heat oil in a Dutch oven or roasting pan over medium-high heat. Add meat and brown on all sides. Add seasonings and 1 inch cooking liquid. Bring to a simmer. Cover and cook on low heat or in oven. Add vegetables 45 minutes before the end of cooking, if desired.	1-inch cubes: 1–1½ hours 2-inch cubes: 1½–2½ hours

VEAL

Veal, the meat from calves slaughtered by four months of age, is a very lean meat. The texture and taste of veal are very appealing to most people. The challenge is to cook it well enough to leave it moist and juicy without overcooking it.

Veal from milk-fed calves should be smooth and creamy with a tinge of pink. It is, in general, very tender. Veal from grass-fed calves has a more pronounced flavor, darker meat, and a chewier texture. Whether buying formula-fed or grass-fed veal, look for slightly moist, pale pink to reddish meat and slightly yellow fat.

Cuts of Veal

Veal has six primal cuts: breast, leg, loin, rack, shank, shoulder.

Breast. The breast is a less expensive cut of meat that is usually braised. It can be boned, stuffed, or roasted with the ribs left in. It's very flavorful, but also rather chewy and bony.

Leg. The leg of veal is similar to the leg of lamb and the round of beef. It consists of top sirloin, top round, eye round, and bottom round. Cutlets are usually cut from this section, and often the meat from the leg is boned and made into roasts.

Loin. The loin is the most tender cut of veal and also the most expensive. The best steaks and chops come from the loin. The loin section is just behind the rack (ribs) on the top back of the animal. You can recognize loin chops by their T-bone shape, with the tenderloin on one side.

Rack. Rack of veal is similar to rack of lamb. It usually consists of 8 ribs or trimmed individual chops that are called rib chops. Rib chops have a curved bone that runs the length of the chop.

Shank. The shank is the foreleg of the animal. It is usually cut into rather small crosswise sections. Veal shank is the base for the famous Italian dish osso buco and is primarily braised.

Shoulder. The shoulder has more fat than other cuts but is very flavorful. It is often boned and either tied into a roast or stuffed. Always ask for shoulder when making a stew.

Cooking Veal with Flavor

The final cooking temperature of veal should be 140°F–155°F, or medium done. This means removing a veal roast from the oven when the internal temperature reaches 135°F to 150°F.

Braising. Braising is the perfect way to cook large cuts of veal, since it cooks the meat slowly while leaving it moist. For wonderful results, simmer the meat in veal or chicken stock with wine, milk, or cream. To make osso buco, simmer the shank in a wine stock with tomatoes, onions, carrots, celery, garlic, and lemon peel. The best cuts for braising are the tougher, more flavorful cuts, such as shoulder, rump, breast, sirloin, and shank.

Broiling. Broiling can dry out veal before it browns. Thus it isn't recommended for all cuts of veal. Chops should be cut at least 1½ inches thick or the meat will be too dry.

Grilling. Grilling is a good choice for thick chops and steaks. For extra flavor, try coating the meat with an herb rub or spice mix, and serve with a salsa or chutney.

Pan-Frying and Sautéing. The best ways to cook veal chops, veal steaks, or medallions of veal are to pan-fry or sauté them. Buy chops 1¼ to 1½ inches thick, medallions about ¾ inch thick. The medallions can be pounded into escalopes and pan-fried or sautéed.

Pat the meat dry before adding it to the pan. I like to sauté veal in a generous 2 tablespoons of butter and 2 tablespoons oil in a large skillet. The veal will release delicious juices to make a pan sauce. After searing the meat in the butter and oil over high heat, reduce the heat to medium and let the veal cook in its own juice until done. Remove the meat from the pan, and add about ½ cup veal or chicken stock to the pan. Boil it until the liquid thickens to a nice syrupy consistency.

Roasting. Roasting can be done quickly, at a high oven temperature, which browns the meat on the outside while leaving it pink, moist, and juicy in the center. This method is perfect for the more tender and expensive cuts of veal, like the loin and rib. Slow-roasting is best suited for the cheaper and less tender cuts, like the shoulder, leg, and breast. Slow-roasting cooks veal to an even pink color, without browning, leaving the meat moist and juicy.

To make a sauce for roasts, remove the finished roast from the pan and let it stand under a loose tent of aluminum foil. Add ½ cup white wine and ½ cup chicken stock to the roasting pan and place over a burner. Bring to a boil, scraping up any burnt bits from the bottom of the pan. Boil for 1 to 2 minutes, until the pan juices have a syrupy consistency. Pour the sauce over the roast.

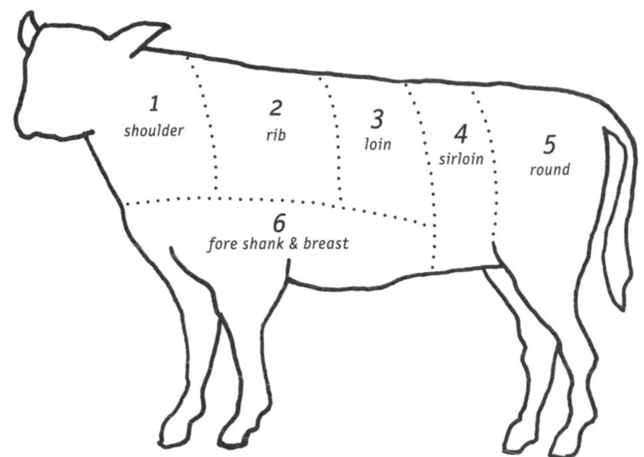

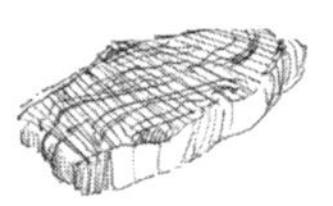
blade steak (1)

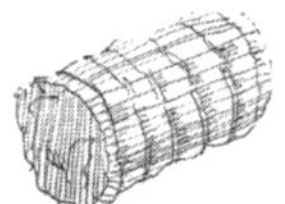
boneless breast roast (6)

boneless shoulder roast (1)

boneless shoulder steak (1)

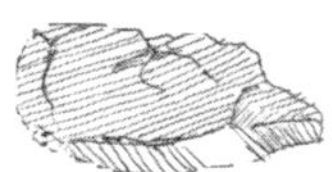
boneless sirloin steak (4)

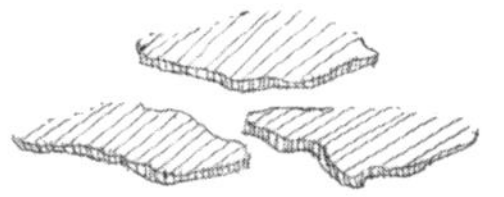
cutlet/scallops (5)

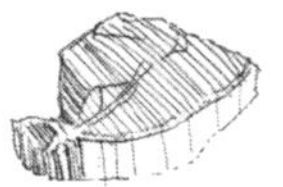
loin chop (3)

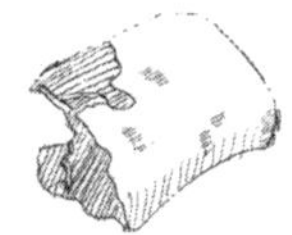
loin roast (3)

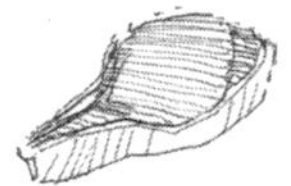
rib chop (2)

riblet (6)

rib roast (2)

top round steak (5)

TIMINGS: Veal

NOTE: The cooked temperatures for veal are for medium (140°F–155°F). The timing of veal depends on the age of the animal when killed. The younger the meat, the faster it will cook.

TYPE	*METHOD*	*INSTRUCTIONS*	*TIMING*
BREAST Stuffed; 3–4 pounds	BRAISE	Stuff the pocket of the breast with the dressing of your choice. Brush meat with oil. Place in a large Dutch oven and brown on all sides. Add 1 inch braising liquid to the pan and seasonings and simmer over low heat until meat reaches an internal temperature of 155°F–160°F.	1½–2½ hours
	GRILL	*To Grill (Indirect Method):* Prepare a medium-hot fire in the grill. Push all the coals to one side and place a drip pan on the other side. Rub breast with oil and season well. Place on greased grill over the drip pan, cover, and grill, adding more coals as needed, until the meat reaches an internal temperature of 140°F–155°F.	2–2½ hours
	ROAST	Preheat oven to 425°F. Stuff the pocket of the breast with the dressing of your choice. Rub the meat with oil and place in roasting pan. Roast until meat reaches an internal temperature of 155°F–160°F. Let stand covered loosely with foil 20 minutes before serving.	1–1½ hours, plus 20 minutes standing time

TYPE	METHOD	INSTRUCTIONS	TIMING
CHOPS Loin, Rib; ¾ inch	PAN-FRY	Dust chops with seasoned flour, dip in egg wash, and coat with crumbs. Heat ¼ inch oil in a large heavy skillet over medium-high heat. Fry on both sides, turning once.	First side: 3–4 minutes Second side: 1–2 minutes
	SAUTÉ	Heat butter and/or oil in a large skillet over medium-high heat. Add chops and sear on both sides, about 2 minutes per side. Reduce the heat to medium and continue cooking until the meat is tender, turning the chops again.	4 minutes per side
CHOPS Loin, Rib; 1 inch	BRAISE	Heat butter and/or oil in a large skillet over medium-high heat. Add chops and brown about 2 minutes on each side. Add seasoning and 1 inch braising liquid, cover, reduce heat, and simmer until tender. (Timing depends on age of veal.)	20–40 minutes
	GRILL	Prepare a medium-hot fire in the grill. Rub each chop with oil and season well. Place on grill and sear the chops on both sides. Then move to a cooler area on the grill and finish cooking until tender, turning once.	6–7 minutes per side
	GRILL	*To Grill (Indirect Method):* Prepare a medium-hot fire in the grill. Push all the coals to one side and place a drip pan on the other side. Rub each chop with oil and season well. Place on greased grill over the drip pan and grill, turning once, until the chops reach an internal temperature of 160°F.	7–8 minutes per side

TYPE	*METHOD*	*INSTRUCTIONS*	*TIMING*
CHOPS Loin, Rib; 1 inch (*cont'd.*)	SAUTÉ	Heat butter and/or oil in a large skillet over medium-high heat. Add chops and sear on both sides, about 2 minutes per side. Reduce the heat to medium and continue cooking until the meat is tender, turning the chops again.	7–8 minutes per side
CHOPS Loin, Rib; 1½ inch	BRAISE	Heat butter and/or oil in large skillet over medium-high heat. Add chops and brown about 3 minutes on each side. Add seasonings and 1 inch braising liquid, cover, reduce heat, and simmer until tender. (Timing depends on age of veal.)	20–40 minutes
	GRILL	Prepare a medium-hot fire in the grill. Rub each chop with oil and season well. Place on greased grill 3 inches above the coals and sear the chops on both sides, about 2 minutes per side. Then move to a cooler area on the grill and finish cooking until tender, turning once.	7–7½ minutes per side
	SAUTÉ	Heat butter and/or oil in a large skillet over medium-high heat. Add chops and sear on both sides, about 2½–3 minutes per side. Reduce the heat to medium and continue cooking until the meat is tender, turning the chops again.	7–8 minutes per side
CUTLETS, MEDALLIONS, LOIN STEAKS ¾ inch	DEEP-FRY	Heat 3 inches of oil to 375°F. Dust meat with seasoned flour, dip in egg wash, and coat with crumbs. Deep-fry until golden brown, turning once.	3–5 minutes per side

TYPE	METHOD	INSTRUCTIONS	TIMING
	GRILL	Prepare a medium-hot fire in the grill. Brush or rub the meat with oil and season well. Grill 3 inches from coals for 1 minute per side. Move to a cooler area of grill for remainder of cooking time, turning once more.	2–3 minutes per side
	PAN-FRY	Dust with seasoned flour, dip in egg wash, coat with crumbs. Heat ¼ inch oil in a large heavy skillet over medium-high heat. Fry on both sides, turning once.	2–2½ minutes per side
	SAUTÉ	Heat butter and/or oil in a large heavy skillet over medium-high heat. Add the meat and sear on both sides, about 2 minutes per side. Reduce heat to medium and continue cooking until the meat is tender, turning again.	4–6 minutes
	STIR-FRY	Cut meat into ¼-inch-thick strips. Add to hot oil in wok and cook over high heat, stirring constantly.	3–5 minutes
CUTLETS, MEDALLIONS, SCALLOPS Pounded to ¼ inch or thinner	GRILL	Prepare a medium-hot fire in the grill. Brush or rub meat with oil and season well. Grill 4 inches from coals, turning once. Do not overcook. Sprinkle with lemon juice when done.	2 minutes per side
	PAN-FRY	Season meat well. Heat ⅛ inch oil in a large heavy skillet over high heat. Fry on both sides, turning once.	30–60 seconds per side
	SAUTÉ	Heat butter and/or oil in a large skillet over medium heat. Sauté on both sides until done. Remove from pan. Pour juices over meat.	1–3 minutes

TYPE	*METHOD*	*INSTRUCTIONS*	*TIMING*
CUTLETS, MEDALLIONS, SCALLOPS Pounded to ¼ inch or thinner (*cont'd.*)	STIR-FRY	Cut meat into ¼-inch-thick strips. Add to hot oil in wok and cook, stirring constantly.	1–3 minutes
ROASTS Leg of veal, Round, Rump, Sirloin, Top; boneless 3–4 pounds	BRAISE	Brush meat with oil. Place in a large Dutch oven and brown on all sides. Add 1 inch braising liquid and seasonings and simmer over low heat until the meat is tender and reaches an internal temperature of 155°F–160°F.	2–2½ hours
	ROAST	*To Slow-Roast:* Preheat oven to 450°F. Tie roast with twine and rub the entire surface with oil. Sprinkle with salt and pepper. Place roast fat side up on a rack in a roasting pan. Roast 10 minutes at 450°F. Reduce heat to 250°F. Continue roasting until the internal temperature reaches 145°F. Remove roast and let stand covered loosely with foil 20 minutes before slicing.	2–2¾ hours, plus 20 minutes standing time
ROASTS Loin, boneless; 3–4 pounds	ROAST	*To Fast-Roast:* Preheat oven to 425°F. Tie roast with twine and rub the entire surface with oil and seasonings. Place roast fat side up on a rack in a roasting pan and cook until the internal temperature reaches 130°F–145°F. Remove and let stand loosely covered with foil 20 minutes before slicing.	45–55 minutes, plus 20 minutes standing time

TYPE	METHOD	INSTRUCTIONS	TIMING
	ROAST	*To Slow-Roast:* Preheat oven to 450°F. Tie roast with twine and rub the entire surface with oil. Sprinkle with salt and pepper. Place roast fat side up on a rack in a roasting pan. Roast for 10 minutes at 450°F. Reduce heat to 250°F. Continue roasting until the internal temperature reaches 130°F–145°F. Remove roast and let stand covered loosely with foil 20 minutes before slicing.	1¼–1¾ hours, plus 20 minutes standing time
	BRAISE	Heat oil in a large Dutch oven over medium-high heat. Add roast and brown on all sides. Add seasonings and 1 inch braising liquid and simmer over low heat until tender.	1½–2 hours
ROASTS Rib (rack), Bone in; 5–7 pounds	ROAST	*To Fast-Roast:* Preheat oven to 425°F. Tie roast with twine and rub the entire surface with oil. Sprinkle with salt and pepper. Place roast fat side up on a rack in a roasting pan and cook until the internal temperature reaches 130°F–145°F. Remove and let stand loosely covered with foil 20 minutes before slicing.	1¼–1½ hours, plus 20 minutes standing time
	ROAST	*To Slow-Roast:* Preheat oven to 450°F. Tie roast with twine and rub the entire surface with oil. Sprinkle with salt and pepper. Place roast fat side up on a rack in a roasting pan. Roast 10 minutes at 450°F. Reduce heat to 250°F. Continue roasting until the internal temperature reaches 130°F–145°F. Remove roast and let stand covered loosely with foil 20 minutes before carving.	1¾–2 hours, plus 20 minutes standing time

TYPE	METHOD	INSTRUCTIONS	TIMING
SHANKS	BRAISE	Preheat oven to 200°F. Heat butter and oil in a large Dutch oven or large skillet over medium-high heat. Add shanks and brown on all sides, about 3 minutes per side. Add seasonings and 1 inch braising liquid. Cover pan and place in oven. Braise until tender.	1–2 hours, depending on size
SHANKS Osso buco; 1–1½ inches	BRAISE	Preheat oven to 325°F with rack in lower third of oven. Heat oil in a large Dutch oven over medium heat. Brown shanks on all sides. Remove and add vegetables. Sauté until soft. Return shanks to the pot with 1 inch braising liquid (stock, tomatoes, wine) and seasonings. Increase heat to high. Bring to a boil. Cover pot. Place in oven and cook, turning 3 times, until shanks are tender.	1–1¾ hours
ROASTS Shoulder, boneless— Veal square, Chuck, Chuck shoulder clod; 2½–3 pounds	BRAISE	Preheat oven to 350°F. Heat oil in a large Dutch oven over medium heat. Brown roast on all sides. Add seasonings and 1 inch braising liquid. Bring to boil and baste meat. Cover pot. Place in oven and braise until tender and internal temperature reaches 155°F–160°F.	1½–2 hours
ROASTS Shoulder, bone in— Blade roast, Arm roast; 3–4 pounds	BRAISE	Preheat oven to 350°F. Heat oil in a large Dutch oven over medium heat. Brown roast on all sides. Add seasonings and 1 inch braising liquid. Bring to boil and baste meat. Cover pot. Place in oven and braise until tender and internal temperature reaches 155°F–160°F.	1½–2 hours

TYPE	*METHOD*	*INSTRUCTIONS*	*TIMING*
STEAKS Blade; ¾–1 inch	BRAISE	Heat butter and/or oil in large skillet over medium-high heat. Add steak and brown about 3 minutes on each side. Add seasonings and 1 inch braising liquid, cover, reduce heat, and simmer until tender.	45–50 minutes
	BROIL	Preheat broiler. Brush steak with oil. Broil 4 inches from heat, turning once.	12–14 minutes
STEWING MEAT Shoulder	BRAISE	Cut meat into 1–2-inch cubes. Dust with seasoned flour. Heat oil in a large Dutch oven over medium-high heat. Brown meat on all sides. Add seasonings and 1 inch braising liquid, cover, and simmer over low heat until tender. Add vegetables 45 minutes before the end of cooking time, if desired.	1½–2 hours
	STEW	Cut meat in 1–2-inch cubes. Dust with seasoned flour. Heat oil in a large Dutch oven over medium-high heat. Brown meat on all sides, then remove from pot. Add vegetables and sauté until soft. Return meat to pot. Add braising liquid to cover meat, cover pot, and simmer over low heat until tender. Add vegetables 45 minutes before end of cooking time, if desired.	1½–2 hours

LAMB

When buying lamb, look for meat that is pink and finely textured. The ends of the bones should be red and moist, the fat should be white and well trimmed, and there should be no odor.

In the United States, lamb is certified and is guaranteed to be less than 1 year old. Baby or milk-fed lamb is certified to be 6 to 8 weeks old; spring lamb is between 3 and 5 months old and is slaughtered between March and early October. It is possible to buy older lamb, tougher and gamier in taste than young lamb. Yearling lamb comes from a sheep between 1 and 2 years old and mutton comes from one that is 2 years old or older.

The meat has a thin layer of white membrane tightly surrounding it. This membrane is called the fell; it is usually removed before cooking, as it tends to make the flavor stronger.

Most lamb is tender, especially the cuts from the loin and rib. The tender cuts are best served rare to medium rare. Cuts from the shoulder are tougher and are best cooked to medium.

Cooked Temperatures

The temperature of cooked meat will continue to rise after the meat has been removed from the heat. To achieve perfectly cooked meat, use the timing charts to estimate cooking times and an instant-read thermometer to determine exactly when the meat is done. The temperatures below represent those at which you will want to remove the meat from the heat. Let it stand under a loose tent of aluminum foil, and the temperature will continue to rise about 5 degrees.

The cooked temperatures for lamb are:

DONENESS	TEMPERATURE	DESCRIPTION
Rare	120°F–130°F	Meat is soft and bright pink to red in center. Very juicy.
Medium-rare	130°F–135°F	Meat is pink in center and has begun to turn gray at edges. Firmer, but still juicy.
Medium	140°F–150°F	Meat is pink in center, gray at edges. Texture is firm.
Medium-well	155°F–165°F	Meat is uniformly gray, pinkish tint near bones.
Well done	170°F	Meat is overcooked unless it is fatty and very juicy.

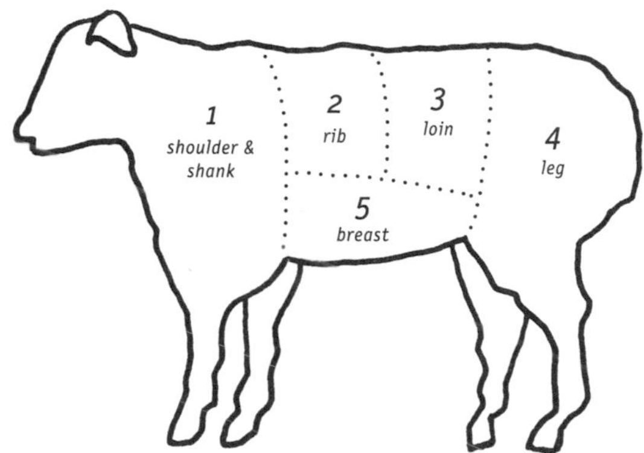

arm chop (1)

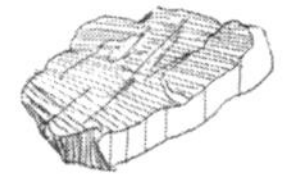
blade chop (1)

boneless shoulder roast (1)

French-style rib roast (2)

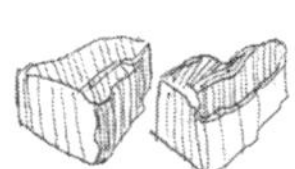
loin chop (3)

loin roast (3)

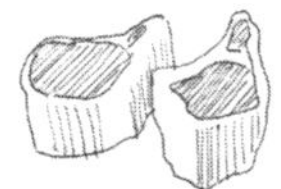
rib chop (2)

rib roast (2)

shank half of leg (4)

sirloin chop (4)

top round roast (4)

whole leg (with shank and sirloin) (4)

TIMINGS: Lamb

CUT	*METHOD*	*INSTRUCTIONS*	*TIMING*
BREAST 3–4 pounds	BRAISE	Heat oil in a large Dutch oven. Add meat and brown both sides. Add seasonings and 1 inch braising liquid. Reduce heat and simmer covered. Cut ribs before serving.	1½ hours
	GRILL	Prepare a medium-hot fire in the grill. Push the coals to one side and place a drip pan on the other side. Grill breast over pan with the lid off, basting often.	1–1½ hours
CHOPS Arm, Blade, Leg, Shoulder; 1 inch	BRAISE	Heat oil in a Dutch oven over medium-high heat. Add chops and brown well on both sides. Add seasonings and 1 inch cooking liquid and bring to a simmer. Cover and cook slowly over low heat.	40–45 minutes
	BROIL	Preheat the broiler. Lightly oil the chops and place on the preheated broiling pan. Broil 3 inches from the heat, turning once.	Rare: 4–5 minutes per side Medium-rare: 5–6 minutes per side Medium: 6 minutes per side Well: 8 minutes per side

CUT	METHOD	INSTRUCTIONS	TIMING
	GRILL	Prepare a medium-hot fire in the grill. Place on greased grill 4 inches from coals and grill, turning once.	Rare: 4–5 minutes per side Medium-rare: 5–6 minutes per side Medium: 6–7 minutes per side Well: 8–10 minutes per side
	PAN-BROIL	Preheat heavy iron skillet over high heat. Lightly oil chops and add to hot pan. Cook on both sides, turning once.	Rare: 3½ minutes per side Medium-rare: 4 minutes per side Medium: 5 minutes per side Well: 6 minutes per side
CHOPS Loin, Rib, Sirloin; 1 inch	BROIL	Preheat the broiler. Lightly oil chops and place on the preheated broiling pan. Broil 2 inches from the heat, turning once.	Rare: 3–3½ minutes per side Medium-rare: 3½–4 minutes per side Medium: 4–5 minutes per side Well: 6–7 minutes per side

CUT	METHOD	INSTRUCTIONS	TIMING
CHOPS Loin, Rib, Sirloin; 1 inch *(cont'd.)*	PAN-BROIL	Preheat heavy iron skillet over high heat. Lightly oil chops and add to hot pan. Cook on both sides, turning once.	Rare: 2½–3 minutes per side Medium-rare: 3–3½ minutes per side Medium: 3½–4 minutes per side Well: 4–5 minutes per side
	GRILL	Prepare a medium-hot fire in the grill. Place on greased grill 4 inches from coals and grill, turning once.	Rare: 3–3½ minutes per side Medium-rare: 3½–4 minutes per side Medium: 4–5 minutes per side Well: 6–7 minutes per side
CHOPS Loin, Rib, Sirloin; 1½ inches	BROIL	Preheat the broiler. Lightly oil chops and place on the preheated broiling pan. Broil 2 inches from the heat, turning once.	Rare: 5–6 minutes per side Medium-rare: 6–6½ minutes per side Medium: 6½–7 minutes per side Well: 7–8 minutes per side

CUT	METHOD	INSTRUCTIONS	TIMING
	PAN-BROIL	Preheat heavy iron skillet over high heat. Lightly oil chops and add to hot pan. Cook on both sides, turning once.	Rare: 4½–5½ minutes per side Medium-rare: 5–6 minutes per side Medium: 6–6½ minutes per side Well: 6½–7 minutes per side
	GRILL	Prepare a medium-hot fire in the grill. Place on a greased grill 4 inches from coals and grill, turning once.	Rare: 5–6 minutes per side Medium-rare: 6–6½ minutes per side Medium: 6½–7 minutes per side Well: 7–8 minutes per side
CHOPS Loin, Rib, Sirloin; 2 inches	BROIL	Preheat the broiler. Lightly oil chops and place on the preheated broiling pan. Broil 3 inches from the heat, turning once.	Rare: 8 minutes per side Medium-rare: 8½–9 minutes per side Medium: 9–10 minutes per side Well: 11 minutes per side

CUT	METHOD	INSTRUCTIONS	TIMING
CHOPS Loin, Rib, Sirloin; 2 inches (*cont'd.*)	PAN-BROIL	Preheat heavy iron skillet over high heat. Lightly oil chops and add to hot pan. Cook on both sides, turning once.	Rare: 6–7 minutes Medium-rare: 7–8 minutes Medium: 8–9 minutes Well: 9–10 minutes
	GRILL	Prepare a medium-hot fire in the grill. Place on greased grill 5 inches from coals and grill, turning once.	Rare: 8 minutes per side Medium-rare: 8½–9 minutes per side Medium: 9–10 minutes per side Well: 11 minutes per side
CROWN ROAST Approximately 12 ribs	ROAST	*To Roast Stuffed:* Let your butcher prepare the crown roast. Fill roast with stuffing. Preheat oven to 350°F. Place meat in a roasting pan and rub with oil and seasoning. Roast until the internal temperature reaches 125°F–130°F. Continue cooking a little longer for medium or well done, checking frequently. Remove from oven, cover loosely with foil, and let stand 10 minutes before carving.	Rare: 10–11 minutes per pound Medium-rare: 12–13 minutes per pound Medium: 13–15 minutes per pound Well: 18–20 minutes per pound, plus 10 minutes standing time

CUT	METHOD	INSTRUCTIONS	TIMING
GROUND LAMB PATTIES ½ inch	BROIL	Preheat the broiler. Broil 3 inches from the heat, turning once.	Rare: 2 minutes per side Medium-rare: 3–4 minutes per side Medium: 4–5 minutes per side Well: 6 minutes per side
	PAN-BROIL	Preheat lightly oiled heavy iron skillet over medium-high heat. Cook on both sides, turning once.	Rare: 2 minutes per side Medium-rare: 3–4 minutes per side Medium: 4–5 minutes per side Well: 6 minutes per side
	GRILL	Prepare a medium-hot fire in the grill. Place on greased grill 4 inches from coals and grill, turning once.	Rare: 2 minutes per side Medium-rare: 3–4 minutes per side Medium: 4–5 minutes per side Well: 6 minutes per side

CUT	METHOD	INSTRUCTIONS	TIMING
GROUND LAMB PATTIES ¾ inch	BROIL	Preheat the broiler. Broil 3 inches from the heat, turning once.	Rare: 3–4 minutes per side Medium-rare: 4–4½ minutes per side Medium: 5–6 minutes per side Well: 6–7 minutes per side
	PAN-BROIL	Preheat lightly oiled heavy iron skillet over medium-high heat. Cook on both sides, turning once.	Rare: 3–4 minutes per side Medium-rare: 4–4½ minutes per side Medium: 5–6 minutes per side Well: 6–7 minutes per side

CUT	METHOD	INSTRUCTIONS	TIMING
	GRILL	Prepare a medium-hot fire in the grill. Place on a greased grill 4 inches from coals and grill, turning once.	Rare: 3–4 minutes per side Medium-rare: 4–4½ minutes per side Medium: 5–6 minutes per side Well: 6–7 minutes per side
KABOBS From leg of lamb or shoulder	BROIL	Preheat broiler. Cut the meat into 1–2-inch cubes and arrange on skewers. Broil 6 inches from heat, turning and basting often.	Rare: 8–10 minutes Medium-rare: 14–17 minutes Medium: 20–25 minutes Well: 25–30 minutes
	GRILL	Prepare a medium-hot fire in the grill. Cut the meat into 1–2-inch cubes and arrange on skewers. Brush with oil or marinade. Grill 3 inches from coals on a greased grill, turning and basting often.	Rare: 8–10 minutes Medium-rare: 12–15 minutes Medium: 16–20 minutes Well: 20–24 minutes
LEG OF LAMB Bone in; 4–6 pounds	BRAISE	Heat oil in a large Dutch oven over medium-high heat. Add lamb and brown well. Add seasoning and 1 inch cooking liquid and bring to a simmer. Cover and cook slowly over low heat, basting 3 times during cooking.	1½–2 hours

CUT	METHOD	INSTRUCTIONS	TIMING
LEG OF LAMB Bone in; 4–6 pounds (*cont'd.*)	GRILL	*To Grill (Indirect Method):* Prepare a fire in the grill, letting the coals burn down to a medium-low fire. Push the coals to one side of the grill and set a drip pan on the other side. Set the cooking grate 6 inches from heat. Place the roast over the drip pan and grill with the lid down, basting often and turning several times. Add more coals as needed. Cover loosely with foil and let stand 10 minutes before carving.	2–3 hours, plus 10 minutes standing time
	ROAST	Preheat oven to 325°F. Place meat on a rack in a roasting pan. Insert meat thermometer in leg. Rub lamb with oil and seasonings and roast. Remove from oven, cover loosely with foil, and let stand for 10 minutes before carving.	Rare: 10–11 minutes per pound Medium-rare: 12–13 minutes per pound Medium: 13–15 minutes per pound Well: 18–20 minutes per pound

CUT	*METHOD*	*INSTRUCTIONS*	*TIMING*
LEG OF LAMB Bone in; 7–8 pounds	ROAST	*To Fast-Roast:* Preheat oven to 450°F. Rub roast with oil and seasonings. Place on rack in a large roasting pan. Put roast in oven and reduce heat to 325°F. Roast until desired doneness when tested with an instant-read thermometer. Remove from oven, cover loosely with foil, and let stand 10 minutes before carving.	Rare: 10–11 minutes per pound Medium-rare: 12–13 minutes per pound Medium: 13–15 minutes per pound Well: 18–20 minutes per pound, plus 10 minutes standing time
LEG OF LAMB Half, Butterflied; 2–3 pounds	BROIL	Cover lamb with oil and seasoning mixture. Place meat on rack in broiler pan, cover with waxed paper, and let stand 2 hours. Preheat broiler. Place meat on preheated broiler pan, remove waxed paper, and grill 4 inches from the heat, turning once. Remove from broiler, cover loosely with foil, and let stand 10 minutes before slicing.	Rare: 12–15 minutes per side Medium-rare: 15–17 minutes per side Medium: 18–20 minutes per side, plus 2 hours, 10 minutes standing time

CUT	METHOD	INSTRUCTIONS	TIMING
LEG OF LAMB Half, Butterflied; 2–3 pounds (*cont'd.*)	GRILL	Cover lamb with oil and seasoning mixture. Cover with waxed paper and let stand 2 hours. Prepare a medium-hot fire in the grill. Grill 6 inches from coals with lid on, turning once, until meat reaches the internal temperature of 125°F–130°F for rare. Continue cooking for a little longer for medium or well-done lamb, checking frequently. Remove from grill, cover loosely with foil, and let stand 10 minutes before slicing.	Rare: 15–17 minutes per side Medium-rare: 18–20 minutes per side Medium: 20–22 minutes per side, plus 2 hours, 10 minutes standing time
LEG OF LAMB Steaks; ¾ inch	BROIL	Preheat broiler pan. Place steaks on pan and broil 4 inches from heat, turning once.	Rare: 2 minutes per side Medium-rare: 3 minutes per side Medium: 4–5 minutes per side Well: 6 minutes per side
	GRILL	Prepare a medium-hot fire in the grill. Place on greased grill 4 inches from coals and grill, turning once.	Rare: 2 minutes per side Medium-rare: 3 minutes per side Medium: 4–5 minutes per side Well: 6 minutes per side

CUT	METHOD	INSTRUCTIONS	TIMING
	SAUTÉ	Pound lamb as you would veal. Marinate in refrigerator overnight. Pat dry before cooking. Heat oil and/or butter in large skillet over high heat. Cook quickly over high heat, turning once.	Rare: 2½–3 minutes per side Medium-rare: 3–3½ minutes per side Medium: 3½–4 minutes per side Well: 5–6 minutes per side
	STIR-FRY	Cut meat into ¼-inch thick strips. Add to hot oil in wok and cook over high heat, stirring constantly.	Rare: 3 minutes Medium-rare: 3½–4 minutes Medium: 4½ minutes Well: 5 minutes
LOIN Saddle roast, Boneless; 1½–2 pounds	ROAST	Preheat oven to 425°F. Heat large heavy skillet, without fat, over high heat. Place roast in skillet and brown on all sides, about 4 minutes. Place skillet in oven and roast until the internal temperature reaches 125°F–130°F. Continue cooking a little longer for medium or well-done lamb, checking frequently. Remove from oven, cover loosely with foil, and let stand 10 minutes before carving.	Rare: 11–12 minutes per pound Medium-rare: 13–14 minutes per pound Medium: 15–16 minutes per pound Well: 20–25 minutes per pound, plus 10 minutes standing time

CUT	METHOD	INSTRUCTIONS	TIMING
LOIN Saddle roast, Bone in; 5 pounds	ROAST	Preheat oven to 500°F. Place meat in roasting pan, top side up. Roast until the internal temperature reaches 125°F–130°F. Continue cooking a little longer for medium or well-done lamb, checking frequently. Remove from oven, cover loosely with foil, and let stand 10 minutes before carving.	20–30 minutes, plus 10 minutes standing time
RACK OF LAMB 7–8 ribs; 2 pounds	GRILL	Prepare a medium-hot fire in the grill. Place rack on greased grill 4 inches from coals, meat side up. When bottom is browned, about 15 minutes, turn and grill meat side down, moving rack as needed to avoid flare-ups. Grill until well browned, or when internal temperature reaches 125°F–130°F. Remove from grill, cover loosely with foil, and let stand 15 minutes before carving.	30–35 minutes, plus 15 minutes standing time
	ROAST	Preheat oven to 425°F. Pat meat dry. Heat large heavy skillet without fat over high heat. Place roast in skillet meat side down. Sear 2 minutes per side. Pour off any fat. Place in oven bone side down. Roast until the internal temperature reaches 125°F–130°F. Continue cooking a little longer for medium or well-done lamb, checking frequently. Remove from oven, cover loosely with foil, and let stand 10 minutes before carving.	Rare: 10–11 minutes per pound Medium-rare: 12–13 minutes per pound Medium: 13–15 minutes per pound Well: 18–20 minutes per pound, plus 10 minutes standing time

CUT	METHOD	INSTRUCTIONS	TIMING
SCALLOPS Cut from saddle or leg; ¼ inch	SAUTÉ	Heat butter and/or oil in a large skillet over medium heat. Add lamb and cook, turning once.	From saddle: 4–5 minutes per side From leg: 2–3 minutes per side
SHANKS	SIMMER	Dust shanks with seasoned flour. Heat oil in a Dutch oven over medium-high heat. Add shanks and brown on all sides. Add seasonings and 1 inch braising liquid, cover, and simmer. Turn 2 or 3 times during cooking.	1½–1¾ hours
SHOULDER ROAST Rolled; 4–5 pounds boneless, 8–9 pounds, bone in	BRAISE	Preheat oven to 325°F. Heat oil in a large Dutch oven. Add meat and brown on all sides. Add seasonings and 2 inches braising liquid. Cover and simmer in the oven.	Boneless: 2–2½ hours Bone in: 3–3½ hours
STEW MEAT, NECK	STEW	Cut boneless pieces into 1–2-inch cubes. Dust meat with seasoned flour. Heat oil in a large Dutch oven and brown a few pieces at a time and set aside. Brown aromatic vegetables (onions, carrots, etc.). Return meat to pot and cover with water, broth, or liquid. Cook slowly over low heat. Add vegetables during last 45 minutes of cooking, if desired.	1½–2 hours

PORK AND HAM

The meat of pig encompasses the fresh meat (pork), the cured meat (ham and bacon), and all the trimmings, which are used mainly for sausage.

When buying pork, look for meat that is moist and reddish pink with white fat. Avoid meat that is a pale pink-gray. The meat should be lean, firm to the touch, and fine-grained.

Cuts of Pork

Pork has four main areas from which meat is taken: the belly, the ham, or leg, the loin, and the shoulder.

Belly. The belly, or underside, of the pig is usually used for bacon and spareribs.

Leg. The leg, or ham, yields hams as well as leg cuts, such as leg cutlets and top leg roast. The leg, also known as "fresh ham," can be cooked whole with bone, or whole without bone or cut into steaks. Pigs' feet or hocks are usually braised.

Loin. Pigs have two loins, on either side of the back, and each weighs about 20 pounds. The loin is a very lean area. When cooking, add fat to keep the meat moist. The loin area of the pig includes the ribs, loin, and sirloin. The chops, rib roast, loin roast, and the ribs are cut from the loin area. The meat labeled "center cut" is the best cut from the center of the loin.

Shoulder. The shoulder of the pig is fatty and is often used to make fresh sausage or ground pork. The best way to cook the whole shoulder is by braising it.

About Ham

"Fresh ham" is a cut from the hind leg of the pig that has not been cured or smoked. "Ham" or "cooked ham" is that same portion of the pig that has been cured or smoked.

Today, unless ham is labeled "fresh ham" it can describe any cut of pork that has been put through a preserving process of curing with salt or aging with smoke. When you buy ham, make sure you know what type of ham you're buying. Some hams are partially cooked and should say clearly on the label that you must cook them to 155°F to 160°F before eating. Others will say "Fully Cooked" or "Ready to Eat" or "Ready to Serve." These are known as "fully cooked hams" and can be eaten as is, but are better tasting if baked and glazed. Imported hams such as Parma ham or prosciutto have been dry-cured and can be eaten as is.

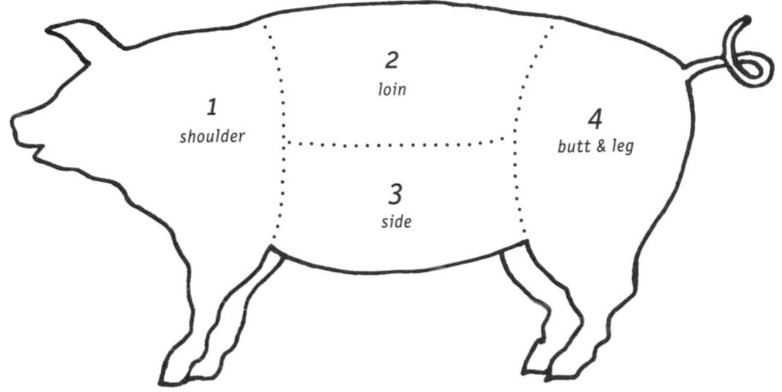

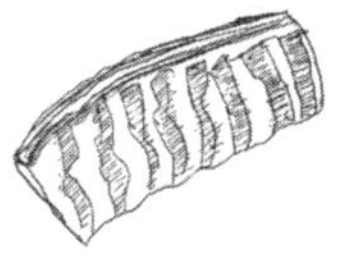
back ribs (2)

boneless sirloin steak chop (2)

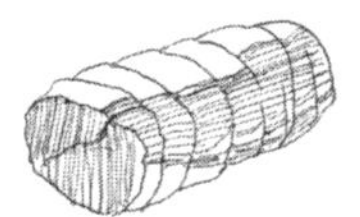
boneless top loin roast (2)

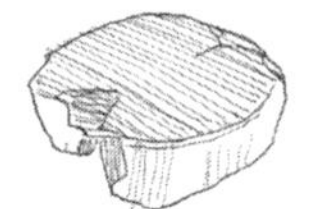
butterfly chop (2)

country-style ribs (2)

loin chop (2)

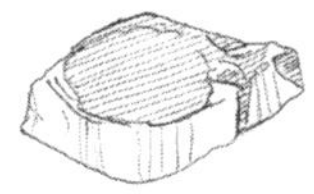
rib chop (2)

rib crown roast (2)

sirloin chop (2)

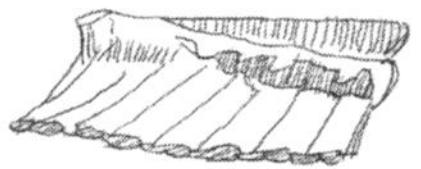
spareribs (3)

tenderloin (2)

top of shoulder (1)

Cooking Pork

Today's pork is a leaner meat that is also more tender than the pork of the past—the pigs are brought to market at a younger age. The worst thing you can do to pork is overcook it, which is what many people do. At one time pork was cooked to internal temperatures of 175°F to 185°F because of the fear of trichinosis. The meat usually came out gray, dry, and overcooked. But the trichina worm is killed at 137°F. If you cook pork to an internal temperature of 160°F, you can be absolutely sure that it is safe to eat, and the meat will be tender and succulent. For roasts, this means removing the meat from the heat when the internal temperature reaches 150°F to 155°F and letting it stand as the internal temperature continues to rise. Fattier cuts, such as ribs, should be cooked until well done, to 165°F.

If the ham has not been precooked or partially cooked, cook it for at least 18 to 25 minutes per pound in a preheated 350°F oven. With a meat thermometer, make sure the internal temperature is at least 160°F before serving it. If the ham has been precooked, the meat should still be cooked, for at least 10 minutes per pound. This will assure that the meat is heated through, and will give it more flavor. A simple basting sauce for ham is a mixture of 1 cup orange juice, 1 cup brown sugar, and 1 cup dry mustard.

Judging Doneness

Pork must be thoroughly cooked; therefore, the final temperatures for pork—after standing—are only for medium (155°F–165°F) to well done (180°F–185°F). When roasting, remove meat from the oven when the meat thermometer registers 10 degrees less than the desired temperature. The meat will continue to cook while standing.

TIMINGS: Pork

TYPE	*METHOD*	*INSTRUCTIONS*	*TIMING*
CHOPS Blade; ¾–1 inch	BRAISE	Preheat oven to 350°F. Heat oil in a large Dutch oven over medium-high heat. Add the chops and brown on both sides. Drain off excess oil. Add 1 inch braising liquid, seasonings, and precooked vegetables, if desired. Cover and bake for 15 minutes. Remove cover and continue the braise until meat is tender and the internal temperature reaches 150°F–155°F.	35–45 minutes
CHOPS Loin, Rib, Sirloin, Top loin—Bone in; ½ inch	BRAISE	Heat oil in a large Dutch oven over high heat. Add chops and sear on both sides. Add seasonings and ½ inch braising liquid. Cover, reduce heat to low, and cook until tender, turning once.	11–14 minutes
	GRILL	Prepare a medium-hot fire in the grill. Place chops on a greased grill 4 inches from coals. Brush with oil or butter. Sear on the first side. Cover grill. Cook 3 minutes. Then turn and sear the second side. Brush with oil or butter, cover grill, and cook until done.	8 minutes
	PAN-FRY	Dust the chops with seasoned flour. If desired, dip in egg wash and coat with crumbs. Heat oil in a heavy skillet over medium-high heat. Add chops and brown on both sides, turning once.	3–4 minutes per side

TYPE	METHOD	INSTRUCTIONS	TIMING
CHOPS Loin, Rib, Sirloin, Top loin—Bone in; ½ inch *(cont'd.)*	SAUTÉ	Heat oil in a heavy skillet over medium-high heat. Add chops and brown on both sides. Reduce the heat and continue cooking until meat is no longer pink inside.	8 minutes
CHOPS Loin, Rib, Sirloin, Top loin—Bone in; ¾ inch	BRAISE	Heat oil in a large Dutch oven over high heat. Add chops and sear on both sides. Add seasonings and ½ inch braising liquid. Cover, reduce heat to low, and cook until tender, turning once.	11–14 minutes
	GRILL	Prepare a medium-hot fire in the grill. Place chops on a greased grill 4 inches from coals. Brush with oil or butter. Sear on the first side. Cover grill. Cook about 4 minutes. Then turn and sear the second side. Brush with oil or butter, cover grill, and cook until done.	8–10 minutes
	PAN-FRY	Dust chops with seasoned flour. If desired, dip in egg wash and coat with crumbs. Heat oil in a heavy skillet over medium-high heat. Add chops and brown on both sides, turning once.	4–5 minutes per side
	SAUTÉ	Heat oil in a heavy skillet over medium-high heat. Add chops and brown on both sides. Reduce the heat and continue cooking until meat is no longer pink inside.	10 minutes
CHOPS Loin, Rib, Sirloin, Top loin—Bone in; 1 inch	BAKE	Preheat oven to 250°F. Heat oil in a large heavy skillet over medium-high heat. Add chops and sear 1 minute on each side. Cover skillet and place in oven. Bake until tender. Let stand for 5 minutes before serving.	10 minutes, plus 5 minutes standing time

TYPE	*METHOD*	*INSTRUCTIONS*	*TIMING*
	BRAISE	Heat oil in a large Dutch oven over high heat. Add chops and sear on both sides. Add seasonings and ½ inch braising liquid. Cover, reduce heat to low, and cook until tender, turning once.	11–14 minutes
	GRILL	Prepare a medium-hot fire in the grill. Place the chops on a greased grill 4 inches from coals. Brush with oil or butter. Sear on the first side. Cover grill. Then turn and sear the second side. Brush with oil or butter, cover grill, and cook until done.	5–6 minutes per side
	PAN-FRY	Dust chops with seasoned flour. If desired, dip in egg wash and coat with crumbs. Heat oil in a large heavy skillet over medium-high heat. Add chops and brown on both sides, turning once.	5–6 minutes per side
	SAUTÉ	Heat oil in a large heavy skillet over medium-high heat. Add chops and brown on both sides. Reduce heat and continue cooking until meat is no longer pink inside.	12 minutes
CHOPS Loin, Rib, Sirloin, Top loin—Bone in; 1½ inches	BAKE	Preheat oven to 250°F. Heat oil in a large heavy skillet over medium-high heat. Add chops and sear 1 minute on each side. Cover skillet and place in oven. Bake until tender. Let stand 5 minutes before serving.	15 minutes, plus 5 minutes standing time
	BRAISE	Heat oil in a large Dutch oven over high heat. Add chops and sear on both sides. Add seasonings and 1 inch braising liquid. Cover, reduce heat to low, and cook until tender, turning once.	11–14 minutes

TYPE	METHOD	INSTRUCTIONS	TIMING
CHOPS Loin, Rib, Sirloin, Top loin—Bone in; 1½ inches (*cont'd.*)	GRILL	Prepare a medium-hot fire in the grill. Place chops on a greased grill 4 inches from coals. Brush with oil or butter. Sear on the first side. Cover grill. Then turn and sear the second side. Brush with oil or butter, cover grill, and cook until done.	7–8 minutes per side
	PAN-FRY	Dust the chops with seasoned flour. If desired, dip in egg wash and coat with crumbs. Heat oil in a large heavy skillet over medium-high heat. Add chops and brown on both sides, turning once.	7–8 minutes per side
CHOPS Loin, Rib, Sirloin, Top loin—Bone in; 1½ inches (*cont'd.*)	SAUTÉ	Heat oil in a large heavy skillet over medium-high heat. Add chops and brown on both sides. Reduce the heat and continue cooking until meat is no longer pink inside.	14–16 minutes
CHOPS Loin, Rib, Sirloin, Top loin— Bone in; Double cut, 2–2½ inches	BRAISE	Heat oil in a large Dutch oven over high heat. Add chops and sear on both sides. Cover, reduce heat to low, and cook 20 minutes, turning frequently. Add 1 inch braising liquid, cover, and simmer.	1¼ hours total
CHOPS Loin, Rib, Sirloin, Top loin— Boneless; ½ inch	BRAISE	Heat oil in a large Dutch oven over high heat. Add chops and sear on both sides. Add seasonings and 1 inch braising liquid. Cover, reduce heat to low, and cook until tender, turning once.	10–14 minutes
	DEEP-FRY	Heat oil to 375°F. Dust chops with seasoned flour, dip in egg wash, and coat with crumbs or dip into batter. Deep-fry until golden brown. Drain on paper towels before serving.	1½–2 minutes

TYPE	***METHOD***	***INSTRUCTIONS***	***TIMING***
	GRILL	Prepare a medium-hot fire in the grill. Place the chops on a greased grill 4 inches from coals. Brush with oil or butter. Sear on the first side. Cover grill. Cook about 2 minutes. Turn and sear the second side. Brush with oil or butter, cover grill, and cook until done.	4–6 minutes
	PAN-FRY	Dust the chops with seasoned flour. If desired, dip in egg wash and coat with crumbs. Heat oil in a large heavy skillet over medium-high heat. Add chops and brown on both sides, turning once.	2–3 minutes per side
	SAUTÉ	Heat oil in a large heavy skillet over medium-high heat. Add chops and brown on both sides. Reduce heat and continue cooking until meat is no longer pink inside.	6 minutes
	STIR-FRY	Cut chops into ¼-inch-thick strips. Add to hot oil in wok and cook, stirring constantly.	3 minutes
CHOPS Loin, Rib, Sirloin, Top loin—Boneless; ¾ inch	BRAISE	Heat oil in a large Dutch oven over high heat. Add chops and sear on both sides. Add seasonings and 1 inch braising liquid. Cover, reduce heat to low, and cook until tender, turning once.	11–14 minutes
	GRILL	Prepare a medium-hot fire in the grill. Place the chops 4 inches from coals. Brush with oil or butter. Sear on the first side. Cover grill. Cook about 3 minutes. Turn and sear the second side. Brush with oil or butter, cover grill, and cook until done.	6–8 minutes

TYPE	*METHOD*	*INSTRUCTIONS*	*TIMING*
CHOPS Loin, Rib, Sirloin, Top loin—Boneless; ¾ inch (*cont'd.*)	PAN-FRY	Dust chops with seasoned flour. If desired, dip in egg wash and coat with crumbs. Heat oil in a heavy skillet over medium-high heat. Add chops and brown on both sides, turning once.	3–4 minutes per side
	SAUTÉ	Heat oil in a skillet over medium-high heat. Add chops and brown on both sides. Reduce the heat and continue cooking until meat is no longer pink inside.	8 minutes
	STIR-FRY	Cut meat into ¼-inch strips. Add to hot oil in wok and cook, stirring constantly.	3 minutes
CHOPS Loin, Rib, Sirloin, Top loin—Boneless; 1 inch	BRAISE	Heat oil in a large Dutch oven over high heat. Add the meat and sear on both sides. Add seasonings and 1 inch braising liquid. Cover, reduce heat to low, and cook until tender, turning once.	11–14 minutes
	GRILL	Prepare a medium-hot fire in the grill. Place the chops on a greased grill 4 inches from coals. Brush with oil or butter. Sear on the first side. Cover grill. Cook about 4 minutes. Turn and sear the second side. Brush with oil or butter, cover grill, and cook until done.	8–10 minutes
	PAN-FRY	Dust the chops with seasoned flour. If desired, dip in egg wash and coat with crumbs. Heat oil in a heavy skillet over medium-high heat. Add chops and brown on both sides, turning once.	4–5 minutes per side
	SAUTÉ	Heat oil in a skillet over medium-high heat. Add meat and brown on both sides. Reduce the heat and continue cooking until meat is no longer pink inside.	10 minutes

TYPE	METHOD	INSTRUCTIONS	TIMING
	STIR-FRY	Cut meat into ¼-inch strips. Add to hot oil in wok and cook, stirring constantly.	3 minutes
CHOPS Loin, Rib, Sirloin, Top loin—Boneless; 1½ inches	BRAISE	Heat oil in a large Dutch oven over high heat. Add chops and sear on both sides. Add seasonings and 1 inch braising liquid. Cover, reduce heat to low, and cook until tender, turning once.	11–14 minutes
	GRILL	Prepare a medium-hot fire in the grill. Place chops on a greased grill 4 inches from coals. Brush with oil or butter. Sear on the first side. Cover grill. Cook about 6 minutes. Turn and sear the second side. Brush with oil or butter, cover grill, and cook until done.	12–14 minutes
	PAN-FRY	Dust chops with seasoned flour. If desired, dip in egg wash and coat with crumbs. Heat oil in a large heavy skillet over medium-high heat. Add chops and brown on both sides, turning once.	6–7 minutes per side
	SAUTÉ	Heat oil in a large heavy skillet over medium-high heat. Add chops and brown on both sides. Reduce the heat and continue cooking until meat is no longer pink inside.	12–14 minutes
	STIR-FRY	Cut meat into ¼-inch strips. Add to hot oil in wok and cook, stirring constantly.	3 minutes

TYPE	METHOD	INSTRUCTIONS	TIMING
HAM HOCKS AND PIGS' FEET, FRESH	BRAISE	Heat butter and/or oil in a large Dutch oven. Add feet and brown on all sides. Add 1 inch braising liquid, seasonings, and vegetables, if desired. Bring to a simmer. Cover pan and braise until meat is tender.	1½–1¾ hours
	BROIL	Preheat broiler. Rub braised or stewed hocks with butter. Roll in parsley and crumbs. Broil 6 inches from heat, turning once.	Until golden
	STEW	Wash under cold running water. Place in large pot and cover with cold water. Add vegetables and seasonings and bring to a boil. Skim water. Reduce heat to simmer, cover pot, and cook over low heat until meat is tender.	1¾–2 hours
HAM HOCKS AND PIGS' FEET, SMOKED	STEW	Place in large pot with water to cover, seasonings, and aromatic vegetables. Bring to a boil, reduce heat, and simmer until tender.	1¾–2 hours
KABOBS 1½-inch chunks cut from Loin, Shoulder, Sirloin, Tenderloin	GRILL	Prepare a medium-hot fire in the grill. Trim away all visible fat. Arrange on skewers and brush with marinade or seasoned oil. Sear over the hottest part of the fire to brown each side quickly. Then move to cooler area of grill, cover, and continue grilling until kabobs are cooked through and reach an internal temperature of 155°F.	9–12 minutes

TYPE	*METHOD*	*INSTRUCTIONS*	*TIMING*
RIBS Spare, Country-style, Back ribs; 6 pounds; 2 racks	BAKE	Preheat oven to 300°F. Place ribs in single layer on baking sheet and season well. Cover with foil and bake, basting occasionally, until meat is tender and begins to pull away from bone. The internal temperature should reach 165°F–175°F.	1¼–1½ hours
	BARBECUE	Prepare a medium-low fire in the grill. Push the coals to one side and place a drip pan on the other side. Place ribs over drip pan and cover grill. Maintain a temperature inside the grill of 220°F–250°F, adding more coals and wood chips as needed. Baste and turn occasionally; barbecue until tender and meat begins to pull away from bones. Cover and let stand 20–40 minutes before serving.	2–2½ hours, plus 20–40 minutes standing time
	GRILL	Bake ribs first. Prepare a medium-hot fire in the grill. Brush ribs with barbecue sauce. Grill 5 inches from coals, with grill lid on. Turn once.	5–10 minutes per side
	ROAST	Preheat oven to 425°F. Place ribs on a rack in roasting pan and season well. Brush on glaze and roast, turning ribs after the first 45 minutes and brushing on more glaze.	30 minutes per pound

TYPE	*METHOD*	*INSTRUCTIONS*	*TIMING*
ROASTS Crown; 5–8 pounds	ROAST	Preheat oven to 325°F. Place roast in a roasting pan and roast uncovered. Halfway through roasting time, add the stuffing and cover with foil. Foil also can be added to the bone tips to prevent burning. Remove all foil for last 15 minutes of roasting. Remove from the oven when the internal temperature reaches 150°F–155°F. Cover loosely with foil and let stand 15 minutes before carving.	20–22 minutes per pound, plus 15 minutes standing time
ROASTS Leg of pork, whole—fresh ham, Bone in or boneless; 15–20 pounds	ROAST	Preheat oven to 450°F. Place roast skin side up in a shallow roasting pan on lowest rack in oven. Roast for 15 minutes. Reduce heat to 325°F and continue roasting until meat reaches an internal temperature of 150°F–155°F. Remove from oven, cover loosely with foil, and let stand 15 minutes before carving.	4¾–5 hours, plus 15 minutes standing time
ROASTS Leg of pork, Rump end or Center cut—fresh ham; 4–6 pounds	ROAST	Preheat oven to 325°F. Place roast in shallow roasting pan and add 1 cup stock or water. Roast until meat reaches an internal temperature of 145°F–155°F, basting occasionally. Add more liquid if pan becomes dry. Remove from oven, cover loosely with foil, and let stand 15 minutes before carving.	20–22 minutes per pound, plus 15 minutes standing time

TYPE	METHOD	INSTRUCTIONS	TIMING
ROASTS Loin; Boneless; 2½–3 pounds	GRILL	Prepare a medium-hot fire in the grill. Push all the coals to one side and place a drip pan on the other side. Brush the meat with oil and place over the drip pan. Cover the grill and grill until the internal temperature reaches 150°F–155°F. Remove the meat, cover loosely with foil, and let stand 15 minutes before slicing.	20–22 minutes per pound, plus 15 minutes standing time
	ROAST	Preheat oven to 450°F. Place the meat on a rack in roasting pan. Roast for 10 minutes, then reduce the heat to 250°F. Roast until internal temperature reads 150°F–155°F. Remove the meat from the oven, cover loosely with foil, and let stand 15 minutes before slicing.	22–25 minutes per pound, plus 15 minutes standing time
ROASTS Loin; Rolled; 3–5 pounds	BRAISE	Heat oil in a large Dutch oven over medium-high heat. Add meat and sear on all sides. Add 2 inches braising liquid. Cover and let simmer. Baste the meat with liquid during braising, adding more as needed.	2–2½ hours
	GRILL	*To Grill Indirectly:* Prepare a medium-hot fire in the grill. Push all the coals to one side and place a drip pan on the other side. Brush the meat with oil and place over the drip pan. Cover the grill and grill until the internal temperature of the meat reaches 150°F–155°F. Remove the meat, cover loosely with foil, and let stand 15 minutes before slicing.	20–22 minutes per pound, plus 15 minutes standing time

TYPE	*METHOD*	*INSTRUCTIONS*	*TIMING*
ROASTS Loin; Rolled; 3–5 pounds	ROAST	Preheat oven to 350°F. Place fat side up on a rack in a roasting pan. Rub with salt and pepper. Roast uncovered until the internal temperature of the meat reaches 150°F–155°F. Remove from the oven, cover with loosely with foil, and let stand 15 minutes before slicing.	20–22 minutes per pound, plus 15 minutes standing time
ROASTS Loin; Bone in; 5–6 pounds	ROAST	Preheat oven to 450°F. Place fat side up on a rack in a roasting pan. Rub with salt and pepper. Roast for 15 minutes, then reduce oven temperature to 250°F. Roast uncovered until the internal temperature of the meat reaches 150°F–155°F. Remove from oven, loosely cover with foil, and let stand 15 minutes before carving.	105–115 minutes, plus 15 minutes standing time
ROASTS Picnic shoulder, fresh—Shoulder ham; Boneless	ROAST	Preheat oven to 325°F. Place ham in a roasting pan and roast, basting occasionally with pan juices, until the internal temperature reaches 165°F. Remove from oven, cover loosely with foil, and let stand 15 minutes before slicing.	25–30 minutes per pound, plus 15 minutes standing time
ROASTS Picnic shoulder, smoked—Shoulder ham; Bone in or boneless	ROAST	Preheat oven to 325°F. Place ham in a roasting pan and roast, basting occasionally with pan juices, until the internal temperature reaches 165°F. Remove from oven, cover loosely with foil, and let stand 15 minutes before carving.	25–30 minutes per pound, plus 15 minutes standing time

TYPE	METHOD	INSTRUCTIONS	TIMING
ROASTS Shoulder, Butt; Boneless; 3–5 pounds	BRAISE	Heat oil in a large Dutch oven over medium-high heat. Add meat and sear on all sides. Add seasonings and 1 inch braising liquid. Cover and let simmer, basting often, until meat is tender and the internal temperature reaches 160°F–165°F. Remove from oven, loosely cover with foil, and let stand 15 minutes before slicing.	1¾–2½ hours, plus 15 minutes standing time
	ROAST	Preheat oven to 450°F. Place meat on a rack in roasting pan. Roast for 10 minutes. Reduce heat to 350°F and roast until internal temperature reaches 170°F. Remove from oven, cover loosely with foil, and let stand 15 minutes before slicing.	35 minutes per pound plus 35 minutes, plus 15 minutes standing time
	STEW	Cut meat into 3-inch cubes. Heat oil in a large Dutch oven over medium-high heat. Add meat and brown. Add seasonings, braising liquid to cover, and vegetables, if desired. Simmer until tender.	1 hour
ROASTS Shoulder, bone in; 5–7 pounds	BARBECUE	Prepare a medium-low fire in the grill. Push the coals to one side and place a drip pan on the other side. Place meat over drip pan and cover grill. Maintain a temperature inside the grill of 220°F–250°F, adding more coals and wood chips as needed. Baste and turn occasionally and barbecue until the meat shreds easily with a fork inserted near the bone. Remove outer skin (cracklings) and pull meat away from bone.	6–8 hours

TYPE	*METHOD*	*INSTRUCTIONS*	*TIMING*
ROASTS Shoulder, bone in; 5–7 pounds (*cont'd.*)	BRAISE	Heat oil in a large Dutch oven over medium-high heat. Add meat and sear on all sides. Add seasonings and 1 inch braising liquid. Cover and let simmer, basting often, until meat is tender and the internal temperature reaches 160°F–165°F. Remove from heat and let stand for 15 minutes before slicing.	1¾–2½ hours, plus 15 minutes standing time
	ROAST	Preheat oven to 450°F. Place meat on a rack in roasting pan. Roast for 10 minutes. Reduce heat to 350°F and roast until internal temperature reaches 170°F. Remove from oven, cover loosely with foil, and let stand 15 minutes before carving.	30 minutes per pound plus 30 minutes, plus 15 minutes standing time
STEAKS Cut from shoulder or Boston butt; ¾ inch	BRAISE	Preheat oven to 350°F. Heat oil in a large heavy skillet over medium-high heat. Add steaks and brown on both sides. Drain off excess oil. Add seasonings, 1 inch braising liquid, and precooked vegetables, if desired. Cover and bake 15 minutes. Remove cover and continue baking until meat is tender and the internal temperature reaches 150°F–155°F.	35–45 minutes
	BROIL	Preheat broiler. Arrange steaks on preheated broiler pan. Broil 3 inches from heat, turning once, until the internal temperature reaches 150°F.	5–6 minutes per side
	GRILL	Prepare a medium-hot fire in grill. Place steaks on greased grill 4 inches from coals and grill, turning once, until the internal temperature reaches 150°F.	5–6 minutes per side

TYPE	METHOD	INSTRUCTIONS	TIMING
SUCKLING PIG 10–15 pounds	ROAST	Ask your butcher to prepare the pig. Make sure it's cleaned and all organs are removed. Preheat oven to 350°F. Place an apple in pig's mouth. Rub the entire pig with oil or fat. Sprinkle with salt and pepper. Stuff the cavity with a breadcrumb recipe and sew it shut. Place the pig on its stomach on a rack in a large oiled roasting pan. Tie the front legs with knees bent to the rack. Stretch hind legs backward and tie together. Cover ears and tail with foil. Cut the back of the pig in long diagonal cuts about 3 inches apart. Roast, basting every 15 minutes with butter, until pig releases juices; then start basting with juices from the pig. Roast about 2½ hours. Remove foil and continue roasting until internal temperature reaches 165°F, basting every 15 minutes. Remove from oven and let stand 15 minutes before carving.	3 hours, plus 15 minutes standing time
TENDERLOIN CUTLETS OR MEDALLIONS ½ inch	SAUTÉ	Heat butter and/or oil in a large skillet over high heat. Add medallions and sear, on both sides, turning once.	1½ minutes per side
	BROIL	Preheat broiler. Place medallions on preheated broiler and brush with seasoned oil or marinade. Broil 4 inches from heat, turning once.	1½ minutes per side
	GRILL	Prepare a medium-hot fire in the grill. Brush medallions with seasoned oil or marinade and grill 4 inches from coals, turning once.	1½ minutes per side

TYPE	*METHOD*	*INSTRUCTIONS*	*TIMING*
TENDERLOIN CUTLETS OR MEDALLIONS 1 inch	BROIL	Preheat broiler. Place medallions on preheated broiler and brush with seasoned oil or marinade. Broil 4 inches from heat, turning once.	2 minutes per side
	GRILL	Prepare a medium-hot fire in the grill. Brush medallions with seasoned oil or marinade and grill 4 inches from coals, turning once.	2 minutes per side
	SAUTÉ	Heat butter and/or oil in a large skillet over high heat. Add medallions and sear on both sides, turning once.	2 minutes per side
TENDERLOIN, WHOLE 1–1¼ pounds	BROIL	Preheat the broiler. Coat meat with oil and roll in herbs or spice mix. Place tenderloin on rack over shallow broiling pan. Broil 4 inches from heat, turning once, until meat reaches an internal temperature of 150°F–155°F. Remove from broiler, cover loosely with foil, and let stand 5 minutes before slicing.	5–6 minutes per side, plus 5 minutes standing time
	GRILL	Prepare a hot fire in the grill. Coat tenderloin with oil and dust with herbs or spice mix. Sear meat on both sides over the hottest area of the grill, 4 inches from the coals, turning once, about 2½ minutes per side. Move to a cooler area of the grill and grill, turning occasionally, until tenderloin reaches an internal temperature of 150F°–155°F. Remove from grill, cover loosely with foil, and let stand 5 minutes before slicing.	15–17 minutes, plus 5 minutes standing time

TYPE	METHOD	INSTRUCTIONS	TIMING
	GRILL	Prepare a medium-hot fire in the grill. Butterfly the meat by cutting lengthwise down the center and pounding to a thickness of ½ inch. Coat meat on both sides with oil and dust with herbs or a spice mix. Grill 4 inches from the coals, turning once, until tenderloin reaches an internal temperature of 150°–155°F. Remove from grill, cover loosely with foil, and let stand 5 minutes before slicing.	4–5 minutes per side, plus 5 minutes standing time
	GRILL	*To Grill (Indirect Method):* Prepare a medium-hot fire in the grill. Push the coals to one side and place a drip pan on the other side. Coat tenderloin with oil and roll in herbs or spice mix. Place the meat directly over the coals and sear on both sides, 1½ minutes per side. Then move meat over drip pan, cover grill, and cook, turning occasionally until the internal temperature reaches 150°F–155°F. Remove tenderloin from grill, cover loosely with foil, and let stand 5 minutes before slicing.	11–16 minutes, plus 5 minutes standing time
	PAN-FRY	Heat oil in a large skillet over medium-high heat. Dust meat with seasoned flour. Sear tenderloin, turning once, then reduce heat and cook gently until meat reaches an internal temperature of 150°F–155°F. Remove from skillet, cover loosely with foil, and let stand 5 minutes before slicing.	7–8 minutes, plus 5 minutes standing time

TYPE	METHOD	INSTRUCTIONS	TIMING
TENDERLOIN, WHOLE 1–1¼ pounds *(cont'd.)*	ROAST	Preheat oven to 500°F. Place meat on a rack in roasting pan and season well. Brush on glaze and roast until tenderloin reaches an internal temperature of 150–155°F. Remove meat from oven, cover loosely with foil, and let stand 5–10 minutes before slicing.	18–22 minutes, plus 5–10 minutes standing time

TIMINGS: Ham and Bacon

TYPE	METHOD	INSTRUCTIONS	TIMING
COUNTRY HAM Whole or half	BAKE	Place ham in a large pot and cover with cold water. Soak 24–48 hours, changing the water once or twice. Scrub ham and rinse well. Return to pot, cover with fresh cold water, and bring to a boil. Reduce heat and simmer until bone is loose, 2½–3 hours. Let ham cool in liquid, then drain. Remove skin and fat. Let stand 30 minutes and preheat oven to 350°F. Arrange meat side up on a rack in a roasting pan. Brush with glaze. Bake 30 minutes or until meat reaches an internal temperature of 140°F. Cover loosely with foil and let stand 30 minutes before carving.	Presoak: 24–48 hours Simmer: 2½–3 hours Bake: 30 minutes Standing Time: 1 hour
HAM, FRESH Bone in; 10–14 pounds	ROAST	Preheat oven to 325°F. Place ham in a roasting pan and roast, basting occasionally with pan juices, until the internal temperature reaches 150°F–155°F. Remove from oven, cover loosely with foil, and let stand 15 minutes before carving.	25–30 minutes per pound, plus 15 minutes standing time

TYPE	METHOD	INSTRUCTIONS	TIMING
HAM, PARTIALLY COOKED Boneless; 12–14 pounds	GRILL	Prepare a medium-hot fire in the grill. Push all the coals to one side and place a drip pan on the other side. Place ham over the drip pan. Cover the grill. Grill until the ham reaches an internal temperature of 150°F–155°F. Remove from grill, cover loosely with foil, and let stand 20 minutes before slicing.	25–30 minutes per pound, plus 20 minutes standing time
	ROAST	Preheat oven to 325°F. Remove skin. Trim away all but ½-inch layer of fat. Place meat, fat side up, in roasting pan. Roast until the ham reaches an internal temperature of 150°F–155°F. If glazing is desired, increase the temperature to 425°F during the last 15 minutes and brush with glaze. Brush on more glaze every 5 minutes. Remove from oven, cover loosely with foil, and let stand 20 minutes before slicing.	25–30 minutes per pound, plus 20 minutes standing time
HAM, FULLY COOKED Boneless	BAKE	*To Bake Glazed:* Preheat oven to 350°F. Place ham on a rack in a roasting pan, fat side up. Bake until the ham reaches an internal temperature of 130°F, about 1 hour. Spread glaze or sauce over ham. Stud ham with cloves and/or place pineapple rings on ham. Return to oven. Bake 1 more hour, basting every 15 minutes. Remove from oven, cover loosely with foil, and let stand 20 minutes before slicing.	2 hours, plus 20 minutes standing time

TYPE	*METHOD*	*INSTRUCTIONS*	*TIMING*
HAM, FULLY COOKED Boneless (*cont'd.*)	GRILL	Prepare a medium-hot fire in the grill. Push all the coals to one side and place a drip pan on the other side. Place ham over the drip pan. Cover the grill. Grill until the ham reaches an internal temperature of 140°F. Remove from grill, cover loosely with foil, and let stand 20 minutes before slicing.	10–15 minutes per pound
	ROAST	Preheat oven to 325°F. Place ham in roasting pan and glaze or baste while roasting. Roast until the ham reaches an internal temperature of 140°F. Remove from oven, cover loosely with foil, and let stand 20 minutes before slicing.	10–15 minutes per pound, plus 20 minutes standing time
HAM STEAKS Partially cooked; ¾–1 inch	BAKE	Preheat oven to 325°F. Brush steaks with glaze or cover with herb paste or spice rub. Bake, uncovered, until heated through.	20 minutes
	BROIL	Preheat broiler. Place meat in broiler pan 4 inches from heat with fat facing back of broiler. Broil, turning once.	9 minutes per side
	BRAISE	Heat a lightly greased Dutch oven over medium-high heat. Add steaks and brown on both sides. Pour the drippings from the pan, then add seasonings and 1 inch braising liquid. Cover, reduce heat to simmer, and cook, turning the meat once.	20 minutes
	GRILL	Prepare a fire in the grill and let the coals burn down to medium low. Place the steaks 5 inches from the coals and grill, turning once.	10 minutes per side

TYPE	*METHOD*	*INSTRUCTIONS*	*TIMING*
	PAN-BROIL	Heat a heavy skillet over high heat. Add steaks and brown on both sides.	6–7 minutes per side
	PAN-FRY	Heat a lightly greased heavy skillet over medium-high heat. Add steaks and brown on both sides.	8 minutes per side
HAM STEAKS Fully cooked; ½–¾ inch	BROIL	Preheat broiler. Place meat in broiler pan and broil 4 inches from heat.	3–5 minutes
	GRILL	Prepare a fire in the grill and let it burn down to medium-low coals. Grill 4 inches from coals. Do not turn.	4–5 minutes
	PAN-BROIL	Heat heavy skillet over high heat. Add steaks and brown on both sides.	3 minutes per side
	PAN-FRY	Heat a lightly oiled heavy skillet over low to medium heat. Add meat and sauté on both sides until brown.	2–3 minutes per side
BACON	BROIL	Place bacon strips on cold broiling pan or rack. Broil 4–6 inches from the heat, turning often. Drain on paper towels before serving.	10–15 minutes
	ROAST	Preheat oven to 400°F. Place bacon on rack in roasting pan uncovered. Do not turn. Blot with paper towels before serving.	20 minutes
	SAUTÉ	Add bacon to cold skillet and cook over medium to low heat until crisp, turning once. Drain on paper towels before serving.	8–10 minutes
BACON, CANADIAN Whole	ROAST	Preheat oven to 325°F. Place bacon on rack in roasting pan uncovered. Do not turn. Roast until the internal temperature reaches 160°F.	35 minutes per pound

TYPE	*METHOD*	*INSTRUCTIONS*	*TIMING*
BACON, CANADIAN Slices, ⅛–¼ inch	BROIL	Place in a cold broiler pan. Broil 4 inches from heat, turning often.	6–8 minutes
	SAUTÉ	Lightly oil a large skillet and heat over medium heat. Add the bacon and sauté until browned and heated through, turning often.	3–5 minutes

SAUSAGES

Sausages can be found in almost every nation around the globe because they provide a way to preserve meat for short or long periods without refrigeration. Most traditional sausages are pork-based, with beef or veal added. Health-conscious societies have an assortment of fish, poultry, and vegetable sausages available as well.

Types of Sausage

Sausages are divided into three categories.

Cooked Sausage. Cooked sausage may be smoked or cooked by some other method. The texture of these sausages ranges from very fine, such as frankfurters, to coarse, such as cooked salami. These cooked sausages are safe to eat without further cooking, but most, like frankfurters, are best steamed, poached, grilled, or fried. Mortadella, bologna, and liverwurst are examples of a few that are served without further cooking. Cooked smoked sausages with a coarse texture, such as kielbasa, are best pan-fried, grilled, or broiled. These sausages are less perishable than fresh sausage, but should be cooked within 3 to 5 days of purchase.

Dry or Semidry Fully Cured Sausage. Sausage made from fresh meat that is cured and dried during processing can be eaten without further cooking. Fully dried sausage, such as pepperoni, will even keep unrefrigerated. Semidry sausage, such as summer sausage and Thuringer, are ready to eat but require refrigeration. They should be used within 2 to 3 weeks.

Fresh (Uncooked) Sausage. Usually made from ground or chopped meat combined with herbs and spices, fresh sausage has a slightly coarse texture. It may come as bulk sausage, links, or patties. Fresh sausage links are best when they are poached, simmered, or slowly pan-fried, then grilled or broiled. Never microwave fresh sausage links; they will burst. Pan-frying is best for thick fresh sausages because it drains off much of the fat. When pan-frying or grilling fresh sausage links without precooking, you must allow for longer cooking times. Most sausages contain pork, so they should be cooked until well done, to an internal temperature of at least 140°F. Fresh sausage is perishable and should be cooked within 2 days of purchase.

A Guide to Sausage

FRESH UNCOOKED SAUSAGES

- Bratwurst. A German sausage made from pork and veal and flavored with ginger, nutmeg, and coriander or caraway seeds. It's best poached or simmered first, then grilled or broiled.
- Chorizo. A Mexican pork sausage seasoned with garlic and chiles, usually cooked without the casing.
- Country sausage (pork sausage). The American breakfast sausage comes in bulk, link, and patty form. It is often flavored with sage and pepper. It is best slowly pan-fried or simmered first, then broiled or grilled.
- Gayette. A French sausage made from pork liver, bacon, and garlic. The shape is flat. Usually baked and served cold.
- Italian sausage (hot or sweet). This pork sausage is typically flavored with garlic and fennel. The hot version also has chile peppers. Italian turkey sausage has become increasingly available. This sausage is best pan-fried or simmered first, then broiled or grilled.
- Kishke. A Jewish-American sausage made of beef, matzo meal, fat, and onions.

PRECOOKED SAUSAGES

- Bauerwurst. A coarse German sausage made with beef and pork. It is smoked and highly seasoned.
- Bockwurst. A German sausage that is off-white in color, similar to a frankfurter in texture, but larger and thicker. Made with veal or veal and pork.
- Boudin blanc. A white French sausage made from poultry, veal, pork, or rabbit and mixed with breadcrumbs.
- Bratwurst (precooked). A German sausage that is off-white in color and made from pork. The texture of the meat is coarse.
- Frankfurter (wiener). A fine-textured sausage that may be made from beef, pork, chicken, or turkey.
- Kielbasa. A Polish pork sausage flavored with garlic and smoked. Sold in medium-size to large links. Turkey kielbasa is also available.

- Knackwurst. A German sausage made from beef and pork and flavored with garlic. It is a fine-textured meat similar to a frankfurter, but larger and thicker.

CURED AND DRIED SAUSAGES

- Cervelat. A French sausage made from chopped pork and/or beef and seasoned with herbs and spices. It is preserved by curing, drying, and smoking and has a semidry, moist, soft texture.
- Chorizo. A Spanish pork sausage mildly flavored with chiles. Resembles pepperoni in size and shape.
- Pepperoni. The air-dried Italian sausage that is favored on pizza. It can be quite spicy.
- Salami. Italian sausage made from pork and/or beef, highly seasoned with garlic and spices and air-dried.

TIMINGS: Sausage

TYPE	*METHOD*	*INSTRUCTIONS*	*TIMING*
ANDOUILLETTE (pork, veal) Fresh raw	BAKE	Preheat oven to 350°F. Place the sausages on a rack in a baking pan with ½ inch water in bottom of pan. Bake uncovered.	10–45 minutes, depending on size
	GRILL	Prepare a medium-hot fire in the grill. Poach or pan-fry the sausages, but do not prick them before cooking; the drippings cause flare-ups. Place the sausages on a greased grill 6 inches from coals. Sear on all sides, then cover grill and cook slowly, turning often for even browning.	7–15 minutes

TYPE	METHOD	INSTRUCTIONS	TIMING
ANDOUILLETTE (pork, veal) Fresh raw (*cont'd.*)	PAN-FRY	Heat a large heavy skillet over medium heat with a light film of oil. Place sausages side by side in pan. Cover. Shake pan occasionally to brown sausage evenly.	5–15 minutes
	PAN-FRY	*To Pan-Fry/Simmer:* Bring ½ cup of water or liquid to a boil in a covered pan. Reduce to a simmer. Add sausages side by side in pan and simmer gently 8–10 minutes. Pour off liquid and discard. Return sausages to pan and brown them over low heat uncovered. Shake the pan occasionally until browned evenly.	15–20 minutes total
	POACH	Bring water, beer, or other liquid to boil in a covered pot. Reduce heat. When water is at a simmer, add sausage. Cover pot and simmer slowly.	10–20 minutes
	SAUTÉ	Heat a little butter and/or oil in a large skillet over medium heat. Place sausages side by side in pan. Gently shake pan or turn sausages to brown evenly.	6–12 minutes
	STEW	Add sausages to simmering liquid. Cover and stew.	30–45 minutes
BAUERWURST (spicy pork or pork/beef, very coarse textured) Precooked	GRILL	Prepare a medium-hot fire in the grill. Do not prick sausage; the drippings cause flare-ups. Place on a greased grill 6 inches from coals. Sear sausage on all sides, then cover grill. Cook, turning sausage often for even browning.	5–10 minutes

TYPE	METHOD	INSTRUCTIONS	TIMING
	PAN-BROIL	Heat a large, heavy skillet over medium heat with a light film of butter and oil. Place sausages in pan. Cover. Shake pan occasionally to brown sausages evenly.	5–6 minutes
	PAN-FRY	Preheat large nonstick skillet. Add sausage. Cook over medium heat, moving sausage occasionally to brown evenly.	5–7 minutes
	PAN-FRY	*To Pan-Fry/Simmer:* Bring ½ cup of water or liquid to a boil in a covered pan. Reduce to a simmer. Add sausages side by side in pan and simmer gently 8–10 minutes. Pour off liquid and discard. Return sausages to pan and brown them over low heat uncovered. Shake the pan occasionally until browned evenly.	15–20 minutes total
	POACH	Bring water, beer, or other liquid to boil in a covered pot. Reduce heat. When water is at a simmer, add sausage. Cover pot and simmer slowly.	5–7 minutes
	ROAST	Preheat oven to 350°F. Place poached sausage in a roasting pan with 2 inches of water. Roast uncovered.	15–20 minutes
	SAUTÉ	Heat a little butter and/or oil large skillet over medium heat. Place sausages side by side in pan. Gently shake pan or turn sausages to brown evenly.	5–7 minutes

TYPE	METHOD	INSTRUCTIONS	TIMING
BOCKWURST (veal, pork) Precooked	GRILL	Prepare a medium-hot fire in the grill. Do not prick sausage; the drippings cause flare-ups. Place on a greased grill 6 inches from coals. Sear sausage on all sides, then cover grill. Cook, turning sausage often for even browning.	5–10 minutes
	PAN-BROIL	Heat a large, heavy skillet over medium heat with a light film of butter and oil. Place sausages in pan. Cover. Shake pan occasionally to brown sausages evenly.	5–6 minutes
	PAN-FRY	Preheat large nonstick skillet. Add sausage. Cook over medium heat, moving sausage occasionally to brown evenly.	5–7 minutes
	POACH	Bring water, beer, or other liquid to boil in a covered pot. Reduce heat. When water is at a simmer, add sausage. Cover pot and simmer slowly.	5–7 minutes

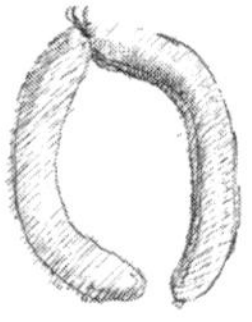

frankfurter

boudin blanc

bratwurst

TYPE	*METHOD*	*INSTRUCTIONS*	*TIMING*
BOUDINS BLANC (pork, veal, rabbit, chicken, cream, onions, eggs, bread crumbs, and/or rice) Precooked	BAKE	Preheat oven to 350°F. Place the sausages on buttered greaseproof baking pan.	10–20 minutes,
	GRILL	Prepare a medium-hot fire in the grill. Do not prick sausage; the drippings cause flare-ups. Place on a greased grill 6 inches from coals. Sear sausage on all sides, then cover grill. Cook, turning sausage often for even browning.	5–10 minutes
	PAN-BROIL	Heat a large, heavy skillet over medium heat with a light film of butter and oil. Place sausages in pan. Cover. Shake pan occasionally to brown sausages evenly.	5–6 minutes
	PAN-FRY	Preheat large nonstick skillet. Add sausage. Cook over medium heat, moving sausage occasionally to brown evenly.	5–7 minutes
	PAN-FRY	*To Pan-Fry/Simmer:* Bring ½ cup of water or liquid to a boil in a covered pan. Reduce to a simmer. Add sausages side by side in pan and simmer gently 8–10 minutes. Pour off liquid and discard. Return sausages to pan and brown them over low heat uncovered. Shake the pan occasionally until browned evenly.	15–20 minutes total

TYPE	METHOD	INSTRUCTIONS	TIMING
BOUDINS BLANC (pork, veal, rabbit, chicken, cream onions, eggs, bread crumbs, and/or rice) Precooked (*cont'd.*)	POACH	Bring water, beer, or other liquid to boil in a covered pot. Reduce heat. When water is at a simmer, add sausage. Cover pot and simmer slowly.	5–7 minutes
	STEW	Add sausages to simmering liquid. Cover and stew.	30–45 minutes
BRATWURST (pork and/or veal) Fresh raw	BAKE	Preheat oven to 350°F. Place the sausages on a rack in a baking pan with ½ inch water in bottom of pan. Bake uncovered.	10–45 minutes, depending on size
	GRILL	Prepare a medium-hot fire in the grill. Poach or pan-fry the sausages but do not prick them before cooking; the drippings cause flare-ups. Place the sausages on a greased grill 6 inches from coals. Sear on all sides, then cover grill and cook slowly, turning often for even browning.	7–15 minutes
	PAN-FRY	Heat a large heavy skillet over medium heat with a light film of oil. Place sausages side by side in pan. Cover. Shake pan occasionally to brown sausage evenly.	5–15 minutes

TYPE	METHOD	INSTRUCTIONS	TIMING
	PAN-FRY	*To Pan-Fry/Simmer:* Bring ½ cup of water or liquid to a boil in a covered pan. Reduce to a simmer. Add sausages side by side in pan and simmer gently 8–10 minutes. Pour off liquid and discard. Return sausages to pan and brown them over low heat uncovered. Shake the pan occasionally until browned evenly.	15–20 minutes total
	POACH	Bring water, beer, or other liquid to boil in a covered pot. Reduce heat. When water is at a simmer, add sausage. Cover pot and simmer slowly.	15–20 minutes
BRATWURST (pork and/or veal) Precooked	BAKE	Preheat oven to 350°F. Place the sausages on a rack in a baking pan with ½ inch water in bottom of pan. Bake uncovered.	10–20 minutes, depending on size
	GRILL	Prepare a medium-hot fire in the grill. Do not prick sausage; the drippings cause flare-ups. Place on a greased grill 6 inches from coals. Sear sausage on all sides, then cover grill. Cook, turning sausage often for even browning.	5–6 minutes
	PAN-BROIL	Heat a large, heavy skillet over medium heat with a light film of butter and oil. Place sausages in pan. Cover. Shake pan occasionally to brown sausages evenly.	5–6 minutes
	PAN-FRY	Preheat large nonstick skillet. Add sausage. Cook over medium heat, moving sausage occasionally to brown evenly.	5–7 minutes

TYPE	*METHOD*	*INSTRUCTIONS*	*TIMING*
BRATWURST (pork and/or veal) Precooked (*cont'd.*)	POACH	Bring water, beer, or other liquid to boil in a covered pot. Reduce heat. When water is at a simmer, add sausage. Cover pot and simmer slowly.	5–7 minutes
BREAKFAST SAUSAGE (country sausage, pork) Fresh raw links and patties	BAKE	Preheat oven to 350°F. Place the sausages on a rack in a baking pan with ½ inch water in bottom of pan. Bake uncovered.	10–45 minutes, depending on size
	GRILL	Prepare a medium-hot fire in the grill. Poach or pan-fry the sausages but do not prick them before cooking; the drippings cause flare-ups. Place the sausages on a greased grill 6 inches from coals. Sear on all sides, then cover grill and cook slowly, turning often for even browning.	7–15 minutes
	PAN-BROIL	Heat a large, heavy skillet over medium heat with a light film of butter and oil. Place sausages in pan. Cover. Shake pan occasionally to brown sausages evenly.	5–6 minutes
	PAN-FRY	Preheat large nonstick skillet. Add sausage. Cook over medium heat, moving sausage occasionally to brown evenly.	5–7 minutes

TYPE	METHOD	INSTRUCTIONS	TIMING
	PAN-FRY	*To Pan-Fry/Simmer:* Bring ½ cup of water or liquid to a boil in a covered pan. Reduce to a simmer. Add sausages side by side in pan and simmer gently 8–10 minutes. Pour off liquid and discard. Return sausages to pan and brown them over low heat uncovered. Shake the pan occasionally until browned evenly.	15–20 minutes total
CERVELAT (smoked, minced) Precooked	PAN-FRY	Slice sausages into ⅛-inch- to ¼-inch-thick pieces and brown in a skillet.	4–5 minutes
FRANKFURTER (hot dog; pork and/or beef) Precooked	GRILL	Prepare a medium-hot fire in the grill. Do not prick sausage; the drippings cause flare-ups. Place on a greased grill 6 inches from coals. Sear sausage on all sides, then cover grill. Cook, turning sausage often for even browning.	5–6 minutes
	PAN-FRY	Preheat large nonstick skillet. Add sausage. Cook over medium heat, moving sausage occasionally to brown evenly.	5–7 minutes
	POACH	Bring water, beer, or other liquid to boil in a covered pot. Reduce heat. When water is at a simmer, add sausage. Cover pot and simmer slowly.	5–7 minutes
	SAUTÉ	Heat a little butter and/or oil in a large skillet over medium heat. Place sausages side by side in pan. Gently shake pan or turn sausages to brown evenly.	5–7 minutes

TYPE	METHOD	INSTRUCTIONS	TIMING
FRANKFURTER (chicken, turkey, venison) Precooked	PAN-FRY	Preheat large nonstick skillet. Add sausage. Cook over medium heat, moving sausage occasionally to brown evenly.	5–7 minutes
	GRILL	Prepare a medium-hot fire in the grill. Do not prick sausage; the drippings cause flare-ups. Place on a greased grill 6 inches from coals. Sear sausage on all sides, then cover grill. Cook, turning sausage often for even browning.	5–10 minutes
	POACH	Bring water, beer, or other liquid to boil in a covered pot. Reduce heat. When water is at a simmer, add sausage. Cover pot and simmer slowly.	5–7 minutes
	SAUTÉ	Heat a little butter and/or oil large skillet over medium heat. Place sausages side by side in pan. Gently shake pan or turn sausages to brown evenly.	5–7 minutes
	STEAM	Place on steaming rack above boiling water. Cook covered.	4–5 minutes
GAYETTES (pig's liver, fat, bacon, garlic, spices) Fresh raw	BAKE	Preheat oven to 350°F. Place the sausages on a rack in a baking pan with ½ inch water in bottom of pan. Bake uncovered.	10–45 minutes, depending on size
	GRILL	Prepare a medium-hot fire in the grill. Poach or pan-fry the sausages but do not prick them before cooking; the drippings cause flare-ups. Place the sausages on a greased grill 6 inches from coals. Sear on all sides, then cover grill and cook slowly, turning often for even browning.	7–15 minutes

TYPE	METHOD	INSTRUCTIONS	TIMING
	PAN-FRY	Heat a large heavy skillet over medium heat with a light film of oil. Place sausages side by side in pan. Cover. Shake pan occasionally to brown sausage evenly.	5–15 minutes
	PAN-FRY	*To Pan-Fry/Simmer:* Bring ½ cup of water or liquid to a boil in a covered pan. Reduce to a simmer. Add sausages side by side in pan and simmer gently 8–10 minutes. Pour off liquid and discard. Return sausages to pan and brown them over low heat uncovered. Shake the pan occasionally until browned evenly.	15–20 minutes total
	POACH	Bring water, beer, or other liquid to boil in a covered pot. Reduce heat. When water is at a simmer, add sausage. Cover pot and simmer slowly.	10–20 minutes
ITALIAN SAUSAGE Fresh raw	GRILL	Prepare a medium-hot fire in the grill. Poach or pan-fry the sausages but do not prick them before cooking; the drippings cause flare-ups. Place the sausages on a greased grill 6 inches from coals. Sear on all sides, then cover grill and cook slowly, turning often for even browning.	7–15 minutes
	PAN-BROIL	Heat a large, heavy skillet over medium heat with a light film of butter and oil. Place sausages in pan. Cover. Shake pan occasionally to brown sausages evenly.	5–6 minutes

TYPE	METHOD	INSTRUCTIONS	TIMING
ITALIAN SAUSAGE Fresh raw (*cont'd.*)	PAN-FRY	Heat a large heavy skillet over medium heat with a light film of oil. Place sausages side by side in pan. Cover. Shake pan occasionally to brown sausage evenly.	5–15 minutes
	PAN-FRY	*To Pan-Fry/Simmer:* Bring ½ cup of water or liquid to a boil in a covered pan. Reduce to a simmer. Add sausages side by side in pan and simmer gently 8–10 minutes. Pour off liquid and discard. Return sausages to pan and brown them over low heat uncovered. Shake the pan occasionally until browned evenly.	15–20 minutes total
	SAUTÉ	Heat a little butter and/or oil in a large skillet over medium heat. Place sausages side by side in pan. Gently shake pan or turn sausages to brown evenly.	6–12 minutes
KIELBASA (pork, beef, fat, spices, garlic) Fresh raw	BAKE	Preheat oven to 350∞ F. Place the sausages on a rack in a baking pan with ½ inch water in bottom of pan. Bake uncovered.	10–45 minutes, depending on size

Polish kielbasa

Italian sausage

knackwurst

TYPE	METHOD	INSTRUCTIONS	TIMING
	GRILL	Prepare a medium-hot fire in the grill. Poach or pan-fry the sausages but do not prick them before cooking; the drippings cause flare-ups. Place the sausages on a greased grill 6 inches from coals. Sear on all sides, then cover grill and cook slowly, turning often for even browning.	7–15 minutes
	PAN-BROIL	Heat a large, heavy skillet over medium heat with a light film of butter and oil. Place sausages in pan. Cover. Shake pan occasionally to brown sausages evenly.	5–6 minutes
	PAN-FRY	*To Pan-Fry/Simmer:* Bring ½ cup of water or liquid to a boil in a covered pan. Reduce to a simmer. Add sausages side by side in pan and simmer gently 8–10 minutes. Pour off liquid and discard. Return sausages to pan and brown them over low heat uncovered. Shake the pan occasionally until browned evenly.	15–20 minutes total
	POACH	Bring water, beer, or other liquid to boil in a covered pot. Reduce heat. When water is at a simmer, add sausage. Cover pot and simmer slowly.	10–20 minutes
	ROAST	Preheat oven to 350°F. Place poached sausage in a roasting pan with 2 inches of water. Roast uncovered.	15–20 minutes
	STEW	Add sausages to simmering liquid. Cover and stew.	30–45 minutes

TYPE	*METHOD*	*INSTRUCTIONS*	*TIMING*
KIELBASA (pork, beef, fat, spices, garlic) Precooked	GRILL	Prepare a medium-hot fire in the grill. Do not prick sausage; the drippings cause flare-ups. Place on a greased grill 6 inches from coals. Sear sausage on all sides, then cover grill. Cook, turning sausage often for even browning.	5–10 minutes
	PAN-BROIL	Heat a large, heavy skillet over medium heat with a light film of butter and oil. Place sausages in pan. Cover. Shake pan occasionally to brown sausages evenly.	5–6 minutes
	PAN-FRY	*To Pan-Fry/Simmer:* Bring ½ cup of water or liquid to a boil in a covered pan. Reduce to a simmer. Add sausages side by side in pan and simmer gently 8–10 minutes. Pour off liquid and discard. Return sausages to pan and brown them over low heat uncovered. Shake the pan occasionally until browned evenly.	15–20 minutes total
	ROAST	Preheat oven to 350°F. Place poached sausage in a roasting pan with 2 inches of water. Roast uncovered.	15–20 minutes
	SAUTÉ	Heat a little butter and/or oil large skillet over medium heat. Place sausages side by side in pan. Gently shake pan or turn sausages to brown evenly.	5–7 minutes
KISHKE (pork, beef fat, garlic, highly spiced) Fresh raw	GRILL	Prepare a medium-hot fire in the grill. Poach or pan-fry the sausages but do not prick them before cooking; the drippings cause flare-ups. Place the sausages on a greased grill 6 inches from coals. Sear on all sides, then cover grill and cook slowly, turning often for even browning.	7–15 minutes

TYPE	METHOD	INSTRUCTIONS	TIMING
	PAN-BROIL	Heat a large, heavy skillet over medium heat with a light film of butter and oil. Place sausages in pan. Cover. Shake pan occasionally to brown sausages evenly.	5–6 minutes
	PAN-FRY	Heat a large heavy skillet over medium heat with a light film of oil. Place sausages side by side in pan. Cover. Shake pan occasionally to brown sausage evenly.	5–7 minutes
	POACH	Bring water, beer, or other liquid to boil in a covered pot. Reduce heat. When water is at a simmer, add sausage. Cover pot and simmer slowly.	10–20 minutes
	ROAST	Preheat oven to 350°F. Place poached sausage in a roasting pan with 2 inches of water. Roast uncovered.	15–20 minutes
	STEW	Add sausages to simmering liquid. Cover and stew.	30–45 minutes
KNACKWURST (lean pork, beef, fresh pork fat, cumin, garlic) Precooked	GRILL	Prepare a medium-hot fire in the grill. Do not prick sausage; the drippings cause flare-ups. Place on a greased grill 6 inches from coals. Sear sausage on all sides, then cover grill. Cook, turning sausage often for even browning.	5–10 minutes
	PAN-FRY	*To Pan-Fry/Simmer:* Bring ½ cup of water or liquid to a boil in a covered pan. Reduce to a simmer. Add sausages side by side in pan and simmer gently 8–10 minutes. Pour off liquid and discard. Return sausages to pan and brown them over low heat uncovered. Shake the pan occasionally until browned evenly.	15–20 minutes total

TYPE	*METHOD*	*INSTRUCTIONS*	*TIMING*
KNACKWURST (lean pork, beef, fresh pork fat, cumin, garlic) Precooked (*cont'd.*)	SAUTÉ	Heat a little butter and/or oil large skillet over medium heat. Place sausages side by side in pan. Gently shake pan or turn sausages to brown evenly.	5–7 minutes
PORK SAUSAGE American (pork, cardamom, salt, pepper, coriander, nutmeg), Fresh raw; and English (pork, salt, pepper), Fresh raw	GRILL	Prepare a medium-hot fire in the grill. Poach or pan-fry the sausages but do not prick them before cooking; the drippings cause flare-ups. Place the sausages on a greased grill 6 inches from coals. Sear on all sides, then cover grill and cook slowly, turning often for even browning.	7–15 minutes
	PAN-BROIL	Heat a large, heavy skillet over medium heat with a light film of butter and oil. Place sausages in pan. Cover. Shake pan occasionally to brown sausages evenly.	5–6 minutes
	PAN-FRY	Heat a large heavy skillet over medium heat with a light film of oil. Place sausages side by side in pan. Cover. Shake pan occasionally to brown sausage evenly.	5–15 minutes
	PAN-FRY	*To Pan-Fry/Simmer:* Bring ½ cup of water or liquid to a boil in a covered pan. Reduce to a simmer. Add sausages side by side in pan and simmer gently 8–10 minutes. Pour off liquid and discard. Return sausages to pan and brown them over low heat uncovered. Shake the pan occasionally until browned evenly.	15–20 minutes total

TYPE	METHOD	INSTRUCTIONS	TIMING
	SAUTÉ	Heat a little butter and/or oil in a large skillet over medium heat. Place sausages side by side in pan. Gently shake pan or turn sausages to brown evenly.	6–12 minutes
RABBIT SAUSAGE (boiled roaster rabbit) Fresh raw	PAN-FRY	Heat a large heavy skillet over medium heat with a light film of oil. Place sausages side by side in pan. Cover. Shake pan occasionally to brown sausage evenly.	5–15 minutes
	POACH	Bring water, beer, or other liquid to boil in a covered pot. Reduce heat. When water is at a simmer, add sausage. Cover pot and simmer slowly.	10–20 minutes
SAUCISSON (best cuts of prime pig and veal, usually contains under 5% fat) Precooked	BAKE	Preheat oven to 350°F. Place the sausages on a rack in a baking pan with ½ inch water in bottom of pan. Bake uncovered.	10–45 minutes, depending on size
	GRILL	Prepare a medium-hot fire in the grill. Do not prick sausage; the drippings cause flare-ups. Place on a greased grill 6 inches from coals. Sear sausage on all sides, then cover grill. Cook, turning sausage often for even browning.	5–10 minutes
	PAN-BROIL	Heat a large, heavy skillet over medium heat with a light film of butter and oil. Place sausages in pan. Cover. Shake pan occasionally to brown sausages evenly.	5–6 minutes

TYPE	METHOD	INSTRUCTIONS	TIMING
SAUCISSON (best cuts of prime pig and veal, usually contains under 5% fat) Precooked (*cont'd.*)	PAN-FRY	*To Pan-Fry/Simmer:* Bring ½ cup of water or liquid to a boil in a covered pan. Reduce to a simmer. Add sausages side by side in pan and simmer gently 8–10 minutes. Pour off liquid and discard. Return sausages to pan and brown them over low heat uncovered. Shake the pan occasionally until browned evenly.	15–20 minutes total
	POACH	Bring water, beer, or other liquid to boil in a covered pot. Reduce heat. When water is at a simmer, add sausage. Cover pot and simmer slowly.	5–7 minutes
SEAFOOD SAUSAGE (pureed raw fish or shellfish, cream, egg whites) Precooked	GRILL	Prepare a medium-hot fire in the grill. Do not prick sausage; the drippings cause flare-ups. Place on a greased grill 6 inches from coals. Sear sausage on all sides, then cover grill. Cook, turning sausage often for even browning.	5–10 minutes
	PAN-FRY	Preheat large nonstick skillet. Add sausage. Cook over medium heat, moving sausage occasionally to brown evenly.	5–7 minutes
	POACH	Bring water, beer, or other liquid to boil in a covered pot. Reduce heat. When water is at a simmer, add sausage. Cover pot and simmer slowly.	5–7 minutes
	SAUTÉ	Heat a little butter and/or oil large skillet over medium heat. Place sausages side by side in pan. Gently shake pan or turn sausages to brown evenly.	5–7 minutes

TYPE	*METHOD*	*INSTRUCTIONS*	*TIMING*
TOULOUSE (pork, wine, garlic, seasonings) Fresh raw	BAKE	Preheat oven to 350°F. Place the sausages on a rack in a baking pan with ½ inch water in bottom of pan. Bake uncovered.	10–45 minutes, depending on size
	GRILL	Prepare a medium-hot fire in the grill. Poach or pan-fry the sausages but do not prick them before cooking; the drippings cause flare-ups. Place the sausages on a greased grill 6 inches from coals. Sear on all sides, then cover grill and cook slowly, turning often for even browning.	7–15 minutes
	PAN-BROIL	Heat a large, heavy skillet over medium heat with a light film of butter and oil. Place sausages in pan. Cover. Shake pan occasionally to brown sausages evenly.	5–6 minutes
	PAN-FRY	*To Pan-Fry/Simmer:* Bring ½ cup of water or liquid to a boil in a covered pan. Reduce to a simmer. Add sausages side by side in pan and simmer gently 8–10 minutes. Pour off liquid and discard. Return sausages to pan and brown them over low heat uncovered. Shake the pan occasionally until browned evenly.	15–20 minutes total
	POACH	Bring water, beer, or other liquid to boil in a covered pot. Reduce heat. When water is at a simmer, add sausage. Cover pot and simmer slowly.	10–20 minutes
	STEW	Add sausages to simmering liquid. Cover and stew.	30–45 minutes

TYPE	*METHOD*	*INSTRUCTIONS*	*TIMING*
WEINERWURST (45% lean pork, 30% beef, water, spices, 25% fat)	GRILL	Prepare a medium-hot fire in the grill. Do not prick sausage; the drippings cause flare-ups. Place on a greased grill 6 inches from coals. Sear sausage on all sides, then cover grill. Cook, turning sausage often for even browning.	5–10 minutes
	PAN-FRY	Preheat large nonstick skillet. Add sausage. Cook over medium heat, moving sausage occasionally to brown evenly.	5–7 minutes
	POACH	Bring water, beer, or other liquid to boil in a covered pot. Reduce heat. When water is at a simmer, add sausage. Cover pot and simmer slowly.	10–20 minutes
	SAUTÉ	Heat a little butter and/or oil large skillet over medium heat. Place sausages side by side in pan. Gently shake pan or turn sausages to brown evenly.	5–7 minutes
WEISSWURST (veal, cream, eggs)	POACH	Bring water, beer, or other liquid to boil in a covered pot. Reduce heat. When water is at a simmer, add sausage. Cover pot and simmer slowly.	5–7 minutes

VARIETY MEATS

Variety meats are also called innards or organ meats. They're the meats that include brains, heart, kidneys, liver, sweetbreads, tongue, and tripe. In many parts of the world, organ meats are considered delicacies, but in America only liver is a fairly common dish. The other variety meats are often found in expensive or ethnic restaurants around the country but can be hard to find outside of a specialty butcher shop. If you've never had them before, you may be surprised by how delicious they can be.

The freshness of variety meat is of the utmost importance. Be sure to shop at a good butcher shop and order them in advance; that way, they are more likely to be fresh. These meats perish faster than any other type of meat, so they should be cooked within 24 hours of purchase. Avoid any with greenish color, strong smell, or slimy surfaces. Always wash thoroughly before using.

Types of Variety Meats

Brains. Brains are a very delicate meat and must be bought very fresh. They should be plump and have a moist, shiny, pink surface. A good test of freshness is to see how easily the outer membrane is removed—the easier, the fresher. Calf brains are considered to be the most delicious, but beef, lamb, and pork brains are also excellent. Brains are usually braised, poached, or sautéed; they should be firm when done with no transparent center.

Heart. Heart has a firm texture and rich flavor, similar to liver. The cavity of the heart is perfect for a variety of stuffings. Heart is lean, so slow cooking is best. Braising or stewing keeps it moist and tender. Lamb, veal, and pork hearts are the favorites.

Kidneys. Beef, veal, lamb, and pork kidneys should be plump, firm, dense, and encased in a shiny membrane. Avoid any that have a strong odor. Veal kidneys are the choice of connoisseurs; lamb kidneys are a close second. Kidneys have a taste similar to liver; they are usually braised or sautéed.

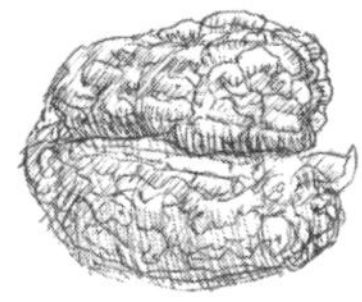

brain

sweetbreads

duck's liver

Liver. Calf's liver is mild and tender and should be broiled, sautéed, or pan-fried. Lamb's liver is less delicate and tends to be drier, but it also can be sautéed. Chicken livers are very mild and delicate and are usually sautéed. Pig's liver has a strong and pronounced flavor; you can sweeten the taste by soaking it in milk for 1 hour before cooking. Liver should have a bright, shiny surface when you buy it.

Cook liver until the internal temperature reaches 140°F. It will still be pink in the center.

Sweetbreads. Sweetbreads are the most expensive and delicate of the organ meats. They are the thymus glands of young calves and lambs. They must be soaked and cooked on the day of purchase. They should be cooked quickly; often they are sautéed with egg and breadcrumbs. Calf's sweetbreads are preferred.

Tongue. Tongue comes from beef, pork, veal, and lamb, but beef tongue is considered to have the best flavor. Small tongues (under 3 pounds) have better flavor than large tongues. Tongue may be cooked fresh, smoked, or pickled. It is often served sliced and hot but can be served cold as well.

Tripe. Tripe is the muscular stomach lining of an animal that chews its cud. Only beef tripe is generally available in this country. The two most common types of tripe are smooth and honeycomb, but the honeycomb tripe is preferred. Tripe is usually sold cleaned, soaked, and scalded, but further blanching may be required before cooking. Both French and Italian cookbooks have excellent recipes for tripe.

TIMINGS: Variety Meats

TYPE	*METHOD*	*INSTRUCTIONS*	*TIMING*
BRAINS Calf, Lamb, Pig, and Beef; Whole		*Preparation:* Rinse thoroughly 2–3 times, then soak for 2 hours in water and lemon juice. For a firm texture, poach the brains by covering them with cold water in a saucepan. Add the juice of a lemon or a couple of tablespoons of white vinegar. Bring to a slow simmer and simmer 10–15 minutes. *Note:* Poach brains before other methods of cooking	

TYPE	METHOD	INSTRUCTIONS	TIMING
	BRAISE	Preheat oven to 350°F (optional). Brown brains in butter and/or oil in a Dutch oven. Add ½ inch braising liquid and seasonings to pan. Cover tightly. Slowly simmer on top of the stove or place in oven.	15–20 minutes
	BROIL	Preheat the broiler. Brush brains with melted butter. Broil 4 inches from heat until brown. Do not turn.	10–15 minutes
BRAINS Slices or pieces	DEEP FRY	Preheat oil to 375°F. Dip slices of brains in batter and deep-fry. Drain on paper towels before serving.	2–3 minutes
	SAUTÉ	Poach the brains to firm the texture (see *Preparation* above). Heat butter over medium heat, add brains, and cook 3 minutes per side. Reduce heat and cover. Cook another 3–4 minutes.	9–10 minutes
HEART Beef, Lamb, Veal, Pork; Whole		*Preparation:* Wash thoroughly under cold water. Cut away any arteries, fat, or connective tissue.	
	BRAISE	Preheat oven to 350°F (optional). Heat butter and/or oil in a Dutch oven over medium heat. Add heart and brown well. Add ½ inch braising liquid and seasoning. Cover tightly. Simmer slowly on top of stove or in oven.	Beef: 2½ hours Lamb, pork, veal: 1½–2½ hours
	POACH	*To Poach:* Cover the heart with water. Add 1 teaspoon salt for each quart of water. Simmer over low heat until tender.	Beef: 3–3½ hours Lamb, pork, veal: 2½ hours

TYPE	*METHOD*	*INSTRUCTIONS*	*TIMING*
HEART Lamb or Veal; Slices	SAUTÉ	Slice heart in half lengthwise, then into ½-inch slices crosswise. Heat butter and/or oil in large skillet over medium heat. Add heart slices and sauté slowly, turning frequently until done.	5 minutes
KIDNEYS Lamb, Veal; Whole		*Preparation:* Wash thoroughly. Trim away the white membrane that covers the kidneys. Snip the fat where meat is attached and remove it, if desired. Make sure the ducts have been removed completely from center. Juice should run pink when pierced.	
	BRAISE	Preheat oven to 350°F (optional). Heat butter and/or oil in a saucepan over medium heat. Add the kidneys and brown well. Add ½ inch braising liquid and seasonings. Cover tightly. Simmer slowly on top of stove or in oven.	30–40 minutes
	BROIL	Preheat the broiler. Cut kidneys in half or in ½-inch slices. Dip them in butter and sprinkle with salt and pepper. Broil 3 inches from heat until brown, turning once.	Halves: 2–4 minutes per side Slices: 1–2 minutes per side
	ROAST	Preheat oven to 450°F. Leave fat on kidneys. Place kidneys in a well-greased roasting pan and roast.	30–40 minutes per pound
	SAUTÉ	Split kidneys lengthwise. Cut into ½-inch slices, if desired. Heat butter in a large skillet over medium heat. Add kidneys and sauté, turning frequently.	Halves: 4–6 minutes Slices: 2–4 minutes

TYPE	*METHOD*	*INSTRUCTIONS*	*TIMING*
LIVER, CALF'S		*Preparation:* Wash thoroughly. Trim away any exposed veins, ducts, or connective tissue. Peel away the thin outer membrane.	
	BRAISE	Preheat oven to 350°F (optional). Heat butter and/or oil in a large Dutch oven over medium heat. Add liver and brown on both sides. Add ½ inch braising liquid and seasonings to pan. Cover tightly. Simmer slowly on top of stove or in oven.	30–40 minutes
	BROIL	Preheat broiler. Cut liver into ½-inch slices. Broil 3 inches from heat, turning once.	2 minutes per side
	PAN-FRY	Cut liver into ½-inch slices. Dust with seasoned flour. Heat oil and/or butter in large skillet over medium heat. Add liver and pan-fry, turning once.	2–3 minutes per side
	SAUTÉ	Cut liver into ¼-inch slices. Dust with seasoned flour. Heat oil and/or butter in a large skillet over medium heat. Add liver and sauté, turning once.	1–2 minutes per side
LIVER, CHICKEN	GRILL	Prepare a hot fire in the grill. Toss the livers with oil. Thread onto skewers if small. Place on grill 4 inches from coals and grill until crusty brown, turning once.	2–3 minutes per side
	SAUTÉ	Heat butter in a large skillet over high heat. Add livers in a single layer. Sauté until livers begin to release juices into pan.	Small: 1½–2 minutes Large: 4–6 minutes

TYPE	METHOD	INSTRUCTIONS	TIMING
SWEETBREADS Calf's; Whole		*Preparation:* Soak for 2 hours in several changes of cold water; rinse. Cover with cold water in a large pot of water. Add the juice of 1 lemon. Bring to a boil and blanch 3 minutes. Drain and remove skin and membrane but be careful not to break sweetbreads. Pat dry. They must be cooked on the day of purchase.	
	BRAISE	Preheat oven to 350°F (optional). Heat oil and/or butter in a large Dutch oven or pot. Add sweetbreads and brown on all sides over medium heat. Add ½ inch braising liquid and seasonings. Bring to a simmer. Cover tightly. Simmer slowly in oven or on top of stove.	30–40 minutes
	POACH	Place prepared sweetbreads in a pot and cover with a court-bouillon. Bring the liquid to a simmer and simmer gently, uncovered.	20–30 minutes
SWEETBREADS Slices and pieces	BROIL	Preheat broiler. Split sweetbreads and season well. Dip in egg wash and roll in crumbs. Broil 4 inches from heat until well browned on both sides, turning once.	4–5 minutes per side
	DEEP-FRY	Preheat oil to 375°F. Dip slices in batter and deep-fry until golden. Drain on paper towels before serving.	3–4 minutes
	SAUTÉ	Trim and slice into ¼-inch slices. Dust with seasoned flour. Melt butter in a sauté pan over medium-high heat. Add sweetbreads and brown on both sides.	3–5 minutes

TYPE	*METHOD*	*INSTRUCTIONS*	*TIMING*
TONGUE, FRESH, PICKLED, OR SMOKED Beef, 4–6 pounds; Veal, 1–1½ pounds; Pork, 1 pound; Lamb, ¾ pound		*Preparation:* Scrub well with a stiff brush under running water. Soak tongue in cold water to cover for 2 hours. If the tongue has been pickled or smoked, blanch it in simmering water to cover for 10 minutes. Drain and immerse in cold water. After cooking, cool the tongue enough to handle it. Then split the skin and peel it off. Trim away the bones and gristle.	
TONGUE SLICES	BAKE	Preheat oven to 350°F. Place poached tongue slices in greased baking pan. Brush with melted butter. Place in oven and bake.	20–30 minutes
	BRAISE	Preheat oven to 400°F. Heat butter in a large Dutch oven. Add poached tongue and brown on both sides. Add vegetables or sauce. Add 1 inch white wine and cover. Bring to a boil. Cover and place in oven to finish cooking. Drain the tongue and slice.	45–60 minutes per pound
	POACH	Add to a large pot of boiling water along with seasonings. Partially cover and simmer gently until tender.	Beef: 3–4 hours Veal: 1½–2 hours Pork: 1–1½ hours Lamb: 1 hour
TRIPE		*Preparation:* Tripe is sold parboiled. Soak it 5–10 minutes in cold water. Rinse and cut into strips. Try not to overcook or it becomes tough: Place tripe in a large pot and cover with court-bouillon. Bring to a simmer and simmer until tender—anywhere from ½ to 2 hours. Time will depend on how long tripe has been blanched before it was sold.	

TYPE	METHOD	INSTRUCTIONS	TIMING
TRIPE *(cont'd.)*	BROIL	Preheat broiler. Dip poached tripe strips in melted butter and roll in crumbs. Broil 3 inches from heat, until lightly browned, turning once.	2–3 minutes per side
	DEEP-FRY	Heat oil to 365°F. Cut poached tripe strips into serving size pieces and dip into batter. Deep-fry until golden. Drain on paper towels before serving.	3–4 minutes
	SAUTÉ	Cut poached tripe strips into 2-inch pieces. Melt butter in a large skillet over medium-high heat. Add the tripe and sauté until browned.	4 minutes

GAME

Game was once referred to as meat hunted in the wild. But much of today's game is farm-raised. Farm-raised game tends to be more tender than wild game and lacks the assertive "gamy" flavor that people associate with wild game.

Types of Game

The game most like to be sold in the stores or popularly hunted are buffalo, rabbit, venison, and boar. The category of game also includes game birds, which are discussed in the poultry chapter (see pages 150–71).

Buffalo. Farm-raised American buffalo, or bison, is increasingly available in supermarkets and specialty food stores. The meat is considered a very healthful alternative to beef, containing 30 percent less cholesterol and about half the calories and fat of beef. The same cuts available for beef (steaks, chops, roasts, and ground meat) are available for buffalo. Beefalo, a cross between beef cattle and buffalo, is also available. Beefalo is a red meat that tastes like beef but is lower in fat. It can be used interchangeably with buffalo.

Rabbit. Most of the rabbit sold in the United States is raised domestically and often comes packaged and cut up into pieces. Young rabbits that weigh between 2 and 3½ pounds are called fryers, and larger rabbits, at 4 to 6 pounds, are called roasters. The hindquarters have more meat than the front quarters.

Wild rabbits and hares (a larger relative) are the most commonly hunted small game in the United States. Their white meat is lean and requires moist cooking, such as stewing and braising. These animals commonly carry tularemia, or rabbit disease, so wear gloves when handling the uncooked meat.

Venison. Most of the venison one finds comes from deer, but venison can come from any antlered animal (antelope, caribou, elk, moose). Much of the venison today is farm-raised fallow or red deer from the United States and Europe or red deer from New Zealand, which goes under the brand name Cervena. Farm-raised venison tends to be more tender and less gamy in flavor that wild venison.

Wild Boar. Wild boar is almost impossible to find in this country, but if you do find it, treat it as you would pork. If the boar has been skinned, marinate it. Make sure wild boar and farm-raised boar is cooked beyond 140°F so that there is no danger from trichinosis. Always serve the meat medium or well done.

Cooking Game with Flavor

It used to be common practice to marinate wild game for a few days to tenderize the meat and mask its gamy flavor. This certainly isn't necessary for today's farm-raised game. If you do marinate, 1 hour at room temperature or up to 24 hours in the refrigerator is sufficient. Although a red wine marinade is traditional, buttermilk-based marinades are particularly good at masking the gamy flavor of wild venison and wild boar.

Buffalo. Substitute buffalo in any beef recipe, but cook at slightly lower temperatures. Serve steaks and roasts rare or medium rare. The meat and juices will appear redder than those of beef because of the high iron content of the blood.

Rabbit. The taste is very much like chicken, and you can substitute domestic rabbit in any chicken recipe. Wild rabbit has a much stronger flavor. Wild rabbit and hare can be marinated for up to 24 hours in the refrigerator before cooking with moist heat, such as braising or stewing.

Rabbits can be roasted whole, but usually they are cut into 6 or 8 pieces (2 forelegs, 2 hind legs, and 2 to 4 saddle or loin pieces). Treat farm-raised rabbit like chicken: Roast or grill the fryers and braise or stew the roasters.

Venison. The tender cuts are the saddle, loin, and tenderloin—these cuts can be broiled, sautéed, or grilled quickly to rare or medium-rare. Braising is best for meat from the shoulder, neck, or leg.

Wild venison benefits from marinating in a red wine– or buttermilk-based marinade for 1 hour at room temperature or up to 24 hours in the refrigerator.

Wild Boar. The meat is dark and very intensely flavored, with practically no fat. Substitute wild boar in any pork recipe, cooked until medium or well done.

TIMINGS: Game

TYPE	*METHOD*	*INSTRUCTIONS*	*TIMING*
BUFFALO GROUND MEAT	BROIL	Preheat broiler. Form meat into patties at least ½ inch thick. Place on preheated broiler pan and broil 4 inches from heat, turning once.	4 minutes per side
	GRILL	Prepare a medium-hot fire in grill. Form meat into patties at least ½ inch thick. Place on greased grill 4 inches from coals and grill, turning once.	4 minutes per side

TYPE	METHOD	INSTRUCTIONS	TIMING
	PAN-BROIL	Preheat a heavy skillet over high heat. Form meat into patties ½ inch thick. Add patties to skillet and cook, turning once.	4 minutes per side
BUFFALO POT ROAST Chuck; 4–5 pounds	BRAISE	Preheat the oven to 350°F. Dust the meat with seasoned flour. Heat oil in a Dutch oven over medium-high heat. Add the meat and brown on all sides. Add seasonings and 1 inch braising liquid. Cover and simmer, adding vegetables, if desired, during last 45 minutes of cooking time.	2½–3 hours
BUFFALO RIBS 3–3½ pounds	BARBECUE	Prepare a medium-low fire in the grill. Push the coals to one side and place a drip pan on the other side. Place meat over drip pan and cover grill. Maintain a temperature inside the grill of 220°F–250°F, adding more coals and wood chips as needed. Baste and turn occasionally and barbecue until tender.	5½ hours
	GRILL	Prepare a medium-low fire in the grill. Season ribs and place on grill 6 inches above coals. Grill, turning frequently, until juices run clear and ribs are crispy and tender.	45–60 minutes
BUFFALO STEAKS Rib-eye, T-bone	BROIL	Preheat broiler. Place steaks on preheated pan and broil 4 inches from heat until rare or medium rare, turning once.	3–4 minutes per side
	GRILL	Prepare a medium-hot fire in the grill. Grill 4 inches from the coals until rare or medium rare, turning once.	3–4 minutes per side

TYPE	*METHOD*	*INSTRUCTIONS*	*TIMING*
BUFFALO TENDERLOIN 4 pounds	ROAST	Preheat oven to 325°F. Remove silverskin from meat. Brush with oil and season well. Place in roasting pan fat side up and roast uncovered until internal temperature reaches 135°F. Remove from oven, cover loosely with foil, and let stand 15 minutes before serving.	50–60 minutes,
RABBIT, FARM-RAISED	BRAISE	Cut rabbit into 6–8 serving pieces. Preheat the oven to 350°F. Dust the rabbit with seasoned flour. Heat oil and/or butter in a large Dutch oven. Add the rabbit and brown on all sides. Add 1 inch braising liquid and seasonings. Cover. Place in oven and simmer until tender.	1 hour
	ROAST	Cut rabbit into 6–8 serving pieces. Preheat oven to 400°F. Brush rabbit with oil and season well. Place in a shallow roasting pan and roast uncovered until leg and thigh pieces are tender.	20–30 minutes
RABBIT, FARM-RAISED Loins; 1 pound	BROIL	Preheat broiler. Brush loins with oil and season well. Place in preheated broiling pan and broil 4 inches from heat, turning once.	10 minutes per side
	GRILL	Prepare a medium-hot fire in the grill. Brush with oil and season well. Grill 4 inches from coals, turning once.	10 minutes per side

TYPE	METHOD	INSTRUCTIONS	TIMING
RABBIT, WILD HARE	BRAISE	Preheat the oven to 350°F. Cut rabbit into 6–8 serving pieces. Dust with seasoned flour. Heat oil and/or butter in a large Dutch oven. Add rabbit and brown on all sides. Add 1 inch braising liquid and seasonings. Cover. Place in oven and simmer until tender.	1–1½ hours
	STEW	Cut rabbit into 6–8 serving pieces. Dust with seasoned flour. Heat oil and/or butter in a large Dutch oven. Add rabbit and brown on all sides. Add braising liquid to cover and seasonings. Cover and simmer until meat is tender. Add vegetables 45 minutes before the end of cooking, if desired.	50–60 minutes
VENISON, LARGE PIECES	BRAISE	Preheat oven to 350°F. Dust meat with seasoned flour. Heat oil and/or butter in a large Dutch oven. Add venison and brown on all sides. Add 1 inch braising liquid and seasonings. Cover. Place in oven and simmer until tender.	20 minutes per pound
VENISON LEG 5–8 pounds	BRAISE	Preheat oven to 350°F. Rub leg with lard or butter. Season well. Heat oil and/or butter in large Dutch oven and brown on all sides. Add 1 inch beef broth or other braising liquid. Cover tightly. Place pot on lowest rack in oven and simmer until tender.	1½–2½ hours

TYPE	*METHOD*	*INSTRUCTIONS*	*TIMING*
VENISON LEG 5–8 pounds (*cont'd.*)	ROAST	Preheat oven to 450°F. Generously coat meat with melted butter and herbs, then place on a rack in a roasting pan. Roast 20 minutes. Reduce heat to 325°F. Add 2 cups chicken stock or red wine. Roast uncovered, basting frequently until internal temperature reaches 125°F–130°F for rare or 130°F–140°F for medium rare. Remove from oven, cover loosely with foil, and let stand 15–20 minutes before serving.	Bone-in: 12 minutes per pound Boneless: 15 minutes per pound, plus 15–20 minutes sranding time
VENISON LOIN Boneless; 3–5 pounds	ROAST	Preheat oven to 425°F. Brush meat with oil. Place on a rack in a roasting pan and roast uncovered until the internal temperature reaches 125°F–130°F for rare or 130°F–140°F for medium rare. Remove from oven, cover loosely with foil, and let stand 15–20 minutes before serving.	Rare: 7 minutes per pound Medium-rare: 8 minutes per pound Medium: 10 minutes per pound
	ROAST	Preheat oven to 350°F. Heat butter and/or oil in a large skillet over medium heat. Add the meat and sear on all sides. Place in a shallow roasting pan and roast uncovered until the internal temperature reaches 125°F–130°F. Remove from oven, cover loosely with foil, and let stand 15–20 minutes before serving.	15 minutes, plus 15–20 minutes standing time
VENISON POT ROAST Top round or shoulder roast; 3–4 pounds	BRAISE	Preheat oven to 350°F. Dust meat with seasoned flour. Heat oil and/or butter in a large Dutch oven. Add venison and brown on all sides. Add 1 inch water or braising liquid and seasonings. Cover. Place in oven and cook until tender, adding vegetables during last 45 minutes, if desired.	2–2½ hours

TYPE	METHOD	INSTRUCTIONS	TIMING
VENISON STEAKS OR CHOPS From loin	BROIL	Preheat broiler. Brush steaks or chops with oil and season well. Broil 4 inches from heat, turning once. Steaks and chops are done when the internal temperature reaches 125°F.	5 minutes per side
	GRILL	Prepare a medium-hot fire in the grill. Brush steaks or chops with oil and grill 4 inches from coals until tender, turning once. Steaks and chops are done when the internal temperature reaches 125°F.	5 minutes per side
	PAN-FRY	Place in a hot well-oiled heavy skillet. Sear on both sides over high heat, turning once. Steaks and chops are done when the internal temperature reaches 125°F.	3–5 minutes per side
	SAUTÉ	Heat oil or butter in a large heavy skillet over medium-high heat. Add steaks or chops and sauté, turning once. Steaks and chops are done when the internal temperature reaches 125°F.	3–5 minutes per side
WILD BOAR CHOPS	BROIL	Preheat broiler. Brush chops with oil and season well. Broil 4 inches from heat, turning once. Cook until medium to well done.	6–7 minutes per side
	GRILL	Prepare a medium-hot fire in the grill. Brush chops with oil and grill 4 inches from coals until tender, turning once. Cook until medium to well done.	6–7 minutes per side

TYPE	*METHOD*	*INSTRUCTIONS*	*TIMING*
WILD BOAR STEW MEAT OR BONELESS SHOULDER MEAT	STEW	Cut meat into 1½-inch cubes. Heat oil in a large Dutch oven over medium-high heat. Brown meat on all sides. Add seasonings and braising liquid to cover. Cover and simmer over low heat until meat is tender. If desired, add vegetables 45 minutes before the end of cooking time.	2 hours

3 Pressure Cooking

In a pressure cooker, you can cook foods in about one-third the time of regular stovetop cooking, while retaining flavor, nutrients, and texture. Some people shy away from pressure cooking because of disaster stories they have heard about exploding pots. But the current generation of pressure cookers is a far cry from the ones used in the past. They are made of new materials that seal the steam under the lid and are perfectly safe and easy to use. The valves are designed so that the excess steam will escape before any buildup can occur.

Pressure cookers come in many different styles, from deluxe to standard, and there are many variations depending on the model. Always consult the manufacturer's manual to get maximum results from your cooker. The standard industry-size cooker is 6 quarts.

Times for pressure cooking are given in ranges, even though you can't look inside the pot and taste for doneness. You will have to make a decision on whether to go with the shorter or longer time period, depending on the size and freshness of the ingredients, as well as how you like your foods cooked. Grains cooked for the shorter amount of time will be chewier; vegetables cooked for the shorter amount of time will be crunchier. Don't worry—you can always return the pot to the burner for more cooking.

Steam under pressure raises the temperature in the cooker above 212°F, which is the highest temperature attainable by boiling water at sea level. Most pressure cookers have controls enabling you to cook at 5, 10, or 15 pounds of pressure, thus increasing the temperature inside.

How to Use Your Pressure Cooker

First, read your manual. Models vary, and instructions vary from model to model. What follows are only the most general of instructions:

All ingredients should be cut into uniform pieces. Add the correct amount of liquid. Your manual will usually recommend a minimum amount of liquid. Never use less than the recommended amount. Stocks, juices, and sauces are considered liquid; oil is not.

Timing begins once pressure is reached. Always adjust the heat to maintain the pressure specified in the table or recipe. Generally this is done by lowering the heat after the correct pressure has been reached. You may have to adjust the heat often to be sure the correct amount of pressure is maintained.

Releasing Steam

When the cooking time is over, steam must be released before the pressure cooker can be safely opened. New pressure cookers have steam release buttons or latches that allow steam to escape. The lid will open easily after all the steam is released. This is a useful feature, especially when cooking delicate foods. On standard models, you can use these two methods for releasing steam:

Quick Cool. For the quick release of pressure on standard models, carefully carry cooker to the sink, release the lock as the manufacturer directs, then run cold water over the lid of the cooker. Once the pressure is released, shake the pot several times before opening the lid.

Slow Cool. Slow release of pressure can be done by sliding the pressure cooker off the burner and allowing it to stand until it cools enough for the pressure to be released. This can take 15 minutes, and the extra time can cause food to overcook. Use this method only where indicated.

Pressure and Cooking Temperatures

5 pounds (low): At 5 pounds of pressure, the temperature maintained inside the pressure cooker is 220°F. This temperature is recommended for cooking custards and puddings and some delicate fruit.

10 pounds (medium): At 10 pounds of pressure, the temperature maintained inside the pressure cooker is 235°F–240°F. This temperature is recommended for cooking most poultry and shellfish.

13 pounds (medium-high): At 13 pounds of pressure, the temperature maintained inside the pressure cooker is 240°F–245°F. This temperature is recommended for certain types of rice, desserts, and some very firm fruits and vegetables.

15 pounds (high): At 15 pounds of pressure, the temperature maintained inside the pressure cooker is 250°F. This temperature is recommended for cooking most soups, cereals, fresh and frozen vegetables, dried beans, legumes, dried fruit, rice, meat, and wild game.

Pressure Cooking Tips

- Foods that cook well in a pressure cooker: Rice, risotto, beans, vegetables, stew, soups, dried fruits.
- Foods to avoid cooking in a pressure cooker: Cranberries, rhubarb, split peas, applesauce, oatmeal, fish, pasta, and certain grains (millet).
- Carefully read the manufacturer's manual to get to know how your pressure cooker works.

- The cooking process can be stopped at any time. To interrupt the cooking, place the pressure cooker under cold running water. Shake the pot several times, then remove the lid by tilting it away from you, allowing the steam to escape away from your face and body.
- When preparing soups and stocks, release pressure slowly.
- The heat diffuser is a metal plate or wire that prevents direct contact between the bottom of your cooker with the burner. It usually comes with the cooker and should be used when cooking pasta, rice, cereals, or beans.
- Don't use high heat to bring up the pressure when cooking rice, cereals, or other foods that are apt to froth while cooking. Add 1 tablespoon oil to avoid the buildup of foam.
- Make sure to bring up pressure slowly and use the heat diffuser.
- When you want to cook two or more vegetables at the same time, it's not necessary to put them in separate containers, because one flavor will not invade the other.
- When cooking ingredients with different cooking times, cook the food with the longer timing first. Interrupt the timing by releasing the steam as directed. Then add the more quickly cooked ingredients, redevelop steam, and continue to cook.
- Sticking can occur with dishes that call for little liquid. To make sure this does not happen, use a heat diffuser.
- If the lid will not open, place the cooker over low heat to develop some pressure. Release steam rapidly and remove the lid. Sometimes a seal will form on the lid long after pressure is gone and the lid will open only after pressure is formed, then released.
- Wash your pressure cooker with soap and hot water. Make sure the valve is very clean. Rinse, dry, then rub mineral oil on rubber surfaces. This adds to the longevity of the rings. Most rubber rings will last for approximately 150 uses. Always store your pressure cooker with the lid unlocked.

DRIED BEANS AND LEGUMES

All dried beans, including lentils, must be presoaked before cooking in the pressure cooker to prevent foaming and clogging (see box below). Dried beans will double in volume when soaked. Add 1 tablespoon cooking oil per 1 cup beans to prevent foaming.

Always be sure that the vent of your pressure cooker is open and the hole is clear. Check that the pressure cooker is less than two-thirds full of water or liquid and has at least 1½ inches of clear space between the contents and rim of cooker. After cooking, let the pressure drop on its own before removing the cover. Always use a heat diffuser when cooking beans, and use the **Slow Cool Method** of releasing steam (page 293). The timings in the chart below are based on cooking with 15 pounds of pressure. Always consult your manual for instructions on cooking and handling.

Three Ways to Presoak

Conventional Soaking. Soak dried beans overnight: Place measured beans in bowl. For every 1 cup beans, add 2 cups water. Let stand for at least 6 hours or overnight. Drain and cook.

Quick Soak Method #1. Combine 4 cups water, 1 cup dried beans, and 1 teaspoon salt in pressure cooker. Secure lid. Over high heat, develop steam to high pressure (15 pounds) and cook 2 minutes. Quickly reduce the pressure by running cold water over the pressure cooker. Remove the lid. Drain the beans and cook as directed.

Quick Soak Method #2. Combine 4 cups water, 1 cup dried beans, and 1 teaspoon salt in pressure cooker. Cover pressure cooker and bring up to low pressure (5 pounds). Remove the pressure cooker from the heat and allow the cooker to release pressure on its own. Uncover and let stand 4 hours. Drain the beans and cook as directed.

TIMINGS:
Dried Beans and Legumes

TYPE BEANS	*AMOUNT BEANS*	*AMOUNT WATER*	*POUNDS PRESSURE*	*PRESSURE RELEASE*	*TIMING*
ADZUKI	1 cup	2 cups	15 pounds (High)	Slow Cool	3–5 minutes
BLACK BEANS	1 cup	2 cups	15 pounds (High)	Slow Cool	5–8 minutes
BLACK-EYED PEAS	1 cup	2 cups	15 pounds (High)	Slow Cool	4–10 minutes
CANNELLINI	1 cup	2 cups	15 pounds (High)	Slow Cool	4–6 minutes
GARBANZO BEANS (Chickpeas)	1 cup	2 cups	15 pounds (High)	Slow Cool	4–9 minutes
GREAT NORTHERN	1 cup	2 cups	15 pounds (High)	Slow Cool	4–9 minutes
KIDNEY	1 cup	2 cups	15 pounds (High)	Slow Cool	4–9 minutes
LENTILS	1 cup	2 cups	15 pounds (High)	Slow Cool	4–9 minutes
LIMA BEANS	1 cup	2 cups	15 pounds (High)	Slow Cool	3–5 minutes
NAVY	1 cup	2 cups	15 pounds (High)	Slow Cool	3–5 minutes
PINTO	1 cup	2 cups	15 pounds (High)	Slow Cool	3–5 minutes

TYPE BEANS	AMOUNT BEANS	AMOUNT WATER	POUNDS PRESSURE	PRESSURE RELEASE	TIMING
SOYBEANS	1 cup	2 cups	15 pounds (High)	Slow Cool	30–35 minutes
SPLIT PEAS	1 cup	3 cups	15 pounds (High)	Slow Cool	6–10 minutes

RICE

Rice dishes are perfect for cooking in the pressure cooker. Allow the steam to reduce slowly at the end of the cooking time (see **Slow Cool Method** of releasing steam, page 293). The added moisture improves the texture and creates very fluffy rice. Always use a heat diffuser so that the starch settling on the bottom of the pot does not burn.

For all types of rice, allow 2¼ cups broth or liquid for each 1 cup rice. Add 1 teaspoon salt and 1 tablespoon oil. (For risotto, add 2 tablespoons oil.)

TIMINGS: Rice

TYPE RICE	*AMOUNT RICE*	*AMOUNT LIQUID*	*POUNDS PRESSURE*	*PRESSURE RELEASE*	*TIMING*
ARBORIO	1 cup	2¼ cups	15 pounds (High)	Slow Cool	15–20 minutes
BASMATI RICE	1 cup	2¼ cups	13 pounds (Medium-high)	Slow Cool	5–7 minutes
CONVERTED RICE	1 cup	2¼ cups	13 pounds (Medium-high)	Slow Cool	5–7 minutes
LONG-GRAIN RICE	1 cup	2¼ cups	13 pounds (Medium-high)	Slow Cool	5–7 minutes
LONG-GRAIN BROWN RICE	1 cup	2¼ cups	15 pounds (High)	Slow Cool	15–25 minutes
WILD RICE	1 cup	2¼ cups	15 pounds (High)	Slow Cool	25–30 minutes

GRAINS

Grains are easily cooked in a pressure cooker. Begin by toasting the grains to bring out their nutty flavor: Place the grains in the dry pressure cooker over medium heat. Stir for 3 to 4 minutes, until the grain smells fragrant and appears lightly toasted. Stir in 1 tablespoon oil for each cup of grain. Add 4 to 4½ cups boiling liquid and use the chart below for timing. Add 3 cups water and 1 tablespoon oil for each additional cup of grain. Do not fill the pressure cooker beyond the halfway mark. When the cooking time is up, use the **Quick Cool Method** of releasing steam (page 292) and run the pot under cold running water. Drain immediately once the grains are cooked. Unlike what occurs with stovetop cooking, the grains will not absorb all the liquid.

Grains such as millet, amaranth, and quinoa are difficult to cook in a pressure cooker. Consult a pressure cooker recipe book for these grains.

TIMINGS: Grains

NOTE: The amount of liquid and the timings are given in ranges because some people like their grains chewier than others. Use less liquid and less time for chewy grains. If the grains are too chewy for your taste, replace the lid and return the pot to high pressure for another few minutes.

TYPE GRAIN	AMOUNT GRAIN	AMOUNT LIQUID	POUNDS PRESSURE	PRESSURE RELEASE	TIMING
BARLEY	1 cup	4–4½ cups	15 pounds (High)	Quick Cool	18–20 minutes
WHOLE BARLEY	1 cup	4–4½ cups	15 pounds (High)	Quick Cool	50–55 minutes
BULGUR	1 cup	4–4½ cups	15 pounds (High)	Quick Cool	5 minutes
JOB'S TEARS	1 cup	4–4½ cups	15 pounds (High)	Quick Cool	20–22 minutes
OAT GROATS	1 cup	4–4½ cups	15 pounds (High)	Quick Cool	25–30 minutes

TYPE GRAIN	*AMOUNT GRAIN*	*AMOUNT LIQUID*	*POUNDS PRESSURE*	*PRESSURE RELEASE*	*TIMING*
TRITICALE	1 cup	4–4½ cups	15 pounds (High)	Quick Cool	25–30 minutes
RYE BERRIES	1 cup	4–4½ cups	15 pounds (High)	Quick Cool	25–30 minutes
WHEAT BERRIES	1 cup	4–4½ cups	15 pounds (High)	Quick Cool	35–40 minutes

DRIED FRUIT

Pressure cooking dried fruit results in ready-to-eat stewed fruit. You can replace some or all of the water with fruit juice, if desired. Add sweetener after cooking; sugar will prevent the fruit from becoming fully tender. After cooking, a little lemon juice or a pinch of salt will bring out the flavor of the fruit.

TIMINGS: Dried Fruit

NOTE: Timings are given in ranges because some people like their fruit chewier than others. If the fruit is too chewy for your taste, replace the lid and return the pot to high pressure for another few minutes.

TYPE DRIED FRUIT	*AMOUNT FRUIT*	*AMOUNT WATER*	*POUNDS PRESSURE*	*PRESSURE RELEASE*	*TIMING*
APPLES	1 pound	2 cups	15 pounds (High)	Quick Cool	4–6 minutes
APRICOTS	1 pound	2 cups	15 pounds (High)	Quick Cool	3–6 minutes
DATES	1 pound	2 cups	15 pounds (High)	Quick Cool	6–10 minutes
FIGS	1 pound	2 cups	15 pounds (High)	Quick Cool	6–10 minutes
PEACHES	1 pound	2 cups	15 pounds (High)	Quick Cool	3–5 minutes
PEARS	1 pound	2 cups	15 pounds (High)	Quick Cool	4–7 minutes
PRUNES	1 pound	2 cups	15 pounds (High)	Quick Cool	5–6 minutes
RAISINS	1 pound	2 cups	15 pounds (High)	Quick Cool	5 minutes

VEGETABLES

The chart below is a general guide to pressure cooking vegetables. It is geared to average-sized vegetables bought in the market. If you have a garden and pick vegetables fresh, you may want to use less time for cooking.

Always be sure the vent of your pressure cooker is open, the hole is clear, and the pressure cooker is less than two-thirds full. Use the trivet that comes with your pressure cooker to keep the vegetables out of the water. You can also set a metal steaming basket in the pressure cooker, as long as the vegetables don't stick up above the two-thirds level in the pressure cooker. Use the **Quick Cool Method** (page 292) when cooking all vegetables.

TIMINGS: Fresh Vegetables

NOTE: Timings are given in ranges because some people like their vegetables crunchier than others. Use the shorter time if your vegetables are very fresh and you like them crunchy. If the vegetables are too crunchy for your taste, replace the lid and return the pot to high pressure for another few minutes.

TYPE VEGETABLE	*INSTRUCTIONS*	*AMOUNT WATER*	*POUNDS PRESSURE*	*PRESSURE RELEASE*	*TIMING*
ARTICHOKES	Trim bottom. Cut off 1 inch from the top.	1 cup	15 pounds (high)	Quick Cool	9–10 minutes
ASPARAGUS	Cut off woody ends. Leave spears whole.	½ cup	15 pounds (high)	Quick Cool	½–2 minutes
BEANS, GREEN AND WAX	Remove ends. French-cut or leave whole.	½ cup	15 pounds (high)	Quick Cool	½–2 minutes
BEANS, SHELL Lima, Fava, etc.	Shell.	½ cup	15 pounds (high)	Quick Cool	½–2 minutes

TYPE VEGETABLE	*INSTRUCTIONS*	*AMOUNT WATER*	*POUNDS PRESSURE*	*PRESSURE RELEASE*	*TIMING*
BEETS	Trim stems to 1-inch length. After cooking, let cool and slip off skins.	½ cup	15 pounds (high)	Quick Cool	12–15 minutes
BROCCOLI	Cut off tough part of stalk. Remove wilted outer leaves and peel off tough part of stem. Cut lengthwise into spears.	½ cup	15 pounds (high)	Quick Cool	½–2 minutes
BROCCOLI RABE	Trim off all tough and wilted leaves and tough part of stems. Cut into 1-inch pieces.	½ cup	15 pounds (high)	Quick Cool	½–2 minutes
BRUSSELS SPROUTS	Remove wilted leaves. Cut an X on the bottoms for even cooking.	½ cup	15 pounds (high)	Quick Cool	2–3 minutes
CABBAGE	Remove outside leaves and inner core. Cut into 1½-inch pieces.	½ cup	15 pounds (high)	Quick Cool	3–7 minutes
CARROTS	Scrub or peel. Leave small carrots whole; cut larger carrots into ¼-inch rounds.	whole carrots: 1 cup; sliced carrots: ½ cup	15 pounds (high)	Quick Cool	4–6 minutes 1½–2 minutes

TYPE VEGETABLE	*INSTRUCTIONS*	*AMOUNT WATER*	*POUNDS PRESSURE*	*PRESSURE RELEASE*	*TIMING*
CELERY	Remove leaves. Leave whole or chop into pieces.	½ cup	15 pounds (high)	Quick Cool	1½–2 minutes
CELERY ROOT (Celeriac)	Peel. Cut into slices or strips.	½ cup	15 pounds (high)	Quick Cool	2–3 minutes
CORN ON THE COB	Remove husk and silk.	½ cup	15 pounds (high)	Quick Cool	2–4 minutes
GREENS Beet, Collard, Escarole, Kale, Mustard, Turnip greens	Wash thoroughly in several changes of water.	½ cup	15 pounds (high)	Quick Cool	2–3 minutes
KOHLRABI	Peel and cut into ½-inch cubes.	1 cup	15 pounds (high)	Quick Cool	1–2 minutes
ONIONS	Peel. Leave onions 2 inches in diameter or smaller whole. Cut large onions in halves or quarters.	1 cup	15 pounds (high)	Quick Cool	5 minutes
PARSNIPS	Scrape or peel. Leave whole.	1 cup	15 pounds (high)	Quick Cool	7 minutes
PEAS, GREEN	Shell.	½ cup	15 pounds (high)	Quick Cool	1–2 minutes
POTATOES	Scrub. Do not peel new potatoes; leave whole.	1 cup	15 pounds (high)	Quick Cool	8–10 minutes

TYPE VEGETABLE	INSTRUCTIONS	AMOUNT WATER	POUNDS PRESSURE	PRESSURE RELEASE	TIMING
SPINACH	Wash thoroughly in several changes of water.	½ cup	15 pounds (high)	Quick Cool	½–1 minute
SQUASH, WINTER Acorn, Buttercup, Golden nugget, Spaghetti	Peel and cut into 2-inch chunks.	1½ cups	15 pounds (high)	Quick Cool	10–14 minutes
SWEET POTATOES	Scrub and leave whole.	1 cup	15 pounds (high)	Quick Cool	8–10 minutes
TURNIPS AND RUTABAGAS	Peel and cut into 1-inch slices or cubes.	½ cup	15 pounds (high)	Quick Cool	2–3 minutes

SHELLFISH

Generally, people cook shellfish in a pressure cooker with vegetables, rice, or other ingredients. For the timing of complicated recipes, consult a cookbook. The amount of liquid used may depend on the recipe and the amount of ingredients used with the shellfish.

All shellfish should be thawed before it is placed in the pressure cooker. Cook under high pressure of 15 pounds. Use the **Quick Cool Method** of releasing steam (page 292) for all shellfish by running the pressure cooker under cold water.

TIMINGS: Shellfish

TYPE SHELLFISH	*SIZE OR AMOUNT*	*AMOUNT WATER*	*POUNDS PRESSURE*	*PRESSURE RELEASE*	*TIMING*
CLAMS	Medium	1 cup	15 pounds (High)	Quick Cool	3 minutes
CRAB LEGS	6–8 ounces	1 cup	15 pounds (High)	Quick Cool	2 minutes
LOBSTER TAIL	6–8 ounces	1 cup	15 pounds (High)	Quick Cool	5 minutes
	12–14 ounces	1 cup	15 pounds (High)	Quick Cool	8 minutes
SCALLOPS	Small	1 cup	15 pounds (High)	Quick Cool	1 minute
	Medium or Large	1 cup	15 pounds (High)	Quick Cool	2 minutes
SHRIMP	Small	1 cup	15 pounds (High)	Quick Cool	1 minute
	Medium	1 cup	15 pounds (High)	Quick Cool	2 minutes
	Large	1 cup	15 pounds (High)	Quick Cool	3 minutes

POULTRY

Poultry blends well with other ingredients when cooked in the pressure cooker, so it is often cooked with vegetables or rice. You may want to consult a cookbook for your favorite dishes, because the amount of liquid and the length of the timings will vary depending on the ingredients used. Poultry can be browned before cooking (sear the poultry for 3–4 minutes in hot oil). Or, after cooking, it can be browned under the broiler until the skin is nice and crisp.

In general, allow 10 minutes of pressure cooking for every 2 inches of thickness. Use the **Quick Cool Method** of releasing steam (page 292).

TIMINGS: Poultry

TYPE POULTRY	*PART OR SIZE*	*AMOUNT WATER*	*POUNDS PRESSURE*	*PRESSURE RELEASE*	*TIMING*
CHICKEN	Whole (4–5 pounds)	1 cup	10 pounds (Medium)	Quick Cool	25–30 minutes
	Serving-size pieces, skin removed	1 cup	10 pounds (Medium)	Quick Cool	8–10 minutes
	Breast halves with bone	1 cup	10 pounds (Medium)	Quick Cool	10–12 minutes
	Breast pounded to fillets	1 cup	10 pounds (Medium)	Quick Cool	2–3 minutes
	Drumsticks with skin removed	1 cup	10 pounds (Medium)	Quick Cool	9–10 minutes
	Thighs (2 inches thick)	1 cup	10 pounds (Medium)	Quick Cool	10 minutes
	Thighs or breasts, boneless, frozen	1 cup	10 pounds (Medium)	Quick Cool	5–7 minutes

TYPE POULTRY	*PART OR SIZE*	*AMOUNT WATER*	*POUNDS PRESSURE*	*PRESSURE RELEASE*	*TIMING*
DUCK	Cut into pieces	1 cup	10 pounds (Medium)	Quick Cool	8–10 minutes
PHEASANT	Cut into pieces	1 cup	10 pounds (Medium)	Quick Cool	7–10 minutes
PIGEON	Halved	1 cup	10 pounds (Medium)	Quick Cool	25–30 minutes
ROCK CORNISH HENS	1¼–1½ pounds	1 cup	10 pounds (Medium)	Quick Cool	8–10 minutes
TURKEY	Drumsticks	1 cup	10 pounds (Medium)	Quick Cool	15–20 minutes
	Half breast with bone	1 cup	10 pounds (Medium)	Quick Cool	25–30 minutes
	Leg quarter	1 cup	10 pounds (Medium)	Quick Cool	25–30 minutes

MEAT

Most meat cooked in the pressure cooker is combined with vegetables, potatoes, or other ingredients. Consult a cookbook for stews and meat dishes, because the amount of liquid used and the timings will vary depending on the type and amount of other ingredients used.

In general, cut the meat into uniform-size pieces and sear in oil and/or butter for 3 minutes. This seals in juices and adds color as well as flavor. Limit the size of roasts to 3 to 4 pounds or less. Allow slightly more cooking time for cuts with bones. Reduce the steam slowly at the end of cooking cycle unless "Quick Cool" is noted. For more information on the methods for releasing steam, see page 292.

TIMINGS: Beef

CUT BEEF	*SIZE OR AMOUNT*	*AMOUNT WATER*	*POUNDS PRESSURE*	*PRESSURE RELEASE*	*TIMING*
BEEF STEW	1½-inch cubes	4 cups	15 pounds (High)	Slow Cool	16–20 minutes
BLADE ROAST	2–3 pounds	2 cups	15 pounds (High)	Slow Cool	20 minutes per inch thickness
BRISKET Whole	2–3 pounds	2 cups	15 pounds (High)	Slow Cool	20 minutes per inch thickness
Flat cut	2–3 pounds	2 cups	15 pounds (High)	Quick Cool	9 minutes
CHUCK ROAST	3 pounds	2 cups	15 pounds (High)	Slow Cool	35 minutes

CUT BEEF	*SIZE OR AMOUNT*	*AMOUNT WATER*	*POUNDS PRESSURE*	*PRESSURE RELEASE*	*TIMING*
CORNED BEEF	3 pounds	4 cups	15 pounds (High)	Slow Cool	60 minutes or 20 minutes per inch thickness
FLANK STEAK	¼ inch thick	1½ cups	13 pounds (Medium-high)	Slow Cool	20 minutes
LIVER, SLICED	¼ inch thick	2 cups	15 pounds (High)	Quick Cool	5 minutes
MEATBALLS	¼ inch round	1 cup	13 pounds (Medium-high)	Slow Cool	10 minutes
OXTAIL	1-inch to 3-inch cross sections	3 cups	13 pounds (Medium-high)	Slow Cool	For stock: 18–20 minutes
ROLLED RIB ROAST	3 pounds	2 cups	15 pounds (High)	Slow Cool	30 minutes
ROUND STEAK	¼ inch thick	1 cup	15 pounds (High)	Quick Cool	4 minutes
	½ inch thick	1 cup	15 pounds (High)	Quick Cool	10 minutes
	1 inch thick	1½ cups	15 pounds (High)	Slow Cool	25 minutes
	2-inch cubes	1 cup	15 pounds (High)	Slow Cool	18 minutes
SHORT RIBS	¾ inch thick	1½ cups	15 pounds (High)	Slow Cool	25 minutes
SHANKS	2–3 pounds	1½ cups	15 pounds (High)	Slow Cool	18–20 minutes

TIMINGS: Veal

CUT VEAL	SIZE OR AMOUNT	AMOUNT WATER	POUNDS PRESSURE	PRESSURE RELEASE	TIMING
BREAST	1–2 pounds	1 cup	15 pounds (High)	Quick Cool	8 minutes per inch thickness
CHOPS	¼ inch thick	1 cup	15 pounds (High)	Quick Cool	2 minutes
	½ inch thick	1 cup	15 pounds (High)	Quick Cool	2 minutes
CUTLETS	¼–½ inch thick	½ cup	15 pounds (High)	Quick Cool	10 minutes per inch thickness
ROAST	3 pounds	1 cup	15 pounds (High)	Slow Cool	45 minutes
RUMP	3–4 pounds	1 cup	15 pounds (High)	Quick Cool	8 minutes per inch thickness
SHOULDER	3–4 pounds	1 cup	15 pounds (High)	Quick Cool	8 minutes per inch thickness
VEAL STEAK	½–¾ inch thick	1 cup	15 pounds (High)	Quick Cool	6–8 minutes
	1 inch thick	1 cup	15 pounds (High)	Quick Cool	10 minutes
STEW MEAT	1-inch cubes	2 cups	15 pounds (High)	Quick Cool	8 minutes per inch thickness

TIMINGS: Lamb

CUT LAMB	SIZE OR AMOUNT	AMOUNT WATER	POUNDS PRESSURE	PRESSURE RELEASE	TIMING
CHOPS	¼ inch thick	1 cup	15 pounds (High)	Slow Cool	2 minutes
	½ inch thick	1 cup	15 pounds (High)	Slow Cool	5 minutes
LEG	3 pounds	1 cup	15 pounds (High)	Slow Cool	35–45 minutes
NECK	2–3 pounds	1 cup	15 pounds (High)	Slow Cool	10 minutes
RIBLETS	2–3 pounds	1 cup	15 pounds (High)	Slow Cool	10 minutes
SHANKS	split in half	1 cup	15 pounds (High)	Slow Cool	10 minutes
SHOULDER	3–4 pounds	1 cup	15 pounds (High)	Slow Cool	10 minutes
STEW MEAT	1-inch cubes	1 cup	15 pounds (High)	Slow Cool	10 minutes

TIMINGS: Pork and Ham

CUT PORK	SIZE OR AMOUNT	AMOUNT WATER	POUNDS PRESSURE	PRESSURE RELEASE	TIMING
PORK PICNIC SHOULDER, UNCOOKED	3–4 pounds	2 cups	15 pounds (High)	Slow Cool	30 minutes
HAM SHANK, UNCOOKED	3–5 pounds	2 cups	15 pounds (High)	Slow Cool	35–45 minutes

CUT PORK	*SIZE OR AMOUNT*	*AMOUNT WATER*	*POUNDS PRESSURE*	*PRESSURE RELEASE*	*TIMING*
HAM STEAKS, UNCOOKED	1 inch thick	2 cups	15 pounds (High)	Quick Cool	9–12 minutes
	2 inches thick	2 cups	15 pounds (High)	Quick Cool	12–20 minutes

TIMINGS: Game

TYPE GAME	*SIZE OR AMOUNT*	*AMOUNT WATER*	*POUNDS PRESSURE*	*PRESSURE RELEASE*	*TIMING*
RABBIT	whole	2 cups	15 pounds (High)	Slow Cool	12–15 minutes
VENISON	3–4 inches thick	2 cups	15 pounds (High)	Slow Cool	30–40 minutes

SOUPS

One of the best ways to use a pressure cooker is to make soups in it. Flavors blend well to give you slow-simmered flavor in a fraction of the time it normally takes.

TIMINGS: Soups

NOTE: All timings are for a 6-quart pressure cooker. Fill the pressure cooker to less than three-quarters of its capacity. If the soup contains grains, the cooker should be filled only half full. Use the Slow Cool Method of releasing steam (page 293).

TYPE SOUP	AMOUNT WATER	POUNDS PRESSURE	PRESSURE RELEASE	TIMING
BEANS, PRESOAKED	12 cups	15 pounds (High)	Slow Cool	20 minutes
BEANS, PRECOOKED	12 cups	15 pounds (High)	Slow Cool	10 minutes
BEEF	12–16 cups	15 pounds (High)	Slow Cool	60 minutes
CHICKEN	12–16 cups	15 pounds (High)	Slow Cool	30–35 minutes
FISH	12–16 cups	15 pounds (High)	Slow Cool	10–12 minutes
GRAINS	12 cups	15 pounds (High)	Slow Cool	15–60 minutes
HAM	12–16 cups	15 pounds (High)	Slow Cool	30–35 minutes

4 Microwave Cooking, Defrosting, and Reheating

Many changes and improvements have been made to the microwave oven over the years, but those improvements haven't changed the way most people think about microwave cooking. The fact is that microwaves are used mostly for thawing frozen food or warming leftovers. One of the problems cooks have with microwave cooking is that they can't see, touch, or hear the food they are cooking. In spite of these and many other drawbacks, the microwave is here to stay.

Timing food, in general, is difficult; in a microwave, however, it is even more challenging. First of all, there is no standardization of microwave ovens; they vary tremendously in power output. The size of the food and the container it's cooked in affects the timing for most foods. Therefore, use the times provided in this chapter as a guideline for your own experiments with the microwave oven.

Cooking in the Microwave

Just as burners on stoves can be adjusted for level of heat, most microwaves have **power settings** that enable you to control the intensity of the microwave. The range of intensity is usually given as a percentage, with 100 percent power for the highest intensity and 10 percent power for the lowest. Most foods are cooked at 100 percent power and defrosted at 30 percent power.

One way microwave cooking varies significantly from stovetop cooking is in the necessity for **standing time.** Standing time allows the food to finish cooking. When the cooking time is completed, remove the food from the microwave, place the dish on a heat-resistant surface, and keep the container covered. Let the food stand for the time called for in the charts.

If you think the food is going to be undercooked, even with the standing time, return it to the microwave for additional cooking. Don't just give the food more standing time. On the other hand, try to avoid overcooking food; the food will continue cooking while it stands.

Judging When Microwaved Food Is Done

When food steams throughout the dish, not just at the edge, the food is heated through. The center of the bottom of the dish will be quite hot to the touch. Beyond these measures, you can judge when food is cooked by conventional means—looking, feeling, and tasting or using an instant-read thermometer. Fish will be opaque and flake easily with a fork. The thigh joints of poultry should move easily and juices should run clear and yellow, not pink. Meat should show no pink color on the outside.

What Microwaves Do Well

- Defrost foods.
- Warm up leftovers.
- Steam (moist-heat cooking) vegetables, fish, shellfish, and white meat of poultry.
- Cook bacon.
- Poach fruit.
- Make and reheat sauces.
- Make and reheat soups.
- Make candy.
- Melt chocolate.
- Blanch fruit and tomatoes for easy peeling.

What Microwaves Do *Not* Do Well

- Brown food or make it crispy.
- Blend flavors.
- Cook meat. (The microwave steams meat, plus large portions of juices are lost.)
- Cook beans and pasta. (These cook well in small amounts, but take too long and have a tendency to cook unevenly.)
- Cook eggs.
- Bake.

You may choose to use the microwave for cooking foods on the "Don't" list anyway. Therefore, some of them will be listed in the microwave timing section. If you like microwave cooking, I urge you to experiment with the cooking and timings and wish you good luck.

Tips for Safe and Efficient Microwave Use

- Don't use metal in the microwave. The only exception: You can use 2-inch-wide (and no wider) strips of aluminum foil to shield food that is getting overcooked.
- Always use a dish or container that is microwave safe.
- Round or oval-shaped casseroles or dishes work best. Square-cornered cookware concentrates the energy, so food tends to overcook in the corners.
- Don't operate a microwave empty.
- Use only plastic wrap, paper, and paper towels labeled microwave safe. Waxed paper is okay.
- Do not let plastic wrap touch the food you are cooking. Use it only as a cover, leaving 1 inch of space between the food and the wrap.
- When containers are covered with plastic wrap, vent the steam by turning the wrap back at one corner to allow steam to escape.
- Potatoes, sausages, and other foods that can explode while microwave cooking should be pricked with a fork before cooking.
- Arrange food so that the thickest areas are toward the outside of the dish. (Food cooks more quickly at the outer edge of the dish.)
- Cover all foods while cooking. To trap steam, use a lid or plastic wrap. To trap heat, but not steam, use waxed paper.
- When covering with waxed paper, cut the sheet generously enough to trap the ends of the paper under the dish to secure it.
- Cook for the shortest amount of time indicated, then check to see if the food needs more time.
- When stirring food, stir from the outside toward the center of the dish.
- Most foods require turning, stirring, or rearranging at least once during cooking, because food in a microwave cooks from top to bottom and from outside to inside.

- When cooking food that has both thin and thick areas, such as poultry and certain cuts of meat, make a shield with a thin piece of aluminum foil and cover thin areas so they don't overcook.
- Small quantities will cook faster than large ones. (Example: 1 potato may bake in 4 minutes, while 8 potatoes will bake in 20 minutes.)
- Smooth, compact foods, such as a rolled pot roast, will microwave more evenly than irregularly shaped poultry or fish.
- Refrigerator-cold and frozen foods take longer to cook than those at room temperature.
- Many foods require standing time, while still covered, to finish cooking after they are removed from the microwave.
- When reheating food, turn or stir two or three times.
- When reheating food with gravy, cover with waxed paper; without gravy, a paper towel can be used.
- When reheating bread or rolls, wrap loosely in a paper napkin or towel.
- For stews and braises, you will achieve superior results if you brown the foods on top of the stove and then transfer them to the microwave to finish cooking.
- Meat cooked in a microwave will not brown. To brown microwave-cooked meats, transfer them to the broiler or grill for the final few minutes of cooking.
- Microwave chicken and meat on special microwave-safe roasting racks, which are deeply ridged plastic racks, set in baking dish. This allows fat to drain away from meat.

Microwave Power Settings

650–800-WATT MICROWAVE	*POWER LEVEL*	*OVEN OR STOVETOP*
100–90% power	High	425°F–500°F or high on stovetop
80% power		375°F–425°F or high on stovetop
70% power	Medium-high	350°F–375°F or medium-high on stovetop
60–50% power	Medium	300°F–350°F or medium on stovetop
40–30% power	Medium-low	225°F–300°F or medium-low on stovetop
20% power	Low	200°F–225°F or low on stovetop
10% power		150°F–200°F or lowest setting on stovetop

RICE

TIMINGS: Rice

Cooking rice in a microwave reduces the time needed and enables you to cook and serve in the same bowl, if desired.

NOTE: All timings are based on using mid- and full-size microwave ovens in the 600- to 700-watt range. In ovens less than 600 watts, increase cooking times by 10–15 percent. In those over 700 watts, check the manufacturer's timing guide. Timings are given in ranges. If your microwave is in the 600-watt range, use the longer times. If it is in the 700-watt range, use the shorter times.

TYPE	INSTRUCTIONS	POWER	TIMING	STANDING TIME
WHITE RICE 1 cup	Combine with **2 cups water** in a 2-quart microwave-safe bowl. Cover.			
Long-grain		100% (High) + 50% (Medium)	5 minutes 9–10 minutes	 5 min
Short-grain, Arborio		100% (High) + 50% (Medium)	4–6 minutes 9–10 minutes	 5 min
Basmati		100% (High) + 50% (Medium)	4–5 minutes 7–8 minutes	 5 min
BROWN RICE 1 cup	Combine with **2½ cups water** in a 2-quart microwave-safe bowl. Cover.			
Long-grain		100% (High) + 50% (Medium)	5 minutes 28–30 minutes	 5 min
Short-grain		100% (High) + 50% (Medium)	5 minutes 28–30 minutes	 5 min
Basmati		100% (High) + 50% (Medium)	5 minutes 26–28 minutes	 5 min

TYPE	*INSTRUCTIONS*	*POWER*	*TIMING*	*STANDING TIME*
BROWN RICE (*cont'd*) Converted		100% (High) + 50% (Medium)	5 minutes 28–30 minutes	5 min
WILD RICE 1 cup	Combine with **2 cups water** in a 2-quart microwave-safe bowl. Cover tightly with plastic wrap. After microwaving, pierce plastic to vent, then cover with a plate and let stand.	100% (High)	12 minutes	15 min

FRESH AND FROZEN VEGETABLES

Because steaming is a fine way to cook vegetables, the microwave can be used to cook both fresh and frozen vegetables. It allows vegetables to retain their color, flavor, and vitamins. Always wash and trim fresh vegetables before cooking. Most of them should be allowed to stand, covered, to finish cooking.

TIMINGS: Fresh Vegetables

NOTE: All timings are based on using mid- and full-size microwave ovens in the 600- to 700-watt range. If your microwave is in the 600-watt range, use the longer timings. If it is in the 700-watt range, use the shorter.

VEGETABLE	*INSTRUCTIONS*	*POWER*	*TIMING*	*STANDING TIME*
ARTICHOKES 6–8-ounce globes	Cut stems flush with bottoms. Cut off prickly tips. Wrap artichokes separately in plastic food wrap. Turn over about halfway through. Test for doneness after minimum time by piercing wrap with fork.			
1		100% (High)	3–5 minutes	3 min
2		100% (High)	5–7 minutes	3 min
4		100% (High)	10–13 minutes	4 min
ASPARAGUS	Combine in a dish with ¼ **cup water.** Cover. Rotate dish once while cooking.			
⅓ pound (6–7 spears)		100% (High)	2½–3 minutes	3 min
1 pound (15–20 spears)		100% (High)	3–4 minutes	3 min
2 pounds (36–40 spears)		100% (High)	8–10 minutes	3 min

VEGETABLE	*INSTRUCTIONS*	*POWER*	*TIMING*	*STANDING TIME*
BEANS, GREEN	Combine in a dish with **2 tablespoons water.** Cover.			
¼ pound		100% (High)	5–6 minutes	2 min
½ pound		100% (High)	7–10 minutes	2 min
1 pound		100% (High)	10–15 minutes	3 min
BEETS	Prick the skins of whole beets, or cube or slice. Place in a dish with **¼ cup water.** Cover. Stir twice while cooking.			
⅓ pound (2 small)		100% (High)	6–8 minutes	3 min
¾ pound (3 medium)		100% (High)	12–14 minutes	3 min
1½ pounds (6 medium)		100% (High)	16–20 minutes	3 min
BROCCOLI SPEARS	Combine in a dish with **1 tablespoon water** and cover. Rotate or stir at least once while cooking. Uncover during standing time.			
¼ pound		100% (High)	3–4 minutes	2 min
½ pound		100% (High)	5–7 minutes	2 min
1 pound		100% (High)	10–15 minutes	2 min
BROCCOLI RABE	Chop broccoli rabe. Combine in a dish with **3 tablespoons water.** Cover. Stir once while cooking.			
¼ pound		100% (High)	4–5 minutes	None
½ pound		100% (High)	5–7 minutes	None
1 pound		100% (High)	7–9 minutes	None

VEGETABLE	INSTRUCTIONS	POWER	TIMING	STANDING TIME
BRUSSELS SPROUTS (1 inch in diameter)	Combine in a dish with **3 tablespoons water.** Cover. Stir at least once during cooking time.			
¼ pound		100% (High)	3 minutes	3–4 min
½ pound		100% (High)	4–6 minutes	3 min
¾–1 pound		100% (High)	6–8 minutes	3 min
CABBAGE, GREEN OR RED	Cut into wedges and place in a dish with wide ends facing out. Or shred and place in dish. Add **3 tablespoons water.** Cover. Stir once during cooking.			
1½ cups shredded		100% (High)	3–5 minutes	3 min
3 cups shredded		100% (High)	5–6 minutes	3 min
2 wedges (1 quart)		100% (High)	5–7 minutes	2–3 min
4 wedges (1½ quarts)		100% (High)	8–10 minutes	2–3 min
8 wedges (2–3 quarts)		100% (High)	10–12 minutes	2–3 min

VEGETABLE	INSTRUCTIONS	POWER	TIMING	STANDING TIME
CARROTS, REGULAR OR BABY	Cut regular carrots into 1-inch chunks; leave baby carrots whole. Combine in a dish with **2 tablespoons water.** Cover; stir once during cooking.			
⅓ pound		100% (High)	4–5 minutes	2 min
⅔ pound		100% (High)	6–8 minutes	2 min
1⅓ pounds		100% (High)	8–10 minutes	2 min
2 pounds		100% (High)	10–15 minutes	2 min
⅔ cup strips		100% (High)	5–6 minutes	3 min
1⅓ cups strips		100% (High)	6–8 minutes	3 min
CAULIFLOWER	Leave whole or cut into florets. Combine in a dish with **1 tablespoon water.** Cover. Rearrange or stir once during cooking.			
1½-pound head		100% (High)	7–10 minutes	3 min
2-pound head		100% (High)	12–15 minutes	3 min
1 cup florets (¼ pound)		100% (High)	3–4 minutes	2 min
2 cups florets (½ pound)		100% (High)	4–6 minutes	3 min
4 cups florets (1 pound)		100% (High)	8–10 minutes	3 min
CELERY	Cut into 1½-inch slices. Combine in a dish with **¼ cup water.** Cover. Stir once during cooking.			
¼ pound		100% (High)	4–6 minutes	2 min
½ pound		100% (High)	6–8 minutes	2 min
1 pound		100% (High)	9–10 minutes	3 min

VEGETABLE	INSTRUCTIONS	POWER	TIMING	STANDING TIME
CELERY ROOT (Celeriac)	Cut into 1½-inch cubes. Combine in a dish with **¼ cup water.** Cover.			
1 pound		100% (High)	4–5 minutes	3 min
CORN, WHOLE KERNEL	Spread kernels evenly in a dish. Add 2 tablespoons water. Cover with waxed paper.			
¾ cup		100% (High)	3–4 minutes	None
1½ cups		100% (High)	4–5 minutes	None
3 cups		100% (High)	7–8 minutes	None
CORN ON THE COB	Place on a plate. Add **2 tablespoons water.** Cover with waxed paper. Rearrange once during cooking.			
1 ear		100% (High)	3 minutes	2–3 min
2 ears		100% (High)	3–4 minutes	3 min
4 ears		100% (High)	5–6 minutes	3 min
EGGPLANT	Cut eggplant in half and place halves with cut sides up in a dish. Cover. Microwave until eggplant is soft.			
1¼–1½ pounds		100% (High)	8–10 minutes	None
FENNEL	Combine in dish with **¼ cup water.** Cover. Stir or arrange once while cooking.			
½ bulb		100% (High)	2 minutes	4–6 min
1 bulb		100% (High)	6–8 minutes	2 min
2 bulbs		100% (High)	9–10 minutes	3 min
GARLIC	Not recommended.			

VEGETABLE	INSTRUCTIONS	POWER	TIMING	STANDING TIME
GREENS (Beet greens, Chicory, Collard, Escarole, Kale, Mustard, Radicchio, Swiss chard, Turnip greens)	Place greens in dish still wet from washing. Cover. Stir once during cooking.			
½ pound		100% (High)	2½–3½ minutes	None
1 pound		100% (High)	4–6 minutes	None
2 pounds		100% (High)	7–9 minutes	None
3 pounds		100% (High)	10–12 minutes	None
KOHLRABI	Cut into ½-inch cubes. Combine in a dish with **¼ cup water.** Cover.			
⅔ cup		100% (High)	4–5 minutes	3 min
1½ cups		100% (High)	6–7 minutes	3 min
2½ cups		100% (High)	8–9 minutes	3 min
LEEKS	Cut into 1-inch slices. Place in a dish with **¼ cup water.** Cover.			
½ pound		100% (High)	5–7 minutes	3 min
1 pound		100% (High)	7–9 minutes	3 min
2 pounds		100% (High)	9–12 minutes	3 min

VEGETABLE	INSTRUCTIONS	POWER	TIMING	STANDING TIME
MUSHROOMS (Button, Chanterelles, Enoki, Morels, Oyster, Porcini, Shiitake)	Cut into 1½-inch slices. Combine in a dish with **2 tablespoons butter** and **1 tablespoon oil.** Cover. Stir 2–3 times during cooking.			
½ pound		100% (High)	2 minutes	None
¾ pound		100% (High)	2–3 minutes	None
1 pound		100% (High)	4–5 minutes	None
OKRA	Slice 1 inch thick. Combine in a dish with **¼ cup water.** Cover. Stir once during cooking.			
¼ pound		100% (High)	1 minute	2–3 min
½ pound		100% (High)	3½–4 minutes	1 min
1 pound		100% (High)	1 minute	5–6 min
ONIONS, SMALL WHITE	Place in a dish with **¼ cup water.** Cover.			
¼ pound		100% (High)	4–5 minutes	3 min
½ pound		100% (High)	5–7 minutes	3 min
1 pound		100% (High)	7–10 minutes	3 min
PARSNIPS	Cut into 3-inch chunks. Combine in a dish with **¼ cup water.** Cover. Stir once during cooking.			
6 ounces		100% (High)	3–4 minutes	2 min
¾ pound		100% (High)	4–6 minutes	3 min
1½ pounds		100% (High)	7–9 minutes	3 min

VEGETABLE	INSTRUCTIONS	POWER	TIMING	STANDING TIME
PEAS, GREEN	Combine in a dish with ¼ **cup water.** Cover. Stir once during cooking.			
⅔ cup		100% (High)	2–2½ minutes	None
1⅓ cups		100% (High)	3–5 minutes	None
2⅔ cups		100% (High)	5–7 minutes	None
PEAS, SUGAR, SNAP AND SNOW	Combine in a dish with ¼ **cup water.** Cover. Stir once during cooking.			
1 pound		100% (High)	5–8 minutes	None
PEPPERS, SWEET	Combine rings or strips in a dish with ¼ **cup water.** Cover. Stir once during cooking.			
1		100% (High)	2–3 minutes	None
2		100% (High)	4–6 minutes	None
4		100% (High)	6–8 minutes	None
PEPPERS, HOT	Not recommended.			
POTATOES Baked (5 ounces each)	Prick potatoes with fork. Place on paper towel. Turn over once during cooking.			
1		100% (High)	3 minutes	4–5 min
2		100% (High)	7–9 minutes	3 min
4		100% (High)	11–13 minutes	3 min
POTATOES Boiled	Peel and quarter potatoes. Combine in a dish with ¼ **cup water.** Cover. Stir once during cooking.			
1		100% (High)	3–4 minutes	2–3 min
2		100% (High)	4–6 minutes	2–3 min
4		100% (High)	7–9 minutes	3 min

VEGETABLE	INSTRUCTIONS	POWER	TIMING	STANDING TIME
POTATOES, SWEET	Prick potatoes with fork. Place on paper towel. Turn over once during cooking.			
1		100% (High)	4–5 minutes	3 min
2		100% (High)	6–8 minutes	3 min
4		100% (High)	10–12 minutes	3 min
RUTABAGAS	Cut in ½-inch cubes. Combine in a dish with **¼ cup water.** Cover, stir 2–3 times during cooking.			
1 cup		100% (High)	5–7 minutes	3 min
2 cups		100% (High)	9–11 minutes	3 min
4 cups		100% (High)	12–14 minutes	3 min
SPINACH	Chop spinach. Place in a dish still wet from washing. Cover. Stir once during cooking.			
1 pound		100% (High).	3 minutes	4–6 min
SQUASH, SUMMER (Yellow, Zucchini)	Slice ¼ inch thick. Combine in a dish with **1 teaspoon water.** Cover. Stir once during cooking.			
1 cup		100% (High)	2–4 minutes	3 min
SQUASH, WINTER (Acorn)	Prick on top, place on paper towel. Turn once during cooking. Or cut in half, remove seeds and fibers, and place cut side down in dish with **2 tablespoons water.** Cover, rearrange once during cooking.			
1 pound		100% (High)	3 minutes	4–5 min
TOMATOES	Halve and place in round dish. Cover. Rearrange once during cooking.			
2		100% (High)	1–2 minutes	None
4		100% (High)	2–3 minutes	None
6		100% (High)	3–4 minutes	None

VEGETABLE	*INSTRUCTIONS*	*POWER*	*TIMING*	*STANDING TIME*
TURNIPS	Cut into ½-inch cubes. Combine in dish with **¼ cup water.** Cover. Stir once during cooking.			
5 ounces		100% (High)	4–5 minutes	3 min
¾ pound		100% (High)	5–7 minutes	3 min
1½ pounds		100% (High)	7–9 minutes	3 min

TIMINGS: Frozen Vegetables

FROZEN VEGETABLE	*INSTRUCTIONS*	*POWER*	*TIMING*	*STANDING TIME*
ASPARAGUS 10-ounce package	Combine in dish with **1 tablespoon water.** Cover. Separate after 3 minutes.	100% (High)	6–8 minutes	2 min
BEANS, GREEN 10-ounce package	Combine in dish with **1 tablespoon water.** Cover. Stir after 3 minutes.	100% (High)	5–7 minutes	2 min
BEANS (LIMA) 10-ounce package	Combine in dish with **1 tablespoon water.** Cover. Stir after 3 minutes.	100% (High)	6–9 minutes	2 min
BROCCOLI 10-ounce package	Combine in dish with **2 tablespoons water.** Cover. Stir after 3 minutes. Uncover during standing time.	100% (High)	5–7 minutes	2 min
BRUSSELS SPROUTS 10-ounce package	Combine in dish with **2 tablespoons water.** Cover. Stir after 3 minutes.	100% (High)	6–8 minutes	2 min

FROZEN VEGETABLE	*INSTRUCTIONS*	*POWER*	*TIMING*	*STANDING TIME*
CARROTS 2 cups	Combine in dish with **1 tablespoon water.** Do not cover. Stir after 3 minutes.	100% (High)	5–7 minutes	2 min
CAULIFLOWER FLORETS 10-ounce package	Combine in dish with **1 tablespoon water.** Cover. Stir after 3 minutes.	100% (High)	4–6 minutes	2 min
CORN ON THE COB 2 ears	Place in glass or ceramic pie plate with **2 tablespoons water.** Cover. Rearrange after 4 minutes.	100% (High)	6–8 minutes	2 min
CORN KERNELS 10-ounce package	Combine in dish with **2 tablespoons water.** Cover. Stir after 2 minutes.	100% (High)	4–6 minutes	2 min
OKRA, WHOLE OR SLICED 10-ounce package	Combine in dish with **2 tablespoons water.** Cover. Stir after 3 minutes.	100% (High)	6–8 minutes	2 min
PEAS, GREEN 10-ounce package	Combine in dish with **1 tablespoon water.** Cover. Stir after 3 minutes.	100% (High)	6–8 minutes	2 min
SPINACH, LEAF OR CHOPPED 10-ounce package	Place in dish. Add no water. Cover. Stir after 3 minutes.	100% (High)	6–8 minutes	2 min
SQUASH, SUMMER 10-ounce package	Place in dish. **Add 2 tablespoons water.** Cover. Stir after 3 minutes.	100% (High)	6–8 minutes	2 min

FROZEN VEGETABLE	*INSTRUCTIONS*	*POWER*	*TIMING*	*STANDING TIME*
SQUASH, WINTER 10-ounce package	Combine in dish. Add no water. Cover. Stir after 3 minutes.	100% (High)	6–8 minutes	1 min
TURNIPS 10-ounce package	Combine in dish with **2 tablespoons water.** Cover. Break apart and stir after 3 minutes.	100% (High)	8–10 minutes	2 min

POACHING FRUIT

Microwave ovens can be used to poach fruit. For the syrup mixture, combine ¼ cup sugar with 1½ cups liquid (fruit juice, water, wine, etc.) in a 4-cup glass measure. Cover and microwave at 100 percent power (HIGH) for 5 minutes. Let stand 3 minutes and stir to dissolve any sugar that is not yet dissolved. Add the fruit, cover, and microwave according to the chart below.

TIMINGS: Poaching Fruit

FRUIT	*INSTRUCTIONS*	*POWER*	*TIMING*	*STANDING TIME*
APPLES ½ pound (1½ cups sliced)	Add peeled, cored, and sliced apples to hot syrup and cover.	100% (High)	3 minutes	None
APRICOTS ½ pound (1 cup halves)	Add apricot halves to hot syrup and cover.	100% (High)	2 minutes	None
BLUEBERRIES AND HUCKLEBERRIES ½ pound (2 cups)	Add to hot syrup and cover.	100% (High)	1 minute	None
CHERRIES ½ pound (2 cups pitted)	Add pitted cherries to hot syrup and cover.	100% (High)	1–2 minutes	None
CRANBERRIES ½ pound (2–3 cups)	Add 2 tablespoons sugar to hot syrup along with cranberries and cover.	100% (High)	4 minutes	None
NECTARINES ½ pound (1 cup sliced)	Add sliced nectarines to hot syrup and cover.	100% (High)	3 minutes	None

FRUIT	*INSTRUCTIONS*	*POWER*	*TIMING*	*STANDING TIME*
PEACHES ½ pound (1¼ cups sliced)	Add peeled, sliced peaches to hot syrup and cover.	100% (High)	3 minutes	None
PEARS ½ pound (1⅓ cups sliced)	Add peeled, cored, and sliced pears to hot syrup and cover.	100% (High)	4 minutes	None
PLUMS ½ pound (1 cup quartered)	Add quartered plums to hot syrup and cover.	100% (High)	5 minutes	None
PRUNES ½ pound (15–20)	Add pitted prunes to hot syrup and cover.	100% (High)	3 minutes	None
RASPBERRIES ½ pound (2 cups)	Add to hot syrup and cover.	100% (High)	1 minute	None
RHUBARB ½ pound (2 cups sliced)	Add to hot syrup. Stir 2 or 3 times during cooking.	100% (High)	4 minutes	None
STRAW-BERRIES ½ pound (2 cups halved)	Add hulled and halved strawberries to hot syrup and cover.	100% (High)	1 minute	None

BLANCHING AND TOASTING NUTS

To blanch nuts, such as almonds, hazelnuts, Brazil nuts, or pistachios, arrange the nuts in a single layer, and add water as specified. When the nuts are cool enough to handle, place inside a dish towel and rub to remove the skins. The advantage of "toasting" in a microwave is that there is little chance of scorching the nuts; the disadvantage is they don't brown well.

TIMINGS: Blanching Nuts

AMOUNT	INSTRUCTIONS	POWER	TIMING	STANDING TIME
4 ounces	Arrange nuts in a single layer in a shallow dish and add 2 tablespoons water. Cover tightly.	100% (High)	1½ minutes	None
8 ounces	Arrange nuts in a single layer in a shallow dish ¼ cup and add water. Cover tightly.	100% (High)	3 minutes	None
1 pound (2 cups)	Arrange nuts in a single layer in a shallow dish and add ½ cup water. Cover tightly.	100% (High)	6 minutes	None

TIMINGS: Toasting Nuts

NOTE: For toasting nuts, arrange skinned nuts in a single layer in a shallow dish. Do not cover. Pine nuts should be stirred twice during the toasting.

NUT AND AMOUNT	*POWER*	*TIMING*	*STANDING TIME*
ALMONDS 1 cup	100% (High)	5 minutes	None
MACADAMIA NUTS 1 cup	100% (High)	4 minutes	None
PEANUTS 2 cups	100% (High)	3 minutes	None
PEANUTS 4 cups	100% (High)	4 minutes	None
PECANS 1¼ cups	100% (High)	4½ minutes	None
PINE NUTS 1 cup	100% (High)	8–10 minutes	None
WALNUTS 1¼ cups	100% (High)	4½ minutes	None

FISH AND SHELLFISH

When you cook seafood in a covered dish in the microwave, you are basically steaming the fish. For added flavor, brush with melted butter and lemon juice and sprinkle with salt and pepper. You can also sprinkle with fresh herbs. Or brush with sesame oil and soy sauce for an Asian flavor. If you like, flavor the soy sauce with minced garlic and/or ginger and sprinkle the fish with chopped scallions.

TIMINGS: Fish

TYPE	*INSTRUCTIONS*	*POWER*	*TIMING*	*STANDING TIME*
WHOLE FLATFISH 1 pound	Remove head and tail from fish. Sprinkle with salt and pepper inside and out. Prick skin all over. Brush fish with melted butter and lemon juice. Place in casserole and cover. Halfway through cooking, turn fish.	100% (High)	3–4 minutes per pound	5 min
FISH FILLETS 1 pound	Place in glass or ceramic pie plate or casserole. Turn under thin area of fillets for even cooking. Cover with plastic wrap.	70% (Medium-high)	4–6 minutes	2 min
FISH STEAKS 1-inch thick 1 pound	Place in glass or ceramic pie plate or casserole. Cover with plastic wrap. Turn over halfway through cooking.	70% (Medium-high)	5–7 minutes	2 min

TIMINGS: Shellfish

TYPE	*INSTRUCTIONS*	*POWER*	*TIMING*	*STANDING TIME*
CLAMS, LITTLENECK 1 pound	Place in ceramic or glass pie plate with shell hinges facing toward edge of plate. Rotate halfway through cooking. Discard clams that do not open.	70% (Medium-high)	5–6 minutes	None
CLAMS, CHERRYSTONE 1 pound	Place in ceramic or glass pie plate with shell hinges facing toward edge of plate. Rotate halfway through cooking. Discard clams that do not open.	70% (Medium-high)	1–1½ minutes	None
OYSTERS 1 pound	Place in dish. Rearrange halfway through cooking.	100% (High)	2–5 minutes	None
CRAB CLAWS Precooked and frozen; 12 claws	Place in dish with tips toward center. Cover with plastic wrap.	100% (High)	3–4 minutes	None
MUSSELS 1 pound	Place in dish. Rearrange halfway through cooking.	100% (High)	2½–3½ min	None
SCALLOPS 1 pound	Place in glass or ceramic pie plate and cover with plastic wrap. Turn over halfway through cooking.	70% (Medium-high)	4–6 minutes	None
SHRIMP, IN SHELL 1 pound	Arrange shrimp around edge of glass or ceramic pie plate plate with tails toward center. Rotate halfway through cooking.	70% (Medium-high)	4–6 minutes	None

TYPE	*INSTRUCTIONS*	*POWER*	*TIMING*	*STANDING TIME*
SHRIMP, SHELLED 1 pound	Arrange shrimp around edge of glass or ceramic plate with tails toward pie the center. Cover with plastic wrap. Turn over halfway through cooking.	100% (High)	4–6 minutes	None

POULTRY

You won't be able to use the microwave to roast chicken or turkey, but it does a fine job of steaming. For added flavor, brush skinless poultry with melted butter and lemon juice and sprinkle with salt and pepper. You can also sprinkle with fresh herbs. Or brush with sesame oil and soy sauce for an Asian flavor. If you like, flavor the soy sauce with minced garlic and/or ginger and sprinkle the poultry with chopped scallions.

If you want to cook poultry with its skin, it may benefit from a few minutes in a hot oven or under a broiler to crisp the skin.

TIMINGS: Poultry

NOTE: The internal removal temperature refers to the internal temperature of the poultry after microwaving and before standing time. If, after the allotted microwave time, the poultry has not reached the necessary internal temperature, return to the microwave for a few minutes before standing.

TYPE	*INSTRUCTIONS*	*POWER*	*TIMING*	*INTERNAL REMOVAL TEMP.*
WHOLE CHICKEN	*Instructions:* Place breast down on microwave roasting rack set in shallow dish. Cover with plastic wrap. Turn over halfway through cooking. During standing time, cover loosely with aluminum foil.			
Roaster 4–8 pounds		100% (High), 50% (Medium)	10 minutes plus 10–12 minutes per pound; 10 minutes standing	175°F–180°F
Broiler/Fryer ¼ chicken		100% (High)	5–6 minutes per pound; 5 minutes standing	175°F–180°F

TYPE	*INSTRUCTIONS*	*POWER*	*TIMING*	*INTERNAL REMOVAL TEMP.*
Broiler/Fryer ½ chicken		100% (High)	6–7 minutes per pound; 5 minutes standing	175°F–180°F
Broiler/Fryer 3–4 pounds		100% (High)	7–9 minutes per pound; 5 minutes standing	175°F–180°F
CHICKEN PARTS WITH BONE	To cook wings, remove tips and split in two. Place the parts on a plate skin side down, with the meatiest pieces toward the edge of the plate. Cover with plastic wrap. Turn halfway through cooking and rearrange the pieces for even cooking.			
Drumsticks		100% (High)	5–6 minutes per pound; 5 minutes standing	170°F
Breast		100% (High)	4–5 minutes per pound; 5 minutes standing	170°F
Thighs		100% (High)	5–6 minutes per pound; 5 minutes standing	170°F
Wings		100% (High)	4–5 minutes per pound; 5 minutes standing	170°F

TYPE	INSTRUCTIONS	POWER	TIMING	INTERNAL REMOVAL TEMP.
CHICKEN, BONELESS BREASTS 4–5 ounces	Place on plate with the meatiest parts to the outside of the plate. Cover with plastic wrap. Turn over halfway through cooking.			
1		100% (High)	2–3 minutes per pound; 5 minutes standing	160°F
2		100% (High)	3½–5 minutes per pound; 5 minutes standing	160°F
4		100% (High)	7–9 minutes per pound; 5 minutes standing	160°F
6		100% (High)	9–12 minutes per pound; 5 minutes standing	160°F
WHOLE CORNISH GAME HEN 1–2 pounds	Place on plate breast down. Cover with plastic wrap. Turn halfway through cooking.	100% (High)	6–8 minutes per pound; 5 minutes standing	170°F
WHOLE CAPON 6–9 pounds	Place on plate breast down. Cover with plastic wrap. Turn halfway through cooking.	100% (High) 50% (Medium)	10 minutes 10–12 minutes per pound; 5 minutes standing	175°F–180°F

TYPE	*INSTRUCTIONS*	*POWER*	*TIMING*	*INTERNAL REMOVAL TEMP.*
WHOLE TURKEY 6–12 pounds	Place breast down on a microwave roasting rack in a shallow dish. Cover with plastic wrap. Turn halfway through cooking.	100% (High) 50% (Medium)	10 minutes 11–13 minutes per pound; 20 minutes standing	175°F–180°F
TURKEY BREAST, BONE-IN 4–6 pounds	Place on plate. Cover with plastic wrap. Turn halfway through cooking.	50% (Medium)	13–15 minutes per pound; 15 minutes standing	170°
TURKEY BREAST, BONELESS 2–4 pounds	Place on plate. Cover with plastic wrap. Turn halfway through cooking.	50% (Medium)	11–15 minutes per pound; 15 minutes standing	160°F
TURKEY LEGS 1 pound	Place on plate with the meatiest part toward the edge of the plate. Cover with plastic wrap. Turn halfway through cooking.	100% (High)	7–9 minutes per pound; 15 minutes standing	175°F

MEAT

When it comes to cooking meat in the microwave, consider whether you are making a dish that will benefit from moist-cooking. In most cases—roasts, steaks, and chops—cooking on the stovetop or in the oven will produce better results. Even braises and stews are best done on a regular stove, as the initial browning step is very important for developing flavor. With these caveats in mind, here are some times for meat cooked by microwave. You can always finish cooking a dish by browning the meat under the broiler or on the grill. Indeed, one of the best uses for a microwave when it comes to meat is to cook spareribs in the microwave, then finish them on the grill.

TIMINGS: Beef

NOTE: The internal removal temperature refers to the internal temperature of the beef after microwaving and before standing time. If, after the allotted microwave time, the beef has not reached the necessary internal temperature, return it to the microwave for a few minutes before standing.
NOTE: Standing time for most beef dishes is about 20 minutes. The internal temperature will rise, completing the cooking process.

CUT	*INSTRUCTIONS*	*POWER*	*TIMING*	*INTERNAL REMOVAL TEMP.*
BRISKET 2¼ pounds	Combine with **1½ cups liquid** and 1 pound vegetables. Cover tightly.	100% (High)	60 minutes; 20–30 minutes standing	155°F
GROUND BEEF 1 pound	Place in dish crumbled. Cover with waxed paper. Stir once while cooking.	100% (High)	4–6 minutes; no standing time	155°F
HAMBURGER 1 pound; 4 patties of ½ pound each	Place on rack. Cover with waxed paper. Turn halfway through cooking.	100% (High)	4–6 minutes; no standing time	

CUT	INSTRUCTIONS	POWER	TIMING	INTERNAL REMOVAL TEMP.
MEATBALLS 1 pound; 8 meatballs	Place in dish. Cover with waxed paper. Rotate halfway through cooking.	100% (High)	6–8 minutes; no standing time	
MEAT SAUCE 2 pounds	Combine ground beef with 4 cups sauce.	100% (High)	5 minutes; no standing time	
POT ROAST Chuck Roast; 2–3 pounds	Cook in **½ cup liquid** in large baking dish. Cover. Turning halfway through cooking time.	50% (Medium)	21–24 minutes per pound; 20 minutes standing time	Well: 150°F
SHORT RIBS 1¼ pounds	Cut into 3-inch-by-2½-inch pieces. Combine with 4–6 tablespoons liquid for every pound of meat. Cover tightly.	100% (High)	12 minutes; 20 minutes standing time	
2½ pounds		100% (High)	25 minutes; 20 minutes standing time	
5 pounds		100% (High)	35 minutes; 20 minutes standing time	
STEW MEAT 2 pounds	Cut meat into 1-inch cubes. Place in a baking dish with **1 cup liquid** and 1 pound vegetables. Cover tightly.	100% (High)	16–20 minutes; 15–20 minutes standing time	

TIMINGS: Veal

NOTE: Standing time for most veal dishes is 15–20 minutes. The internal temperature will rise, completing the cooking process.

CUT	INSTRUCTIONS	POWER	TIMING	INTERNAL REMOVAL TEMP.
ROAST, LOIN Boneless 1½ pounds	Place in a shallow dish with **½ cup braising liquid.** Cover tightly.	100% (High)	6 minutes; 15–20 minutes standing time	135°F
STEW MEAT 2 pounds	Combine with **3 cups braising liquid** and 1 pound vegetables. Cover tightly.	100% (High)	18 minutes; 10 minutes standing time	

TIMINGS: Lamb

NOTE: Standing time for most lamb dishes is 20 minutes. The internal temperature will rise, completing the cooking process.

CUT	INSTRUCTIONS	POWER	TIMING	INTERNAL REMOVAL TEMP.
SHANKS	Cut each shank in half crosswise. Cover tightly.			
1½ pounds; 4 shanks—8 pieces		100% (High)	12 minutes; 15 minutes standing time	
STEW MEAT 2 pounds	Combine with **3 cups braising liquid** and 1 pound vegetables in shallow dish. Cover tightly.	100% (High)	18 minutes; 10 minutes standing time	

TIMINGS: Pork

NOTE: Standing time for pork is 20 minutes. The internal temperature will rise, completing the cooking process.

CUT	INSTRUCTIONS	POWER	TIMING	INTERNAL REMOVAL TEMP.
CHOPS, THICK 1–1½ inches	Place 3½ pounds vegetables in shallow baking dish. Arrange chops in dish with small end toward center of dish. Cover tightly. Turn halfway through cooking.			
4 chops (2 pounds)		100% (High)	16 minutes; no standing time	
CHOPS, THIN ½–¾ inch	Arrange in dish with small end toward center of dish. Cover with **¼ cup sauce** per chop. Cover tightly. Turn halfway through cooking.			
1 chop (⅓ pound)		100% (High)	4 minutes; no standing time	
6 chops (2 pounds)		100% (High)	8 minutes; no standing time	
ROASTS	Place meat on microwave roasting rack. Cover with plastic wrap. Turn over halfway through cooking time. Broil to finish roast.			
Loin Roast; Bone in		70% (Medium-high)	7–11 minutes per pound; 20 minutes standing time	160°F
Loin Roast; Boneless		50% (Medium)	12–14 minutes per pound; 20 minutes standing time	160°F

CUT	*INSTRUCTIONS*	*POWER*	*TIMING*	*INTERNAL REMOVAL TEMP.*
SPARERIBS	Place ribs in shallow dish and brush with sauce. Cover with plastic wrap. Turn over halfway through cooking time. Finish over medium-hot coals in the grill.			
3½ pounds		100% power	20 minutes; finish on grill	

TIMINGS: Ham and Cured Meat

TYPE	*INSTRUCTIONS*	*POWER*	*TIMING*	*STANDING TIME*
BACON	Place between paper towels on a plate or rack. Do not overlap slices.			
Regular slices				
2 slices		100% (High)	1½–2 minutes	1 min
4 slices		100% (High)	3–3½ minutes	2 min
6 slices		100% (High)	4½–5 minutes	3 min
Thick slices				
2 slices		100% (High)	2–2½ minutes	1 min
4 slices		100% (High)	3½–4 minutes	2 min
6 slices		100% (High)	5–6 minutes	3 min
HAM, WHOLE Ready to eat	Slice in ¼-inch pieces. Place in baking dish. Add **¼ cup water or fruit juice** and cover loosely with plastic wrap. Rotate 180° halfway through cooking. Drain. Let stand covered.			
1½–2 pounds		100% (High)	10–12 minutes	5 min
3 pounds		100% (High)	20–22 minutes	5 min

TYPE	INSTRUCTIONS	POWER	TIMING	STANDING TIME
HAM, STEAK Ready to eat	Remove rind and trim fat covering to ⅛ inch. Cut edge every 1 inch to prevent curling. Lay ham steak in casserole. Cover with vented plastic wrap. Halfway through cooking, turn steaks. Let stand covered.			
¼ inch thick; 10½ ounces		50% (Medium)	9–10 minutes	1 min
½ inch thick; 1¼ pounds		50% (Medium)	10½–11½ minutes	2 min
1 inch thick; 2 pounds		50% (Medium)	12–14 minutes	2 min
2 inches thick; 3½ pounds		50% (Medium)	20–25 minutes	3 min
SLICED CANNED HAM	Line up slices side by side in dish. Add **2 tablespoons water** and cover with vented plastic wrap. Rearrange slices about halfway through cooking.			
2 slices; 2–3 ounces		50% (Medium)	1½–1¾ minutes	None
4 slices; 5 ounces		50% (Medium)	2¼–2½ minutes	None
6 slices; ½ pound		50% (Medium)	3–3½ minutes	None

TIMINGS: Sausage

NOTE: Never microwave fresh (uncooked) sausage links. They will burst.

TYPE	*INSTRUCTIONS*	*POWER*	*TIMING*	*STANDING TIME*
COOKED SAUSAGE LINKS	Make diagonal slices in links. Place on paper or dinner plate. Cover with waxed paper. Rearrange halfway through cooking.			
4 frankfurters		100% (High)	1–2 minutes	None
4 cooked sausage links		100% (High)	3–4 minutes	None
BULK SAUSAGE	Place in pie dish. Cover with waxed paper. Turn over halfway through cooking.			
4 patties		100% (High)	4–5 minutes	None

DEFROSTING

Read your microwave oven manufacturer's manual for recommendations on defrosting food. Many of today's microwave ovens have specific defrosting cycles built in. Commercially frozen food should have defrosting instructions on the label. Always follow these carefully. In general, it's best to break up and redistribute frozen food as soon as possible during defrosting. Large items should be turned over and icier pieces should be moved to the outside area of your oven tray. If the food is in a bag, flex the bag so that the food defrosts more evenly. Food should always be tested after the minimum defrosting time to make sure it's defrosting evenly and that some areas are not beginning to cook. After the food is defrosted, let it stand. This allows the ice crystals to melt, contributing to even thawing.

Shielding

It's best to shield vulnerable, quick-cooking, or quick-defrosting areas with small thin foil strips. These small strips of metal are all right to use as long as they are few in number. However, never use metal trays or other metal items in the microwave. Shield any areas that show signs that they are beginning to cook, as well as poultry wings and drumsticks, fish heads and tails, edges of meat roasts, and corners of a casserole dish that start to bubble before the center thaws.

Microwave Defrosting Tips

Fish. Frozen fish defrosts very quickly, so make sure it is still cold after defrosting. The cooking process has already started if fish is warm. The shape of the package and the weight of the fish will have a lot to do in determining how long it must be defrosted. A thick, wide package will take longer than a thin, long package. Make sure to check all fish after the minimum defrosting time. It is better to remove fish early and run it under cold water than defrost it too long. Always defrost at 30 percent power (LOW).

Fruit. Defrost fruit on 50 percent power (MEDIUM) for 2 to 5 minutes. Fruit is better when it's not defrosted completely. Leave ice crystals on the fruit and let stand a short time before eating or cooking. When defrosting commercially frozen fruit, remove all metal or foil before defrosting. If the fruit is in a pouch, place the pouch in a dish; halfway through the defrosting process, try to break the fruit up gently. If the fruit is loose or in a frozen block, place it in a bowl and break it up with a fork at the minimum time of defrosting. When properly defrosted, fruit will be cold, firm, and slightly icy.

Meat. Irregularly shaped cuts thaw unevenly. The shape of the cut and its weight determine the overall defrosting time. Remove any insulated packaging such as Styrofoam trays or paper liners. Unwrap the meat from its plastic wrap. If you find the wrap clinging to the frozen meat, begin defrosting with the wrap still on and remove it as soon as you can. Do not start the timing until the food is completely unwrapped.

After the meat defrosts, it should look moist, soft, and glossy. The fat should be white and ice crystals should be clearly visible. Make sure that all meats are defrosted thoroughly. Otherwise some meat will begin cooking before the rest is defrosted. When defrosting ground meat, remove the soft meat on the outer edges. Let the hard center defrost, then combine the two before cooking.

It's advisable to defrost a roast before cooking. The roast will cook much more evenly. If you intend to cook meat many hours after defrosting it, microwave for the minimum defrosting time only.

Defrost at 30 percent power (LOW).

Poultry. Poultry must be completely thawed before cooking. Remove all metal clamps and giblet package before defrosting. Unwrap bird and place breast down in microwave-safe baking dish. Defrost on 30 percent power (LOW). Halfway through the defrosting time, turn the bird over or rearrange pieces if defrosting sections. If some areas thaw faster or begin to cook, remove from the oven and place it in cold water for the specified standing time.

Shellfish. Frozen shellfish defrosts fairly quickly. If you are defrosting a frozen block of packaged shellfish in its store-bought package, make sure you turn it halfway through the defrosting time, flexing the plastic pouch to break up the shellfish. Try and break off individual pieces if possible. Start large shellfish like lobster with the soft-shell-side up. All shellfish should still be translucent, soft, and cool after defrosting. Always defrost at 30 percent power (LOW).

Vegetables. Most vegetables should be cooked without defrosting or thawing. The exceptions are corn on the cob, which should always be completely thawed, and greens, such as broccoli and leafy greens, which should be partially thawed to cook more evenly. Many vegetables require breaking into separate pieces before cooking.

TIMINGS: Fruit

NOTE: All timings for defrosting are based on using mid- and full-size microwave ovens in the 600–700-watt range. In ovens with less than 600 watts, increase the time about 10–15 percent.

AMOUNT	*INSTRUCTIONS*	*POWER*	*TIMING*	*STANDING TIME*
FRUIT	Place unopened package in shallow dish. Halfway through defrosting, rotate dish 180° and turn over the fruit.			
1 cup		30% (Medium-Low/ Defrost)	1½–2 minutes	5 min
1 pint		30% (Medium-Low/ Defrost)	2½–3 minutes	5 min
1 quart		30% (Medium-Low/ Defrost)	4–5 minutes	5 min

TIMINGS: Fish

NOTE: All timings for defrosting are based on mid- and full-size microwave ovens in the 600–700-watt range. In ovens with less than 600 watts, increase times about 10–15 percent.

UNCOOKED FISH	*INSTRUCTIONS*	*POWER*	*TIMING*	*STANDING TIME*
WHOLE FISH	Place fish in shallow dish. Unwrap and cover with waxed paper. Rearrange fish halfway through defrosting and turn it over. Shield head and tail of large fish with foil strips (see page 353).			
1 pound or less		30% (Medium-Low/ Defrost)	5–6 minutes per pound	5 min
1½–3 pounds		30% (Medium-Low/ Defrost)	7–8 minutes per pound	10 min
3–4 pounds		30% (Medium-Low/ Defrost)	14–16 minutes per pound	15 min
FILLETS	Place fish in shallow dish. Unwrap. Fillets in blocks: Cover with waxed paper. Check corners of blocks halfway through defrosting and remove any warm pieces. After block stands 5 minutes, separate fillets under cool running water. Thin packages of fillets should be separated as soon as possible during defrosting—thick packages only after standing. Ice-glazed fillets: Place on microwave roasting rack in shallow dish and cover with waxed paper. Halfway through defrosting, rearrange fillets.			
Fillets in block; ¼–½ inch thick		30% (Medium-Low/ Defrost)	5–6 minutes per pound	5 min
Ice-glazed fillets; ¾–1 inch thick		30% (Medium-Low/ Defrost)	6–8 minutes per pound	5 min

UNCOOKED FISH	INSTRUCTIONS	POWER	TIMING	STANDING TIME
STEAKS, CHUNKS	Place fish on a rack in shallow dish and unwrap. Cover with waxed paper. Rearrange halfway through defrosting.			
1–1½ inches thick		30% (Medium-Low/ Defrost)	7–9 minutes per pound	5 min

TIMINGS: Shellfish

NOTE: All timings for defrosting are based on mid- and full-size microwave ovens in the 600–700-watt range. In ovens with less than 600 watts, increase the time by 10–15 percent.

SHELLFISH	INSTRUCTIONS	POWER	TIMING	STANDING TIME
CLAMS, SHUCKED AND UNCOOKED	Place container in microwave oven, but transfer to shallow dish as soon as possible and cover with waxed paper. Break frozen clumps apart halfway through defrosting. Stir clams.			
1 pint		30% (Medium-Low/ Defrost)	6–8 minutes	3 min
CRABS	Unwrap and arrange crabs belly up in shallow dish. Cover with vented plastic top or food wrap. Turn crabs over halfway through defrosting.			
Whole crabs in shell		30% (Medium-Low/ Defrost)	8–10 minutes per pound	10 min
Alaska King crab legs; 8–10 ounces		30% (Medium-Low/ Defrost)	6–8 minutes per pound	3 min

SHELLFISH	*INSTRUCTIONS*	*POWER*	*TIMING*	*STANDING TIME*
CRABMEAT, COOKED	Remove any metal rings, twist ties, or foil wrapping from package. Place package in shallow dish. After 1 minute, turn crabmeat over and separate.			
6-ounce package		30% (Medium-Low/ Defrost)	4–5 minutes per pound	3 min
1-pound block		30% (Medium-Low/ Defrost)	10–15 minutes per pound	5 min
LOBSTERS, UNCOOKED	Unwrap and place belly up in a shallow dish. Cover with vented plastic top or food wrap. Turn lobsters over about halfway through defrosting. Rotate dish.			
Whole lobsters in shell		30% (Medium-Low/ Defrost)	8–10 minutes per pound	10 min
ROCK LOBSTER TAILS				
2		30% (Medium-Low/ Defrost)	6–8 minutes per pound	3 min
4		30% (Medium-Low/ Defrost)	10–14 minutes per pound	3 min
6		30% (Medium-Low/ Defrost)	15–18 minutes per pound	3 min
LOBSTER MEAT, COOKED		30% (Medium-Low/ Defrost)	10–12 minutes per pound	5 min

SHELLFISH	*INSTRUCTIONS*	*POWER*	*TIMING*	*STANDING TIME*
OYSTERS, SHUCKED AND UNCOOKED	Begin microwaving in container, but transfer to shallow dish as soon as possible. Cover with waxed paper. Break frozen clumps apart about halfway through defrosting.			
12-ounce container		30% (Medium-Low/ Defrost)	6–8 minutes per pound	3 min
1 pint		30% (Medium-Low/ Defrost)	7–9 minutes per pound	3 min
SCALLOPS	Place scallops in shallow dish and unwrap as soon as possible. Place on microwave roasting rack in dish and cover with waxed paper. Break up block with knife as soon as possible and thaw scallops until slightly soft but still icy. Rinse under cold water to melt remaining ice. Let stand.			
Bay scallops		30% (Medium-Low/ Defrost)	4–5 minutes per pound	5 min
Sea scallops		30% (Medium-Low/ Defrost)	5–7 minutes per pound	5 min
SHRIMP	Place shrimp in shallow dish. Unwrap and separate as soon as possible. Spread shrimp in single layer in shallow dish. Cover with waxed paper. Rearrange about halfway through defrosting. Thaw only slightly. Finish thawing under cold running water, and then let stand.			
Small–medium		30% (Medium-Low/ Defrost)	4–5 minutes per pound	3 min
Jumbo–colossal		30% (Medium-Low/ Defrost)	5–7 minutes per pound	5 min

TIMINGS: Poultry

NOTE: All timings for defrosting are based on mid- and full-size microwave ovens in the 600–700-watt range. In ovens with less than 600 watts, increase times by 10–15 percent.

TYPE	*INSTRUCTIONS*	*POWER*	*TIMING*	*STANDING TIME*
WHOLE CHICKEN	Unwrap and place chicken breast down in shallow dish. Cover with waxed paper. Halfway through defrosting, turn bird over, pour off juices, and shield if beginning to cook. After standing time, run cool water into cavity to remove giblets.			
Roaster 4–8 pounds		30% (Medium-Low/ Defrost)	6–8 minutes per pound	10–20 min
Broiler-Fryer 3–4 pounds		30% (Medium-Low/ Defrost)	6–7 minutes per pound	10 min
CHICKEN PARTS	Unwrap parts and place on microwave roasting rack in shallow dish. Cover with waxed paper. Separate parts and arrange thickest parts toward edge of dish with wings in center. Pour off juices halfway through defrosting.			
Broiler-fryer; Halves, Quarters, Legs, Thighs, Wings		30% (Medium-Low/ Defrost)	5–6 minutes per pound	5 min
Broiler-fryer; Boneless breasts (whole or halves)		30% (Medium-Low/ Defrost)	4–5 minutes per pound	5 min
Sliced boneless breast (roasting chicken)		30% (Medium-Low/ Defrost)	3–5 minutes per pound	5 min

TYPE	INSTRUCTIONS	POWER	TIMING	STANDING TIME
CHICKEN LIVERS	Unwrap and arrange on microwave roasting rack in shallow dish, placing icy pieces around outer edges. Halfway through defrosting, pour off juices. Rinse livers in cool water before standing time.			
1–2 pounds		30% (Medium-Low/ Defrost)	4–6 minutes per pound	5 min
WHOLE DUCK	Unwrap and place duck breast down on microwave roasting rack in shallow dish. Cover with waxed paper. Halfway through defrosting, turn bird over, pour off juices, and shield wings, breastbone, and leg joints with thin foil strips if beginning to cook. After standing time, run cool water into cavity to remove giblets.			
4–5 pounds		30% (Medium-Low/ Defrost)	7–8 minutes per pound	10 min
WHOLE GOOSE	Unwrap and place goose breast down on microwave roasting rack in shallow dish. Cover with waxed paper. About halfway through defrosting, pour off juices and turn bird breast up. Shield wings, breastbone, and leg joints with thin foil strips. After bird has stood for 30 minutes, run cool water into cavity to remove giblets. Finish thawing goose by submerging it in cool water for 1–2 hours, if needed after standing time.			
4–12 pounds		50% (Medium) 30% (Medium-Low/Defrost)	3 minutes per pound plus 3–4 minutes per pound	30–40 min

TYPE	INSTRUCTIONS	POWER	TIMING	STANDING TIME
WHOLE ROCK CORNISH HENS	Unwrap and place hens breast down in shallow dish. Cover with waxed paper. If defrosting more than 2 hens, use microwave oven shelf and stagger dishes. Turn birds breast up about halfway through defrosting. Shield wings, breastbone, and leg joints with thin foil strips if beginning to cook. Pour off juices.			
1–2 pounds		30% (Medium-Low/ Defrost)	6–7 minutes per pound	10 min
WHOLE TURKEY	Unwrap and place turkey breast down on microwave roasting rack in shallow dish. Cover with waxed paper. About halfway through defrosting, pour off juices and turn bird breast up. Shield wings, breastbone, and leg joints with thin foil strips, if beginning to cook. After turkey has stood for 30 minutes, run cool water into cavity to remove giblets. Finish thawing turkey by submerging it in cool water for 1–2 hours if needed after standing time.			
6–12 pounds		50% (Medium) 30% (Medium-Low/Defrost)	3 minutes per pound plus 3–4 minutes per pound	30 min
TURKEY BREAST	Unwrap turkey breast and arrange on microwave roasting rack in shallow dish with skin down. Cover with waxed paper. Halfway through defrosting, pour off juices and turn over.			
Bone in; 4–6 pounds		30% (Medium-Low/ Defrost)	5–7 minutes per pound	10 min
Boneless; 2–4 pounds		30% (Medium-Low/ Defrost)	7–9 minutes per pound	10 min

TYPE	INSTRUCTIONS	POWER	TIMING	STANDING TIME
TURKEY PARTS	Unwrap turkey pieces and arrange on microwave roasting rack in shallow dish with thickest parts toward edge. Cover with waxed paper. Rearrange pieces about halfway through defrosting. Shield where necessary with thin foil strips, if beginning to cook.			
Legs, Thighs, Wings		30% (Medium-Low/ Defrost)	7–6 minutes per pound	10 min
Cutlets, Breast slices, Tenderloin steaks		30% (Medium-Low/ Defrost)	5–7 minutes per pound	5 min
Whole tenderloins		30% (Medium-Low/ Defrost)	6–8 minutes per pound	10 min
GROUND TURKEY MEAT	Unwrap and place in shallow dish. Cover with waxed paper. Break up meat with fork about halfway through defrosting. Remove meat as it is thawed.			
		30% (Medium-Low/ Defrost)	5–7 minutes per pound	5 min

TIMINGS: Meat (Beef, Veal, Lamb, Pork)

NOTE: All timings for defrosting are based on mid- and full-size microwave ovens in the 600–700-watt range. In ovens with less than 600 watts, increase the time about 10–15 percent.

MEAT	*INSTRUCTIONS*	*POWER*	*TIMING*	*STANDING TIME*
BACON, UNCOOKED	Place entire package in shallow dish. Remove thawed pieces halfway through defrosting. Turn package over and rotate 180°.			
		30% (Medium-Low/ Defrost)	4–5 minutes per pound	5 min
BURGERS	Unwrap, separate burgers, and arrange in single layer on plate. Cover with waxed paper. If defrosting more than 2, rearrange about halfway through defrosting.			
1		30% (Medium-Low/ Defrost)	50–60 seconds per pound	3 min
2		30% (Medium-Low/ Defrost)	1¾–2 minutes per pound	3 min
3		30% (Medium-Low/ Defrost)	2–2½ minutes per pound	4 min
4		30% (Medium-Low/ Defrost)	2½–3 minutes per pound	5 min
5		30% (Medium-Low/ Defrost)	3–3½ minutes per pound	5 min

MEAT	INSTRUCTIONS	POWER	TIMING	STANDING TIME
6		30% (Medium-Low/ Defrost)	3½–4 minutes per pound	5 min
CHOPS Bone in or boneless	Unwrap and place meat in shallow dish. Separate chops as soon as possible. Cover with waxed paper. Move thickest parts to edge, bony ones to center about halfway through defrosting.			
Small— 2–8 ounces; ½–1 inch thick		30% (Medium Low/ Defrost)	5–7 minutes per pound	5 min
Large, thin— 9 ounces or more; ½–1 inch thick		30% (Medium-Low/ Defrost)	4–5 minutes per pound	5 min
Large, thick— 9 ounces or more; 1–2 inches thick		30% (Medium-Low/ Defrost)	7–13 minutes per pound	5–10 min
GROUND MEAT	Unwrap, place meat in shallow dish, and cover with waxed paper. Halfway through defrosting, break up frozen block with fork and spread meat.			
½–1 pound		30% (Medium-Low/ Defrost)	5–7 minutes per pound	5 min
2 pounds		30% (Medium-Low/ Defrost)	10–12 minutes per pound	10 min
5 pounds		30% (Medium-Low/ Defrost)	24–26 minutes per pound	20 min

MEAT	INSTRUCTIONS	POWER	TIMING	STANDING TIME
MEDALLIONS Scaloppine, Cutlets	Unwrap and place meat in shallow dish. Separate pieces as soon as possible. Cover with waxed paper.			
		30% (Medium-Low/ Defrost)	5–7 minutes per pound	5 min
ROASTS Bone in or boneless	Unwrap and place on microwave roasting rack in shallow dish. Cover with waxed paper. Check edges halfway through defrosting, shield warm areas with foil strips, and turn roast over.			
Up to 6 pounds		30% (Medium-Low/ Defrost)	10–13 minutes per pound	30 min
SPARERIBS, SHORT RIBS	*Instructions:* Unwrap and place on platter. Cover with waxed paper. Separate racks halfway through defrosting and turn over. Move icy pieces toward edge.			
		30% (Medium-Low/ Defrost)	4–8 minutes per pound	15 min
STEAKS Bone in or boneless	Unwrap and place meat in shallow dish. Separate pieces as soon as possible. Cover with waxed paper. Move thickest parts to edge, bony ones to center about halfway through defrosting.			
Small— 2–8 ounces; ½–1 inch thick		30% (Medium-Low/ Defrost)	5–7 minutes per pound	5 min
Large, thin— 9 ounces or more; ½–1 inch thick		30% (Medium-Low/ Defrost)	4–5 minutes per pound	5 min
Large, thick— 9 ounces or more; 1–2 inches thick		30% (Medium-Low/ Defrost)	7–13 minutes per pound	5–10 min

MEAT	INSTRUCTIONS	POWER	TIMING	STANDING TIME
STEW MEAT	Unwrap and place in shallow dish. Cover with waxed paper. Separate pieces about halfway through. Remove any thawed pieces.			
Chunks, Strips		30% (Medium-Low/ Defrost)	6–9 minutes per pound	5 min
VARIETY MEATS	Unwrap and place in shallow dish. Cover with waxed paper. Separate pieces halfway through. If pieces are thick, turn over three-quarters through defrosting time. Remove pieces as they thaw.			
Kidneys, Sliced liver		30% (Medium-Low/ Defrost)	6–8 minutes per pound	5 min
SAUSAGES	Unwrap and place sausages on plate. Cover with waxed paper. Halfway through defrosting, separate sausages, arrange in circle, and turn over.			
Links (raw, precooked)		30% (Medium-Low/ Defrost)	4–5 minutes per pound	3 min
Patties (raw)		30% (Medium-Low/ Defrost)	4–5 minutes per pound	2 min
Bulk, Roll (raw)		30% (Medium-Low/ Defrost)	4–6 minutes per pound	5 min
Frankfurters (precooked)		30% (Medium-Low/ Defrost)	3–5 minutes per pound	None
Kielbasa, Knackwurst, Bratwurst, Italian (precooked)		30% (Medium-Low/ Defrost)	5–7 minutes per pound	5 min

REHEATING

TIMINGS: Microwave Reheating

PRODUCT	INSTRUCTIONS	STARTING TEMP.	POWER	TIMING
BAKED POTATOES	Cut potato lengthwise, then score several times crosswise. Cover with waxed paper.			
1 serving		Refrigerated	100% (High)	1–2 min
2 servings		Refrigerated	100% (High)	2–3 min
CASSEROLES AND MAIN DISHES (Can't be stirred)	Cover with waxed paper.			
1 serving		Refrigerated	50% (Med)	5–8 min
2 servings		Refrigerated	50% (Med)	8–11 min
1 quart		Refrigerated	50% (Med)	20–25 min
2 quarts		Refrigerated	50% (Med)	30–40 min
(Can be stirred)	Cover with plastic wrap. Stir halfway through.			
1 pint		Refrigerated	100% (High)	6–10 min
1 quart		Refrigerated	100% (High)	10–15 min
2 quarts		Refrigerated	100% (High)	20–25 min
MEAT Chicken pieces, Chops, Hamburgers, Meatloaf slices	Cover loosely with waxed paper.			
1 serving		Refrigerated	70% (Medium-High)	1–2 min
2 servings		Refrigerated	70% (Medium-High)	2–4 min

PRODUCT	INSTRUCTIONS	STARTING TEMP.	POWER	TIMING
MEAT SLICES Beef, Ham, Pork, Turkey	Cover with gravy and/or waxed paper. Check after 30 seconds.			
1 or more servings		Room temperature	50% (Med)	1–2 min per serving
1 or more servings		Refrigerated	50% (Med)	2–2½ min per serving
PIZZA	Place on paper towel on microwave-roasting rack in shallow dish			
1 slice		Room temperature	100% (High)	15–25 sec
2 slices		Room temperature	100% (High)	25–35 sec
1 slice		Refrigerated	100% (High)	25–35 sec
2 slices		Refrigerated	100% (High)	35–45 sec
PLATE OF FOOD	Cover with plastic wrap.			
1 serving meat		Room temperature	70% (Medium-High)	1–2 min
2 servings vegetables		Refrigerated	70% (Medium-High)	2–3 min
RICE AND PASTA	Spread out in shallow dish. Cover. Stir often.			
1 cup		Refrigerated	100% (High)	2–3 min
1 pint		Refrigerated	100% (High)	3–4 min
1 quart		Refrigerated	100% (High)	6–7 min

PRODUCT	INSTRUCTIONS	STARTING TEMP.	POWER	TIMING
SOUP, CLEAR	Pour soup into bowl. Cover with plastic wrap. Stir halfway through reheating time.			
1 cup		Refrigerated	100% (High)	2–3 min
1 can (1½–1¾ cups)		Room temperature	100% (High)	3–5 min
SOUP, CREAM	Pour soup into bowl. Cover with plastic wrap. Stir halfway through reheating time.			
1 cup		Refrigerated	50% (Med)	3–4 min
1 can (1½–1¾ cups)		Room temperature	50% (Med)	4–5 min
VEGETABLES	Spread out in shallow dish. Cover with plastic wrap. Stir once or twice.			
1 serving		Refrigerated	100% (High)	1–1¼ min
2 servings		Refrigerated	100% (High)	1½–2 min
1 pint		Refrigerated	100% (High)	2–2½ min

Part II

STORAGE OF FOOD

Let's face it: The ritual of shopping every day for fresh food to be cooked right away is long gone, so we must preserve the food we buy in the best manner possible. Some is fine stored on the pantry shelf at room temperature (about 70°F), some is best stored in the refrigerator, and some is best in the freezer.

Since the modern-day refrigerator and freezer have come into existence, fresh food has an extended shelf life. Thanks to airtight doors and special compartments that keep food fresh, the quality of fresh food can be maintained longer than ever before. The timings for refrigerator storage are based on temperatures ranging from 34°F to 40°F.

The timings for freezer storage are based on storing frozen foods at 0°F. A stand-up freezer or a chest freezer is likely to reach that temperature, but most refrigerator freezers don't. If the freezer unit in your refrigerator is warmer than 0°F, you should keep your frozen food for a shorter period of time.

Much of the food we buy is stored in a pantry or cupboards. These foods have an extended shelf life and can be consumed even after their optimal storage time. But for the best flavor, texture, and nutrition, use up food before the storage times listed in the charts that follow. *If food shows the slightest signs of spoilage or odor, throw it out.*

1 Shelf Storage

Commercially canned or bottled foods, cereals, baking mixes, pasta, dried beans, mustard, ketchup, and other condiments can be kept safely at room temperature (60°F to 70°F). Make sure they are stored in a dry, cool place and in cabinets away from refrigerator exhaust or a stove. That way you will ensure the quality of the food. Extremely hot (over 100°F) and extremely cold (below 34°F) temperatures can be harmful to canned goods. They should be kept in a place where the relative humidity is around 50 to 60 percent or lower, to prevent rusting of cans and lids.

When in Doubt, Throw It Out

Here are specific signs that the quality of the food inside your jars or cans is compromised, and the food should be discarded.

- Rust on metal lids or on lips of glass jars
- Leaking, bulging, or badly dented cans
- Cans or jars with a foul odor
- Cracked jars
- Jars with loose or bulging lids
- Any container that spurts liquid when you open it.

Generally, most unopened commercially canned and packaged foods have a long shelf life when properly stored and are safe to eat even after years of storage. Low-acid canned goods such as meat, stews, pastas, potatoes, corn, carrots, spinach, beans, beets, peas, pumpkin, and soups (with the exception of tomato) can be stored for at least 2 years and longer. High-acid canned goods, such as tomato products, sauerkraut, fruit, fruit juices, and foods in vinegar-based sauces should be stored from 12 to 18 months.

What to Watch for in Canned and Bottled Foods

Do not taste the food in a container that shows signs of spoilage (listed above). Throw the food and container out. Always clean cans with a soapy cloth and then rinse before opening to prevent contamination.

Cloudiness in canned food liquid often indicates spoilage, especially if it is accompanied by a bad odor. If, after boiling the food, it doesn't smell normal, throw it away. In certain foods that contain starch, like beans and peas, cloudiness may appear but is probably harmless. To be safe, boil the food and be aware of the odor.

TIMINGS: Shelf Storage

These timings are based on unopened cans and packages stored on the pantry shelf at 70°F. If temperatures are higher, use sooner for best quality. After opening canned products, transfer the food into glass or plastic containers and refrigerate. Bottled foods, such as condiments and fruit juices, can stay in their original glass containers, but once opened must be refrigerated. Most products sold in cardboard boxes or similar packaging, such as cereals, baking mixes, and dried pastas, do not require refrigeration after opening. They can remain in their own packaging or be transferred to an airtight plastic container, if you prefer, and stored in a cool, dry place.

PRODUCT	INSTRUCTIONS	SHELF TIME
ALMONDS, IN SHELL	Store in original container.	1 year
ARROWROOT	Store in original container.	1 year
BABY FOOD (in jars)	Store in a cool place.	18 months
BAKING POWDER	Store opened or unopened in original can.	1 year or to expiration date on can
BAKING SODA	Store in original package; keep dry.	12–18 months
BARLEY, PEARL	Store in tightly lidded container.	1 year
BEANS, CANNED	Store in a cool, dry place.	18 months
BEANS, DRIED	Store in airtight container.	1 year
BISCUIT, BROWNIE, AND MUFFIN MIXES	Store in a cool, dry place.	9 months
BOUILLON CUBES, CRYSTALS	Store in tightly closed container.	1 year
BREAD	Store in original wrapper.	4–7 days
BUCKWHEAT GROATS, KASHA	Store in tightly lidded container.	1 month
BULGUR	Store in tightly lidded container.	1 month
CAKE MIXES	Store in a cool, dry place.	9 months Angel food: 1 year

PRODUCT	INSTRUCTIONS	SHELF TIME
CAKES (Without whipped cream or custard)	Wrap well in plastic or foil or store in sealed plastic cake box.	2–3 days
CEREAL, INSTANT HOT	Store in original box or tightly lidded container.	1 year
CEREAL, READY-TO-EAT	Store in original box or tightly lidded container.	Unopened: 1 year Opened: 3 months
CHOCOLATE	Store in freezer for longer storage.	Dark: 1 year Milk: 6 months
CHOCOLATE SYRUP	Store in original container.	Unopened: 2 years Opened: 6 months
COCOA, UNSWEETENED	Store in original container.	18 months
COCOA MIXES	Store in original container.	1 year
COCONUT, FLAKED	Refrigerate after opening.	6 months
COFFEE, GROUND	Store opened cans in refrigerator or freezer.	1 year
COFFEE, FREEZE-DRIED	Store in original container.	Unopened: 6 months Opened: 2–3 months
COFFEE, INSTANT	Store in original container.	Unopened: 1 year Opened: 2–3 months
CONDIMENTS (Ketchup, Mustard, Horseradish, etc.)	Refrigerate after opening.	2–20 months
COOKIES	Store in tightly lidded jar or sealed plastic bag.	1–2 weeks
CORNMEAL	Transfer to an airtight container.	1 year
CORNSTARCH	Store in original package; keep dry.	Indefinitely
CORN SYRUP	Store in original container.	Unopened: up to date on label Opened: 4–6 months
CRACKERS	Store in a cool, dry place.	Unopened: 6 months Opened: 1 month
DEHYDRATED FOODS	Store in original container or airtight jar.	5 years

PRODUCT	INSTRUCTIONS	SHELF TIME
EXTRACTS (Vanilla, Almond, etc.)	Store in original container.	3–4 months
FISH AND SHELLFISH, CANNED	Store in a cool, dry place.	1 year
FLOUR (White, Rice, Semolina)	Transfer to airtight container. Store in a cool, dry place.	6–12 months
FLOUR, WHOLE-WHEAT	Keep in refrigerator or freezer for longer storage.	1 month
FOOD COLORING	Store in original container.	12–20 months
FREEZE-DRIED FOODS	Store in original container or airtight jar.	Indefinitely
FROSTING, CANNED	Store in original container.	18 months
FRUIT, CANNED	Store in a cool, dry place.	18 months Berries, citrus, and juices: 6 months
FRUIT, DRIED	Store in airtight package in cool, dark place.	6 months
GARLIC	Keep cool and dry.	5 weeks
GELATIN (flavored)	Store in original container.	1 year
GELATIN (unflavored)	Store in original container.	3 years
GRITS, HOMINY	Store in tightly lidded container.	1 month
HAZELNUTS, IN SHELL		3 months
HERBS, DRIED	Store in a cool, dark place.	Whole: 1 year Ground: 6 months
HONEY	Store in a cool, dark place.	12–20 months
INFANT FORMULA	Store in original container.	12–18 months
JAMS, JELLIES, PRESERVES	Refrigerate after opening.	12 months
JUICE, FRUIT AND VEGETABLE (in bottles)	Refrigerate after opening.	1 year

PRODUCT	*INSTRUCTIONS*	*SHELF TIME*
JUICE, FRUIT (in boxes)	Store in original container.	4–6 months
KETCHUP, CHILI SAUCE, ETC.	Refrigerate after opening for longer storage.	Unopened: 12 months Opened: 1 month
MAPLE SYRUP	Store opened jars in the refrigerator for 1 year or indefinitely in the freezer.	Unopened: 2 years
MARSHMALLOWS	Store in airtight container.	2–3 months
MARSHMALLOW CREME	Refrigerate after opening.	2 months
MAYONNAISE	Refrigerate after opening.	2–3 months or until expiration date on label
MEATS, CANNED	Store in a cool, dry place.	18 months
MILK, EVAPORATED	Refrigerate after opening.	4–6 months
MILK, SWEETENED CONDENSED	Refrigerate after opening.	4 months
MILK, NONFAT DRY	After opening, transfer to airtight container.	6 months
MILLET	Store in tightly lidded container.	1 year
MOLASSES	Store in a cool, dry place.	12–24 months
MUSHROOMS, DRIED	Store in a cool, dry place.	1 year
MUSTARD	Refrigerate after opening.	12–15 months
NONDAIRY CREAMER	Store in original container.	Unopened: 2 years Opened: 1 year
NOODLES, EGG	Store in original package.	6 months
NUTS, CANNED	Store opened cans in refrigerator or freezer.	6–12 months
OATS, ROLLED	Store in tightly lidded container.	1 month
OIL, OLIVE	Store in a cool, dark place.	4–12 months

PRODUCT	INSTRUCTIONS	SHELF TIME
OIL, SESAME	Store in a cool, dark place.	2 months
OIL, VEGETABLE (Canola, Corn, Peanut, Safflower, Soybean, Vegetable)	Store in a cool, dark place.	Unopened: 1 year Opened: 6 months
OIL, WALNUT	Store in a cool, dark place.	2 months
OLIVES	Refrigerate after opening.	1 year
ONIONS, SHALLOTS	Store in a cool, dark place.	5 weeks
PANCAKE MIXES	After opening, transfer to airtight container.	6–9 months
PASTA, DRIED	Store in original package in a cool, dry place.	12–18 months
PEANUT BUTTER	Store in original container.	Unopened: 1 year Opened: 1 month
PEANUTS, IN SHELL	Store in original container.	Raw: 2 months Roasted: 1 month
PEPPERCORNS	Transfer to an airtight container.	12–14 months
PEPPERS, CANNED	Store in a cool, dry place.	6 months
PEPPERS, DRIED	Store hanging or in a basket to allow air circulation. Keep dry.	1 year
PEPPER SAUCES (Tabasco, Louisiana, etc.)	Discard if turned brown.	1 year
PICKLES	Refrigerate after opening.	12–20 months
PIE CRUST MIX	Keep cool and dry.	8 months
POPCORN, UNPOPPED	Store in an airtight container.	12–15 months
POTATOES	Store in a cool, dark, dry place, such as an unheated cellar. Potatoes will keep 7–10 days at room temperature.	Mature potatoes: 1–2 months New potatoes: 1–2 weeks

PRODUCT	*INSTRUCTIONS*	*SHELF TIME*
POTATOES, INSTANT	Keep in airtight package.	6–12 months
POULTRY, CANNED	Store in a cool, dry place.	1 year
PUDDING, CANS	Store in a cool, dry place.	1 year
PUDDING MIXES	Store in a cool, dry place.	1 year
PUMPKIN	Store in a cool, dark, dry place.	1 month
PUMPKIN SEEDS (in shell)	Store in original container.	2–3 months
QUINOA	Store in tightly lidded container.	1 month
RICE (white, wild)	Transfer to airtight container and store in a cool, dark, dry place.	Indefinitely
RICE (brown)	Transfer to airtight container and store in a cold, dark, dry place.	1 month
RICE MIXES	Keep cool and dry.	1 year
SALAD DRESSINGS	Refrigerate after opening.	10–12 months
SAUCE AND GRAVY MIXES	Keep cool and dry.	1 year
SALT (Table, Kosher, Rock, Sea)	Keep dry.	Indefinitely
SALT (seasoned)	Keep dry.	1 year
SEAWEED (Nori, Hijiki, Kombu, etc.)	Store in a tightly sealed jar or plastic bag.	2–4 months
SHORTENING, SOLID	Keep at room temperature.	1 year
SOUP MIXES	Keep cool and dry.	1 year
SOUPS, CANNED	Store in a cool, dry place.	1 year Beef and tomato: 6 months
SOY SAUCE	Store in original bottle.	1 year
SPICES, DRIED	Store in a cool, dark place.	Whole: 1 year Ground: 6 months
SQUASH (WINTER)	Store in a cool, dark, dry place or refrigerate.	3 weeks

PRODUCT	*INSTRUCTIONS*	*SHELF TIME*
SUGAR, BROWN AND CONFECTIONERS'	After opening, transfer to airtight container.	4 months
SUGAR, GRANULATED WHITE	After opening, transfer to airtight container.	12–20 months
SUGAR SUBSTITUTES	Cover tightly.	2 years
SUNFLOWER SEEDS (in shell)	Store in original container.	2–3 months
SWEET POTATOES	Store in cool, dark, dry place, such as an unheated cellar. Sweet potatoes will keep for about 1 week at room temperature.	2 months
TAPIOCA	Store in tightly lidded container.	1 year
TEA, LOOSE AND BAGGED	Store in a dark place.	6–12 months
TEA, INSTANT	Store in original container.	6–12 months
TOMATOES, FRESH	Ideal storage container is between 50°F and 60°F.	2 days
TOMATO PASTE	Store in a cool, dry place.	1 year
TOMATO SAUCE	Store in a cool, dry, place.	6 month
TURNIPS	Store in a cool, dark, dry place.	1 week
VEGETABLE JUICES, CANNED	Store in a cool, dry place. Transfer to glass bottles once opened and refrigerate.	6 months
VEGETABLES, DRIED	Repackage in airtight container. Store in dark, dry place.	12–20 months
VEGETABLES, CANNED	Store in a cool, dry place.	18 months Sauerkraut and tomatoes: 6 months
VINEGAR	Store in a cool, dark, dry place.	Unopened: 2 years Opened: 1 year

PRODUCT	*INSTRUCTIONS*	*SHELF TIME*
WATER	Make sure the source is uncontaminated. If in doubt, boil for at least 3 minutes or use water-purification tablets. Always store in glass or plastic bottles and inspect them periodically. If any cloudiness occurs, replace.	Indefinitely
WHEAT BERRIES	Store in tightly lidded container.	1 month
WINTER SQUASH	Store whole, uncut squash in a cool, dry place, such as an unheated cellar.	1 month

2 Refrigerator Storage

Most refrigerators hold foods at temperatures between 33°F and 40°F, with special storage areas holding foods at different temperatures. For example, the meat drawer is usually the coldest spot in the refrigerator. When storing foods in the refrigerator, keep them well wrapped and dry; bacteria grow faster on moist surfaces. Clean your refrigerator regularly. Remove spoiled foods immediately to avoid contaminating other foods. The storage times in the following charts are for fresh foods, both cooked and uncooked, stored between 33°F and 40°F. They are arranged by food category.

VEGETABLES

Most vegetables require refrigerator storage. Exceptions are onions; garlic; shallots; whole, uncut winter squash; tomatoes; and potatoes. Most other vegetables are best stored in a perforated plastic bag in the refrigerator crisper between temperatures of 33°F and 40°F. Do not wash vegetables before storing them in the refrigerator.

TIMINGS: Vegetables

VEGETABLE	*INSTRUCTIONS*	*REFRIGERATOR STORAGE TIME*
ARTICHOKES	Store in crisper.	4–5 days
ARUGULA	Place in plastic bag, leaving stems exposed. Secure bag with rubber band to make it airtight. Wrap a wet paper towel around stems and roots and secure with foil or rubber band.	3–4 days
ASPARAGUS	Keep bottoms wet with wet paper towels secured with a rubber band. Store in crisper.	1–2 days
AVOCADOS	Allow to ripen at room temperature. When fully ripe, store in crisper drawer.	10–14 days
BASIL	Cut ¼ inch off stems. Wrap wet paper towel around newly cut stems. Then wrap leaves and towel-wrapped stems in foil or plastic wrap.	3–4 days
BEANS, GREEN AND WAXED	Keep in crisper or moisture-proof wrap.	3–4 days
BEANS, SHELL (lima and fava)	Keep in plastic bags. Do not shell until you are ready to cook.	2 days
BEETS	Remove tops and keep in crisper.	1–2 weeks
BEET GREENS	Place in plastic bag, leaving stems exposed. Secure bag with rubber band, making it airtight. Wrap wet paper towels around stems or roots and secure with foil or rubber band.	4–5 days
BROCCOLI	Keep in crisper.	3–4 days
BROCCOLI RABE	Store in perforated plastic bag in crisper.	3–4 days

VEGETABLE	INSTRUCTIONS	REFRIGERATOR STORAGE TIME
BRUSSELS SPROUTS	Store in plastic bag in crisper.	3–5 days
CABBAGE	Store in plastic bag.	7–8 days
CARROTS	Cut off tops of bunched carrots and store carrots in plastic bags. Leave prepackaged carrots in original plastic bags.	2 weeks
CAULIFLOWER	Store covered loosely in crisper.	4–7 days
CELERY	Store in plastic bag.	2 weeks
CELERY ROOT (Celeriac)	Trim off string roots and stems. Store in plastic bag.	4–7 days
CHAYOTE	Store in plastic bag.	2 weeks
COLLARD GREENS	Store in plastic bag.	6 days
CORN ON THE COB	Blanch or cook; then store loosely in plastic wrap.	3–5 days
CUCUMBER	Store in perforated plastic bag or loose in the crisper.	9 days
EGGPLANT	Store in plastic bag.	3–5 days
ENDIVE	Wrap in a damp cloth or paper towel and place inside plastic bag.	3 days
ESCAROLE	Place in plastic bag, leaving stems exposed. Secure bag with rubber band to make it airtight. Wrap a wet paper towel around stems or roots and secure with foil or rubber band.	3–4 days
FENNEL	Cut off stems with leaves. Store bulbs in plastic bag.	7–10 days
JERUSALEM ARTICHOKES	Store in plastic bag.	2 weeks
KALE	Place unwashed and uncut in sealed plastic bag.	3–4 days
KOHLRABI	Store in plastic bag.	4–5 days

VEGETABLE	*INSTRUCTIONS*	*REFRIGERATOR STORAGE TIME*
LEEKS	Store in plastic bag.	1–2 weeks
LETTUCE (all types)	Place in plastic bag, leaving stems exposed. Secure bag with rubber band to make it airtight. Wrap a wet paper towel around stems or roots and secure with foil or rubber band.	5–7 days
MUSHROOMS	Cover loosely with paper towel or place in brown paper bag. Do not wrap in plastic.	6 days
MUSTARD GREENS	Place unwashed and uncut in sealed plastic bag.	3–4 days
OKRA	Pat dry and store in plastic bag.	3 days
ONIONS	Can be stored loose, but will impart their odor to everything in refrigerator. Not recommended.	2 months
PARSLEY	Place stems in water in jar. Cover top loosely with plastic bag. Store in refrigerator, changing water daily.	7–10 days
PARSNIPS	Remove green tops. Store in plastic bag.	1–2 weeks
PEAS, GREEN	Store in plastic bag; do not shell.	3–5 days
PEAS, SNOW AND SNAP	Store in plastic bag.	3–5 days
PEPPERS	Store in paper bag in crisper.	4–6 days
RADICCHIO	Store in plastic bag.	3–5 days
RADISHES	Remove green tops. Store in sealed plastic bag.	2 weeks
RUTABAGAS	Store in plastic bag.	1–2 weeks
SCALLIONS	Store in plastic bag.	1–2 weeks
SORREL	Rinse in cold water. Pat dry and store in plastic bag.	3–4 days

VEGETABLE	*INSTRUCTIONS*	*REFRIGERATOR STORAGE TIME*
SPINACH	Loosely pack unwashed and uncut spinach in plastic bag. If bought in sealed plastic bag, open bag and discard any wilted or wet leaves. then close bag.	3 days
SQUASH, SUMMER	Store in plastic bag.	4–5 days
SQUASH, WINTER	In a cool root cellar, will keep for 1 month, but will keep only 2 weeks in the refrigerator. Cut pieces should be wrapped in plastic.	Whole: 2 weeks Cut: 2–4 days
SWISS CHARD	Store in plastic bag.	3–5 days
TOMATOES (very ripe only)	Only very ripe tomatoes should be refrigerated. Store uncovered.	2–4 days
TURNIPS	Store in plastic bag.	1 week
WATERCRESS	Wrap in damp paper towel and store in plastic bag.	2–3 days

FRUIT

Since most fruits are picked unripe, it is usually a good idea to leave the fruit out at room temperature for a few days until ripe. To ripen fruit, place in a brown paper bag at room temperature. Turn the bag over daily to ripen the fruit evenly. If an apple or banana is added to other fruit in the bag, the ripening process will quicken.

Check fruit daily in or out of the refrigerator. If any piece shows any sign of spoilage or softness, remove it.

Before the fruit goes into the refrigerator, it is fine to wash it as a general rule, the exceptions being grapes, berries, cherries, and plums, which should not be washed until you are ready to eat them.

TIMINGS: Fruit

FRUIT	*INSTRUCTIONS*	*REFRIGERATOR STORAGE TIME*
APPLES	If washed, dry well before refrigerating in plastic bag.	2–3 weeks
APRICOTS	Keep at room temperature until fully ripe. Refrigerate in plastic bag.	2–3 days
BANANAS	Store at room temperature, away from heat and direct light. A perfectly ripe banana can be refrigerated. Its skin will darken, but flesh will be fine.	4–5 days
BLACKBERRIES	Refrigerate in a single layer, uncovered, on shelf. Do not wash before storing.	1–2 days
BLUEBERRIES	Refrigerate in sealed plastic container.	1–2 weeks
CHERRIES	Refrigerate unwashed in plastic bag.	2–4 days
CRANBERRIES	Remove brown or softening berries. Refrigerate in plastic bag.	1 month
CURRANTS	Refrigerate in uncovered bowl or basket.	1–2 days
FIGS	Refrigerate in plastic bags in coldest part of refrigerator.	1–2 days
GOOSEBERRIES	Refrigerate in sealed plastic container.	1–2 days
GRAPEFRUIT	Refrigerate in perforated plastic bag.	10–14 days

FRUIT	*INSTRUCTIONS*	*REFRIGERATOR STORAGE TIME*
GRAPES	Don't wash before refrigerating. Remove shriveled or damaged grapes. Store in plastic bags in coldest part of refrigerator.	3–5 days
GUAVAS	Allow to ripen at room temperature. Refrigerate in crisper.	2 weeks
KIWIFRUIT	Allow to ripen at room temperature, then refrigerate.	1 week
KUMQUATS	Refrigerate loose in crisper.	3 weeks
LEMONS	Refrigerate in plastic bag.	2–3 weeks
LIMES	Refrigerate in plastic bag or loose in crisper.	2–3 weeks
MANGOES	Fully ripen at room temperature. Refrigerate in plastic bag.	2–3 days
MELONS (Cantaloupes, Casabas, Crenshaws, Honeydews)	Ripen at room temperature for 2–4 days. Refrigerate whole melons in loose plastic bags; tightly wrap cut melons.	Whole: 7–10 days Cut: 1–2 days
NECTARINES	Store in plastic bag in coldest part of the refrigerator.	3–5 days
ORANGES	Will keep at room temperature for several days. Refrigerate in a plastic bag.	10–14 days
PAPAYAS	Ripen fully at room temperature. Refrigerate in a plastic bag.	2 weeks
PEACHES	Refrigerate in plastic bags.	3–5 days
PEARS	Refrigerate in plastic bags.	3–5 days
PERSIMMONS	Ripen in a paper bag with an apple or banana at room temperature. Then store in refrigerator. Refrigerate.	1–2 days
PINEAPPLES	Refrigerate whole ripe pineapple in plastic bag, cut pieces in airtight container.	Whole: 3–5 days Pieces: 7 days
PLUMS	Refrigerate in plastic bag.	3–5 days

FRUIT	*INSTRUCTIONS*	*REFRIGERATOR STORAGE TIME*
POMEGRANATES	Refrigerate loose.	2–3 weeks
QUINCES	Refrigerate in plastic bag.	2–3 weeks
RHUBARB	Remove leaves. Refrigerate cut stalks in plastic bag.	3–5 days
STAR FRUIT	Refrigerate loose on shelves or in crisper.	1 week
STRAWBERRIES	Refrigerate unwashed berries in covered container.	3–5 days
WATERMELONS	Refrigerate whole ripe melon unwrapped, cut pieces in plastic wrap.	Whole: 1 week Cut: 3–4 days

DAIRY PRODUCTS AND EGGS

Dairy products are perishable and should always be stored in the refrigerator (or freezer, in the case of ice cream). Open cans of evaporated and condensed milks and reconstituted dry milk must also be refrigerated. Keep dairy products in closed containers and cheese well wrapped to prevent other odors from penetrating. Homemade puddings and custards made with milk are also perishable; keep them well covered in the refrigerator for 2 to 3 days.

Keeping Dairy Products and Eggs Fresh

- Milk should be stored between 38°F and 40°F. If the expiration date on the container has passed or the milk smells sour, throw it out. Milk should have a sweet taste when fresh.
- Never return unused portions of milk and cream to original containers if they have been sitting out at room temperature.
- All dairy products should be kept away from foods with strong odors, since they absorb odors easily.
- Butter should taste sweet and fresh, and have a uniform color and texture. If a foreign smell is detected, throw the butter out.
- All cheeses should be kept very well wrapped to prevent them from taking on or giving off odors.
- Mold on cheese is not necessarily a sign that the cheese should be discarded. Simply cut away the moldy part (and a generous amount of cheese with it) and use the rest.
- A thin liquid may separate out of yogurt and sour cream. This is not a sign of spoilage. Stir the liquid back in or drain it off.
- Eggs should not be purchased more than 2 weeks prior to intended use. They should not have cracked or dirty shells. They should have grade AA or A on the carton. If the USDA shield is on the carton, it means they have met federal standards.
- Eggs should be stored in their original container in the coldest area of the refrigerator, not on the door. They should be stored between 34°F and 40°F. Fresh eggs should not have an odor, and the written "use by" date on the carton should be followed.

TIMINGS: Dairy Products and Eggs

PRODUCT	*INSTRUCTIONS*	*REFRIGERATOR STORAGE TIME*
BUTTER	Keep covered in butter dish.	1–3 months
BUTTER, CLARIFIED	Keep well covered.	1–3 months
BUTTERMILK	Store in original container.	1–2 weeks
COTTAGE CHEESE	Keep in original container. For best flavor, use within 1 week.	1–3 weeks
CREAM, HEAVY, LIGHT	Store in original container in coldest part of refrigerator.	4 days after "sell by" date
CREAM, ULTRA-PASTEURIZED	Store in original container in coldest part of refrigerator.	1 month
CREAM, WHIPPED (homemade)	Keep well covered.	1 day
CREAM, WHIPPED (aerosol can)	Keep in original container.	4–6 weeks
CREAM CHEESE	Keep tightly wrapped in moisture-proof wrapping.	2 weeks
CRÈME FRAÎCHE	Keep in original container.	4 weeks
CHEESE, HARD	Keep well wrapped in plastic or foil. Hard cheese continues to age and sharpen in flavor. Storage time depends on type of cheese, wrapping, whether cheese is cut or whole, whether cheese is coated in wax.	1–12 months
CHEESE, GRATED HARD	Keep in original container.	Up to 1 year
CHEESE, SEMISOFT	Keep well wrapped in plastic or foil. Storage time depends on type.	2–4 weeks

PRODUCT	*INSTRUCTIONS*	*REFRIGERATOR STORAGE TIME*
CHEESE, SOFT	Keep well wrapped in plastic or foil. Look for "use by" date and follow it.	2–3 days, if fully ripe
CHEESE, PROCESSED	Check label directions.	Unopened: 2 months Opened: 2–4 weeks
HALF-AND-HALF	Keep in original container.	3–4 days
MARGARINE	Store in original wrapping or container.	Opened: 1 month Unopened: 4 months
MILK (Whole, Skim, 2 percent)	Store in original container. Keep tightly closed. Whole milk keeps longer than skim or 2 percent.	5 days beyond "sell by" date on container
MOZZARELLA	Keep well covered.	Fresh: 2–3 days Aged: 2–3 weeks
RICOTTA CHEESE	Keep in original airtight container.	1 week
SOUR CREAM	Keep in sealed container.	1–2 weeks beyond "sell by" date on container.
YOGURT	Keep in sealed container.	1–2 weeks
EGGS		
Whole uncooked	Keep covered. Do not use uncovered egg rack in door of refrigerator. Store with small end down. After 2 weeks, eggs are best in baked goods or for scrambled eggs.	1 month
Hard-cooked	If shelled, wrap in plastic; if unshelled, wrap in foil.	In shell: 2–3 weeks Shelled: 1 week
Whites uncooked	Store in metal airtight container.	7–10 days
Yolks uncooked	Cover with cold water and store in airtight container.	2 days

PRODUCT	INSTRUCTIONS	REFRIGERATOR STORAGE TIME
EGG SALADS AND STUFFED EGGS	Keep tightly covered.	1 day
EGG SUBSTITUTES	Keep in tightly covered container.	5 days

FISH AND SHELLFISH

Fish is the most vulnerable of all foods to spoilage and should be stored around 34°F. If at all possible, fill a drawer in your refrigerator or a large bowl with crushed ice and bury your fish in the ice, still wrapped in its package from the store. If you don't have crushed ice, you can lay the fish on top of ice packs on a platter in the refrigerator. Replace the ice or ice packs daily.

Fish should never have a strong fish odor; it should smell like the sea and not like ammonia. It should be firm and elastic, the gills should be bright red, and the eyes should be clear and moist. If the piece of fish you have differs in any way from these signs, discard it.

Whole clams, oysters, mussels, lobsters, and sometimes crabs are sold live. Lobsters and crabs should show movement. The shells of clams and oysters should be closed. If the shell is slightly open, tap it. If it closes, then it's okay. Like fish, shellfish that has a strong odor should be discarded.

TIMINGS: Fish and Shellfish

FISH AND SHELLFISH	*INSTRUCTIONS*	*REFRIGERATOR STORAGE TIME*
FISH (fresh, uncooked)	Keep tightly wrapped. Bury in ice in refrigerator.	Freshly caught: up to 4 days From the market: 1–2 days
FISH (cooked)	Keep tightly covered.	1 day
FISH (pickled)	Keep in tightly covered container.	1 week
FISH (smoked)	Tightly wrap with waxed paper, then foil.	3–4 days
FISH (canned)	Transfer to an airtight container.	2 days
CLAMS, MUSSELS, OYSTERS	Refrigerate in shallow pan with moist towel covering. Do not place on ice. Refrigerate shucked shellfish in their own liquor in an airtight container.	Live: 1 day Shucked: 1–2 days
LOBSTER AND CRAB	For best storage, pack live creatures in seaweed in specially designed insulated carton. Do not place in or cover with water.	Live: 8 hours Cooked: 1–2 days

FISH AND SHELLFISH	*INSTRUCTIONS*	*REFRIGERATOR STORAGE TIME*
SCALLOPS	Refrigerate in their own liquor in an airtight container in coldest part of refrigerator.	1 day
SHRIMP (shelled or unshelled)	Store on a bed of ice.	Uncooked: 1 day Cooked: 3–4 days
SALADS AND SANDWICH FILLINGS (Tuna, Crab, etc.)	Refrigerate immediately after preparation. Store in a tightly covered container.	1 day
STEWS (Bisques, Chowders, Broth, etc.)	Refrigerate immediately after preparation. Store in a tightly covered container.	1–2 days

POULTRY

Poultry should be stored between 34°F and 40°F. All poultry should be handled carefully because they are often contaminated with salmonella. All counters and utensils should be washed often. Signs of spoilage in poultry are easy to spot. An abnormal odor, darkened wing tips, stickiness under the wings, or a soft flabby skin are signs that the bird should be discarded.

TIMINGS: Poultry

PRODUCT	*INSTRUCTIONS*	*REFRIGERATOR STORAGE TIME*
FRESH WHOLE BIRD (Chicken, Turkey, Duck, Goose, Guinea fowl, Game birds)	Rinse cavity thoroughly with cold water. Wipe dry. Refrigerate loosely wrapped in waxed paper or foil or in covered container. Store giblets separately from bird.	1–2 days
FRESH POULTRY, IN PIECES	Rinse thoroughly with cold water. Wipe dry. Refrigerate loosely wrapped in waxed paper or foil or in covered container.	1–2 days
COOKED POULTRY	Cool and refrigerate within 2 hours after cooking. Remove any stuffing and store separately. Wrap tightly or store in tightly covered container.	2–3 days
CANNED POULTRY	Transfer to tightly covered container.	2 days
BROTH AND STOCK	Cool and refrigerate within 30 minutes after cooking. Store tightly covered. Bring to boiling point before serving.	2 days
SALADS (Chicken, Turkey, etc.)	Refrigerate immediately after preparation. Store in tightly covered container.	1 day
STEWS, PIES, CREAMED DISHES, GRAVIES	Cool and refrigerate within 30 minutes after cooking. Store tightly covered. Reheat to boiling point before serving.	1 day
STUFFING FROM POULTRY	Cool and refrigerate within 30 minutes after cooking.	1 day

FRESH MEAT

All large cuts of meat should carry the USDA stamp or the State Department of Agriculture stamp to ensure that the carcass of the animal was inspected, no signs of illness in the animal were found, and the processing was done under sanitary conditions.

Discoloration may indicate a contaminated cut of meat. Brown, green, or purple coloring is a sign of microbial contamination. The colors black, white, and green may indicate mold or freezer burn. If meat has a sour smell, is very dry, slimy, or sticky to the touch, throw it out.

Beef. Beef should be light cherry red to brownish red in color; don't buy meat that is a very deep purple-red. Beware of meat with dark splotches or yellowed fat with signs of browning or darkening. Discard sticky or wet meat, or meat with an unpleasant odor. Inspect ground beef very closely, because it is the most vulnerable to microbial contamination and deterioration.

Lamb. Lamb should be a light red in color and fat should be white. Watch for any discoloration, especially if it is brownish in color or has a white surface on the lean surface of the meat.

Pork. The lean portion of the meat should be light pink and the rest of the cut should be white and firm. Watch for pale, soft pork that looks watery or has excessive fat. Stick a clean knife into the meat near the bone; if the knife smells sour after you've withdrawn it, throw the cut out.

Veal. Veal may be pale pink to reddish, depending on the age of the animal and its feed. The flesh should be firm and springy, not mushy.

TIMINGS: Fresh Meat

MEAT	*INSTRUCTIONS*	*REFRIGERATOR STORAGE TIME*
ALL MEATS		
Bones	Store in meat drawer in tightly wrapped package.	1–2 days
Cooked dishes (including leftovers)	Refrigerate meat, gravy, and stuffing separately in covered containers.	3–4 days

MEAT	***INSTRUCTIONS***	***REFRIGERATOR STORAGE TIME***
Stock	Store in tightly sealed container.	1–2 days
BEEF	Store in meat drawer in original wrapper. If original wrapper is opened or damaged, wrap meat in butcher paper or waxed paper, then wrap again in foil.	
Cubes or slices		2 days
Ground		1–2 days
Roasts		4–5 days
Steaks or ribs		3–5 days
GAME	Store in original wrapper or waxed paper. Wrap again with foil.	1–2 days
LAMB	Store in meat drawer in original wrapper. If original wrapper is opened or damaged, wrap meat in butcher paper or waxed paper, then wrap again in foil.	
Chops		2–3 days
Cubes or slices		1–2 days
Ground		1–2 days
Roasts		2–4 days
Steaks or ribs		2–3 days
PORK	Store in meat drawer in original wrapper. If original wrapper is damaged or opened, wrap meat in butcher paper or waxed paper, then wrap again in foil.	
Chops		2–3 days
Cutlets or medallions		1–2 days
Ground		1–2 days
Ribs		2–4 days
Roasts		2–4 days
Steaks		2–3 days

MEAT	*INSTRUCTIONS*	*REFRIGERATOR STORAGE TIME*
SAUSAGE	Store in meat drawer in original wrapper or loosely wrapped in butcher paper or waxed paper.	1–2 days
VARIETY MEATS Brains, Heart, Kidney, Liver, Sweetbreads, Tongue, Tripe	Store in meat drawer in original wrapper. If original wrapper is damaged, wrap meat in butcher paper or waxed paper, then wrap again in foil.	1–2 days
VEAL	Store in meat drawer in original wrapper. If original wrapper is damaged, wrap meat in butcher paper or waxed paper, then wrap again in foil.	
Chops		2–3 days
Cubes		1–2 days
Cutlets, scallops, medallions		1–2 days
Roasts		2–4 days
Steaks		2–3 days

CURED AND PROCESSED MEATS

When storing cured and processed meats, read the label for storage advice, "use by" or "sell by" dates, and instructions on whether the meat requires further cooking. Meats sold in vacuum packs should have a "use by" date and generally will keep for longer than meats packed without the vacuum seal.

TIMINGS: Cured and Processed Meats

MEAT	*INSTRUCTIONS*	*REFRIGERATOR STORAGE TIME*
BACON	Store in meat drawer in original wrapper. Wrap opened package in foil.	Unopened: 2 weeks Opened slices: 5–7 days Opened slab: 14–21 days Cooked: 3–4 days
BACON, CANADIAN	Store in original wrapper.	Sliced: 3–4 days Chunk: 1 week
BOLOGNA	Store in original wrapper.	4–7 days
CORNED BEEF	Store in original wrapper. In vacuum-sealed package, it will keep for 7 days beyond "sell by" date. Keep homemade corned beef well wrapped in plastic or foil.	Uncooked: 1 week Cooked: 3–5 days
FRANKFURTERS	Store in original wrapper. In vacuum-sealed package, it will keep for 7 days beyond "sell by" date. Once opened, keep well wrapped in plastic or foil.	4–5 days
HAM	If in vacuum-sealed or heavy plastic wrap, keep in original wrapper. Otherwise, wrap tightly in plastic or foil.	Whole: 1 week Sliced: 2–3 days

MEAT	*INSTRUCTIONS*	*REFRIGERATOR STORAGE TIME*
HAM, CANNED	If unopened, keep in vacuum-sealed can in refrigerator. If opened, wrap tightly in plastic or foil.	Unopened: 6–12 months Opened: 5–7 days
LUNCHEON MEATS, SLICED	In unopened vacuum-sealed packages, luncheon meats will keep for 7 days beyond "sell by" date. Store opened packages tightly wrapped in plastic or foil.	2–3 days
SALAMI AND OTHER DRY OR SEMIDRY SAUSAGES	Keep unopened vacuum-sealed packages for up to 7 days beyond "sell by" date. Store opened packages tightly wrapped in plastic or foil. Dry sausages keep longer than semi-dry sausages.	Whole: 2–6 weeks Sliced: 3 weeks
SALT PORK	Keep in original wrapper until opened. Then wrap tightly in plastic or foil.	30 days
SAUSAGE, COOKED	Keep in original wrapper until opened. Then wrap tightly in plastic or foil.	2–7 days
SAUSAGE, FRESH (Bratwurst, Kielbasa, Linguiça, Country sausage, etc.)	Store in tightly wrapped plastic or foil.	Breakfast sausages: 1 day Others: 1 week

MISCELLANEOUS FOODS

The chart that follows lists the storage times for various foods not covered in the ones above. Many of these products, such as mayonnaise and bottled juices, can be stored unopened on a pantry shelf (see page 374).

TIMINGS: Miscellaneous Foods

PRODUCT	*INSTRUCTIONS*	*REFRIGERATOR STORAGE TIME*
BABY FOOD	Store in original glass jar.	2–3 days
BREADS, SOFT-CRUST (Sliced breads, Tortillas, Pita pockets)	Store in original plastic bags.	4–7 days
CAKES (with custard fillings)	Cover loosely with plastic wrap.	4–5 days
CEREAL (cooked)	Cool, then cover tightly with plastic.	3–4 days
CHEESECAKE	Cover tightly with plastic.	7–10 days
CHILI OR COCKTAIL SAUCE	Store in original glass jar.	2 months
COFFEE (ground)	Store in original can or airtight container.	15 days
CONDIMENTS (Ketchup, Mustard, etc.)	Store in original containers, tightly closed.	3 months
CUSTARDS, MOUSSES, PUDDINGS	Cool quickly and refrigerate within 2 hours. Cover tightly with plastic wrap.	3–5 days
CORNMEAL		Degerminated: 1 year Stone-ground: 2–3 months
FLOUR	Store in airtight container.	White: 1 year Whole-grain: 2–3 months
FRUIT, CANNED	Store in airtight container.	3–5 days

PRODUCT	INSTRUCTIONS	REFRIGERATOR STORAGE TIME
FRUITCAKE	Store tightly wrapped.	2 years
FRUIT JUICES	Store bottled juices and juices in cartons in original containers. Store canned or reconstituted juices in glass or plastic containers.	6–7 days
GELATIN, PREPARED	Store in airtight container.	3–4 days
GRAINS	Store in airtight containers.	4–5 months
JAMS, JELLIES, PRESERVES	Store in glass jars.	6 months
MAPLE SYRUP	Store in glass jars.	3–4 months
MAYONNAISE	Store in glass jars.	3 months
NUTS	Store in airtight container.	In the shell: 3–12 months Shelled: 3–4 months
OILS	Store in glass jars.	Olive: 6–12 months Sesame: 4 months Walnut: 4 months
PASTA	Cover tightly with plastic wrap.	Fresh: 1–2 days Cooked: 3 days
PEANUT BUTTER	Store in original jar. (Note: Homemade peanut butter should be used within 10 days.)	3–4 months
PIES	Cover loosely with plastic wrap.	Fruit: 4–5 days Custard: 2–3 days
PIE SHELLS	Cover with plastic wrap.	Baked: 2–3 days Unbaked: 1 day
PUDDINGS	Cover with plastic wrap.	3–4 days
RICE, BROWN	Store in airtight container.	6 months
RICE, COOKED	Cover with plastic wrap.	3–4 days

PRODUCT	INSTRUCTIONS	REFRIGERATOR STORAGE TIME
TOFU	Store in original unopened container for 3–5 days beyond "sell by" date. If bought loose fresh from bulk container, change water daily.	2 weeks
WHEAT GERM	Store in original glass jar.	2–3 months
YEAST, DRY	Store in original foil wrapper or in tightly sealed jar. Check for "use by" date on packaging.	Up to date on label

3 Freezer Storage

Most foods will retain their original flavor and nutritional value after a few months in the freezer, but some can stay frozen up to a year. Meats, poultry, fish, and cooked foods freeze easily. Fruits and vegetables require special preparation for the freezer, so a book on food preservation should be consulted. The recommended storage times for home frozen products held at 0°F are only approximate, since successful storage depends on many factors. Moisture entering the packaging, the type of container, packaging materials used, and the type of freezer and refrigerator all enter into the timings of foods. A freestanding freezer keeps foods at 0°F or colder. The freezer compartment in your refrigerator usually keeps food at 5° to 25°F, which is not cold enough for long-term storage.

ABOUT THAWING FROZEN FOODS

Always thaw frozen foods in their original container. Most foods thaw best in the refrigerator. To thaw food quickly, use a microwave oven (see page 353). Use all frozen foods immediately after thawing; bacteria can form rapidly in thawed food left at room temperature. Once frozen food is thawed, it spoils more quickly than fresh food.

Fish and Shellfish. Except for shrimp, fish and other shellfish should be thawed before cooking. Shrimp need not be thawed, unless it is to be deep-fried. Fish should be slowly thawed in the original wrapping in the refrigerator. Slowly thawed fish cooks more delicately and loses less moisture than quickly thawed fish. Allow about 8 hours' thawing time in the refrigerator per pound of fish. Shellfish, clams, shrimp, scallops, and oysters take slightly less time, while lobster and crab take slightly longer.

Unthawed fish can be cooked, but it is not recommended. It must be cooked at lower temperatures for a longer time. Frozen fish needs about 1¼ times longer to cook than thawed fish.

Meat. Thawing frozen meats before cooking is recommended, because thawed meats will brown evenly and retain their juices almost as well as fresh meat. Meat can be thawed quickly and safely in the microwave oven or by placing it in a watertight bag and immersing it in cold water until it becomes pliable.

Frozen meat can be cooked before thawing, but this is not recommended. Timing the frozen meat correctly is difficult; figure it will take about 1¼ to 1½ times longer to cook than thawed meats. When broiling frozen meats, be sure to place the meat at least 6 inches below the heat. When roasting frozen meat, a heat thermometer is a necessity.

Poultry. Poultry is best when thawed before cooking, and it must be cooked immediately after thawing. Allow 2 hours thawing time in the refrigerator per pound and keep the bird in its original wrapping. A turkey or large bird weighing 4 and 12 pounds can take from 1 to 2 days to thaw. Birds from 12 to 20 pounds take 2 to 3 days to thaw, and those from 20 to 25 pounds take 3 to 4 days. A faster way to thaw is to leave poultry in its original wrapping, seal it well in a freezer bag, and place it in cold water for up to 10 hours depending on size. Change the water frequently. The bird is thawed when the entire flesh is soft and pliable.

Vegetables and Fruit. Vegetables should be cooked in their frozen state. Fruits are best served while there are still a few ice crystals left in the fruit. This helps eliminate the mushy texture some frozen fruits have when thawed. Frozen fruit can be thawed in the refrigerator, which takes about 8 hours, or at room temperature in about 1 to 2 hours, or, if packaged, 30 minutes sitting in cold water.

Not All Foods Do Well When Frozen

The following is a list of foods that should not be frozen:

- Boiled icings
- Cake frostings (made with egg whites or brown sugar)
- Cheeses (all soft cheeses)
- Cooked pasta
- Cream cheese
- Custards
- Egg-thickened sauces
- Fried foods (become soggy)
- Garlic (becomes very strong)
- Gelatin
- Hard-cooked eggs
- Meringue
- Mayonnaise
- Milk-based sauces
- Spices
- Vegetables: Cabbage, celery, cucumbers, endive, leeks, lettuce, parsley, radishes

Tips for Freezing Foods

- Select high-quality foods and freeze them quickly after purchasing, sealed properly.
- Foods must be sealed in moisture- and vapor-proof wrappings or containers and kept at constant 0°F or below during storage.
- Freeze solid foods in freezer bags, heavy foil, freezer plastic wrap, or laminated freezer wrap.
- Freeze liquid or semiliquid foods in containers that are made of rigid plastic or freezer bags. Always leave at least 1 inch headspace between the food and the lid to allow liquid or semiliquid to expand while freezing.
- Meat can be frozen in its original retail packaging for up to 2 weeks after purchase. For longer storage, rewrap or overwrap.
- All foods should be labeled. Include the date the food was purchased or made and the type of food in the container. Use a pencil or special pen for labeling frozen foods and record the information on tape that will stick to the container even in 0° temperatures. A good masking tape usually is adequate.

VEGETABLES

Before freezing, raw vegetables should be blanched in boiling water to set the color and texture, and immediately cooled in ice water to halt the cooking. Drain well. Pack in freezer bags. The drier the vegetables are when they are packed, the higher the quality of the frozen vegetables.

TIMINGS: Vegetables

VEGETABLE	INSTRUCTIONS	FREEZER STORAGE TIME
ARTICHOKES	Blanch 7 minutes.	8 months
ASPARAGUS	Blanch 2–4 minutes.	8 months
BEANS, GREEN AND YELLOW	Blanch 2–3 minutes.	10 months
BEANS, SHELLED (Lima, Fava, etc.)	Blanch 3–4 minutes.	10 months
BEETS	Cook in boiling water until tender, 20–60 minutes.	10 months
BROCCOLI	Blanch spears 3 minutes.	10 months
BRUSSELS SPROUTS	Blanch whole heads 3–5 minutes.	10 months
CABBAGE	Trim coarse leaves. Cut into medium shreds, thin wedges, or individual leaves. Blanch 1½ minutes.	10 months
CARROTS	Leave baby carrots whole. For larger ones, thinly slice or cut into strips or ¼-inch cubes. Blanch 2–5 minutes.	10 months
CAULIFLOWER	Cut into 1-inch florets. Blanch 3 minutes.	10 months
CELERY	Cut into 1-inch lengths. Blanch 3 minutes.	10 months
CELERY ROOT (Celeriac)	Not recommended for freezing.	
CHAYOTE (Mirliton, Christophene)	Dice. Blanch 2 minutes.	10 months
CORN	Blanch ears 7–11 minutes. Blanch kernels 4 minutes.	10 months
EGGPLANT	Not recommended for freezing.	
FENNEL	Blanch slices 2–3 minutes; blanch whole bulbs 9–10 minutes.	10 months
GREENS (Beets, Chard, Collards, Kale, Spinach, etc.)	Blanch collards 3 minutes. Blanch all other greens 2 minutes.	10 months

VEGETABLE	INSTRUCTIONS	FREEZER STORAGE TIME
HERBS, FRESH	Wash well and pat dry, seal in bags. Can be used in cooked dishes; no longer suitable for garnish. Basil is not recommended.	6 months
JERUSALEM ARTICHOKES	Not recommended for freezing.	
KOHLRABI	Peel off tough skin. Leave whole and blanch 3 minutes, or cut into cubes and blanch 1 minute.	10 months
LEEKS	Not recommended for freezing.	
MUSHROOMS	Steam whole mushrooms 5 minutes, buttons or quarters 3½ minutes, slices 3 minutes.	10 months
OKRA	Blanch whole pods 3–4 minutes.	10 months
ONIONS	Blanch whole onions 3–7 minutes.	10 months
PARSNIPS	Cut into ½-inch cubes. Blanch 2 minutes.	10 months
PEAS, EDIBLE PODS	Blanch 1½–2 minutes.	10 months
PEAS, GREEN	Blanch 1½ minutes.	10 months
PEPPERS, BELL OR SWEET	Cut into halves, strips, or rings. Blanching is optional; blanch halves 3 minutes; strips or rings 2 minutes.	Unblanched: 4–6 months Blanched: 8–10 months
PEPPERS, HOT	Wash and stem.	4–6 months
PLANTAINS	Not recommended for freezing.	
POTATOES	Not recommended for fresh potatoes.	Commercial products: 1 year
RUTABAGAS	Cut into ½-inch cubes. Blanch 2 minutes.	8 months
SUMMER SQUASH	Slice ½ inch thick. Blanch 3 minutes.	10 months
TOMATOES	Peel and core. Use for sauce.	2 months
TURNIPS	Cut into ½-inch cubes. Blanch 2 minutes.	8 months

FRUIT

Pack raw fruits in sugar or a sugar syrup (see below) to maintain good texture. Fruits packed in syrup are generally best for uncooked desserts; those packed in sugar or left unsweetened are better in cooked desserts. To prevent discoloring of fruits, such as apples and apricots, mix ½ teaspoon powdered ascorbic acid (1500 mg) into each quart of syrup. If packing the fruit in sugar, dissolve ½ teaspoon ascorbic acid in 2 to 3 tablespoons water and sprinkle over the fruit before adding the sugar.

To use a **sugar syrup,** place fruit in container and cover with syrup (about ½–⅔ cup per pint of fruit). Press fruit down in syrup before sealing container. To use a **sugar pack,** sprinkle sugar over fruit and mix gently until the juice is drawn out of the fruit and the sugar is dissolved. To use a **dry pack,** simply pack the fruit into a container, seal, and freeze. This final method will yield fruit that is mushy, but is quick and easy.

Making Sugar Syrups for Freezing Fruits

Which sugar syrup to use depends on the sweetness of the fruit to be frozen. A heavy syrup (40%) is recommended for most fruits. Lighter syrups are desirable for milder-flavored fruits and for individuals watching their intake of sugar. To make the syrup, dissolve the sugar in lukewarm water, mixing until clear. Chill before using.

SYRUP	AMOUNT SUGAR	AMOUNT WATER	YIELD
Very light (10%)	½ cup	4 cups	4½ cups
Light (20%)	1 cup	4 cups	4¾ cups
Medium (30%)	1¾ cups	4 cups	5 cups
Heavy (40%)	2¾ cups	4 cups	5⅓ cups
Very heavy (50%)	4 cups	4 cups	6 cups

TIMINGS: Fruit

FRUIT	*INSTRUCTIONS*	*FREEZER STORAGE TIME*
APPLES	Peel, core, and slice. Use 40% syrup, sugar pack (½ cup sugar to 1 quart fruit), or dry pack. Use ascorbic acid to prevent browning.	10–12 months
APRICOTS	Peel, pit, and slice, if desired. Use 40% syrup or sugar pack (½ cup sugar to 1 quart fruit). Use ascorbic acid to prevent browning.	10–12 months
BANANAS	Peel and mash.	3 months
BLACKBERRIES, RASPBERRIES	Sugar pack (¾ cup sugar to 1 quart fruit) or dry pack.	10–12 months
BLUEBERRIES	Dry pack.	10–12 months
CHERRIES, SOUR	Pit. Pack in 50% syrup or sugar pack (¾ cup sugar to 1 quart fruit).	10–12 months
CHERRIES, SWEET	Pit. Pack in 40% syrup.	
CITRUS FRUITS	Peel, separate into sections, remove seeds. Pack in 40% syrup or freeze as sweetened juice.	10–12 months
CRANBERRIES	Dry pack.	10–12 months
CURRANTS	Remove stems. Dry pack. Or pack in 50% syrup or sugar pack (¾ cup sugar to 1 quart fruit).	10–12 months
DATES, FRESH	Split to remove pits. Dry pack.	10–12 months
FIGS	Peel, if desired. Pack in 40% syrup or dry pack. Use ascorbic acid to prevent browning.	10–12 months
GOOSEBERRIES	Remove stems and blossom ends. Dry pack or pack in 50% sugar syrup.	10–12 months
GRAPES	Leave seedless grapes whole, cut other grapes in half and remove seeds. Pack in 40% syrup or freeze as juice.	10–12 months

FRUIT	*INSTRUCTIONS*	*FREEZER STORAGE TIME*
GUAVAS	Peel and cut in half. Pack in 30% syrup.	10–12 months
MANGOES	Peel and slice. Pack in 30% syrup, dry pack, or freeze as sweetened or unsweetened purée.	10–12 months
MELONS	Cut into slices, cubes, or balls. Pack in 30% syrup or dry pack.	10–12 months
PEACHES, NECTARINES	Peel. Pack in 40% syrup or sugar pack (⅔ cup sugar to 1 quart fruit) or freeze as purée. Use ascorbic acid to prevent browning.	10–12 months
PEARS	Peel, core, and slice. Pack in 40% syrup. Use ascorbic acid to prevent browning.	10–12 months
PINEAPPLES	Dry pack.	10–12 months
PLUMS	Cut in halves or quarters and pit. Pack in 40–50% syrup. Use ascorbic acid to prevent browning.	10–12 months
RHUBARB	Trim and cut into convenient-size lengths. Dry pack or pack in 40% syrup.	10–12 months
STRAWBERRIES	Hull. Pack in 50% syrup, sugar pack (¾ cup sugar to 1 quart fruit), or pack as sweetened purée.	10–12 months

MOST OTHER FOODS

No special handling is required for nuts, dairy products, fish, shellfish, poultry, and meats. Make sure these products go into the freezer in airtight containers or in sealed freezer bags. Fish, poultry, and meat should be wrapped in plastic-backed freezer paper and sealed with freezer tape.

TIMINGS: Nuts, Dairy Products, Fish, Shellfish, Poultry, and Meats

PRODUCT	*FREEZER STORAGE TIME*
NUTS	
Almonds, in the shell and shelled	1 year
Brazil nuts, in the shell and shelled	9 months
Cashews, shelled	9 months
Chestnuts, shelled	9 months
Coconuts, grated	6 months
Hazelnuts, in the shell	1 year
Macadamia nuts, shelled	9–12 months
Peanuts	In the shell: 9–12 months Shelled: 6 months
Pecans, in the shell and shelled	1 year
Pine nuts, shelled	6 months
Walnuts, in the shell and shelled	1 year
DAIRY PRODUCTS	
Butter or margarine	9 months

PRODUCT	FREEZER STORAGE TIME
Buttermilk	3 months
Cheese (hard, semisoft, processed)	6 months
Cream (all kinds)	2 months
Cream, whipped	1 month
Ice cream, sherbet, ices	1–3 months
Milk, fresh fluid	1–3 months
Yogurt	1 month
Sour cream	Not recommended
EGGS	
Whole eggs, out of shell	9 months
Whites	1 year
Egg substitutes	1 year
FISH (Fresh, Uncooked)	
Lean white fish (Cod, Haddock, Sole, etc.)	6 months
Fatty fish (Mackerel, Salmon, etc.)	3 months
Cooked fish, all types	2 months
Smoked fish	2 months
SHELLFISH	
Clams, shucked	Shucked: 3 months Cooked: 2 months
Crabs	Uncooked: Not recommended Cooked: 2 months
Lobsters	Uncooked: Not recommended Cooked: 2 months

PRODUCT	FREEZER STORAGE TIME
Mussels, shucked	3 months
Oysters, shucked	3 months
Scallops	3 months
Shrimp	Uncooked: 3 months Cooked: 1 month
Shellfish cooked in sauce	1 month
POULTRY	
Chicken	Whole: 6–8 months Parts: 6–8 months Giblets: 2 months Ground: 3 months Breaded, fried: 4 months Cooked: 1 month Cooked in gravy: 2 months Smoked: 6 months TV dinners: 6 months
Duck or goose	Whole: 4–6 months Parts: 4–6 months Giblets: 1 month Sausage: 1 month Cooked: 3 months Cooked in gravy: 1 month
Game birds	Whole: 6–9 months Parts: 6–9 months Cooked: 2 months
Poultry gravy	6 months
Poultry stock	4–6 months
Poultry stuffing	1 month

PRODUCT	FREEZER STORAGE TIME
Turkey	Whole: 4–6 months Parts: 4–6 months Giblets: 2 months Ground: 3 months Cooked: 2 months Cooked in gravy: 1 month Smoked: 6 months TV dinners: 6 months
ALL MEAT	
Bones	6 months
Cooked	2–3 months
Cooked entrées (casseroles, stews, in gravy)	2–4 months
Stock	2–3 months
TV dinners	2–3 months
BEEF (Fresh, uncooked)	
Cubes for stew	2–4 months
Frankfurters	2 months
Ground beef	3 months
Roasts, ribs, steaks	6–8 months
Sausages	1–2 months
Variety meats (Heart, Kidney, Liver, Sweetbreads, Tongue, Tripe)	2–3 months
BEEF (Cooked)	
Hamburger	2 months
Meatballs, meatloaf	2 months

PRODUCT	*FREEZER STORAGE TIME*
Roasts	Whole: 4 months Sliced: 2 months
Sausages	1 month
Steaks or ribs	2–4 months
Stews in gravy	2 months
Variety meats	1 month
GAME	6–9 months
LAMB (Fresh, uncooked)	
Chops, ribs	6 months
Cubes	3 months
Ground lamb	3 months
Roasts	8 months
Variety meats (Heart, Kidney, Liver, Sweetbreads)	1–2 months
LAMB (Cooked)	
Chops	4 months
Cubes	3 months
Ground lamb	2 months
Rack of lamb	3 months
Roasts	6 months
Stews, in gravy	2 months
PORK (Fresh, uncooked)	
Chops	3 months
Ground pork	1 month

PRODUCT	FREEZER STORAGE TIME
Roasts	4 months
Sausage (fresh)	1 month
Spareribs	2 months
Variety meats (Chitterlings, Heart, Kidney, Liver)	2–4 months
PORK (Cooked)	
Chops	2 months
Meatballs, meatloaf	2 months
Roasts	2 months
Sausage	1 month
Spareribs	2 months
Stews, in gravy	2 months
VEAL (Fresh, uncooked)	
Chops, steaks, ribs	6 months
Cubes	3 months
Cutlets, scallops, medallions	3 months
Ground veal	3 months
Roasts	6 months
Variety meats (Brains, Kidneys, Liver, Sweetbreads)	3 months
VEAL (Cooked)	
Chops	2 months
Meatballs, meatloaf	2 months

PRODUCT	FREEZER STORAGE TIME
Roasts	2 months
Steak	2 months
Stews, in gravy	2 months
CURED AND PROCESSED MEAT	
Bacon (sliced, slab)	Uncooked: 1 month Cooked: 1½ months
Bacon, Canadian	Sliced: 1 month Chunk: 2 months
Bologna	2 months
Frankfurters	2 months
Ham	Whole: 3 months Sliced: 1 month Cooked: 1 month
Luncheon meats, sliced	1 month
Salami, sliced	1 month
Salt pork	Not recommended
Sausage, cooked	2 months
Sausage, fresh	2 months

TIMINGS: Miscellaneous Foods

PRODUCT	FREEZER STORAGE TIME
BREAD DOUGH	2 months
BREADS, SOFT CRUST (Sliced breads, Tortillas, Pita pockets)	4 months

PRODUCT	FREEZER STORAGE TIME
CAKES	Angel, chiffon, frosted: 2 months Cheesecake: 1 month Whipped-cream filled: Not recommended Fruitcakes: 1 year
COFFEE	Ground (opened can): 7–10 days Ground (fresh from beans): 2 weeks Whole beans: 3–4 months
COOKIES	Baked: 9 months Dough: 9 months
CORNMEAL	Degerminated: 1 year Stone-ground: 2–3 months
FLOUR	1 year
FRUIT JUICE	8–12 months
GRAINS	2–3 months
PASTA	Fresh: 2 months Cooked dishes: 2 months
PIES	Fruit, pecan: 6 months Custard: Not recommended Pumpkin: 2 months Shells, unbaked: 2 months
RICE, COOKED	6–8 months
TOFU	2 months
WHEAT GERM	2–3 months
YEAST, FRESH	6 months

Index

A

B

C

D

E

F

G

H

I

J

K

L

M

N

O

P

Q

R

S

T

U

V

W

Y

Z

Conversion Chart

Equivalent Imperial and Metric Measurements

American cooks use standard containers, the 8-ounce cup and a tablespoon that takes exactly 16 level fillings to fill that cup level. Measuring by cup makes it very difficult to give weight equivalents, as a cup of densely packed butter will weigh considerably more than a cup of flour. The easiest way therefore to deal with cup measurements in recipes is to take the amount by volume rather than by weight. Thus the equation reads:
1 cup = 240 ml = 8 fl. oz. 1/2 cup = 120 ml = 4 fl. oz.
It is possible to buy a set of American cup measures in major stores around the world.

In the States, butter is often measured in sticks. One stick is the equivalent of 8 tablespoons. One tablespoon of butter is therefore the equivalent to 1/2 ounce/15 grams.

LIQUID MEASURES

FLUID OUNCES	U.S.	IMPERIAL	MILLILITERS
	1 teaspoon	1 teaspoon	5
¼	2 teaspoons	1 dessertspoon	10
½	1 tablespoon	1 tablespoon	14
1	2 tablespoons	2 tablespoons	28
2	¼ cup	4 tablespoons	56
4	½ cup		110
5		¼ pint or 1 gill	140
6	¾ cup		170
8	1 cup		225
9			250, ¼ liter
10	1¼ cups	½ pint	280
12	1½ cups		340
15		¾ pint	420
16	2 cups		450
18	2¼ cups		500, ½ liter
20	2½ cups	1 pint	560
24	3 cups		675
25		1¼ pints	700
27	3½ cups		750
30	3¾ cups	1½ pints	840
32	4 cups or 1 quart		900
35		1¾ pints	980
36	4½ cups		1000, 1 liter
40	5 cups	2 pints or 1 quart	1120

SOLID MEASURES

U.S. AND IMPERIAL MEASURES		METRIC MEASURES	
OUNCES	POUNDS	GRAMS	KILOS
1		28	
2		56	
3½		100	
4	¼	112	
5		140	
6		168	
8	½	225	
9		250	¼
12	¾	340	
16	1	450	
18		500	½
20	1¼	560	
24	1½	675	
27		750	¾
28	1¾	780	
32	2	900	
36	2¼	1000	1
40	2½	1100	
48	3	1350	
54		1500	1½

OVEN TEMPERATURE EQUIVALENTS

FAHRENHEIT	CELSIUS	GAS MARK	DESCRIPTION
225	110	¼	Cool
250	130	½	
275	140	1	Very Slow
300	150	2	
325	170	3	Slow
350	180	4	Moderate
375	190	5	
400	200	6	Moderately Hot
425	220	7	Fairly Hot
450	230	8	Hot
475	240	9	Very Hot
500	250	10	Extremely Hot

Any broiling recipes can be used with the grill of the oven, but beware of high-temperature grills.

EQUIVALENTS FOR INGREDIENTS

all-purpose flour—plain flour
baking sheet—oven tray
buttermilk—ordinary milk
cheesecloth—muslin
coarse salt—kitchen salt
cornstarch—cornflour
eggplant—aubergine
granulated sugar—caster sugar
half and half—12% fat milk
heavy cream—double cream
light cream—single cream
lima beans—broad beans
parchment paper—greaseproof paper
plastic wrap—cling film
scallion—spring onion
shortening—white fat
unbleached flour—strong, white flour
vanilla bean—vanilla pod
zest—rind
zucchini—courgettes or marrow